The Tinder Box

HOW POLITICALLY CORRECT IDEOLOGY DESTROYED THE U.S FOREST SERVICE

Christopher Burchfield

Also By Christopher Burchfield

Choose Your Weapon—The Duel in California 1847-1861

ISBN: 0692300376
ISBN 13: 9780692300374
@ Christopher Burchfield Stairway Press 2012
Stairway Press 2013
Seneca Books 2014

Seneca Books
martinblewis@senecabooks.com

Cover Design by Guy Corp www.grafix CORP.com
Front Cover Photograph Judy Coffman
Hand Model: Leslie K. Benjamin

To the Working Men of the United States Forest Service

ACKNOWLEDGEMENTS

I would like to thank my wife Genendal Lea Burchfield for her support in this long endeavor. I am also obliged to Chuck Kinsey for his editing skills, and would also like to thank Ken Coffman for his interest in seeing this book made available to the public. Among those employed by the U.S. Forest Service who aided me in assembling this volume, many for personal reasons cannot be cited. Among those who can be cited is the staff at the Federal Records Center, in San Bruno, California who were always courteous and helpful.

There are many others to whom I am deeply indebted for their accounts of personal experiences, the documents they provided, the background they contributed with regard to the forestry management and lore, and the legal framework behind both the Bernardi Consent Decree and the Levitoff Civil Suit. Among them are Jeff Applegate, Pete Barker, Peter Brost, Bob Cermak, Louis Demas, Bob Grate, Leroy Johnson, Gary McHargue, Tom Locker, Britt Smith and Congressman Wally Herger's long time aid, Dave Meurer.

Finally, though I was never privileged to meet him because of his untimely and tragic death, I would also like to thank Jerry Levitoff. The determination he, his partner Bob Grate, and their attorney Louis Demas exhibited through the long years as their case slowly wound its way to the U.S. Supreme Court was remarkable. Theirs was a determination that I hope all who have had their rights as American citizens denied, will display in their own turn.

CB, January 2012

FOREWORD

Bureaucracies are supposed to be apolitical because they are unaccountable. It's why the English called them civil servants. They've changed prompting Mary McCarthy to say, *"Bureaucracy, the rule of no one has become the modern form of despotism."*

New Environmental bureaucracies like the U.S. Forest Service have inherent contradictions. Forests have natural uncontrolled patterns but bureaucracies are about control. Forest fires are natural and necessary, but service tries to stop or at least limit them.

Preventing loss of life is a good idea, but ideas require structures which rapidly become more important than the idea. Create a bureaucracy to solve a problem and invariably it perpetuates and expands the problems to perpetuate itself. Environmentalism was a necessary new paradigm, but also an attractive vehicle for political control. The combination of these conflicts and the new paradigm required delusions to divert from reality.

It's easy to create delusions, but as Michael Crichton wrote:

> *...the greatest challenge facing mankind is the challenge of distinguishing reality from fantasy, truth from propaganda. Perceiving the truth has always*

been a challenge to mankind, but in the informa-
tion age (or as I think of it, the disinformation age),
it takes on a special urgency and importance.

Farhad Manjoo expands on the problem. "Facts no longer matter. We simply decide how we want to see the world and then go out and find experts and evidence to back our beliefs." The Post-Fact society is very active in environmental issues, where ideology trumps science. Environmentalism as the prevailing philosophy went global through the work of the United Nations Environmental Programme (UNEP) and expressed in the Principles identified at the 1992 Rio Conference. A document titled Agenda 21 became the blueprint for environment and development and Principle 15 gave official sanction to ideology, trumping facts and science. It said:

In order to protect the environment the precau-
tionary approach shall be widely applied by States
according to their capabilities. Where there are
threats of serious or irreversible damage, lack of full
scientific certainty shall not be used as a reason for
postponing cost-effective measures to prevent envi-
ronmental degradation.

It's a license for unaccountable bureaucracies to be exploited and manipulated by extremists with their politically correct agenda
–Dr. Tim Ball, author of *The Deliberate Corruption of Climate Science,* and co-author of *Slaying the Sky Dragon: Death of the Greenhouse Gas Theory*

TABLE OF CONTENTS

PREFACE:

MANY LETTERS OF CONDOLENCE

All my dreams have been left in ruins. But I can still Dream –Unknown

ONE OF THE first employees impacted by the Bernardi Consent Decree[1] was Ken Wolstenhom, who had just been promoted to assistant fire truck captain, a GS-05 pay grade. Though the position demands considerable skill and responsibility, the truth is a GS-05 forest service employee earns very little money. Even prior to the decree, fire teams, whether hotshots, members of the engine crews, or helitacks[2] were a financially stricken bunch. Until recently U.S. Forest Service fire captains were paid roughly the same wages as the so-called *tanker slugs* (firemen) employed by the California Department of Forestry (Today known as *CalFire*). The reason the agency pays its firefighters so poorly lies in a series of studies begun in the 1950s. Psychologists learned that a genome existed within a fair percentage of men—giving them the unique capacity to deal with numerous dangers, including that of fighting fires. The commingling of danger, drama, and fraternity that emerges during such crises produces a tremendous wallop of androgens. These create a natural exhilaration as the threat is being attacked, which peaks when the threat is finally vanquished. On the basis of these studies, knowing their firemen were likely return for another season of excitement, the agency made a conscious decision to underpay them.

This is why Wolstenhom returned to work year after year and eventually became a permanent employee. He had also been instilled with the belief that fidelity to organization, hard work, and merit were the only means of getting ahead, three reasons why the extraordinary events that follow overwhelmed him.

He now lives in Wildwood, a timber town in northern California. Now in his late fifties, Ken is a powerfully built fellow, both animated and reflective. Asked when he was first impacted by the Bernardi Decree, he replied:

> *I learned that I was to train a woman to be the assistant captain on the truck—and she had just three months of experience compared to my twenty-seven months. She was a bit over five feet tall, and I could see there was no way she was going to be able to do any physical aspect of the job. But the higher ups in the Cleveland [National Forest] were planning to put her in charge of us grunts without her ever having gone through the misery of being a grunt herself. I carried a lot of anguish with me into that assignment. After all the fires, and having been put in so many precarious situations, I was not going to be the engine boss. I was going to have to train someone else to do the job I had just been promoted to.*

Early in the summer of 1983, a fire broke adjacent to Camp Pendleton about four miles from Wolstenhom's work center.

Because of the rugged terrain and pockmarked road, it took the recently promoted engine captain two hours to reach the site. On arrival the crew found the blaze was just an acre in size, and cool because it was burning within a stretch of grassland. Wolstenhom instinctively decided their best option was to clear a fire line around it and said so.

The woman turned and said, "I'm in charge of the engine crew. Not you. We're going to turn the hose loose." The crew did as told and emptied the truck's three-hundred-gallon tank, but saw that the fire was still spreading. "We'll have to go get more water," said the captain, unfolding a map and pointing to a water hole. Wolstenhom peered at the map and said, "That water hole is empty. Its only filled in winter." The captain refused to believe him, and sure enough, when the truck reached the water hole thirty minutes later, it was parched. The six member crew was thus forced to take the long drive back to the station for water. Well before their return they could see smoke rising from a blaze that had now blackened more than forty acres. As the captain pulled up Wolstenhom said, "We've got to get the other engine units and some helicopters over quick."

"No, we're putting it out ourselves," she said as she pulled the truck adjacent a chaparral thicket, shut off the motor and climbed out. Recognizing it as a dangerous place to leave a truck, Wolstenhom slid into the driver seat and pulled it back into the open. When the captain ordered him to park the truck where she had left it, he declined. A terrific shouting match, replete with screams, curses, and finger pointing, ensued in front of the four firemen, with Wolstenhom's resonate baritone matched against the captain's high pitched soprano. Minutes later, as she broke into tears, he swept the radio from her hand and called in three additional fire crews. Before it was extinguished, what was once a creeping fire of one acre had burned up 4,200 acres, including the patch of chaparral near where the truck had been parked.

The following day as the crews moved toward containment, Ken's project supervisor approached him and asked, "What did you do to her? She was crying." He then added, "You're treading on thin ice. With this new consent decree she is thinking of having you fired."

Even as they spoke, the district ranger was taking down a statement from the captain. The next day he phoned county law enforcement and asked them to send in a council of experts to interview Wolstenhom; in his opinion the firefighter was about to go *postal.* The day after, during the interview, Ken admitted to agents he had done a lot of hollering and swearing, but as he put it: "She was in hysterics, shouting, cursing, threatening me, and more important, a life threatening situation was at hand. I had no alternative." The agents left assured that Ken was not going postal.

Word of the incident rapidly spread through the Cleveland Forest. Contests broke out among fire crew members—each competing to write the most graphic letter of condolence to his parents. As Ken recalled:

> *It was terrible for everyone. The men were writing up mock letters of condolence to their moms and dads over their untimely deaths caused by fire. One even wrote his own obituary, stating that he had always dreamed he would be killed as the result of being led into a fire by a cull.*

Shortly after his interview with the agents, Wolstenhom received a call from the Cleveland Forest Supervisor, directing him to come in for a talk. Ken's immediate supervisor, project supervisor, and Regional Forest Supervisor Zane

Smith were all present at the meeting. The first thing his project supervisor did was hand Ken a list of forty words, phrases and topics he was never to use in the presence of a firewoman. One was: "I could not ask a woman what it was like to be fighting a fire among men."

Over the next twelve years, this list, which over time evolved into a score of variations, was shown to thousands of forest workers. Despite passage of the 1978 Civil Service Law, discharging an incompetent, or in this instance a recalcitrant employee, was problematic. The only sure way of hounding them out of the agency was through humiliation. For hundreds of employees the disgrace of having that word list hoisted aloft, with the demeaning lecture that followed were reasons enough to find employment elsewhere.

The following year, 1984, Wolstenhom first saw the numbers. A total of eight men on the Cleveland Forest were to be promoted to engine captain or assistant engine captain. But all, including Ken, were replaced by what were known as *quota captains* and thrust back into the hot shot crews where they had begun work six years before. He was soon applying for fire positions all over the United States; yet no other national forest in any other region wanted him. "So, one day I went in and tossed my badge onto the supervisor's desk and said I was leaving…I realized, even though I loved firefighting, that nothing was ever going to go right."

To this day he remains certain that he was not hired by any other forest because the Cleveland Forest Supervisor blacklisted him over his confrontation with the engine captain.

INTRODUCTION:

SIGNIFICANT EVENTS IN AMERICA AND

ELSEWHERE

Read it with sorrow and you will feel hate. Read it with anger and you will feel vengeful Read it with paranoia and you will feel confusion. Read it with empathy and you will feel compassion. Don't read it at all and you will never feel a thing
– Paraphrasing Shannon L. Alder

AMONG THE MANY concepts the political left brought to America during the last half of the Twentieth Century was that known as "cultural cringe." It was a term coined in 1930 by a team of Australian sociologists, Brain Head and James Walter, to depict the mortification many well-to-do Australians felt toward their countrymen, as well as the country itself. Specifically, cultural cringe embraces the notion that one's own country occupies a subordinate niche on the world's cultural periphery and that superior moral and intellectual standards reside elsewhere. This peculiar development was transported to America by the Frankfurt School of German scholars during the 1930s. A neo-Marxist group, they set up shop at Columbia

University and from there invested its various disciplines. By 1954 it had established itself in major universities across the United States. The Frankfurt School's central thesis was that Western Civilization, rotten and corrupt though it was, could never be upended by a revolt of the masses, or by the working people as had been taught by Marx and other primitive communists. Too many failures had resulted. The only successful overthrow of a Western Civilization had occurred in Russia with the triumph of the Soviet Union. Yet even that single triumph had not been spearheaded by the workers and downtrodden, but by comfortably situated, prosperous notables such as Lenin, Trotsky, Kamanev, Bukharin, and others. Rather, the Frankfurt School contended that Western Civilization could be upended from within—by its elites only.

Among its most prominent American leaders were Max Horkheimer, Theodore Adorno, Walter Benjamin and Herbert Marcuse. Their two best known publications are *Critical Theory* and *The Authoritarian Personality*. Compiled in hopes of bringing about the destruction of Christianity, the Golden Rule, the family unit and the public's understanding of right and wrong, these volumes took America's universities by storm. One of the Frankfurt School's fellow travelers, Willi Munzenberg, also known as "The Red Millionaire," was quoted as saying with remarkable prescience:

> *to organize the intellectuals and use them to make Western Civilization stink.' Only then, after we have corrupted people's values, and made life impossible, can we impose the dictatorship of the proletariat.*

Though its tenets were powerfully refuted by numerous scholars, as the 1960s advanced into the 1970s, the school and its concepts, known as *postmodernism* or *deconstruction* took a vice-like hold over academia, the television industry and several newspaper chains.

Books critical of the Frankfurt School's multitude of spin-offs and the damage they inflicted on the United States now run into the scores. But there has yet to be published a blow-by-blow account of how they went about demolishing a specific institution. *The Tinder Box: How Politically Correct Ideology Destroyed the U.S. Forest Service* is intended to fill that void.

In this respect I was fortunate, having learned that a stash of documents related to the U.S. Forest Service and the civil suit filed against it were lodged in the Federal Records Storage Center in San Bruno, California. Upon examining the index, I was astonished to find that the case file comprised not just two or three boxes of materials, but thirty-seven, each a foot wide and the length of a shoe box. I also found the thousands of letters, reports, directives and minutes of meetings therein filed in no particular order.

Worse, other than the quarterly report binders, the folders were often unlabeled. The chaos was so far-reaching, it appeared as though the individuals stowing the records wished to discourage the public from conducting any research. Because I was rummaging about for a few key pieces of paper, my initial reaction was one of dismay. However, the dismay soon turned to curiosity, which prompted me to order the first four boxes. A review of the documents revealed information so startling that I was forced to make numerous return visits to San Bruno in order to search through boxes five through six, seven through eleven, twelve through twenty, and so forth. Thus, a quest for a few answers to a few specific questions resulted in a thorough exploration of the archives, and uncovered a blow-by-blow account of how the American Left demolished an essential arm of the U.S. Government.

This led to numerous interviews with those who were once, and a few who are still employed with the forest service. One was Bob Grate, a fire captain for the Lassen National Forest and co-founder of the Male Class Complaint, a major lawsuit filed against the agency because of its repeated violations of the Bernardi Consent Decree. He passed me scores of documents dating from the Male Class's origins in 1989 to its closing in 1998. To these records, dozens more were furnished by Male Class Attorney Louis Demas, Congressman Wally Herger's Chief of Staff Dave Meurer, former Fire Management Officer Tom Locker and others. Two of the interviewed had planned to write a book about the calamity, but for the press of time were unable to proceed.

Some of the material, particularly the measures the forest service initiated to remove long-held protections guaranteed its employees, made for harrowing reading. The maneuvers were such that the agency and its so-called legal opponent, the Equal Rights Advocates, circumvented the very consent decree the district court had endorsed in order to vastly expand their collective agenda. Most of the documents and interviews, though by no means all, cover events in California. Even though the most populous state in the union, approximately 50% of it is public land. Of this, eighteen forests, covering over 20-million acres are managed by the U.S. Forest Service. As many readers from other states well know, though these areas are heavily forested, for up to seven months each year no rain falls, and they lay tinderbox dry.

But more to the point: it was in California that the Bernardi Consent Decree arose, where the bludgeoning of public employees began and evolved into the nationwide horror it did. By and large, the agency's Washington, DC office used California as a vast experimental chamber to undertake its social experiments. Agency mavens then determined—not which practices enhanced their employees' ability to manage the lands—but which would provoke the least resistance to the establishment of a new regime. By 1992, when the Bernardi Decree ended, the agency's formulas for dealing with its more recalcitrant employees on the ground had been all but perfected.

Within four years, the ablest foresters and firemen within the remaining 155 national forests and grasslands spread across 172 million acres in 43 other states were hounded out of the agency as well. Still, in no other region did the U.S. Forest Service resort to the criminal acts engaged in by Region Five (California); nowhere else did resistance to its measures reach such dimensions; and nowhere else was a paper trail of such proportions left to posterity.

Some readers may wonder why this volume is necessary. It is necessary because its beginnings are placed at that very point in time the most momentous issue America now faces, first arose. To some of us the Reagan, first Bush, and Clinton Administrations seem like ancient chapters to American history, almost as old as those of Eisenhower and Kennedy. Yet for many others, scarred by the events of the past third of a century, these administrations seem like they occurred just yesterday. This is because, when the New Left policy makers learned that their notion of how a unit of the U.S. Government ought to perform was without biological, social or moral authority, they set about destroying that agency, however essential it was to the nation's fitness.

In the tradition of the Frankfurt School, it was demolished from within under the direction of its most powerful and influential players. Let it here be emphasized that women, whom the Bernardi Decree was purported to advance, did not destroy it. Many, possessed of a natural intuition, and who were vigilant observers of life about them, did what they could to save the agency. Others, forced to observe the men with whom they worked being systematically purged, resigned. Still other women departed for forest regions to the north and east, and when the virus spread there, also resigned.

Very few of those employed by the U.S. Forest Service when the Bernardi Consent Decree began, have any precise memory of its origins. Among the many I interviewed, only those who departed the agency would speak openly of the obscene events that followed. And even amongst the departed were those who declined interviews, many simply stating they had put the nightmare behind them. "I'm not going to open that closet of skeletons again!" declared one. Amid the rapidly dwindling number of those still employed when the decree was implemented, just two would permit use of their names. All others insisted on anonymity. Not surprisingly, those employees who compromised themselves during the decree's implementation would not agree to interviews.

Chapter 1

OF FORESTS, FIRES AND CHIEFS

Get out into the woods or get out of the Service...
—Gifford Pinchot in a memorandum to his Washington staff.

The man who rises through the Forest Service is of a peculiar breed. He is a woodsman, a scientist, an engineer, an economist, an accountant, a public relations expert and something of a nomad—
Newsweek, June 2, 1952

THROUGH THE SUMMER and autumn of 1871 for five months no rain had fallen over northern Wisconsin. Much of the timber there, a mix of pine, spruce and northern hardwood trees had been leveled to feed the state's sawmills, which in turn supplied the nation with lumber. As a result, for many miles around Peshtigo and other small towns, the landscape was dotted with thousands upon thousands of brush piles, many of which had been intentionally set afire by lumberjacks.

Not surprisingly, the residents of these towns had been suffering from smoke inhalation, causing severe headaches and nausea. On several occasions the main street of Peshtigo, covered in sawdust, had been lit by cascading embers swept across the forest canopy by high winds. There was much foreboding among the populace and the frenzied cries of birds in the forest only made the outlook seem more ominous.

On the night of October 8, 1871—the night the far more celebrated Chicago Fire erupted—the evening air suddenly warmed as a storm system blew in from the Great Plains producing tremendous gusts of wind, but no rain. Worry among the residents turned to fright as they saw the pitch black sky turn to copper. A crown fire had erupted some miles distant and with cyclonic fury was roaring through the forest toward town. Winds tore flaming snags from the tops of trees and sent them sailing across the sky where they dropped onto Peshtigo's sawdust streets by the score.

According to the Reverend Penin, whose buggy was blown onto its side and who survived the catastrophe only by plunging into the Peshtigo River and remaining largely submerged through the night...

> *The neighing of horses, falling of chimneys, crashing of uprooted trees, roaring of winds, the crackling of the fire as it ran with lightening like rapidity from one house to the next—all sounds were there save the human voice. People were dumbstruck with terror.*

Some who fled their cabins in the nearby forest miraculously survived by also immersing themselves in creeks, Many later insisted that as the fire passed over the swamps, the gasses therein exploded into huge fire balls. One wrote of: ...*a great black balloon-shaped object, etched in sharp contrast to the red sky, whirled over the tops of the trees and exploded.*

Strangely enough, a third of the 1.5 million acres scorched by the Peshtigo Fire burned on the Door Peninsula within twenty miles of the town of Green Bay. Yet witnesses insist that the Door Peninsula's own slumbering fires were fanned to fury by the same weather system. Two miles out on Green Bay itself, the deck of a schooner was ignited by falling coals while seven miles away from shore, a flaming plank crashed atop the steamship, Atlanta.

Today, owing to numerous itinerant lumberjacks and homesteaders passing through the area, the number of those who perished in the Peshtigo Fire remains a mystery. Estimates run as high as 2,500—ten times the number who died in the Chicago Fire. Yet because Peshtigo and the dozen other towns scattered through northern Wisconsin were connected to the rest of the world by a single telegraph line incinerated in the blaze, news of the calamity barely reached the outside world.

Through the balance of the 1870s decade similar, though somewhat less destructive fires continued to rip through Northern Wisconsin, Michigan and Minnesota, demonstrating that the lumber interests had learned nothing from the Peshtigo disaster. By-and-large, most Americans still regarded the forests as a source of cash and an impediment to civilization. These thoughts were not shared by a small number of European-trained foresters who a year after the great fire journeyed into northern Wisconsin. Horrified by what they saw and spellbound by the accounts told, many were prompted to wonder if there was something wrong with the way America was managing its forests.

Prodded by these individuals, in 1876 Congress approved a grant of $2,000 and ordered the Department of Agriculture to establish a Division of Forestry. Its mission was to look into the preservation of the nation's forests, now being obliterated at a staggering pace. Further adding to this new interest in forestry, were the inspired writings of such early prophets of nature as John Burroughs, George Perkins Marsh and Henry David Thoreau.

The Division of Forestry remained very limited in scope until 1886 when Bernhard Fernow was appointed head. Congress greatly expanded its budget and Fernow himself turned it into a professional agency by applying scientific research to forestry practices. With conservation sentiment further invigorated by figures such as John Muir, Congress passed a bill enabling the president to set aside public lands for timber management and watershed protection. By 1897 the acreage of these forest reserves had grown to 17 million.

That year, Fernow's office initiated a systematic fire prevention program and tightened regulations on grazing, mining and timber falling. President Grover Cleveland followed by adding 21 million more acres to the reserve system—all in states west of the Great Plains. Despite these acquisitions, the Division of Forestry did not possess actual title to its 38.5 million acres. The acreage itself remained under official ownership of the very antiquated General Land Office, which was, by default, also owner of hundreds of millions of acres throughout the West that were never claimed by homesteaders.

It was staffed by employees intent on making underhanded deals with the sovereigns of the mining, timber and ranching industries. Among the worst examples of land office exploitation was that of permitting timber companies to exchange their cut-over private holdings for virgin timberlands in the reserves. A vociferous critic of this lax style of management was Gifford Pinchot, who in 1898 succeeded Fernow as head of the Division of Forestry. A scion of a wealthy Pennsylvania family, Pinchot had studied forestry in Europe and felt that America with its immense unsettled spaces, required new concepts to manage its natural resources. A witness to the almost complete denuding of Pennsylvania's hardwood forests and

the watershed problems and poverty that followed, he felt
certain that good management of both timber and prairie
country was essential to preserving America's heritage.

In 1905, after much prodding from Pinchot, and over
the opposition of Western land interests, Congress passed a
bill transferring title to the now 85.6 million acres of reserve
land from the General Land Office to Pinchot's Division of
Forestry. Two years later, the Chief, as he was called, designated all reserves as national forests and founded what has
ever since been known as the United States Forest Service.
Still within the Department of Agriculture, it is the oldest of
America's four great land-owning agencies–the others being
the National Park Service, the U.S. Fish and Wildlife Service
and the Bureau of Land Management. He set about organizing a staff of employees who understood the concept of
multiple use conservation and sent them into the forests to
manage them. As dynamic as he was hard working, he gained
the strong support of President Theodore Roosevelt. Both
were avid outdoorsmen with nearly identical political views.
They worked so well together that when the President left
office, he stated that the most effective member of his administration had been Gifford Pinchot.

Pinchot was not the first overseer of forest lands, but
because of the energy he expended in transforming a badly
underfunded, poorly organized agency into one of the most
efficient in the federal government, he is considered the
father of the U.S. Forest Service. A member of the Progressive
Movement and Roosevelt's Bull Moose party, he was a strong
supporter of public utilities, labor unions, women's suffrage
and a larger role for the federal government in managing the
economy. At the same time, he and his fellow progressives
never accepted the notion that a government bureau should
serve as an employment agency for the indolent. Every cent

drawn from the U.S. Treasury was to be well spent, and when the opportunity presented itself, reimbursed.

Although the federal government had taken numerous steps to reduce the patronage method of hire, it still existed in many agencies, including the Department of Agriculture. Appalled by patronage practices, Pinchot immediately adopted the Civil Service System, obliging everyone who applied for work to take a complex civil service examination. The test's complexity was intended not only to determine an applicant's capability, but to reinforce the professional ethos required to meet agency expectations. Only those who possessed the required credentials would be hired; only those whose work was commendable would be promoted. Those who failed to meet Pinchot's standards of hard work and ethics were quickly identified and discharged.

Of those considering a career in forestry, he once wrote…

> *I urge no man to make forestry his profession. But rather to keep away from it if he can. In forestry a man is either altogether at home, or very much out of place…there has been and will always be but one kind of place, one form of experience possible in the profession.*

Only then, the Chief reasoned, could he and his lean Washington staff be assured that their employees sent into the remote West would perform in the most professional manner with minimal oversight. This was one reason why none of his five-hundred employees regarded themselves as wards of the state, and upon signing on quickly departed for their respective forests.

These employees did not include the hundreds of Indian scouts, rodeo performers, Spanish American War veterans and local youths with a passion for the wilderness who were hired for the summer months; or the hundreds of students from Harvard and several other forestry schools that had opened up across America, and who were paid $35 per month through the summer. The students were sent into the field, in Pinchot's words, "that they got the Harvard rubbed off them before they came into contact with the loggers." After graduating most of them became foresters.

Among a list of courses Pinchot required for graduates were dendrology, physiography, and *silvics*, the latter the study of each tree species' relationships to light, soil, moisture, and each other. Though the term silviculture is still used, the word silvics never caught on and *conservation* became the designated term for the discipline. In addition, foresters and district rangers were expected to understand forestry economics, which meant the cutting of timber at a rate commensurate with the forest's ability to regenerate.

Under his leadership, and that of his successors, each supervisor and ranger was responsible for the care of his own horse. The supervisor and ranger, much like the employees reporting to them, were expected to perform heavy labor, estimate the amount of timber in an allotment, manage timber sales, livestock and mining operations, and to survive alone in the wilderness for weeks at a time. Within a few short months, the employees reporting to them had a clear understanding of their mission and were eager to support their ranger or forest supervisor. In turn, no supervisor could release himself from the ultimate responsibility for what occurred on his forest. The buck stopped at his desk, and over the next seventy-five years the buck never passed by that desk. This greatly reinforced the agency's respect among local communities.

Pinchot understood that only by bonding the forests to their adjacent towns, could his organization succeed. With the backing of Congress, he directed each unit to deposit its receipts in a local bank, from which 10% would be drawn annually to support local schools and road systems. Employees were expected to mingle with towns people and to ensure that as many local youths as possible were hired to guide the Harvard undergrads through their summer months.

Today, the term bureaucrat carries such negative connotations, that there is almost no way it can be applied with any credibility. Yet, if anyone who ever lived might fit that appellation it is Pinchot, who was once described by Stewart Udall, Secretary of Interior under President Kennedy, as *a magnificent bureaucrat*. Indeed, his determination and vision created a romantic impression among the public at large, prompting author Hamlin Garland to write the book *Cavanaugh: Forest Ranger*. Largely fiction, it was based on the exploits of a forest ranger in his encounters with hostile stockmen in Colorado and other states throughout the West.

It was during his term as chief that Pinchot's once close friendship with the famed John Muir came to an end, the two taking separate trails with regard to their approach to public land management. Muir and his followers favored preservation, the policy adopted by the National Park Service, while Pinchot continued to favor the multiple-use concept. Strangely enough, shortly after their parting, Pinchot became embroiled in a feud with President Taft's secretary of interior, Richard Ballanger, after he criticized the Secretary's cozy relationship with the timber industry. Taft removed Pinchot from office, a measure that was partially responsible for his defeat in the 1912 election.

Even though Pinchot was now gone from the agency, he continued to wield great influence over the chief foresters who followed. Several were personal friends, while others who knew him by reputation only, sought his advice. His replacement was Harry Solon Graves, an austere, hard-working chief who would not permit anyone to smoke or whistle in his office. Graves spent much of his term restoring relations with the Department of Interior, while at the same time rebuilding morale within the agency, badly damaged by Pinchot's departure.

During his tenure, Congress passed the Weeks Act, authorizing the purchase of cut-over lands in the Eastern United States for inclusion into the forest service. The continued purchase of these and other lands in the West would eventually bring its total acreage to 193 million spread across 175 national forests in 44 states. These figures include twenty national grasslands acquired from destitute farmers during the Dust Bowl of the 1930s. Crops were eliminated from these marginal lands, which were then leased to ranchers for cattle grazing on a sustained basis.

Graves' first year as chief saw the outbreak of a huge fire in the Bitterroot Range on the Idaho-Montana border. Before the fire was checked, it had burned three-million acres and killed ninety firefighters. The disaster captured newspaper headlines across the country, thereby enabling the service to vastly expand its funding, and advance its firefighting techniques. A commission was set up to investigate the origins of fires and determine why some burned with such intensity while others burned only moderately under what appeared to be very similar conditions. Thus was born fire science.

In 1918 Graves was succeeded by William B. Greeley who proved much less amenable to Pinchot's management ideals. Still, under his stewardship Congress added a new branch to the service, the State and Private Land Agency, designed to advise states and private land owners on how to manage their forests. In 1928 he was succeeded by Robert Y. Stewart, whose close friendship with Pinchot enabled the old forester to regain much of his influence. With Stewart in office, Congress passed the McSweeney-McNary Act establishing a series of forest experimental stations across the country. This third division was staffed by scientists whose task was the general study of plant life—uncovering means by which tree growth could be promoted and developing pesticides to control insect infestations.

With the election of Franklin D. Roosevelt, Stewart's team developed a list of projects for the new Civilian Conservation Corps to undertake within the forests. In reviewing the record, one can only conclude that most early foresters, including those serving under Republican administrations, believed in the concept of big government—specifically with regard to their own agency. But federal employees also labored under the concept that government operations could be every bit as effective as those in private industry. In those years, working an eighteen hour day was not uncommon among the personnel of many agencies.

The implementer of Roosevelt's conservation corps was another friend of Pinchot's, Ferdinand Silcox, America's first Southern-born chief forester. Though the Civilian Conservation Corps was denounced by many as a socialistic boondoggle, Silcox's management of the corps resulted in the employment of two- million youths who carved out roads, blazed trails, constructed bridges and erected numerous back-country lookout towers. Prior to that time, when a fire broke out, the local forest staff would race from one home, shop and saloon to the next, deputizing locals to help fight the blaze. But with the inception of the CCC, a sizeable cadre of highly motivated young men became a key component to the agency's firefighting ability. After the CCC was abolished during World War II, the forest service continued to hire and train many more local youths.

By then, the amount of timber acreage felled was being surpassed by the acreage replanted. This was in part owing to the Knutson-Vandenberg Act of 1930 which bound lumber companies to place deposits with the agency for the later planting of seedlings before tree felling could begin. Aircraft patrols over the forests increased markedly and firefighting techniques were advanced to such an extent that between 1910 and 1949 no fires of truly epic proportions erupted. For the first time firefighters were being parachuted out of airplanes. Following the attack on Pearl Harbor, many of these smoke jumpers enlisted in the armed services, and formed the nucleus of several parachute operations, such as Operation Market Garden which followed the D-Day Invasion.

At about this time, Secretary of the Interior Harold Ickes made a determined effort to move the forest service into what he hoped would become an all-embracing Department of Conservation, comprising all the great land owning agencies. But the merger never came about, due in large part to opposition from Pinchot, Silcox and the foresters themselves, who felt their agency's much more extensive holdings would be given short shrift by the more influential proponents of the National Park Service. War's end saw a phenomenal rise in the demand for lumber to build houses for the millions of military personnel who returned home and who, with the aid of the GI Bill, were eager to start families. So great was the pressure for housing, for the first time since the early 1930s, the acreage in removed timber began to outstrip acreage planted.

By then the intrepid, picturesque, horse-mounted, armed and all-knowing forest ranger had become little more than a romantic figure of the past—replaced by specialists such as hydrologists, silviculturists, range managers, geneticists, engineers and entomologists. With the great increase in automobile use and the improvement of roads, it was now far more practical for employees to travel from one section of a forest to another by motor vehicle.

Still, it remained an agency with a character and a mission. Despite the great number of professions necessary to manage a forest, some requiring strikingly different backgrounds, working for the same unit in a remote setting ensured that strong personal bonds developed between employees. This phenomenon was almost unique to the forest service among all government agencies, and a big reason why a 1968 survey found that 85% of its employees stated unequivocally, that once again given the chance, they would choose employment with the same agency. This extraordinary rate of job approval was a big reason why—along with the sale of timber—as late 1970, it was the only government organization, other than the U.S Bureau of Land Management, to turn a profit, an objective not dreamed of today by any department of the U.S. Government.

In 1950, Richard McArdle became chief forester, continuing the service's long standing policy of multiple-use, but with more focus on recreation. During his tenure, the agency began hiring local youths on a much larger scale. Many entered what evolved into the elite hotshot crews trained to actively suppress fires, as opposed to containing them. Though not well-paid and forced to work long, hard hours through the summer months, these teams soon developed a camaraderie not unlike that of a U.S. Army squad. Within seven or eight years many of these youths were being promoted to engine captain.

McArdle was perhaps the most popular chief forester since Pinchot. Testimony to the esteem in which he was held is the following exchange between a cook in Fraser, Colorado and Dwight D. Eisenhower. Learning that the President was headed for Missoula, Montana where the Chief was dedicating a new smoke jumper center, the cook said to the President, "I read where you are going to Missoula. There you will see my boss, Mr. McArdle. Give him my greetings and best wishes." Ike turned to his aide and said, "Any time a cook in the ranks wants to be remembered to a general, then you know it's a good outfit."

In 1962, McArdle was succeeded by Edward Parley Cliff. By then lumber consumption had reached 2.6 billion board feet annually, while across the country twenty-thousand ranchers were grazing seven-million head of livestock on forest lands. Between 1956 and 1970, the number of visitors to the forests jumped by 330%. This increase in recreation foreshadowed a clash between the growing environmental movement and traditional users of the forests—the timber and mining companies, and ranchers.

It was under Cliff's tenure that Congress passed the Wilderness Act of 1964 which placed 9.1 million acres of land within the agency's wilderness system. Still, cutting in non-wilderness lands continued apace, and under his management, a massive controversy erupted when the service engaged in a large clear-cut operation in the Monongahela National Forest in West Virginia. According to Bob Cermak, then supervisor of the nearby George Washington National Forest, "The clear-cut there was indeed awful. It looked like a hurricane had swept through the forest. It was an 800 acre clear cut. Next to a road. It was so unprofessional I couldn't believe it."

The furor created by the Monongahela debacle and another barefaced clear-cut in Montana prompted the service, as a matter of policy, to greatly reduce its clear-cuts.

Still, an environmental crusade had been launched of such magnitude it prompted Congress to pass the National Forest Management Act of 1976, under which agency cutting operations were further restricted. By then, members of numerous environmental organizations had opened up their checking accounts and launched a series of legal battles that continue to this day.

As early as 1972, Chief John Richard McGuire began carrying out many undertakings demanded by the environmentalists. Among several laws he dealt with was the 1973 Endangered Species Act, establishing standards for determining which plant and animal species were in danger of extinction. McGuire shared many of the environmental movement's goals, yet he and his foresters also realized that some of their objectives–most particularly those not yet stated–would be unattainable.

By then other factors were impacting the performance of every agency in the U.S. Government. By far the most significant was the decline of the Civil Service System established by the first U.S. Treasurer, Alexander Hamilton. Much like Teddy Roosevelt and Pinchot many years later, Hamilton held his employees accountable, insisting that only the most highly skilled be hired and only the most able advanced. However, in 1829, President Andrew Jackson ended the civil service by terminating its twenty-thousand employees and declaring, "No man has any more intrinsic right to official station than another...the duties of all public officers are...so plain and simple that men of intelligence may readily qualify themselves for their performance."

Jackson replaced the civil service with what became known as the patronage, or "spoils system." Over the next fifty years, to the victor went the spoils, with each new administration hiring its own staff right on down to the lowest paid custodian.

The dramatic turnovers following every presidential election provided no institutional memory for the incoming employees. All the techniques, values and ethics learned by the previous job holders simply vanished into thin air. In addition, there was no sense of loyalty within the agencies, because job security was so often predicated on election returns. Indeed, following an election, anyone could open a Washington newspaper and find an advertisement such as the following:

> *WANTED—A GOVERNMENT CLERKSHIP at a salary of not less than $1,000 per annum. Will give $100 to any one securing me such a position.*

President James Garfield, who was later assassinated by a thwarted patronage seeker, noted his dismay on finding "hungry office-seekers lying in wait for me like vultures on a wounded bison." Worse, by the end of the Civil War more and more government positions called for employees who possessed a technical, scientific, legal or foreign language background. Following Garfield's assassination, Congress passed the Pendleton Civil Service Act.

From that time onward civil service directors began developing a system directed by economy and efficiency. By 1923, a majority of employees operated under its merit system. Because government employees were less affected by economic cycles than those in private industry, they possessed greater job security. Still, stringent civil service examinations safeguarded the government and taxpayers from hiring the ever present next-to-worthless time-servers. Moreover, an unsatisfactory worker could readily be discharged for absenteeism, failure to meet deadlines, or general churlishness.

Beginning in 1933, however, the lowering of entrance standards by advocates of the New Deal brought many less-than-ideal employees into government. The emergency situation arising from the Second World War exacerbated the problem, and by that conflict's end, tens of thousands of nonproductive employees had found a home in the federal government. In 1949, following a bipartisan congressional study, the Civil Service Commission discharged thousands of these poorly performing employees, thus cutting tax payer expenses and streamlining government operations.

However, with the advent of the Lyndon B. Johnson Administration and the rise of the Employee Relations Board, once more it became increasingly difficult to discharge an unsatisfactory staff member. By 1972 the power of the employee board had grown to such an extent that it was next to impossible to fire an incompetent without his supervisor collecting a dossier of shortcomings a quarter-inch thick. This decline in the quality of employees did not affect all agencies equally. Among those able to maintain the standards of the past were NASA, the Department of Defense, the Department of Interior and the U.S. Forest Service. This was in large part due to the unique nature of their missions. Only those who were eager to deal with all manner of technical, mental and physical challenges, and toil without direct supervision tended to apply for work. Among the outdoor agencies, taking pleasure in small town living was almost a prerequisite for employment.

From their beginnings up into the 1970s, the outdoor agencies were very much a man's world. There were many women secretaries and some administrative assistants, but few female biologists, and no hydrologists, engineers, range managers or foresters. This was almost entirely owing to society's approach toward life. I once interviewed a retired forest service employee who attended Oregon State University in the late 1950s. Curious as to why no women were majoring in forestry or in any related science, he paid a visit to the college dean. In answer to his question as to why there were no women, the dean replied, "Forestry involves a lot of field work. The women—what would they do if they were out there and suddenly had to go to the bathroom?"

The upheaval of the 1960s put an end to this dean's line of thinking regarding women in the woods. Still, America's universities continued to turn out very few female scientists. Caught within a crossfire—the pressure to hire more women and too few woman graduating in the sciences—the forest service began hiring women to fill administrative, personnel and community relations positions previously held by men.

Chief McGuire himself urged the hiring of more women and minorities in forests across the nation. So did a number of regional foresters, who in fact began placing women on their fire crews. A startling example of the newly developing bias occurred as early as 1972, when a forest employee recalled applying for a fire position in New Mexico. Upon finding six separate stacks of applications, he asked the clerk why there were so many. In a matter-of-fact fashion, she told him that one was for women, one for Hispanics, one for blacks, one for Native Americans, one for local white men and the last for white men living elsewhere. He left his application behind, but realized as he departed that he stood no chance of being hired.

Toward the end of his term, Chief McGuire, using words that would one day prove prophetic, said, "Perhaps the greatest challenge facing forestry today is the calendar, namely the arrival of the 21st Century." Whether he was referring to the decay of the Civil Service System, the emerging environ-mental movement, or pressure from women and minority groups for special hiring rights is unclear. Perhaps he meant all three.

Regardless, he could scarcely have known how accurate his observation would prove.

Chapter 2

THE STRANGE ORIGINS OF THE

BERNARDI DECREE

If you are going to sin, sin against God, not the bu-reaucracy. God will forgive you but the bureaucracy won't—Admiral Hyman Rickover

BERNARDI V SECRETARY of Agriculture Earl Butz, as the lawsuit was first known, followed closely on the heels of the 1960s tumult that swept through America's campuses. By 1970, as the epoch receded, members of that same generation began emerging from graduate school and were finding employment in government work, the entertainment and news industries and within various law firms. From these key positions they soon began exerting more real power over America's social fabric than they ever wielded from its streets and campuses.

Among those in its vanguard were many female graduates who by now were convinced that in the past, America had persecuted its women in much the same manner it had persecuted African Americans. This was despite the huge abyss that lay between the manner in which former slaves and women were treated. Women did not have the right to vote, hold political office, or conduct business with the same liberty as men. Nonetheless, prior to 1920, in many respects they had been placed on a pedestal, very similar to the women of Great Britain. Indeed, nowhere else in the world were women treated with as much respect as in the U.K. and U..S. Still, because of the influence of such Frankfurt School writers as Eric Fromm and Kurt Lewin, many women's rights advocates actually believed that their fathers, grandfathers and great-grandfathers had deprived their mothers, grandmothers and great-grandmothers of their rights in the same manner as African Americans. Otherwise, how to account for the dearth of women in so many political positions, the sciences and trades?

Nature, it was thought, could have had little to do with these stark differences; differences that in fact have existed from time immemorial among peoples across the globe, but which feminists chose to ignore. With surprising ease, the women's movement was able to erase from the minds of most Americans the stark physical and psychological distinctions between the sexes. Features that to this day are both routinely observed, and routinely ignored by almost everyone. This schizophrenic practice made it easy for feminists to charge, with deceptive authority, that the lack of women in the professions and trades was the product of a patriarchal society that should be overthrown. Thus arose numerous women's rights organizations, such as the Equal Rights Advocates, based in San Francisco.

That the national forests of California, located in the most remote regions of the state, were soon to become a primary target of the feminist cause remains a source of bitterness among former employees to this day. Regardless, if these employees and the now tens of thousands of their brethren all across the country were to learn the truth behind the

Bernardi Decree, there is no reason to believe it would bring any finality to their loss. What might be expected is that with the facts finally brought to light, the public consciousness might be sufficiently raised to bring an end to practices that have since spread far beyond the forest service.

As far back as 1968 the U.S. Forest Service's Washington Office, without any prompting from Congress, began directing its foresters to hire more women and minorities, even if it meant creating positions that were not essential to operations. The reaction among the nation's nine regional foresters was decidedly mixed. One of the most cooperative was Douglas Leisz, who in 1971 assumed overall management of California's forests (Region Five). Bob Cermak, who had been a supervisor of forests in both Colorado and Virginia, commented on his return to California in 1978 after a ten year absence, "I was amazed at the difference in numbers of women there compared to the other regions. No one came close as Doug Leisz in hiring minorities and women."

Ironically, it was not in Leisz's forests the all-consuming fire that would leave them in cinders first erupted. Rather, it was at the Pacific Southwest Experimental Station's Berkeley office. Recall, the experimental division is a part of the forest service, but a separate entity established in 1928 by passage of the McSweeney- McNary Act. In 1968 its Berkeley office hired Gene (not the feminine Jean) Bernardi, a sociologist with a minor in one of the sciences, at the GS-09 level. It might be useful for the reader to know that a GS-09 is a professional grade that requires either a bachelor's degree or extended work in the field.

A number of forest employees have more or less depicted Bernardi as a scarlet devil, complete with forked tongue, a pair of horns that curve inward, and a dart tipped tail. But a photo reveals her to have been an ordinary looking woman in her mid-forties, wearing heavily rimmed glasses.

The record reveals that women were not well represented in the Berkeley Station's professional staff and that Raymond Emig, the personnel director, may have been under pressure to hire her in order to ward off a legal suit. In May 1969, just ten months after he hired Bernardi, she was promoted to GS-11. The following year, the experimental division established an Equal Employment Opportunity Advisory Panel and appointed her its chief advocate for women and minorities.

Chosen to chair the meetings was geneticist Leroy Johnson who later recalled, "I would travel from Placerville to Berkeley and was always on time for the meetings, but Bernardi never attended a single meeting. We would work hard, put together these equal opportunity plans, but afterward she would protest them, even though she was never present at any meeting...but no one in top management had the intestinal fortitude to force her to attend."

Regardless, in 1972 Bernardi asked to be promoted to GS-12, simply stating that she felt the work she was performing embraced all the responsibilities of that grade. But a desk audit by her supervisor, William Folkman, revealed that her responsibilities had not grown in any appreciable manner. In addition, as a member of the science division—as opposed to administrative—she had not produced a single research paper worthy of publication. After several hearings her request was denied.

In response, Bernardi filed a discrimination complaint with the Department of Agriculture's Equal Employment Opportunity Office in Washington DC. On April 9, 1973, investigator Frank J. Mousseau flew out to Berkeley to begin a probe. There, he learned that Bernardi had rummaged through Folkman's files and pulled out a rough draft of his decision not to promote her. The following day she confronted him with the draft, and went into such a tirade that he was unable to reply; nor was he able to learn how, or when, she gained access to his files. As he told Mousseau, "The belligerent manner in which she reacts in interpersonal relationships would not have been tolerated from a male employee...I have frequently been unable to suggest something to her in the way of help or guidance without her interpreting it as a personal insult to her abilities."

The Washington Office concluded that she had suffered no discrimination. She immediately appealed, and while waiting for a hearing, moved against the experimental station on another front. Using her position as equal opportunity counselor, she launched a class complaint, citing fourteen incidents of discrimination against women and minorities.

Yet more investigators were flown out from Washington. There, during a series of interviews with the thirteen employees suffering the alleged discrimination, they learned that six had never filed a complaint, and that Bernardi had completely misrepresented their sentiments. Another woman stated that Bernardi had strong-armed her into filing a complaint. Yet another based her allegation on the fact that she had taken a college course and not been reimbursed. She was unaware and had not been informed that the experimental station reimbursed for science-related courses only.

Among other unfounded charges was that of an African American man who complained that he had been disciplined for an automobile accident, while a white worker had not. He did not realize, nor was he informed, that the white man had not been responsible for his accident. Another minority was found to have been removed from a key position because he was unable to perform what were considered very critical tasks. The remaining three employees simply complained that they were tired of working in *dead-end jobs*. The fourteenth instance of discrimination involved no individual at all; the station had simply eliminated a position there was no longer a need for. In July 1973, the equal employment office closed Bernardi's third party complaint.

Because she was renowned for her noisy outbursts, had rifled through her supervisor's files, and misrepresented the complaints of ten fellow employees, it is difficult to believe she could have remained in a hostile work environment of her own creation for very long. In truth she held on for some time. In 1974, undoubtedly suffering from the self-induced pressures of office, she requested her employee status be changed from full time permanent, to intermittent permanent. When denied the request, she produced a doctor's certificate stating that she was not to work more than twenty hours a week. Despite appeals from the research station, she declined to divulge the nature of her disability, and was therefore docked. This resulted in her resignation in February 1975.

Regardless, the experimental station, Region Five and the forest service at large continued in their quest to hire more qualified women and minorities. Management's general thrust was to assemble a group of young people who at least expressed a desire to work out-of-doors. College-bound students were encouraged to take forestry related courses, while those not college bound were urged to study trades that might be of use to the agency. Far and away the most important of these was firefighting. Among African Americans, recruiting efforts were unsuccessful because the students possessed cultural backgrounds that made it very difficult for them to connect with life in rural America.

With Hispanics, in Southern California at least, recruiting efforts were much more successful, particularly with regard to firefighting. In fact, by the end of the decade there were a number of Hispanic engine captains, particularly in the forests surrounding the Los Angeles Basin. One of the early hires, Sotero Muniz, went on to become an engineer and then supervisor of the Sierra National Forest. But the agency was even more successful in recruiting white women. This was because increasing numbers of them were taking environmental courses in college, and because the forests were actively recruiting women to replace men in administrative work. Not only within Region Five, but all across the United States, men were slowly being phased out of administrative positions.

The net effect of these changes to forestry operations was negative. This was because many male administrative assistants had been drawn from rigorous disciplines such as firefighting. Rather than opting out of the service after twenty years of fighting fires, many of them, because of their fondness for the agency, remained to serve as advisors and staff assistants. Their all-encompassing knowledge of the terrain, the trails, and vegetation often rendered their judgments invaluable. Yet by the late 1970s some were being prompted to leave. Similarly, young men from outside the organization, though highly qualified for administrative positions, were being turned down out-of-hand. The standard phrase over the telephone was, "We already have a candidate. There's no need to submit."

This does not suggest that a woman applying for the position of wildlife biologist invariably had an advantage. Where field work was concerned, the nine regions and experimental stations tended to apply "gut instinct" as to who would do the best job. Even so, by 1976 Doug Leisz and his California foresters had been practicing outreach to such an extent, the college pipeline for woman had been drained almost dry, in all professions. It was a fact known, yet ignored in Washington D.C.

In early 1974, represented by The Equal Rights Advocates Law Firm, Gene Bernardi filed an equal employment opportunity complaint with the Northern Federal District Court of California, charging that the forest service had not promoted her to GS-12 because she was a woman. Her flawed claim and the fact that it was assumed by the advocates reveals something about that organization. Among its goals was the eradication of discrimination against women in all occupations, equal pay for equal work in all trades, and access for women to vocations that had never been open to them.

On paper these are admirable objectives. But within a very short time the measures the advocates were willing to apply in order to meet these objectives would grow much worse than the problems they were intended to resolve. Their targets were later expanded to include promoting the rights of illegal immigrant women, the enforcement of rigid sexual harassment codes, and advancing the lesbian life style.

The most prominent of its founders was Mary Dunlap, who outlined and presented Bernardi's two complaints. She became a strong advocate of lesbian rights, and in 1977 left the firm to become a professor at Stanford University, where she developed an entire law curriculum focused on sexual orientation. Another founder was Nancy Davis, who graduated from the Boalt Hall School of Law in 1972, and taught at the University of San Francisco. She and Herma Kay did the research for a book titled *Sex Based Discrimination*, co-authored by future U.S. Supreme Court Justice Ruth Bader Ginsberg. Davis would remain a part of Bernardi v the Department of Agriculture longer than any other advocate member. Described as short, trim, and dark haired, she was the organization's most effusive member.

Another associate was Wendy Williams whose specialty remains *gender and law*. She co-authored a book on the subject, and later became a member of the Georgetown Woman's Law and Public Policy Fellowship Program. Finally, though not then a member, Judith Kurtz, who replaced Dunlap after her departure, was for many years perhaps its most effective attorney. Kurtz is portrayed as being of medium height and solidly built, with brown hair. She possessed an imposing court room manner, and among all advocates was most succinct in her use of the English language.

The chances of the advocates prevailing in Bernardi v Secretary of Agriculture Earl Butz, within whose department the forest service and its experimental division still resided, were slim to say the least. But this perhaps testifies to the advocates' mindset, the members of which were eager to bring about sweeping social change to perhaps the most masculine bastion in the United States. That they were willing to represent a client with so a feeble a case, suggests they were trolling for work, not necessarily to pay off mammoth debts, but because they were being underwritten by well-heeled, left-leaning foundations.

Although they failed to enlist any woman employed by the service—other than Gene Bernardi—almost immediately the advocates filed a class action suit, also titled "Bernardi v Butz." On April 29, 1974, just four months after presentation, Northern California District Court Judge Samuel Conti announced his decision: Bernardi did not have a compelling suit. Because no other plaintiffs were listed, neither did she have a class complaint. Each party was charged with covering its own legal expenses.

Undaunted, the advocates appealed both cases before the Ninth Federal Circuit Court of Appeals. They cited a recent U.S. Supreme Court opinion written by Potter Stewart—Chandler v Roudebush. The opinion stated that even though Chandler presented no incriminating evidence of discrimination by Roudebush, if incriminating evidence was suspected, she was entitled to a fresh search for evidence. If uncovered, she was permitted a trial *de novo* (fresh trial).

Almost two years passed. Finally on July 15, 1976, the ninth circuit ruled that the Bernardi Class was entitled to a trial *de novo*. The ruling came about even though no other plaintiff had attached herself to the suit. It was a decision that reached far beyond any reasonable intention of Congress when it passed the 1964 Civil Rights Act, and Chief Justice Stewart's decision in Chandler v Roudebush. In truth, the ninth circuit had granted the advocates a legal fishing expedition without precedent. Systematic discrimination within the Pacific Southwest Experimental Station was highly unlikely, but another disgruntled employee might be found. For Davis, Dunlap and Williams, this should have been easier than shooting sturgeon in a barrel. Nonetheless, they never produced that unhappy employee.

In the midst of their quest, Bernardi turned down an offer by the Berkeley Experimental Station for a rehearing, thus terminating her personal suit. In October 1977, the advocates returned to the Northern District Court with anecdotal evidence of discrimination, but a class action suit that still consisted of the original plaintiff only. Bowing to pressure from the Ninth Circuit Court, District Judge Samuel Conti certified the suit and titled it Bernardi v Bergland, the then Secretary of Agriculture. As matters evolved over the many years, the case would always be legally known as Bernardi v who ever happened to be Secretary of Agriculture.

While West Coast district judges are an ideological mixed bunch, the Ninth Circuit Court of Appeals has long been regarded as the most liberal of the eleven appeals courts in the United States. Since 1978 more of its decisions have been overturned by the U.S. Supreme Court than any other appellate. Between 2002 and 2004 alone the high court over-turned 60 of its 81 decisions coming under review–more than all the other circuits combined. Little wonder judicial schol-ars have recognized it as the one appellate within the United States most determined to supplant the nation's elected offi-cials with rule from the bench.

It might also be useful to note that even though the U.S. Supreme Court overturned 75% of the ninth circuit's deci-sions, it reviews less than two percent of all federal court judgments, meaning that the eleven circuit courts and the district courts beneath them are the final arbiters in 98% of all federal suits filed. Davis, Williams and Kurtz (who had replaced Dunlap) were by now so well bankrolled, they were preparinng to flex additional legal muscle. Indeed, their blueprint now was to expand the Bernardi Class Complaint beyond the six experimental stations and their 250 employ-ees to the entire Region Five (all of California) with its 5,800 permanent and 4,000 seasonal employees—charged with managing 20 million acres of land.

They had met with no success in recruiting for their suit, but in addition to the very friendly ninth circuit, they knew that a benign environment existed among forest sov-ereigns both in San Francisco and Washington, DC. Proof presented itself early in 1979 when the service, and Secretary of Agriculture Robert Bergland, invited the advocates to a face to face meeting at the nation's capital.

There, within this friendly environ, Davis and Kurtz began a general assault, not only against the experimental division, but against the single forest region that had done more to promote women than any other; and an agency of the federal government that had done as much as any other to increase the same numbers. By 1979 the percentage of employees in Region Five who were women had risen to

27.1%. The numbers varied within the other forest regions, but averaged out at 24%. Both percentages speak of first-rate progress by an organization that depended heavily on the professions that men instinctively found most appealing, and those trades that relied so much on physical strength and stamina.

These strides meant little to the advocates, who understood that however much their class complaint was void of clients, Secretary Bergland, and most of the Carter Administration were in sympathy with their mission. In addition, by then there were five deputy chief foresters in Washington, largely urban types, who in fact had lost touch with the forests and their employees. "It was the downfall of the service," said forester Bob Cermak ruefully. "They should have been spending more time out there. All the assistant chiefs failed to get on the ground. They began to see themselves as contacts with the power groups in Washington, instead of making contact with the people at work."

At that first face-to-face meeting it is not difficult to assess what passed through the minds of Secretary Bergland and Chief Forester A. Max Peterson who in 1979 had replaced John McGuire. The Carter Administration had been relentless in its demand that all federal agencies hire more women. Many felt the employment percentages for all bureaus should reflect the female civilian work force at large, whether that agency be the Department of Defense, Department of Interior, Department of State, or the Department of Agriculture.

All of which was in direct contravention of Title VII of the 1964 Civil Rights Act, which was intended to clarify, and underscore Section I of the Fourteenth Amendment—that all persons as individuals, not as group members, would not have their lives, liberty or property reduced without due process of law.

The sponsors of the 1964 Civil Rights Act, U.S. Senators Joseph Clark and Clifford Case, were emphatic that the act ensured no individual persons would be at risk of having their civil rights repealed to satisfy the claims of groups of people. Referring to the importance of individual rights guaranteed by the Constitution, the two wrote, "There is no requirement in Title VII that an employer maintain a racial balance to his workforce. On the contrary, any deliberate attempt to maintain a racial balance, whatever such balance would involve, is a violation of Title VII, because maintaining such a balance would require an employer to hire on the basis of race."

Another supporter of the civil rights act was Senator Hubert H. Humphrey, who vigorously declared, "I will start eating the pages of the law, page by page, if anyone can find a clause that calls for quotas or preferences of racial balance in jobs or education." Working tirelessly to ensure that no quotas would ever insinuate themselves into the act, was Republican Senator Everett Dirksen, who emplaced statutory language to eliminate them. Another Republican Senator, John Tower, added an amendment that ensured stringent employment tests for public employment would continue as always. Finally, in the House of Representatives, Judiciary Committee Chairman Emanuel Celler placed an amendment in the bill, "to prevent the Equal Employment Opportunity Commission from making *any* substantive regulatory interpretations of the act [italics added]."

Incredibly, the following year, Lyndon B. Johnson wrote out executive order 11246, directing federal contractors to compile and present to the federal government racial (later gender) tables drawn from minority talent pools in their area. Historically, presidents invoked executive orders only on occasion. They have the same impact as laws passed by Congress, but upon completion of the president's term, automatically expire—unless renewed by his successor. Because of distraction by the Vietnam War and other Great Society programs, Johnson's order had little impact on government personnel practices.

Yet his directive was given great impetus by Republican President Richard M. Nixon, who within a year of taking office replaced it with Executive Order 11478, directing all federal agencies to prepare an affirmative action plan; the Civil Service Commission was then to follow with a series of *upward mobility programs.* The key provision to Nixon's order was that the Equal Employment Opportunity Office will be "an integral part of every aspect of personnel policy and practice in the employment, development, advancement and treatment of civilian employees of the Federal government."

Nixon's out-and-out subversion of the Fourteenth Amendment and 1964 Civil Rights Act remains little known to the public because of the monumental hatred for him among liberal Democrats and because Republicans were so embarrassed by the order they simply swept it under the carpet. In 1977, when Jimmy Carter settled into office, he took a look at Nixon's executive order, liked what he saw, and rather than allowing it to expire, extended it.

In another event filled with irony, during the Carter years, Congress passed the Civil Service Reform Act of 1978, the contents of which should have forever demolished the dreams of Davis, Kurtz and Williams. The act emphatically stated that the merit system of hiring and promotion, as well as the veteran's benefits provision, would remain in place. Despite President Carter's desire to advance women and minorities, Congress at the time was greatly disturbed by the growing number of incompetents within the federal workforce, and balked at passing any act that would sponsor a program of proportional employee representation.

Rather, it encouraged supervisors to discharge unsatisfactory employees. Among other top objectives was its insistence on employee integrity, the stressing of competitiveness, and full utilization of the promotion-by-merit system. In essence, Congress was attempting to re-establish the strong Civil Service System begun by the Pendleton Act, and with certain interruptions continued through the administrations of Truman, Eisenhower and Kennedy.

But the act also contained a passage that conflicted with the above—specifically that which lies in Title III, Section 310, which states that merit principle supports achieving diversity, since it expects agencies to recruit from a representative pool of applicants. This paragraph, buried deep within the 83 page Civil Service Reform Act of 1978, was seized upon by the Equal Rights Advocates and a multitude of other fringe groups to advance their social agendas, when in truth it did not provide a hole large enough to stick a pin through. Yet within two years the advocates would blow a hole through both the 1964 Civil Rights Act and 1978 Civil Service Reform Act large enough for a Saturn Rocket to pass through. Well aware of the Nixon executive order and the strange paragraph stuck in the 1978 reform act, the Equal Rights Advocates prepared to forge ahead. So too were their *adversaries* at the negotiating table, Chief Forester A. Max Peterson, Region Five Forester Zane Gray Smith, and Secretary of Agriculture Bob Bergland.

Prior to taking his post Bergland had served four terms as a congressman from the state of Minnesota, where he routinely received the endorsement of that state's far left Democratic Farmer Labor Party. Max Peterson was a native of Doniphan, Missouri, who upon taking a degree in civil engineering, entered forest service employment. Heavy set and balding, among the various photos of chief and regional foresters, he looks less like *a man of the woods* than any other. Peterson may have possessed a fondness for civil engineering, but the record reveals that his real passion was social engineering. Zane Gray Smith, who in 1978 replaced Doug Leisz as director of Region Five, was a slightly built man with a receding hair line. He was described as personally pleasant, but comments made by those interviewed include the following: *in over his head, a dreamer,* and *easily distracted.* One fire management officer described him as a company man. "If the chief forester told Smith to cut down all the trees in Region Five, he would have cut them down that same year."

Both sides maneuvered through what is known in legal parlance, as the *discovery phase,* the gathering of evidence for what would seem a most improbable legal event—a class complaint with but one complainant. Then in July 1979, at the urging of Peterson and Smith, the Department of Agriculture and the advocates announced they were entering into a consent decree. This is to say they had agreed to work out their differences before a presiding judge, thereby purportedly rescuing the forest service from an expensive court trial. Bergland, Peterson and Smith took this singular step against the advice of their attorneys at the Department of Justice.

A consent decree is a voluntary agreement by the defendant to cease illegal activities in return for an end of charges brought by the plaintiff. Upon reaching an accord on how the *illegal activities* will be ended, the two parties go before a judge to receive a formal stamp of approval. A decree cannot be modified unless both parties attach their signatures to the modification and go back before the judge to receive his certification.

During its negotiations with the advocates, the forest service prevailed on just two points: one, the advocates agreed that the service was *not guilty* of any illegal activities against women; two, Gene Bernardi was to be dismissed from the suit in exchange for $21,250 to cover her attorney fees. In return, the agency agreed to allow the class complaint to expand from the six Pacific Southwest Research Stations and their 250 employees, to all of Region Five and its ten-thousand employees.

Further, the forest service agreed to employ affirmative action to increase the number of women to approximately the number employed in the U.S. civilian work force. Women were also to be placed on its most important decision making panels. These advances would take place over a five year period, once given the legal sanction of a federal judge.

In addition a court monitor, technically the eyes and ears of the judge, would be granted access to all documents relating to the decree. Providing evidence of how complicit Peterson was in making these concessions, he was appointed *Consent Decree Coordinator.* All these compromises were made against the advice of the Justice Department. Several of its attorneys pointed out that Peterson's agency already had an equal employment program in place; its efforts to promote more women into higher places were a matter of record; further, nowhere had greater strides been made on their behalf than in Region Five—the very locale into which the decree was to expand. "Why punish benign conduct?" the agency was asked.

Worse, given the unique nature of forestry work, to assume the ratio of men and women would anytime soon reflect the nation's urban/suburban workforce was an impossibility. But Peterson and Smith would not listen. Meanwhile, President Carter, at Bergland's urging, ordered the recalcitrant Department of Justice to provide the service with $1.5 million to offset the costs of implementing the decree.

Although certified as a class complaint the year before, no women had thus far come forward, and with Bernardi ejected from her own suit, the advocates were now devoid of a litigant. It was thus the weakest class complaint ever filed–a class complaint without a complainant. It was also one of the strangest consent decrees ever entered into. By definition a consent decree consists of an agreement by which a defendant ceases illegal activities, in return for an end of charges. Yet the forest service's own legal arm had already informed the agency that it had not engaged in any illegal activities. And the Equal Rights Advocates had agreed *to an end to the charges*, admitting that the agency had not been guilty of any past illegal activities against women.

Despite all the foregoing, the advocates prevailed upon their *adversary* to mail Region Five's two-thousand permanent female employees working since 1972 (including all who had departed), notices advising them to enter the complaint. In a surprising turn of events, just thirty-one responded. This prompted a good deal more soul searching within the Justice Department. If barely 1.5% of region's women expressed a desire to join the complaint, just how many oppressed women were out there?

The advocates acknowledged the number of new class members to be disappointing, but argued that other class complaints involving small numbers of litigants had resulted in several social benefits. In truth, as Davis and Kurtz knew, Peterson, Bergland and Smith had long since abandoned their legal team, and taken seats on their side of the table. Having deserted that legal team and 99.9% of Region Five employees, the trio turned and began engaging their collaborators in a dialogue over how much cultural change would be required to improve forestry management.

The only positive results to emerge from the disaster was the fact that no quota system had been set in place, the agency would continue to hire and promote by merit, and the other eight forest regions were exempt from the decree.

Chapter 3

THE GREAT BETRAYAL

Relying on numbers is not good enough. It is to correct organizational structure and to correct attitudes.—Region Five Forester Zane Smith on the Bernardi Decree

WHEN THE EQUAL Rights Advocates returned to San Francisco in late 1979, they carried with them a victory of overwhelming proportions. True enough, Peterson could claim that 80% of his work-force had been spared a groundbreaking social experiment. And the contours of the consent decree had not been narrowly defined enough to initiate an explicit quota system. Still, looking over the hiring figures of the past decade, some real number-crunching was at hand. There were employees who were going to pay for that number-crunching, while great harm would be visited on the forests.

Because Peterson was still conferring with several environmental groups, as he welcomed the aid of Bergland, he was now similarly eager to turn the fine points of working out the decree over to regional director Zane Smith. The details were hammered out between Smith and the advocates in San Francisco. He agreed that within five years the number of women employed in the region would be proportional to the number of women in the American civilian workforce. This would be accomplished through affirmative action and an outreach program that stretched well beyond the usual sources—to universities in other states, forests owned and operated by the various states, and forests owned and operated by private timber firms.

All select advisory panels (usually three professional employees), assigned to evaluate each applicant for promotion or hire would always include at least one woman. What were regarded as artificial barriers to woman seeking promotion were to be struck from each job description. This was a concession that would be taken advantage of time and again by the advocates, who argued that qualifications previously created by the service were of no consequence to forestry operations— when in fact they were very consequential to operations.

The conferees also agreed that gender could be a factor in the hiring and promotion of personnel, but that it would only be used as a tie breaker. When a man and a woman were found equally qualified for a position, the woman would be chosen. This agreement overlooks the fact that human qualifications, much like human personalities, appearances and fingerprints are never quite the same. Still, the plan expressly stated that the rights of male employees could not be trammeled upon; nor would any of the agencies' *firmly rooted employment expectations*, the most important of which was promotion by merit. When the best qualified candidate was decided on, that best qualified candidate, regardless of gender, would receive the promotion. The advocates were also explicitly prohibited from forcing region to hire unqualified personnel to reach its affirmative action goals.

After hammering out their accords, Smith, Davis, Kurtz and Williams sent out memos to each of the eighteen forests and to the six experimental stations announcing they intended to take the consent decree before the Northern District Court for its certification. Word soon spread to the employees, who quickly noted that should the best qualified candidates continue to be promoted, gender parity would never be reached. At least not without violating Title VII of the 1964 Civil Rights Act. The unhappiness was such that both Max Peterson and Zane Smith signed and posted a letter assuring employees that their civil rights would never be violated.

On December 19, 1979, Smith and the advocates appeared in the courtroom of the now familiar Samuel Conti. Appointed a district judge by President Nixon, Conti was described as a short, balding, bespectacled arbiter, who at the time of the hearing appeared to have been in his late fifties. He was a conservative jurist who tended to follow the letter of legislative law, which should have boded well for 99.9% of Region Five and experimental station employees, all of whom over the past year had no one in Washington safeguarding their interests.

One of the first witnesses Conti heard was employee representative Corky Lazzarno, who informed him that the region's forests were already being monitored by an equal employment watchdog group, had implemented an equal employment discovery plan, and in the past had attempted numerous other affirmative action programs. To instate the decree would simply create one more layer of bureaucracy for the region to throw its money at. She also warned of tremendous workload bottlenecks and professional pipeline problems if the decree was advanced as designed.

Other witnesses explicitly stated that one reason men advanced faster than women, was because they were much more eager to relocate to other forests, and indeed other regions. Some warned of the physical disparities between men and women. After listening to further testimony, Conti closed the hearing and scheduled another.

That same December, the National Federation of Federal Employees filed a suit against the decree, stating that the interests of Region Five employees, was at great risk. But suddenly on January 17, 1980, for reasons unknown, the union withdrew its petition. It is altogether puzzling it did so, in view of the fact that Bernardi was still a non-binding agreement, but Secretary Bergland was still at the helm of his agency, and may well have played a role in turning the suit aside.

Letters of protest began pouring into Conti's courtroom, many from women. Ann Dow Hanson of the Modoc National Forest wrote that when she was hired in 1974, she was hired *only* because she was a woman. Warning that "promoting too many women into areas of fire management and engineering would result in declining work quality, and great resentment on the staff," she concluded, "The Decree cannot be honored if veteran's preferences and merit promotion remain a factor." Susan Wickman of Quincy, noting the service's long-established tradition of being straightforward with its employees, wondered why not a single copy of the consent decree could be found in any manager's office. Wickman was onto something. The decree still required a good deal more tweaking before it was to be certified, but in the years to follow only a few hundred well-heeled urban clerks would ever lay eyes on it.

On January 18, 1980, Conti held a second hearing. Of the 2,000 women who had been notified of the class complaint, just 31 opted to join, and of these just three were present in his courtroom. This meant that within the Judge's chambers the staff of the Equal Rights Advocates, now numbering eleven, outnumbered the class members they were representing.

Conti's thoughts on why there were so few plaintiffs might be imagined, but he had already been down that road with the ninth circuit before, and so turned his attention to *needs assessments.* As the decree was certain to cost the tax payers a *bundle,* he wanted concrete results. To achieve those results he ordered the service to draw up a listing of interim goals and time tables to be later presented. He then adjourned.

A full year passed during which time alarm over the decree across Region Five and the experimental stations abated. It is difficult to assess what precisely was taking place at the regional headquarters on Samson Street, San Francisco. The proceedings were so secretive that Bob Cermak, who temporarily assumed Zane Smith's position as regional forester, was never apprised as to what was occurring. During our interview, he admitted that he had no desire to learn what they were up to. He much preferred to be out of town, working in the forests with his foresters.

Most likely "postmodern" forestry was what they were working on. That it took so long for the parties to cobble together their interim goals and timetables also suggests that some in attendance felt certain the decree was unworkable, and that the careers of thousands of their fellow workers would soon be sacrificed.

On February 2, 1981, Conti held another hearing, during which Smith and the advocates spelled out their mechanisms for advancing the consent decree. Region itself would undertake a *needs assessment* that would be complete by November 1, 1981; it would then prepare a plan detailing how both the interim and long term goals would be achieved, to be completed in early 1982. The decree would then be implemented, with each supervisor taking charge of his own forest.

That yet another year would pass before the decree was implemented says something about the work habits of Smith and his regional office, where process had clearly assumed primacy over goals. Conti reacted by scheduling a hearing for May, at which time the parties would present the court their entire program. It is of interest to note that during this key interval, the advocates, embarrassed by the small number of women who had joined their complaint, conducted a second and more detailed round of mailings. This resulted in the enlistment of 175 more current and former regional employees.

On May 1 the Judge was presented an elaborate plan that would not only increase the number of women in Region Five, but greatly increase their numbers in high level positions. Smith then announced that he was hiring an outside consulting firm to design and implement the various programs necessary for success. This was almost as good as admitting that he and his staff had squandered another three months of time. Still, there was progress enough to mollify Conti, who was renowned for his short temper. Both parties agreed that the advocates could file a motion for contempt of court should region fail to fully utilize the Department of Justice's $1.5 million fund. Established too was a grievance procedure for women who faced hiring/promotion abuses. Both sides also agreed to appoint a court monitor who would be entitled access to all documents regarding region's hiring practices. Further, those who had joined the class suit were to be the court monitor's eyes and ears, and were to report any difficulties they encountered.

It thus becomes clear, even at this early date, that Smith and his staff, which included Deputy Regional Forester Warren Davies, and consent decree specialists Elaine Grimm and Gwen Hoover, had endorsed the notion that the court monitor would *not* be a neutral party. Rather, she was to act as a prod for recalcitrant forest service workers. It was a highly irregular concession, because a court monitor is intended to act as a prod only when one party to a consent decree has admitted to legal wrongdoing, which the agency had not.

The decree was projected to end on June 30, 1986, precisely five years after its commencement on July, 1, 1981. At that time the percentage of women employed within all disciplines would reflect the percentage of women in America's work force. No specific quotas had been arrived at, but the lopsidedness of the provisions appear to have astonished Conti, who upon realizing how badly skewed they were, is quoted as saying to Smith, "Are you sure you want to do this? You are making good progress as it is."

Smith affirmed, yes, he wanted to do just this. Conti did not like what he heard, and a witness states that he shook his head, raised his gavel, pointed it at Smith and said: "I will hold you to this!"

The chamber cleared and the advocates and regional team members returned to their offices. Matthew Stuart, a Washington staffer who sat in during the hearing, reported the arrangements back to Chief Peterson, who gave them his nod. Thus, from the courtrooms and cubicles of San Francisco, to the administrative centers of the Washington D.C., events conspired to assure that one side of the negotiating table—representing 99.9% of Region Five's employees—would forever be barred from approaching that table.

Their fate typified the fate of many working class Americans, underscored by Christopher Lasch, author of *The Revolt of the Elites*. According to Lasch, by the late Twentieth Century America was no longer a land of potential uprisings by the working classes. Rather, it had become the land of "revolting elites." The professional and managerial types--those *symbolic analysts,* who were living out their lives in a world as rarified and abstract as it was comfortable—were now leading the revolt. They were leading it by breaking hundreds of laws through trafficking in word manipulation and counterfeit data.

Shortly after their court date, the forest service and advocates agreed that Diane Winokur, of the San Francisco law firm of Winokur and Freeman, would be appointed court monitor. Although obliged to work with Winokur, the Southwest Pacific Research Station–where the entire class complaint arose eleven years before–had earlier decided to adopt its own formula for reaching objectives. Because the events that followed were far more traumatic for America and its forests, the focus of this volume from here on out is the forests.

A poor rendition of a photograph of Diane Winokur reveals a pleasant, beaming face, tightly bound by dark hair. Her semi-annual reports disclose that she was a feminist, a tireless worker who knew very little about forestry, and who found herself in a continual state of astonishment at the road blocks she encountered. Yet she seems to have possessed a sense of reality that neither the advocates, Zane Smith or Max Peterson could ever lay claim to.

With regard to Smith, in historical terms, he possibly saw himself as a sort of Susan B. Anthony of the U.S. Forest Service. The naiveté he demonstrated in reaching out to the advocates, both with regard to objectives and time tables, reveals he had no understanding of the work bottlenecks, personnel pipeline blockages, and the great animosities that would soon tear through his forests like a cyclone.

Evidence as to how close his line of thinking paralleled that of Robert Owen, the English visionary who attempted to establish a socialist utopia in Indiana in 1825, is the following sequence of events he envisioned. He and his staff assumed that the very existence of the decree, beginning July 1, 1981, would create a momentum that in the coming year would increase the number of women employees by 10%.

During the second lap of his Five Year Plan, he determined that the process of educating women with regard to the prospects awaiting them would raise their work force level by another 10%; or in summary to 121 women for every 100 that had been employed in July 1981. For the third year he assumed that the removal of barriers to promotion would have such a resounding effect, the number of women employed would increase by another 25%; or in studied numbers there would be 151.25 women working in region for every 100 in July 1981.

For the fourth year he assumed that through the distribution of quality opportunities—the natural result of three years of success —the number of women would rise another 30%. In real numbers by July 1985 there would be 196.11 women working in the forests for every 100 in 1981.

For year five the focused training and development programs designed to orientate more women toward forestry would increase their numbers an additional 25%, which in turn meant that for every 100 women in July 1981, 245.26 would be employed on the final day of the Five Year Plan. This infers that by June 30, 1986 women would represent 67% of region's work force (in fairness to Smith he did not tabulate the percentages). With numbers like that so easily arrived at, he and his staffers could pretty much sit back and watch Bernardi grow on its own, as if each forest lay within a giant Petri dish, beneath a friendly grow lamp. It is doubtful the hard-boiled women at the office of the advocates took Smith's projections very seriously. But his earnest ruminations about a subject so dear to their hearts, doubtless convinced them that they had his twenty-million acres of timberland pretty well stowed in their handbags.

As Smith later wrote, "Relying on numbers is not good enough. It is to correct the organizational structure, and to correct attitudes." This is to say that Smith suffered from a severe case of cultural cringe. The very organization that had performed with such striking efficiency since the days of Pinchot and Roosevelt was in dire need of repair.

On July 15, 1981, two weeks after the Bernardi Decree went into effect, a tragedy occurred after a fire broke out on the Angeles National Forest. Gilbert Lopez, a fire captain, went in search of an inexperienced pump operator who had become separated from the fire team. Though she later managed to find refuge with another crew, Lopez never returned from his search. His charred remains were found after the fire was extinguished.

In response, Smith sent a letter to all fire captains in the region, warning them that too many fire recruits were being certified without adequate training. In his words, "This situation deeply concerns me because of the wide use of inexperienced firefighters in the region each year. These crew members, although inexperienced, meet minimum training requirements, but lack the firefighting skills that only comes with experience."

After signing the letter, he turned his attention back toward making certain that his forests would continue to supplement their fire crews with inexperienced firefighters who lacked the requisite skills that come only with experience. He did so by hiring a San Francisco consulting firm titled *Urban Management Consultants*. It is astonishing how much authority over the years, Smith and his successors would entrust their agency to persons and organizations with so little knowledge of forestry and rural life. Several months passed before he and the advocates decided that Urban Management's plan had too many infirmities. Another company was sought, but this one possessed similar failings. As a result, the "needs assessment" phase of consent was not reached until April 30, 1982, for a total loss of ten months time (in addition to the fifteen months frittered away before the decree was certified).

The second phase of implementation was the development of interim goals that would guide the agency toward its long term objective. Here region stumbled into the arms of another urban consulting firm, and its agreed-upon time table was not reached until July 26, 1983, leaving the agency two full years behind schedule. The third phase involved arranging the steps necessary to implement both interim and long term goals. The big reason for failure here was the personnel pipeline for women in scores of disciplines had been reduced to a trickle. It was a debacle foreseen by everyone in Washington and San Francisco as early as 1978.

The third-rate quality of the regional staff, the third-rate quality of its consulting firms, and the pipeline fiasco were but three reasons for the agency's failure. Others were a lack of consent decree staff for the individual forests, and an incredulous disbelief on the part of forest supervisors and district rangers that such schemes were being contemplated. The truth is, Smith and his staff had completely abandoned their most vital mission—hands-on management of the forests. Thus their sole recourse was to point fingers at the forest supervisors for wasting time, a failing they were guilty of many times over. When the finger pointing failed, they directed that each forester's performance evaluation be heavily rigged on his success in carrying out the decree.

Two years had now passed since the Carter Administration had been replaced by that of Ronald Reagan. Everything that is known of Reagan suggests that the events unfolding in Region Five, *had he known*, would have been anathema to him. Still, he was one of the few presidents who knew how to slash budgets; and sure enough, the forest service took its whack. Unhappily, as had long been the custom among secretaries of agriculture, his secretary, John Block, was content to allow Peterson and Smith to carve up their budgets as they saw fit—which was why the forests took such a direct hit. Smith and company simply vacuumed money out of each forest's operating budget and placed the funds within either the regional or forest supervisor offices where they were allotted to consent decree work.

Secretary Block is said to have been astonished when he later learned what the agency was up to. But unlike Bergland, and like most of his predecessors, he decided to leave the agency to its own devices. One of the very few quotes he left behind is perhaps indicative of the depth of thought he gave the matter. "There are less politics within the Department of Agriculture than in other cabinet positions, but there is still some politics."

As deeply wounded as Region Five may have been, the wound need not have been mortal, but in July 1982, at a semi-annual compliance meeting, a more sinister development took place. Smith and the advocates added two new clauses to "Article IV" of the Bernardi Decree. By June 30, 1986, sixty general service disciplines and all grades within would have 43% female representation. This meant all eighty ranger districts in the state, from the most remote areas of the Klamath and Modoc National Forests, to the most accessible on the Angeles and Cleveland, would be quota tagged. In addition, by July 1986, 77% of GS-09 administrative positions were to be filled by women. The capitulation took place fourteen months after Judge Conti, with a stern warning to Smith, gave his approval to the much more vague *women in the work force* plan. It took place almost exactly one year after the death of Gilbert Lopez, and the warning letter Smith had addressed to all fire captains, regarding the dangers of employing too many inexperienced firefighters.

Chief Peterson read over and approved the modification to Article IV almost immediately. He then mailed a copy, within a binder of other documents to Secretary Block. Uninterested in matters pertaining to the agency, it would be some years before Block became aware of its existence. Judge Conti learned of the additions to Article IV the following January when Diane Winokur submitted her semi-annual report to the court. One can imagine his wrath upon learning that his courtroom had been circumvented without a hearing. In truth, he never signed it, which of course meant the article never became law. But rather than a grand courtroom fireworks display, he quietly decided to permit Smith to thrash about in what one employee termed, "a bear trap of his own setting."

Implicit with the extralegal incorporation of 43% was the extinction of the Golden Rule, the universally accepted premise, "Do unto others as you would have them do unto you." Dead too was the notion of reciprocity—that everyone has a right to just and equal treatment and a responsibility to ensure that others receive the same just and equal treatment. In their place the agency introduced the lethal *plutonium rule*. Incoming employees would *not* be required to adapt to their senior employee's expectations or traditions—so essential to meeting mission objectives. Rather, the new employees would see to it that the seniors adapted to *their* expectations and innovations.

Chapter 4

THE AVALANCHE

If Prometheus was worthy of the wrath of heaven for kindling the first fire upon earth, how ought all the gods honor the men who make it their professional business to put them out?—John Godfrey Saxe

THE CONSENSUS AMONG the employees of California's forests is that they first heard of the consent decree in 1981—the year of Judge Conti's certification. Everyone knew of Gene Bernardi, although none knew her personally. They only vaguely comprehended the Equal Rights Advocates, presuming them to be some sort of civil rights organization focused on bringing relief to oppressed people.

For reasons already cited, more than three years passed before anyone began feeling consent's effects. During this period rumors were constantly in the air, prompting many discussions. But as the months slipped into years and no orders reached the work stations, the decree, while not written off, was pretty much forgotten. Then in the spring of 1983 events began to roll. Quite naturally, within such a far flung operation as Region Five, they were not wheeled out in any orderly manner, some forests being immediately impacted, while others were not.

Aside from the Cleveland National Forest where Ken Wolstenhom was employed, one of the first to feel the shock was the Angeles National Forest. Totaling 680,000 acres, spread across five ranger districts just north of the Los Angeles basin, the Angeles receives more visitors than any other forest in the nation. It is densely covered in chaparral, renowned for its startling views, the 36,000 acre San Gabriel Wilderness, towering 10,064 Mount Baldy, and a herd of bighorn sheep.

Why the fire teams of these two forests were among the first to be targeted remains a mystery. One reason may have been that a majority of fire crews are seasonal employees, who unlike permanent employees, can be easily discharged, or as was the case in the spring of 1983, simply not called back to work. Perhaps they were chosen because they lay adjacent a densely populated area, where many young women resided. Regardless, for the first time in their careers, front line supervisors were being told they could no longer hire employees on their own. This prerogative had been usurped by consent decree panelists who had set up shop in the same building as their forest supervisor.

Let it be said that these two forests, and every other forest, had great difficulty recruiting women into their crews, because a majority had no desire to fight fires. Thus, from the start consent panelists resorted to deception and outright lying in describing the type of work their new hires would perform. This double-dealing was repeated over and over because so many women, after spending a few weeks on a fire crew, departed.

Yet the effort was so massive that within months the forests were able to hire many women who felt they were capable of becoming firefighters, or to assume the duties of a fire captain with as little as eighteen months training. Unhappily for everyone, the forests in particular, a fair percentage of those who succumbed to the agency's blandishments were rigid feminists, who possessed negative sentiments toward men. Worsening relations further were the consent decree officials themselves, who assured the new hires that should any dispute with a man arise, they would receive the agency's undivided backing.

At the time the decree was detonated, the Angeles counted 390 full time employees, among them Bill Shaw who went to work for the forest in 1977, when the agency was still healthy, and labor intensive projects such as controlled burns and slash cutting were proceeding apace. Though he is now sixty- years-old, sports a head of white hair and a white moustache, he comes across as younger than his years. Perhaps it is his animation and excitability of manner.

He was born in Arcadia, California, where as a boy he and his family routinely camped and hiked in the forests, and came to know many of those employed in them. He would return home after these excursions and as he admitted without embarrassment, fall asleep dreaming about Lassie, Smokey the Bear, or some other animal character associated with the woods. After earning an associate degree in forestry, he went to work on one of the Angeles fire crews, rising to the position of fire engine captain. The pay was poor, particularly considering the high cost of living in the area, but he was working in the woods and that counted more than anything else.

Shaw's initial encounter with the decree was not as jarring as Ken Wolstenhom's. Nor did he experience many of those "touchy feely, study your naval gatherings" that were then impacting so many government agencies. After learning that he would not be able to hire the engine crew he had trained and worked with over the past three years, he was ordered to take on several women.

Despite the extra physical training granted the new hires, Shaw's *bullshit detector* went off immediately. He instinctively knew that very few of them would develop the strength and stamina necessary to haul a fifty-foot length of fire hose up a slope. For the next several years it became routine for him to order his female crew members back down the hill to stand by, while he and his two firemen held off the blaze until one or more other engine units arrived. "That way she would not be a danger to herself or to us," is how he put it. But no matter the year, within weeks he found that the women he had trained, essentially to maintain the trucks, were gone—only to be replaced by two more. "Then they left too. I noticed lots of them during the training were not even listening. Most were too overwhelmed by the thought of the job." This is also to say that although the agency was placing lives and careers on the line, and blowing piles of money, Bill had yet to encounter a real feminist.

And despite the worries and frustrations brought about by the decree, his career seemed to be forging ahead. In 1984 it received a quantum leap when he was appointed temporary fire management officer for the entire Angeles Forest at the GS 11 level. A permanent choice for that position was still pending.

"A year passed and I was informed that I, who had been performing the job for that year, and two other well-qualified candidates, were in the running. It was on a Friday afternoon when I received a call from the Angeles Forest Supervisor, informing me that I had been chosen for the position. It was one of the happiest weekends of my life."

But on Monday morning when I reported to work, I was informed by my supervisor that the regional office in San Francisco had ordered that my promotion be rescinded. A Marjorie Beam, who had worked in an office all her life, got the job I had been promoted to. I was immediately put back down to a GS-07."

It was a cross Bill Shaw would carry the rest of his life, thanks in part to Marjorie Beam herself. Unlike many women suddenly thrust into positions they were unqualified to fill, with the backing of the consent decree panel, she remained the Angeles Forest fire management officer for, in Bill's words, "pretty close to an eternity."

"Years passed, and she remained on the Angeles, and everyone else had to carry her water. Two people to do one job. Both of us would go out on a fire. The only problem was there was only one set of foot prints left on the ground, and those footprints were always mine. No one had any respect for her; no one had any respect for fire management; no one had any respect for the forest, and no respect for the agency. It all drained away."

Underscoring the nature of the plutonium rule that now governs the U.S. Forest Service, Bill stated that over his thirty years with the agency, he fought 558 fires and saw numerous dead bodies. "My replacement, Marjorie Beam, GS-11, never saw a dead body in her life."

Another unit struck early by the consent decree was the 910,000 acre Mendocino National Forest. Located on the western rim of the Sacramento Valley, its most spectacular features are the mysteriously named Yolla Bolly Mountains, reaching heights of 8,000 feet. In the past the forest was a substantial producer of timber and livestock receipts. Even today, it counts among its wildlife bobcats, cougars, wild pigs and a large herd of tule elk.

In the spring of 1983 the fire captains there learned they too could no longer hire their own seasonals, the same fellows whose capabilities they had come to trust over the years. Rather, a staff of consent clerks would do the hiring. To the shock of everyone, a high percentage of firefighters bused in from distant locales were women. Les Bagby, a resident of the Sacramento Valley town of Willows, and a deputy for the Glen County Sheriff Department, was both a fire management, and law enforcement officer on the Mendocino. According to him, "When I went to hire people I found out that I could not hire the ones I wanted. They were trying to reset goals. I was required to hire females to reach a new objective. It was not good for morale, anywhere. They were getting positions they were not qualified for.

Bagby almost immediately turned to the subject of the forests themselves:

> *Controlled burns were not taking place that should have. Chaparral should be burned every twenty five years... from 1985 to my departure there was a steep decline in prescribed burns...a very high percentage of men just left the region for other regions... and the prescribed burns never took place. All the [effort] was going into [the] consent decree. The men and women both greatly disliked how it was implemented; yet it was detonated with such astonishing force no one truly had time to react. A lot of people tried to fight independently in their own way, but there was not the organized effort needed.*"

He departed the agency in 1991, still a relatively young man, to assume the position he now holds.

Yet another unit struck early by the consent decree was the 2.2 million acre Shasta-Trinity National Forest in Northern California. Roughly the size of Yellowstone National Park, home to Mount Shasta, the Trinity Alps and Castle Crags, it was also one of the nation's great timber producers. Perhaps

Region Five felt a need to begin working the Shasta-Trinity because of its high number of employees, 600 permanent and roughly 400 seasonals.

Among the thousands whose careers the Bernardi Decree terminated was Britt Smith's. A native of Eugene, Oregon, he possessed an educational background in music and physics. In 1978 he was hired by the Sierra National Forest, and four years later transferred to the Big Bar District of the Shasta-Trinity, where he became a fuels technician. By 1984 it had become clear to Britt that women all around him were assuming positions they had no business assuming. Still, he remained with the agency as a fuels technician, writing up reports on timber conditions, mapping sections of the district, operating a bulldozer and monitoring the cleanup operations of timber companies. Later, in hopes of gaining a promotion, he transferred to a fire crew. Yet, despite a series of outstanding performance ratings, by 1988 he was still a seasonal employee with a lowly GS-05 rating.

"At end of that year they finally offered me a permanent position on a fire truck at the GS-03 level. I had been a GS-05 fuels technician with my own pickup truck, and all those responsibilities, but once again I was going to be a grunt on an engine crew. And with a two dollar cut in pay...

"At about that same time they placed a brand new woman with no experience related to the job on the engine crew; she was brand new to the forest service, and was very out of shape. I was to train her even though she had no experience, and it was known that the turnover rate among women was extraordinarily high...I thought about not taking the demotion/promotion. At a GS-03 level, at the rate guys were progressing, I would be sixty years old before I became a fire captain. And by the time you're sixty years old, you're too old to fight fires."

He continued, "At Big Bar we had been mopping up a fire for several weeks when we suddenly went on standby [status]. There were several women on the crew and there were many personal problems, including one with a woman who would not, and could not, work. One morning I suddenly grabbed my pack and left, hitchhiking all the way to Red Bluff, then took a bus to Fresno, and then to the North Fork District on the Sierra Forest. I had walked off the job which was regarded as a big 'no no.'"

There, a newly appointed female district ranger prepared his severance papers. At the time she drew them up, she was well aware that the manager of the agency's air tanker base in Fresno had badly wanted Smith to work for him. But she declined to inform him of the option, and thus his career ended. "The agency stacked the deck against me. I had worked hard all my life, and until consent had always been rewarded for my hard work. Nothing like this had ever happened before."

Nothing like this has happened to Britt Smith since. He now works in the private sector.

Jim Burton's introduction to the Bernardi Decree was not as explosive as some of the others. Nonetheless, as Burton, employed in succession by the Lassen and Modoc National Forests, remarked, "It went off like a neutron bomb. I was promoted to a GS-06 [assistant engine captain] position aboard a fire truck. In a most bizarre twist to the rules as I understood them, I was then told that I would have to return to my old job as a GS-05. But I was also told to train a woman who would then alone be considered for the position I was supposed to be promoted to."

Burton told his supervisor that he would not train her, but managed to keep his job. Shortly after, several women were assigned to cut brush with his fire crew. Yet because none could start their chainsaws, the men were forced to start the saws for them. After a few minutes of cutting, the women would shut their saws down in order to rest. This had a negative effect on the men who were too often forced to shut off their saws to aid the women in again starting theirs. Worse, the men understood full well that despite the inability of the women to perform, they were being paid the same wages. Much like an automobile engine running low on oil seizes up—work on the brush clearing units began to seize up.

Another fire captain who learned he could no longer hire his own crew was Bob Grate who worked on the Lassen National Forest. Encompassing over one million acres, the Lassen Forest is roughly ten times the size of the more famous Lassen Volcanic National Park, which it completely surrounds. Because of its mean elevation, it receives more precipitation than any other forest in California. For this reason and because it has an excellent network of forest roads, it is often referred to as the Asbestos Forest. Still, because of drier blocks of land near Susanville, and its chaparral choked western slopes, over the years the Lassen has had its share of great fires.

Grate was greatly disturbed to learn that his project supervisor had assigned three women to his crew, leaving only himself and one longtime partner with any experience. Following several weeks of training, he led his new employees into the woods to begin clearing slash. Much as Jim Burton had discovered, Grate found that despite all the training, none of the women could start their chainsaws. In addition, they could not cut slash for more than fifteen minutes before shutting down.

"While they rested we continued clearing, until some twenty minutes later when one of the women would signal they were ready to begin again. Then we would shut off our saws to start up theirs, and the routine was repeated over and over again." As the days passed into weeks Grate's slash clearing operations ground to a halt.

"Finally one morning I went into the project supervisor's office and told him about the lack of progress being made. Not only was I concerned about the lack of brush being cleared, I was worried about fires. So worried I informed the supervisor that should we encounter a fire Roger and I judged too large for us to handle alone, I was calling in additional fire crews."

"'It's that bad?' the project manager asked."

"It's that bad!" retorted Grate who added, "And every day, after two hours of work, we're returning to the fire house, to spend the rest of the day eating cookies and drinking milk." The project manager was so confounded by Grate's *cookies and milk* alert, he was speechless. Though six hours of cookies and milk proved to be a metaphor, in fact after two hours of thinning slash, the work day was over. Other than a few small firefights in which he and his crew acted as auxiliaries, the team spent the balance of the season polishing the trucks, sweeping the firehouse floor and running errands for others.

Though only a GS-07 fire captain, Grate was well known in the other forests. During the 1970s he developed a demanding physical routine he felt was needed to extinguish fires quickly and keep injuries and fatalities to a minimum. They made so much sense that by 1980 other fire captains on other forests had adopted them. In 1984, when region began hiring firefighters whose physical capacities were not remotely close to Bob's standards, he became exceptionally outspoken in defending those practices. As he explained...

"One of a captain's duties is to ensure that every member of his crew is in excellent physical shape. Several times a week we led the crews on long hikes ranging up and down mountain slopes, across streams and through brush. A good captain always takes note if someone is lagging. If it happens a second time they are warned. If no improvement is made after the fourth or fifth warning, they are removed from the crew. The reason is that without the basic stamina, that crew member is very unlikely to come to the aid a fellow firefighter in danger, and are themselves a threat to the life of anyone else compelled to come to their rescue."

Despite the experience of 1983, the following year Grate found himself assigned two more women. One day he entered his project supervisor's office and told him that he was removing them because they could not keep pace with the balance of his crew. His supervisor responded by saying "You can't do that." "Yes I can. Unless *you* attach a letter to my recommendation for removal, stating that '*yes*', they must remain a part of my crew."

"Personnel won't approve of that."

"Well, either you, or personnel will have to attach your letter to my discharge papers stating that you are reinstating those women. In order that should they get killed or someone else gets killed, you take the full responsibility." The women were taken off his crew and given another assignment. It is worthy of note however that Grate possessed more than his share of *grit*. Many fire captains simply acquiesced.

Not every employee shared the anger of other interviewees. One of the exceptions was Pete Barker who worked for the Shasta-Trinity Forest. A tall easygoing good looking fellow, who possessed a blasé attitude toward the consent decree, he holds no ill feelings toward anyone in particular. He simply enjoyed working on a fire crew in remote Trinity County and freely owns up to the fact that he did not pay much attention to what was going on anywhere else. In his words, "I never harbored a lot of dreams about getting ahead."

Barker also found some of the firewomen pleasing to work with. This factor alone, more than offset the fact that as an engine captain, he was often forced to assign duties by sex. "Usually the guys ran the saws and the gals stacked the brush. 'Hack and stack' is what we called it. I thought C.D. was a big joke in the beginning. They gave us training sessions. It wasn't too bad. The women who were incompetents and screw ups were replaced. But they had to be replaced by new ones who had to be trained all over again. A couple gals did turn out pretty good."

When asked what benefit consent brought the forests, Barker pondered a moment, grinned, and said, "The uniforms. After consent they had to issue the women special uniforms to fit their forms."

"Their figures?"

"Yeah, their figures," he said grinning. "Some of them looked pretty good." Still, when asked about the agency's efficiency at the time of his retirement (2007), as opposed to when he began work in 1977, he guessed it was running at 50% capacity. Then in Barkeresque fashion, with a grin and a shrug he added, "But that wasn't my problem."

It is important to note that prior to Bernardi, the forest service routinely interfaced with other agencies in fighting wildfires. These included the Bureau of Land Management, the U.S. Park Service, and the various state park and forest systems. The truth is, for many years the other agencies had looked upon the U.S. Forest Service as the last word in fire professionalism. Unfortunately these multi-jurisdictional missions exposed the agency's dramatic increase in the hiring of women. The result was an equally precipitous drop in confidence among the other organizations regarding the service's capabilities.

The year 1984 brought a further moment of truth to forest personnel, when it was learned the job announcements that had always been posted on the bulletin boards at each work station had vanished. The question was repeatedly asked, "Where are the announcements?" The excuses passed down by upper management and personnel were as differing and tentative as the individuals themselves. But no matter the quality of their obfuscations, within days everyone knew they had gone *sub rosa* for objectionable reasons.

A long time employee who chose to remain anonymous shook his head as he spoke. "Everything went secret. Secrecy was being used against us. Secrecy became a tool. Sure, in the past your supervisor or even your project manager could be a real asshole. Some were rude, others were abrupt, and some maybe forgot to tell you some aspect of your assignment. But almost everyone tried to be upfront....from the forest supervisor right on down to the recreation crew foreman.

"Sometimes jobs did get posted when you knew goddamned well the chances were that a buddy working for the particular forester would be picked up. But at least you had the chance to decide for yourself. There weren't any secret jobs being invented for only certain types of people. That was what was so creepy about consent. It was a creepy operation."

The announcements had of course been withdrawn because region wished to block overqualified men from applying until the requisite number of women had been hired. 1984 was the year all supervisors in all departments through all eighteen forests and all eighty ranger districts, learned they were no longer permitted to do their own hiring. 1984 meant a lot more to them than leafing through a copy of George Orwell's classic on the subject.

Thus did Region Five lurch off its rails. Women, of course, had served on fire crews in limited numbers since 1972. The initial inconvenience caused some grumbling, but according to those interviewed, the grumbling was limited to only a few individuals only, largely because of the women themselves. Through subtle acknowledgment of their physical limitations, light banter, and in many instances downright good looks, a majority were accepted. Whatever *man hours* lost, were compensated for by what some referred to as *eye candy*.

But when the Region Five's engine chiefs learned their freedom to hire had been removed, they took it personally, and their outlook toward women did a 180 degree turn. It was also taken personally by local youths, who quickly learned that even though they were highly experienced, they had not made the seasonal roster simply because they were men. Finally, many of the newly hired women did not possess the sparkling personalities of their pre-consent counterparts.

Chapter 5

A BREADTH OF KNOWLEDGE

Confusion, uncertainty, fear, and rule by the amoral: a reference to the four horsemen of the Apocalypse
—Unknown

IN EARLY 1984 Zane Smith and his staff finally completed their interim goals study and determined what steps were necessary to implement them. That March A. Max Peterson signed off on the plan and within a year began administering *moderate* doses of the consent decree to forests all across the United States.

By this time, the regional office in San Francisco was placing large numbers of women in its budget, planning, and consent decree committees while in the forests a program known as *focused placement* was implemented. After a year of intense training in any discipline of a new employee's choice, they would receive a promotion, regardless of competence.

Another tool Smith's staff developed was that of identifying new employees with the potential to be placed in an *accelerated development program.* Those thought suited were sent to college to earn a degree in forestry or a related discipline with all costs covered by the U.S. Forest Service. In the past, the agency had occasionally sent promising young men to college, but on an *ad hoc* basis only.

A third program, one that would prove enormously damaging to forestry operations, was called *potential to perform.* Here, in evaluating a candidate for promotion, the supervisor was told to confer *potential to perform necessary duties* the precise same weight as actual on-the-job performance. Thus, by 1984, many new employees who displayed *on paper potential to perform* were being promoted over men who had actually performed those tasks for two, three and four years. The program badly damaged morale in the offices, but when extended into the field, the effect was devastating. Within two years women were being promoted to fire management officer. Though the agency was increasingly relying on the use of contractors to fly their aircraft, many fire management officers were skilled pilots of both airplanes and helicopters.

"Has potential to fly an airplane or helicopter," mused one employee. "That would be like Delta Airlines hiring a pilot with the potential to fly an airplane. Either you can and have flown an airplane. Or you can't and haven't flown an airplane. The lives of hundreds of people depend on it!"

Another tool was the implementation of *human resource skills.* It was already known that women smile more often than men, speak in softer voices, have higher pitched voices, are more indirect in their observations and less forward in their criticisms. Thus it was decided these *human resource skills* would be placed on an equal footing with technical skills, such as determining how many board feet of lumber were present in a stand of timber, how many cattle should graze a 10,000 acre allotment, or how much additional water might flow over a spillway should two more inches of rain fall over the next twenty-four hours.

In the selection of new employees, the service also decided to impart extra credit for those who had taken courses in feminist studies—a barrier that left almost every man applying for a job or promotion at a disadvantage. This program would do much to advance the agency's feminization. In addition, through the medium of bulletin board postings, equal rights meetings, office meetings, and *tailgate* meetings, field employees were lectured on the importance of clerical work. That is, firefighters, foresters, engineers and recreation specialists were no longer permitted to disrespect clerical workers as they had allegedly done in the past. Finally, workshops were routinely held at ranger stations to discuss local norms and traditions. For example, it was known that a high percentage of forest personnel preferred listening to country music tapes while in the field. In many instances work crews were told to make allowances for any sort of music their female counterparts might prefer. At these workshops the various lists of words, phrases and topics men were not to use in the presence of women were often presented for their benefit.

There was also the *outside skills bank*. When Smith and the advocates surreptitiously pledged that 43% parity would be reached in all disciplines and pay grades within discipline, women were under-represented in a total of sixty. To help correct this reality, his consent decree committee, and consent specialists working at the forest level, were directed to review the personnel listings of universities, state and local governments, and private firms throughout the United States in search of prospective women employees, and list them according to profession.

Quite a number were found: some in teaching, some working for foundations, others who had recently become mothers. All received letters coaxing them to relocate in sunny California, there to begin a new life in what many (at the time) considered a golden land of opportunity. Initially thought to be a real bonanza, it was soon found that many *discovered women* had no desire to transfer into a remote town to work in a dark forest, even if that dark forest happened to be located in sunny California.

Among additional projects was the *shared jobs* concept. This involved permitting a new hire to occupy two positions at once. Very often the employee would be assigned to work in the recreation department in the morning and in administration during the afternoon. In essence, the employee would be circulating through the campgrounds and dealing with forest visitors during the morning, then answering the telephone and editing letters in the office until check-out time. Because recreation work can be physically demanding and requires contact with an always inquiring, but not always polite public, the real intent of the afternoon portion of *shared jobs* was to allow the employee relief from the stress built up while on morning patrol. The shared job plan's greatest drawback was that it reduced the number of employees in the field who could deal with the public on a sustained basis.

There was also the *part time employment* program. Part time employment was in fact already a reality throughout the forest service. Between November and May, most of America's more northerly and high elevation forests lie under a deep blanket of snow and receive few visitors. Over the years, in order to retain many valuable job holders, these forests employed members of staff for seven or eight months a year before laying them off. They then collected unemployment benefits while at the same time receiving health and retirement benefits, which is to say they were equal in status to a twelve month employee.

But in this instance the consent committee decided to extend the part time concept to such low elevation and relatively snow-free locales as the Angeles, Cleveland, Los Padres and San Bernardino Forests. In essence, the forest staffs were being told to replace their seasonal employees (men) whose health and retirement benefits were not paid for by the public, with part time employees (women), whose health and retirement benefits would be paid for by the public.

There also arrived the *weekend worker* concept, which within a few short years turned into a public relations fiasco. The rationale, as explained by region, was that long time employees, who spent their weekends keeping the district ranger stations open to the public, and patrolling the campgrounds, might enjoy their weekends off. This would allow many new employees to gain at least sixteen additional hours of work each week.

But administrators soon found that few new job holders were willing to accept weekend work. Weekends were a time for getting together with friends and family back home. Worsening matters, the veteran employees, men and women both, very often declined to return to the ranger stations or campgrounds. As one wit put it, "It was like Safeway closing down their stores on Saturday and Sunday." As always, the real victim in this experiment was the public. Many ranger stations across the United States are now routinely closed on weekends. Near some forests an office is maintained in conjunction with another land-owning agency, or perhaps a local environmental group. And, except for the heavily used off highway vehicle areas, it is uncommon for a weekend camper to encounter a recreation specialist anywhere in a forest.

Three additional ventures, although they involved small numbers of people, also badly damaged morale and forestry operations. Sometime in 1984 the San Francisco office discovered that the *priority placement* program was slowing the increase of women in the all-important GS-11 through GS-13 levels. A priority placement occurs when a very demanding job in one of the forests requires filling. In the past, the forest supervisor and his staff would scramble through the listings of other forests until they found an employee willing to assume this all-important position.

However, the regional office determined, on its own, that the demands of these priority placements were exaggerated. In the interests of promoting the decree, the forest supervisors were simply ordered to appoint women. According to postmodern forestry concepts, the newly appointed women, given a little time, could learn to perform these tasks well enough. Suffice to say there was never enough time allotted them to learn the tasks. Not only was damage done to forest operations, but a number of potentially capable women left the agency altogether.

1984 was also the year region struck at *direct assignments.* Similar to a priority placement, a direct assignment occurs when a critical technical skill has suddenly arisen somewhere. In this instance, the skills are much more focused and less broadly defined. The assigning of many improperly trained women technicians to fill these direct assignments also damaged forest operations, resulted in the profound disillusionment of many, and the loss of additional personnel.

In another blow to long time employees, region launched an assault on *lateral placement.* Almost the opposite of a priority placement, a lateral placement occurs when an employee working in a very demanding position for a long period of time is rewarded with transfer to a more tranquil desk. In 1984 Smith and company simply turned these *tranquil desks* over to newly promoted GS-11 female employees.

All in all, by mid-1985 the forest service had launched thirteen profoundly discriminatory programs under the presumed authority of a few scraps of extra-legal paper titled Article IV, in violation of the Fourteenth Amendment, Title VII of the 1964 Civil Rights Act, and the Bernardi Decree itself.

That year Region Five's two leading figures were featured in prominent interviews in the *Southwest Pacific NewsLog*, the regional newsletter. Both Zane Smith and Assistant Director Warren Davies went so far as to state that the new programs were open to men. Yet a little further down the same pages the two hedged in their respective columns by stating that the new programs would *one day* be open to men.

Work in the forests was now being seriously hampered. Project managers, increasingly burdened with paperwork, were no longer getting into the field. First line supervisors, though still able to get into the field, were finding less time to monitor their employees who worked on ranger districts that often encompassed 250,000 acres.

By contrast, their employees were spending ever more time in the field, where some had begun engaging in recreational pursuits, as opposed to work. The forests had always been friendly environments, which is the very reason they had chosen to work in them. As the months passed on, they became ever-more friendly, a pastoral refuge from the hostile work environment of a forest headquarters, ranger station, or work center. In the sardonic words of one employee, "It's a big woods out there." Upon appearing at the office in the morning, he and increasing numbers of his co-workers simply piled into their trucks, and headed into the woods to recreate.

Yet there was very little management could do about it. Prior to then the overwhelming majority of employees could be counted upon to perform. For over eighty years the three touchstones of forest service culture had been hard work, a sense of mission, and most importantly trust. As 1985 advanced into 1986, those touchstones began to die. That year a letter from a supervisor from the Stanislaus National Forest appeared, highlighting yet another reason the culture was dying. After noting the dramatic increase in numbers of women and minorities in his district, he wrote, "People tend to like other people whose personality traits and values are similar to their own." It is a phenomenon etched into every human soul, and more ancient than history itself.

Meanwhile, Court Monitor Diane Winokur pressed ahead with her duties. As early as mid-1982, she set out on a tour of the forests, visiting all eighty ranger districts. The letters, directives and reports she left behind indicate that she really thought the consent decree would succeed. In 1984, after she made a second and more thorough circuit, she reinforced her supposition by stating that because the service had long since established itself as a dynamic organization capable of adapting to any emergency, consent at 43% was eminently achievable. In her words, "Crisis management is endemic to the forest service—fires and floods."

In addition to discussing with each forest supervisor the programs earlier detailed, she informed them that an audit should be performed for every position within each unit. Positions were to be upgraded if it was found that women would benefit from the upgrading; positions were to be downgraded if it was found that men were benefiting from the status quo. Finally, as the regional office had already done by memo, she reminded each forest supervisor that his performance evaluation would be heavily dependent on his success in implementing the decree. This edict could not have endeared her to many, but by late that year all understood that Winokur had the full backing of the regional office, and *assumed* she had the legal backing of the district court.

Still, as she completed her 1984 tour doubts began to emerge. Despite the new programs unveiled, several that markedly increased the number of women working in offices, the forests were reacting to the decree at great variance with no particular pattern emerging. The most cooperative units were the Inyo, Lassen, Los Padres, and San Bernardino Forests, the six experimental stations, and Smith's own headquarters on Samson Street, San Francisco, which in that year alone hired 19 women and 13 men, for a female percentage of 59.4%. The success of the last two forests and the experimental stations can be explained by their proximity to large population centers, while the Lassen's success can be accounted for by the presence of one, Richard Henry, a strong promoter of the consent decree from the beginning. It is possible a progressive forester also presided over the distant Inyo.

Among the least cooperative forests were the Angeles, Eldorado, Mendocino, Modoc, Sierra and Tahoe. The first two, strangely enough, were located near heavily populated areas, where the recruitment of women should have been relatively easy. The other four were quite remote, particularly in regard to the Modoc. In 1986 the Tahoe, perhaps reacting to criticism of its lackluster performance, appointed Geri B. Larson as its forest supervisor, the first woman ever to hold that position.

Larsen possessed a solid background in budgeting, and had previously been an assistant supervisor, but according to those interviewed she did not possess the breadth of knowledge necessary to supervise a forest. *Breadth of Knowledge*, ever since the service's founding had been that singular yardstick relied upon when choosing the best employee to get the job done. This is not to suggest that every man who became a forest supervisor was a crown jewel to the organization. Over the years some had been alcoholics, others temperamentally ill-suited, while others, owing to favoritism, did indeed slip beneath the *breadth of knowledge* radar screen.

One instance of their malfeasance involved a senior forester on the Helena National Forest in Montana, who received a prank phone call directing him to light a number of fuzees at a prescribe burn location. Without confirming the phone caller's identity, the fire officer did as told, and ended up setting an out-of-control fire that burned up 4,000 acres. In California's Sierra National Forest, a private firm was contracted to plant 2,000 acres of trees following a fire. Some months later it was discovered that the company, after being compensated, had planted trees just twenty-feet feet inward from the burn perimeter; leaving the entire core—about 80%—barren. The employee was transferred to another forest to save himself and the Sierra Forest further embarrassment.

The above incidents are reminders that prior to the decree the U.S. Forest Service, was never quite the faultless operation many are fond of reminiscing about. Indeed, the scores of components that comprise managing enormous tracts of land, such as a forest district, each possessed of its own unique features, guarantees that blunders will occur. The goal is to keep the blunders to a minimum.

Still, as Diane Winokur had also learned, one reason the decree was not being properly implemented was that too many employees, as a matter of inclination, felt obliged to manage their timber projects, maintain fire control and implement recreation programs. Added to this were a multitude of environmental studies, essential to avoiding the legal hazards certain to arise if the studies were not conducted. This prompted her to complain that whenever the foresters saw a conflict between consent and forestry, "there is little momentum toward consent."

In fact, many district rangers, middle management supervisors and front line supervisors remained in a state of disbelief. Disbelief that they, and their longtime associates, who over the years, again and again had proven their worth, were being denied promotions they had earned. *Downgrading* a position if it would break a man's hopes of retaining it? *Upgrading* a position if it would break a man's hopes of remaining employed? These contrivances ran against the grain of every human instinct. What one interviewee termed the agency's *guiding principle of deconstruction*, another called its *policy of personal destruction.*

For them, the agency's vaunted reputation for overcoming all obstacles to achieve objectives was the most compelling argument for leaving it alone. One of the smoothest-running government organizations conceived, and one of just two that had turned a profit during the last half of the Twentieth Century, was now being told that it was *broke.*

By the end of 1985 more than two dozen women, with just one year of experience, had been promoted to fire captain over men with five and six years of experience. The traumatic reaction among fire crews upon learning of Ken Wolstenhom's experience on the Cleveland Forest had by now in varying degrees been replicated across every forest in the state. The result was a hostile work environment that by mid-season led to a high number of seasonal employees of both sexes departing. In turn, this led to skeleton fire crews under the stewardship of some very inexperienced fire captains.

Winokur professed astonishment at finding that many women working on the physically demanding hotshot crews were intimidated by both the nature of their work and the negative sentiments of those around them. To remedy the situation, she suggested they be placed in pairs in order to provide "gender relief." Yet the pairing of two under-trained women in a unit that may have counted as few as five team members was a safety hazard in itself and a threat to everyone on the crew. This was but one of hundreds of unintended consequences now unfolding.

In a paragraph inside one of her semi-annual reports, she discussed trimming the Harvard Step Test. Long employed by the agency, the Harvard Step Test required each firefighter candidate to rapidly step up and down on a seventeen-inch box for a five minute period, and then have his pulse read. The object was to eliminate applicants without the stamina to fight fires. At this point, Winokur suggested only that women be given extra time and coaching to pass the test.

By now she was only too familiar with the *pipeline problem* anticipated years before. So few women were graduating from college in disciplines like fire science, forestry, engineering and hydrology the situation was reckoned as hopeless. In one report she frankly admitted that women, whether working in fire, timber, resources, or recreation were so physically challenged they could not effectively wield rock bars, picks, post hole diggers, or pipe cutters. Worse, less than ten-percent were adept with a chain saw.

What is so surprising about Winokur's findings is that she was so surprised. This may have reflected the fact that she herself had never resided in a household, or an environment, where men had committed themselves to physical work. Nonetheless, her frankly written notes suggest she was capable of learning through observation, something her forest service counterparts in San Francisco never could. One feels that had she been aware of these physiological problems, she would have convinced both the advocates and Zane Smith that Article IV was a fool's errand.

She discovered other problems as well. For one, the classes being taught to first and second line managers regarding the multifaceted programs that had been developed required repeating over and over again. This was very often because her students were so distracted about what work was *not being carried out* on their districts, they never really grasped the material.

Finally, across the board in every department, the concept of *potential to perform* was having a very negative impact on newly hired women. Many of the men passed over for promotion—scores of whom had performed the tasks for years—openly detested their replacements. Few other employees familiar with the position believed that any women in their midst possessed *job integrity*. Giving them advice was thought a waste of time; worse, in an organization renowned for its fidelity, it was regarded as an act of betrayal. In dismay Winokur reported that the term "'Qualified' is now an albatross around the neck of every woman. Many women fear being promoted."

Despite all their disagreeable findings, by 1985 Winokur and Smith, with the aid of the forest supervisors, had raised the number of new female hires dramatically. A 43% quota was reached in 26 out of 60 disciplines and grade levels. Not less than 36.4% of the GS-05 through GS-09 grade promotions had been issued to women.

Among clericals, GS-05 through GS-07, women constituted an astonishing 84% of new hires. Among other achievements, they now constituted 55% of personnel specialists, 55% of public affairs specialists, 60% of administrators, and 80% of contract specialists. The downside to these triumphs, of course, was the loss of ability to perform a multitude of tasks beyond the office door. Until then, these positions had been filled by older men who had worked in the forest for years and comprised what was known as the "forest militia." These militia members who had once served as an inspiration for younger employees were now being told to pack their wisdom into a sack and hit the road.

This was often a wrenching event because the forest service had always been their home. Pinchot's famous dictum, "In forestry a man is either altogether at home, or very much out of place...there has been and will always be, but one kind of place, one form of experience possible in the profession," was as instinctive as it was instructive.

Its significance was underscored by a long-time silviculturalist on the Sequoia National Forest who chose to remain anonymous. In response to a question regarding the rapid promotion of women, he said, "Over time the organization will deteriorate. If someone is in over his head, he lacks confidence. He'll be threatened by suggestions and won't feel comfortable dealing with resources and people. Just being bright isn't good enough. You have to have experience too. I can make a decision because I have a feel for the land. That took years to develop. Lack of experience will lead to bad decisions."

He was of course referring to that familiar term, *breadth of knowledge* which itself leads to the sharing of knowledge. Bill Shaw, who also worked as fuels technician on the San Bernardino Forest, explained how in the 1970s and early 1980s it was not unusual to have a dozen fuel technicians cruising or hiking the forest in search of locales in need of thinning and clearing by resource crews. In his words:

> *Very often a forest botanist was in search of particular species of plant. He would describe the plant to us fuel technicians. In our explorations, we sometimes came across that plant, placed a flag next to it, and on returning to the office told the botanist about it.*
>
> *Knowledge of the fuel conditions was absolutely necessary. If you know what kind of conditions you have, the crews are much better prepared to fight the fires. And in addition, the botanist's interest in the plant life got much more spread around. Everyone, the foresters, fuels boss, range manager, fire management officer, fire captains, and botanists all read the reports we wrote up.*

This was why more than a few employees developed something more than a passing interest in the San Bernardino's rare and little known plant species.

The reduction in the number of old-hand foresters was not the only bit of good news to reach the regional office in early 1985. While overall GS-07 ratings were down 18%, the number of women working at that level rose to 31%. Among the professions, 33% of archeologists and an astonishing 48.6% of accountants hired were women.

Still, with the good news came the bad. Just 16% of the landscape architects, 23% of the geologists, and 33% of the biologists were women. The percentages in engineering, surveying and hydrology were minute and underscored the fact that 43% female representation in every profession, and grade within, would never be realized. This forced Zane Smith to write, "...we all agree on the small likelihood of making the statistical gains envisioned by the Decree; thus the qualitative portion of the evaluation becomes all the more important."

This admission that his own *revolt of the elites* had failed was written just a few months after Chief Forester Max Peterson signed off on it. Aware that Judge Conti was likely aware of his back-stair agreement with the advocates, he and his staff decided that if region simply met an overarching *umbrella quota* of 43%, it would please the court. Which is why by 1985, the number of administrative, personnel and public relations positions filled by women had reached such astronomical proportions. Yet as he continued to misread Davis, Kurtz and Williams, he continued to misread the Judge, never suspecting that the stealth betrayal of his own organization was regarded by Conti as a stealth betrayal of his courtroom.

Though the Department of Justice had pledged $1,500,000 to cover expenses until June 30, 1986, funding for the consent decree ran out sooner than anyone imagined. In September of 1984, Attorney General designate Edwin Meese announced that payments would cease on the 30th of the month. Winokur was embarrassed by the expense totals and attributed them to the failed urban consultants the forest service had employed. She also blamed general inflation, a particularly sharp rise in travel expenses and the hitherto unknown fact that each of the eighteen forests was unique and thus required its own implementation plan. Chief Peterson, upon learning that he would now be financing the decree, asked Smith how much he would need. Smith replied that monthly costs would average $300,000, but could go much higher.

Late in 1984 Winokur reported to the advocates and the district court that in her opinion Region Five had made a good faith effort to fulfill the terms of the decree, and on January 1, 1985 tendered her resignation. Her efforts, and those of the advocates and regional office, had met with remarkable success. The most deceptive package of hiring/promotional arrangements ever devised by a government agency, had enabled them to surpass more than two dozen quota tables.

But she had found the complexity of forest operations daunting and under the parameters she was working, felt even those quotas might not be sustained. She had demonstrated that many more women could be signed on. The problem was that a significant number resented being hired to fill positions they were not equipped to fill. By the time Winokur presented her resignation, hundreds had already departed, meaning each district on each forest was being forced to backfill the same, newly vacated position, all over again. Congress and its compensator, the taxpayers, were never made aware of this enormously time consuming, and costly task.

On May 1, 1985, the forest service, represented by David Glass, went before Magistrate Claudia Wilkin whom Judge Conti had temporarily placed in charge of the decree. Turning a legal event as badly mutilated as the Bernardi Decree over to Wilken raises a few questions, because federal magistrates are in essence junior judges. Their creation in 1968 was intended to allow district judges to focus on major legal challenges, while assigning less complex court cases to them. Some legal professionals have argued that too many important cases have ended up in the chambers of these junior judges. Yet the preponderance of evidence suggests that by 1980 most magistrates were legally competent. The question here is whether Wilken was one of them. Succeeding chapters will provide ample evidence for the readers to draw their own conclusions.

Glass argued that the consent decree had been carried out in good faith, and asked that it be ended on June 30, a year ahead of calendar. With women now occupying so many administrative, personnel and policy making positions, and with the support of Diane Winokur, Smith and Glass both felt certain they would prevail. At hearing's end however, Wilken announced that a decision would not be forthcoming until June 30.

On that day Judge Conti entered the chamber, took his seat, and as Glass read out his report, scarcely listened. He had long possessed the ability to carefully peer about his courtroom and upon recognizing a face he happened to associate with some past transgression, wave his gavel at the visage and bark at it over the suddenly remembered offense. This was a big reason why after Glass resumed his seat, the Judge immediately turned to Smith and after savagely berating him for failing to implement the decree, denounced him for squandering the Department of Justice's funds twenty months ahead of the calendar.

Finally, making reference to Smith's now extralegal Article IV, he declared that the service had failed in "striving to implement the Decree to the greatest extent possible in its long term goal of eliminating under representation of women at 43% in each of the job series." He ordered the decree continued until June 30, 1986 when he would hold another hearing.

Conti had known of Smith's clandestine quota system for more than two years—a big reason he was no longer an impartial jurist, but an implacable enemy. Twice during 1980 and 1981 he had offered Smith maneuvering room against the advocates, maneuvering room he badly needed, and rejected. In truth, the Judge had seen enough of the bustling old do-gooder to last two lifetimes. If he and his agency wished to engage his courtroom in a game of legal charades, he was willing and eager. At a number of hearings in the years to come, while Article IV lay resting in his study unendorsed and gathering dust, Conti, when commenting, would refer to it as the consent decree *as amended*.

The problem was that by consigning Zane Smith's life to a living hell, he was consigning the lives of thousands of others to hell, and placing California's forests at great risk.

Chapter 6

A NEW FOREST SERVICE MANUAL

Unless words have specific, precise identifiable and common meanings, how is it possible to conceive of ideas such as freedom, oppression, resistance and the like. If it is no longer possible to formulate abstract ideas and communicate them, then action and creativity are no longer possible and control is absolute and complete.

—George Orwell

THE ADVOCATES AND the forest service were now conducting a search for another court monitor. Finally, in May 1985 they agreed on Attorney Jeannie Meyer, who with Jacqueline H. Cables, worked out of an office in San Francisco. With regard to the new monitor, among those who encountered her, there exists a collective amnesia on the subject of her appearance (a photo has been retrieved). What *did not* undergo collective amnesia were her voice and manner: shrill and unbending, as gnarly as they were unfinished. One forester declared that he would rather fight a cabin full of angry badgers than sit across a conference table from Meyer. Judging from her demeanor in her photo, that employee's assessment was correct.

Why she was selected is unknown. All that is known is that the same hardnosed misandrogonists who were in control of the advocates in 1981 were still in control in 1985. And that the same misandrogonists who bargained away the forest service's rights in 1981 had extended their grasp even further. Indeed, the Washington Office sent a *consent decree liaison officer* out to California, whose most important task was to accompany Meyer on her excursions into the various forests. It is quite possible that in the selection of Meyer, Zane Smith, who by now sorely wanted out from under the decree, was sabotaged by feminists on his staff.

Nationwide, the woman's movement was flexing its political muscle in a manner never before seen on the world stage. Entire sections of bookstores were now given over to feminist writings. One of the most popular authors was Peggy McIntosh, known in some circles as the *Pol Pot* of the American education system. In her *Unpacking the Invisible Knapsack* she claimed that white men had 46 advantages over women and minorities that they took for granted, and proposed that each white man take a 23 step recovery program for the benefit of the country.

As noted earlier, Region Five and the entire U.S. Forest Service had entered a period of financial instability. Because the Washington Office proved unable to underwrite Smith as had been presumed, it turned to the General Accounting Office for help. Its first two applications were rejected—the GAO stating that the clerical expenses of implementing the consent decree (as opposed to the cost of managing the forests), were much too high. However, once *informed* that the overhead had been *ordered* by the Northern District Court of California, the GAO set aside another $1,500,000 to cover costs through September 30, 1988.

On November 5, 1985 a withdrawal from the fund was applied to a symposium held at the Hyatt Hotel in Berkeley attended by consent decree staffers, the advocates and the court monitor. Over the course of the three day confab, a series of panel discussions were held regarding women in the forest, and region's admitted failure to implement the Bernardi Decree. A sign of how shamefaced the forest service felt about its failure was the presence of Max Peterson's assistant, Dale Robertson, who had flown out from Washington. At the Hyatt he gave an extensive talk on the subject of *Tradition and Values in our Present and Future World.*

Two procedural hand grenades were detonated following Robertson's talk. Each forest would now have at least one female counselor present not only when interviewing a woman for promotion, but whenever a discussion was undertaken regarding her career path. If no counselor was available on the forest or an adjacent forest, an out-of-region person would be flown in (for example from the Custer National Forest in Montana). The cost of the flight, and board and motel room was to be drawn upon the local forest's operating expenses. "There will be no excuses," warned consent decree staffer Paul Guilkey, whose idea it was.

Another decree specialist was Margaret Briscoe-Blake who determined that rather than the forest supervisor, each district ranger would assume the hiring responsibilities of his district. Whenever a position opened with the *potential for promotion criteria,* he was to personally contact all prospective employees in whatever state they resided. No man or what were deemed *unsuitable women* were to lay eyes on the announcement. Unhappily, Briscoe-Blake's plan never really got off the ground, because there were eighty district rangers in California, many of whom were conservatives, as opposed to eighteen forest supervisors, most of whom were now progressive.

The region also announced that its *ad hoc* consent panel was being replaced by a full time 122 member Regional Consent Decree Committee, responsible for developing new programs, compiling new reports, interpreting those reports, and facilitating the flow of said reports to all forest clerks. A document dated August 24, 1988 notes that at one regional consent meeting, of 124 members present, just eight were men.

In order to ensure consent work was thoroughly understood by all personnel, a consent decree committee was to be set up on each forest, with at least one representative at each ranger station. The quantity varied from unit to unit. A sampling revealed that the Cleveland Forest committee was staffed by thirteen, while the Angeles Forest was staffed by twelve. In May 1988, the Shasta-Trinity Forest committee in Redding, having mushroomed to such an extent, appropriated the entire fourth floor of the supervisor's building.

Yet as the years advanced, and the decree fell out of favor among more and more women, the meetings at the forest level became poorly attended. In addition, the hundreds of *new* women recruited each year found themselves so overwhelmed by their assignments, they quite naturally found good reasons not to attend.

The Hyatt confab ended with renewed pledges from everyone to work harder to correct the forest service's past injustices, and to continue dismantling its corrosive male culture. Well before the meeting, Jeannie Meyer was hard at work on what she had titled *The Consent Decree Handbook*. Unlike the crisp format presented by most handbooks, her manual reads like a confused recapitulation of Equal Rights Advocate complaints. Still, within one short year her handbook would, for all practical purposes, replace the once venerable *Forest Service Manual* as the last word in forestry instruction.

By dint of some great stroke of irony, a reference to Title VII of the Civil Rights Act of 1964 appears in its very first paragraph. Yet the entire balance of the book is devoted to exploring various means by which Title VII might be circumvented. The new monitor's method of tallying and indexing the agency's different professions was at great variance with Winokur's, who originally listed sixty disciplines and grades in which women were under-represented. By January 18, 1986, the day Meyer issued her manual, the number of positions and grades in which women were under-represented had grown to ninety. According to an article in the *San Bernardino Bear Facts* quarterly, by August 1988 the number of positions targeted for rationing had reached 102.

That same article went on to report that at a recent compliance meeting, 39 more positions were soon to be added. Finally, at a later meeting the forest service agreed to affix eleven additional positions, making for the fantastic total of 152 professions and grades within, targeted for reallocation. All of which suggests that great confusion reigned among the consent panelists as to which, where, and when a position was to be targeted for affirmative action. Among the last added to the agenda were such professions as equipment specialist, draftsperson, cartographer, engineer, and construction inspector. Testimony to Meyer's state of mind is the fact that on one page of her manual she made passing note of the engineering profession. Three pages further on she wrote, "There is no woman's pipeline for engineering. The region must work with engineering to strategize ways to provide more opportunities for women."

It is of interest to note that the term strategy is rooted in the word stratagem, "a trick, scheme, or device used for deceiving an enemy in war; any trick or deception." Widespread use of the word *strategy* by Meyer, the regional and forest consent committees, is by itself an admission that they intended to develop whatever tricks, schemes or devices were necessary to reduce the percentage of men in the workforce to 57%.

The Meyer Manual also launched the so called MARS plan, an improvement over the poorly designed Outside Skills Bank. One of its most enhanced features was the ability to track down all women in America's other eight forest regions who possessed degrees in forestry or any related subject, thus enabling California to divest other regions of their female professionals. Chief Peterson, whose stratagem was to dramatically increase the number of women in all his regions, could not have been pleased with the MARS development.

Regardless, it was also much more effective than its predecessor in seeking out women employed by the fifty states, and in private firms. Running parallel with MARS was a system known as *FEEDERS*, by which women, who at one time or another had been merely overheard to express an interest in forestry, were tracked down and contacted at their homes or places of employment.

The Meyer Manual also emphasized the point that new employees were to be given special latitude in choosing where they wished to live and work. The most innovative change here was in the selection of fire crews. Three years of misfortune and embarrassment had convinced many that firefighting was not a woman's forte. Thus, another bomb was detonated when staffers very discreetly began passing word that women were to be placed in auxiliary positions only, even though they would be drawing the same wages as the men actually fighting the fires.

In addition, many were to be placed in such relatively fire-free forests as the Lassen and Six Rivers, as opposed to the very combustible Los Padres and Sequoia. It is interesting to note that in the Eldorado Forest, then under the supervision of Jerold Hutchings, for one year at least, firewomen were not obliged to fight fires—if they felt doing so *would threaten their well-being*. These changes of policy proved temporary. For reasons unknown, in 1988 region reversed itself and again began assigning women to front line duty and the more fire-prone forests.

Meyer further stressed that each unit was to cover a new employee's time lost through illness for up to six months, a benefit no other government employee was entitled to. Another program she launched was CAW (Charge As Worked), implemented to pay for the transportation and per diem expenses of employees on temporary learning or teaching assignments.

Turning to the already failed and much hated *potential to perform* program, the Meyer Manual launched an offensive against the *Red Card*. For many years the Red Card, carried by each member of a fire crew, stated which duties—some dangerous, all arduous—a firefighter was capable of performing. Owing to cronyism, the Red Card was not quite the perfect document it appeared to be. However, if a firefighter's card stated that he could land a helicopter on a 2000 square foot opening in a forest, everyone could be pretty well assured he could do just that. Meyer was now insisting that any women who had the *potential* to land a helicopter on a 2000 square foot opening in a forest should immediately have her Red Card state she could.

Whether piloting a helicopter or directing a fire assault, this directive posed such a threat to life that it was ignored in most districts. When it was followed, as on some, it had a devastating effect on the morale of crews who promptly concluded that no woman in their midst was properly credentialed. Because most crew members were seasonal employees, the retention of young men was now as problematic as the retention of women. By 1988 just half of region's firemen were remaining through the season, resulting in severe erosion of employee performance and an extraordinary rise in training expenses. Again, these losses were never reported to Congress, or its financiers, the tax payers.

More was to come, this time from the Washington Office. At a November 25, 1985 meeting, a panel at the nation's capital directed that all forests in the United States debase the Harvard Step Test. Instead of taking the seventeen-inch box exercise, new employees would be permitted to take the less strenuous fifteen-inch box test. Later, many forests, seriously lagging in their gender apportioning, would reduce the height of the new employee box to thirteen-inches. Strangely enough, this debasement and the deterioration of other standards would cost the lives of more firefighters outside of California than within. The reasons will be later explained.

In addition, all through 1985, 1986 and 1987, first line managers were forced to attend workshops for instruction on the finer points of the Meyer *Consent Decree Handbook*. Reaching beyond the list of words and phrases men were no longer able to use in a woman's presence, was the elimination of sexist language, such as *fireman*. Meyer felt any term that included the suffix *man* diminished women. Other expressions thought diminishing to women were *he* and *him*.

"He-ism," in Meyer's words, was rampant throughout the forests and harmful to female morale. Thus *he* was stricken from forest correspondence other than when referring to a specific individual. Around the offices, firehouses, shops,

and in the forests beyond, employees, when referring to an
unknown third party, were directed to apply such circuitous
terms as *the person in the shop, that person, those persons,* or *the
individual over there.*
When discussing sexuality employees were ordered to
use the term *gender* as opposed to *sex.* The word sex was said
to have arisen out of artificial constructs developed during
Biblical times in order to keep women subjugated. *Gender*
would eliminate this construct. Further, when referring to
a man or woman, employees were told to use the terms *male*
and *female,* techno-scientific expressions much better suited
for a discussion of fruit flies, mosquitoes or crustaceans.
Oddly, to this day the entire nation continues to employ
these two very cold and detached terms.
The Meyer Handbook sought to correct even more
subtle offenses. As the author explained, *plays a passive role,
polite, pleasant and caring* were all women's terms. *Business like*
and *professional in manner* were men's terms. However sub-
liminal these words might appear, they were sexist in nature
and must be eliminated from the workplace vocabulary.
The expression *team player* was also thought sexist. Yet the
Meyer Manual is imprecise as to what term should replace
it. Indeed, managers were encouraged to apply *team building*
exercises, *encourage team participation,* and to *foster more coop-
eration.* Yet all three phrases foster the notion of a *team player,*
the very concept Meyer was seeking to eradicate.
Interestingly, supervisors were also told to encourage
employees to *increase their ownership of decisions.* The term
ownership of decisions appears quite often in regional correspondence, and may in fact have been an attempt to eliminate the more precise term, *responsibility.* Another buzz word
was *empowerment,* apparently employed in hopes of prompting new employees to feel more powerful about themselves.

Futuring appears as well, and supervisors were instructed to encourage new employees, seeking a career path, to engage in *futuring.*

This postmodern prattle left many older employees in a state of amusement.

In addition, the manual instructed each supervisor to adjust their new employee's work schedule to enable her to study those technical and college courses most likely to advance her career. As many as possible were to be appointed to *teams and committees,* including those involved in human resource management. To quote Meyer: "With more women in decision making, the decisions will get better."

The measure of her quote can be judged by the work of two committees, largely composed of women, who were ultimately responsible for the placement of two ranger stations. When the Plumas Forest decided to move its Feather River District Headquarters out of Oroville, fifteen miles into the mountains—where the forest was in fact located—both the forest and regional consent committees objected so strenuously, the plan was shelved.

Conversely, with the advance of consent, the Grindstone District of the Mendocino Forest, located in remote Stonyford, all but emptied out, becoming a work station for fire and recreation employees only. Both the forest and regional consent committees felt that Stonyford was much too remote to retain the requisite number of women. Today, all but a few district employees now report to Willows, 38 miles removed from their place of work.

Another handbook initiative was the elimination of *exceeds acceptable standards,* from an employee's evaluation rating. It is now known that Meyer and the regional consent committee felt that *exceeds acceptable standards* stimulated the natural competitiveness in men, while women were likely to be intimidated by the term. Employees were also advised that fifty per cent of their annual evaluation would be weighed in favor of *human resource skills,* and their commitment to implementing the decree. The seven technical criteria for evaluating employees remained in place, but jointly comprised just 50% of the overall evaluation.

Like other sections of the Meyer Manual, this measure was not always followed and many supervisors, with a wink and nod from their project managers, continued to apply the traditional method of evaluation. In an attempt to avert this expected sleight of hand, the consent handbook explicitly granted the monitor access to all notes and memorandum compiled by supervisors pertaining to personnel work. Again, this directive was not always followed and many memorandums were *misplaced* or later *corrected.*

Finally, the Meyer Handbook announced that the U.S. Office of Personnel Management had all but dismantled its competitive approach to the hiring of employees (referred to as the X-118 criteria). Much like the *dumbing down* of college grades, this meant the continued dumbing down of government personnel—yet another blow to Congress's heroic, hapless and hopeless 1978 effort to resuscitate its workforce.

In March 1986 a meeting of first line managers from several forests was held in Redding at the headquarters of the Shasta-Trinity Forest. There, it was reported that "The enormous amounts of time expended on paperwork, and in coaching their new employees was negatively impacting their ability to manage the forests." And, "The institutionalizing processes and procedures supporting the decree so that it becomes the central system that controls the forest service was wreaking havoc in them."

The Regional Consent Decree Committee in San Francisco chose to ignore the report.

Shortly afterward, first line supervisors from all eighteen forests sent the regional office a letter complaining about the huge number of new office employees who "lacked the capacity to approach highly complex and sensitive analysis of issues, or unusual situations not normally encountered in an office environment." The letter went on to state that because so many new employees lacked familiarity with resource management, they should be obliged to spend real time in the field, learning about forestry and thus make a contribution to the workplace.

The Regional Consent Decree Committee ignored this proposal as well.

Another event that took place in Redding, signaling strong opposition to the consent decree, arose from a gaff committed by the regional office. Personnel Specialist Wayne Strom had been sent north to give a presentation to first and second line supervisors on *Successfully Incorporating Women and Minorities into Your Organization.* Instead, Strom made the four following points, all of which must have traumatized many on the regional staff.

Point One: What are the causes to resistance to change? His answer, "A high percentage of new ideas do not pass the test of time. Some do. And those that do should be and are adopted. That is why there is often resistance to change." In essence, Strom was stating that most of the consent committee's new ideas would not pass the test of time.

Point Two: Overcoming cultural barriers: "It is true that urban minorities and women who are accustomed to working inside cities and buildings find cultural barriers difficult to overcome when they are transferred to often extremely rural localities. They are likely to have great difficulty in overcoming this barrier." As region already knew, converting an urban employee into a backcountry employee is fraught with challenges.

Point Three: Building a commitment to successful change. Strom stated that "This can be done by being open and forthright with all your employees." Ever since 1983, the agency had utilized every deception known to tyranny to double cross its employees.

Point Four Why do some change efforts fail? Strom's answer: "Some efforts fail because either the changes were no good to start with, or because those implementing the changes were not open and forthright with their employees."

One can only conclude that Wayne Strom was a plant, whose presentation was arranged by a remnant of the regional staff intent on rescuing the agency from further decomposition.

The day the Bernardi Consent Decree was to end, July 31, 1986, finally arrived. But the Equal Rights Advocates, noting that the service was not remotely close of filling its quota tables—at the time numbering 102—charged the agency with contempt of court and asked for an extension. Absent from the district court that day was Judge Conti who—after what must have been some very detailed instructions—tossed Region Five back into the lap of Magistrate Wilken.

In their contempt filing, the advocates charged that region had failed to live up to its good faith pledge, and in recent negotiations had failed to extend the decree, as requested. Attorney David Glass, again representing the service, countered by complaining about Monitor Meyer's abrasive manner. Wilken ignored Glass, and listened to Meyer as she reported a lack of monitoring on the forests and a lack of responses to her inquiries from them; when the forests did respond they very often misled her. Further, the mulishness of forest employees was such that many continued to focus their attention on fighting fires, marking timber and such eccentric projects as the Northern Spotted Owl Plan—all the while failing to implement the decree.

One of the most unique features about Monitor Meyer, the advocates, and the regional consent committee was their ignorance of resource management. Another was their patrician savagery toward men. Moreover, they had found the agency's longtime women employees a huge embarrassment. One of the indignities Meyer was fond of tossing at them was, "You're a good old boy in women's clothing." Within the year she and the advocates would be directing their patrician savagery toward Hispanic, and African American men as well.

If the residents of the communities surrounding the forests had learned of Meyer's charges at the hearing—specifically the incidental nature of firefighting—a political earthquake would have ripped across the California firmament. Yet her accusations remained off the television circuit—the news organizations having long since concluded that Bernardi was nothing more than a fight between two mice.

The hearing continued with Meyer at full cry, until finally Wilken adjourned court. On October 28, she reconvened and startled the forest service by ruling that it was indeed in contempt of court, and that the consent decree would be extended for an indefinite period. She then ordered that Meyer's wages be increased to $100 per hour and that the agency create a special fund for her and her aid, Jacqueline Cables, to the amount of $360,000.

There followed yet another surprise. Nancy Davis of the Equal Rights Advocates reported that between June 11, 1985 and May 15, 1986 she had spent more than 137 hours working on the decree and was entitled to compensation. Magistrate Wilken saw merit in her petition and ordered the service to award its legal adversary the sum requested— amount not stated in documents. What had for so long been known as the consent decree was now being referred to as the *contempt decree*.

Meanwhile, back in Washington, DC, while President Reagan was focusing his attention on the Soviet Union and its emergent leader, Mikhail Gorbachev, his cabinet members were engaged in a quiet feud over affirmative action. When Attorney General Edwin Meese decided to rescind Richard Nixon's Executive Order 11478, he was strenuously opposed by Secretary of Labor William Brock, as well as the Office of Federal Contract Compliance, now solidly in the hands of progressive liberals. In the end Brock prevailed, and Meese, himself still unaware of the demolition taking place on public lands, never brought the dispute to Reagan's attention.

One cabinet member who decided it was time to act was Secretary of Agriculture John Block. Having finally leafed through the binder Max Peterson had sent him two years before, he was startled to learn what had been occurring on his watch. He reacted by writing a letter to Judge Conti, arguing that the forest service had substantially complied with the decree. He also pointed out that it was "unlawful in certain key respects, and in virtually every respect ill-advised and unworkable."

His letter had no effect on the Judge.

Unhappily, Block, Meese and Donald Regan were among a large assemblage of mild-mannered conservatives who remained unaware of the uncompromising nature of the affirmative action industry. Many others serving in the Reagan Administration also felt that if they simply shut up, the whole issue would crumble from the weight of its own iniquity. Reagan himself, able to recognize the unbending nature of Communist totalitarianism abroad, seems not to have been aware of the unbending nature of the totalitarians, who now comprised a majority of his employees just below the cabinet level.

These attitudes within the administration prevailed at a time Americans, by overwhelming margins, opposed the establishment of an affirmative action spoils system every bit as corrosive as that of the Nineteenth Century. Had Reagan, Meese, and Regan turned affirmative action into the great national issue it should have become, its now indelible stain on the nation's social fabric would have long since faded away.

Chapter 7

THE GENDER HOSTILE TOOL HUNT

A woman needs a man like a fish needs a bicycle.
—Irina Dunn, Australian journalist; this quote is
often erroneously attributed to Gloria Steinman

*Single mindedness is all very well in cows and ba-
boons. In an animal claiming to belong to the same
species as Shakespeare it is simply disgraceful.*
—Aldous Huxley

IN 1987 SECRETARY of Agriculture John Block was replaced
by Richard E. Lyng. Alarmed over reports of Region Five's recent reversals and aware that what Block had long thought
a minor brush fire had burst into a firestorm of major proportions, Lyng sought to have Zane Smith removed from office. Let it be said that Smith was a very discouraged man in
search of relief. He was thus kicked upstairs to Washington
D.C, where he reported for work a year or so, before retiring.

Lyng did not appear to have had any specific objectives
in mind and was only aware that the longer Smith remained
in place, the more rapidly Region Five disintegrated. He
was replaced by Paul Barker, former supervisor of the Los
Padres Forest, and who over the years had built up quite a

reputation for integrity. About this time Max Peterson also decided to retire. He was succeeded by Dale Robertson, one of his assistant chiefs.

If Barker had any notions of restoring integrity to the region, he was quickly disabused by his staff as well as by Robertson who inherited Peterson's circle of Washington functionaries. After bringing Barker onboard, the regional consent committee, the advocates and monitor, with Chief Robertson's blessing, forged ahead. One of their newest projects was the opening of a research center inside each forest headquarters. In essence, this was a reading room or library stocked with books on subjects ranging from cultural diversity, to the career needs of women and the shortcomings of a world dominated by men. Among the twenty books listed as required inventory was *Woods Working Women, Sexual Integration in the US Forest Service,* and *What Color is Your Parachute?*

Because of resentment among personnel at the lower level, and because the library grant request was very poorly written, the forests often purchased material that had little to do with women's issues and truly dealt with forestry; nor were men forbidden from entering these *libraries.* During the late morning and afternoon one, two, or even three fellows, who in former times would have been in the field, might be seen sitting at a table, leafing through whatever volume caught his fancy.

Much like Diane Winokur before her, Jeannie Meyer quickly discovered that many forest service tools were hostile to women. In dealing with the crisis, she may well have taken a leaf from Daisy Chin-Lor, director of Avon Products multicultural planning division, who in her numerous writings argued that white male norming was no longer acceptable in a multicultural society. It was unreasonable to assume that women and other minorities could perform in the same manner as white men. In her words, "If I were planting a garden and I wanted to have a number of flowers, I would never think of giving every flower the same amount of sun, the same amount of water and the same soil. I'd be sure to groom and cultivate each individual breed of flower differently."

This quote presented the perfect rationale for Meyer to launch her assault against Region Five's stock of tools.

Each forest was ordered to undertake what was termed a *tool sensing survey* conducted by an independent *Female Subject Matter Expert.* Appointed by the Equal Rights Advocates, it was her duty to seek out and identify those implements favoring one sex over the other. The expert was then to submit her list to the forest consent committee, the regional consent committee and the monitor. Many tools such as chainsaws, rock bars, McClouds and Pulaskis[3] are universal to all forests, but as each unit has its own unique character, suffice to say that each had its own unique piece of gender-hostile gear.

Strangely enough, among the first problems highlighted by the Female Subject Matter Expert (her name was never attached to any document), was within the San Francisco regional office and did not directly involve unfriendly tools. Several new employees reported that the book shelves were much too high for easy access. The problem was remedied by a crew of men who were summoned from below, told to disassemble the shelves and replace them with new, lower furnishings. Also at the regional office, other new employees reported having great difficulty opening its five drawer file cabinets without the use of a stool. Region obliged by purchasing a large number of four drawer bureaus.

In September 1988, Acting Assistant Regional Forester Margaret Nicholson reported that women in the regional office were unable to open and close many windows. Two months later Norwood Robertshaw, in charge of *Lands and Real Estate Management* reported that new employees were opening and closing the windows at will. Shortly after, in an effort to accommodate the safety concerns of new employees, the regional office began turning the complex lights on one hour earlier each morning and leaving them on one hour later each night.

In addition, the sensory expert discovered that the regional office, the eighteen forest supervisor offices and eighty ranger stations were using audio/visual equipment and carts that were much too bulky for new employees to transport. The problem was solved by the region wide purchase of lightweight monitors, half-inch VCRs and lighter carts. In what can only be construed as an artful dodge, a high number of ranger stations quietly continued utilizing their older and heavier pieces of equipment.

The sensing expert also discovered that many of the chairs and tables throughout the over three-hundred office complexes were of standard height, could not be adjusted and that female employees could not accommodate themselves to this *fixed nature furniture.* Thus, all urban and forest offices were ordered to scrap their chairs and tables and replace them with adjustable furnishings. Again, a high number of district rangers ignored the directive and clandestinely went about utilizing *fixed nature furnishings.*

Finally, the San Bernardino Forest issued an order stating that its *smaller employees* were to arrive at and leave their places of work in pairs. If a co-worker could not be located, they were to wait until an older, larger employee was found to escort them off the premises. The San Bernardino office further advised that new employees, upon arriving home, were to call their supervisors to assure them of their safe arrival.

Towering book shelves, five drawer file cabinets, bulky slide projectors, fixed nature furniture, windows that refused to open and close; employees fearful of leaving the workplace unaided, for almost a century the women of the forest service had rarely encountered these difficulties. Few had been afraid to mount a stool and if a newly painted window could not be opened, or a slide projector proved too unwieldy, they were not afraid to ask a man for help.

Among the hundreds of reports and pieces of correspondence dealing with gender-hostile tools, it should be stressed that the terms women and female were almost never used. Instead euphemisms such as *smaller persons, small forest persons, new persons, new forest persons, new employees* and *small people* were employed. These graceless circumlocutions lend credence to George Orwell's many observations about the crippling effect on the public's perception of reality, when its leaders are no longer able to communicate in a clear-cut manner.

While region officially proclaimed there were no differences between men and women, the consent decree's multitude of court dockets, correspondence—legal and personal—and densely noted quarterly reports reveal that within every forest the differences were manifest. They also served to remind me of a series of truths regarding the differences between men and women. For centuries, the societies of Great Britain, France and Anglican North America have known of these truths, but veiled them behind a polite and genteel mantle known as *chivalry*. It was but one of many characteristics unique to Western Civilization.

Among the hundreds of gender discrimination encounters the sensory expert came across, were the hundred-pound sacks of grass seed, mulch and borax found in various storehouses. "In order to accommodate smaller persons" purchasers were told to order fifty pound sacks only. The hundred-pound sacks already on hand were to be manually broken down into fifty pound units. As events soon proved, even after these steps were taken, two new forest employees were required to lift each sack.

The specialist also found that many tools used to fight fires and maintain trails, such as shovels, mattocks, McClouds and Pulaski's were too heavy for smaller persons to wield without risk of injury. New and improved tools were called for. Thus, in October 1988, George Roby of the Angeles Forest reported he had purchased several trenching tools called *combs* that would allow smaller employees to "dig trenches without having to bend over."

Already present was a shovel known as the *rhino* developed at the Boise, Idaho Resource Center. Possessed of a short handle, and a smaller, sharper blade, this was perhaps the only implement in the forest service's stash of tools that was female friendly. Yet it was the men, not women, who found them most useful for directing powerful blows that could slice through buck brush, chamise and even manzanita while clearing a fire line. Curiously, the term *rhino* never caught on and a male employee in the midst of a thicket, suddenly needing one, by habit would shout out, "Ladies shovel! Over here! Ladies shovel!" Upon learning of this, consent decree coordinator for the Lassen National Forest, Deena Bible, forbid (without success) the crews from using that term.

Rock bars, those heavy, spear-shaped instruments used for smashing rocks while digging holes, were found much too heavy for female employees. Here the monitor advised that smaller and lighter rock bars be purchased, presumably to break up smaller rocks into smaller pieces. But many districts, rather than reinventing every shovel, mattock,

McCloud and rock bar demanded by Meyer, simply urged their new employees to work at a more leisurely pace.

The service had been wrestling with the issue of women and chainsaws for years. With the advance of the decree the situation only worsened. In an effort to accommodate women, the regional consent committee ordered each forest to purchase small chainsaws. The lightest proved to be a 10.8 pound *Homelite* with a twelve-inch bar. But operating even a 10.8 pounder proved an impediment, as almost every new forest person was forced to shut down their saws after fifteen minutes of work. Even worse was the often spoken of *fear factor*. This arose from the sharp snap that results from pulling the starter rope and multiple kickbacks owing to unforeseen knots encountered while cutting up tree branches. Over the years kickbacks have resulted in many injuries.

It should be noted that a number of female employees were capable of operating chainsaws with bars as long as sixteen inches for considerable periods of time without fear. They tended to be robust women who had cut firewood as children and whose fathers—employed by either the forest service or a timber company—had by example removed the fear factor from them. Let it be said that they, and their pre-consent counterparts in the offices, looked upon the hunt for gender hostile tools with scorn.

Among other issues the sensory expert uncovered was the following. Despite Max Peterson's 1985 edict, a number of districts were still employing the standard seventeen-inch Harvard Step Test for all firefighters. Monitor Meyer henceforth directed that while the seventeen-inch box was to remain in place for men, fifteen-inch boxes were to be substituted for women without exception. At the time of her edict, many men well into their forties were still working on the fire crews because thousands of desk jobs had been closed off to them. A number argued that they too were entitled to utilize the fifteen-inch box test, protesting that *a firefighter is a firefighter.* But the agency, all the while pretending that a *firefighter was a firefighter,* refused to permit these upper-middle-aged men to take the less strenuous fifteen inch test–an open admission of the vast difference between a fireman and a firewoman.

An October 1988 memo from Assistant Regional Director Joyce Muroaka, stated that new female employees throughout Region Five now had a thirteen-inch box option for the Harvard Test. As she explained, this was "to account for, and render irrelevant structural differences between the genders." In truth, Muroaka's directive rendered the structural differences between men and women all the more apparent.

The sensory expert also found the mops employed for cleaning firehouses and shops too large for smaller persons to wield; they would have to be replaced with smaller mops. Hammers and wrenches were also judged too cumbersome for the arms and hands of smaller employees. Here the forests never responded to the expert's complaints in any particular manner. While some did nothing with regard to hammers and wrenches, others indeed purchased smaller wrenches for women to loosen the same three-quarter-inch nuts that men were loosening. The reduction in torque only led to additional wrist sprains.

The expert was emphatic in her criticism of lug wrenches and vehicle jacks which were much too heavy for new persons to operate. The forests responded by saying they would equip their vehicles with star wrenches, reducing the amount of torque required to turn the lug nuts. These star wrenches never proved to be the magic tool they were imagined and eventually their purchase was restricted to fire trucks and buses.

Thus, most new female employees, whether examining a range allotment or cruising a section of forest for timber, upon experiencing a flat tire were forced to radio the closest work station for service. Though a great expense to the taxpayer, by 1988 most men on the forests no longer regarded these *missions* as annoying. With their hopes for advancement long since gone up in smoke, many were eager to drop their *assignments* to go in search of the stranded forester. Upon reaching her and replacing the flat tire, time and again they would transform a forty-five-minute drive back to the office into a four-hour ramble over the ridges. Gary McHargue, employed by the service from 1975 through 2002, estimates that over his career he went in search of, and changed the tires of sixty new employees.

Another barrier to implementing consent was the much too heavy electro fish shocker used to stun fish for purposes of study. Indeed, the sensory expert's grievances were endless. Paint guns too burdensome, portable water pumps too large and seismographs too heavy. Worst of all were the portable augers and gas powered rock drills, which were far too unwieldy for smaller persons to operate with any effectiveness.

In the course of the sensing expert's visits, she found the number of forklifts used for hoisting boxes and crates in short supply and almost none equipped with power steering. The weather instruments, posted at various locales throughout the forests were invariably placed too high for new employees to reach without benefit of a stool. She also learned that a majority of new hires were intimidated by both the large size of the pickup trucks and the standard transmissions most were equipped with. Today most forklifts are equipped with power steering, the weather instruments have been lowered, and most, but not all trucks are lighter models and come equipped with power steering and automatic transmissions.

Another problem repeatedly encountered were road gates. Placed across forest roads and trails, they are most frequently used to enclose grazing allotments. As the sensoring export reported, many smaller employees found the gates too heavy and because of numerous dents and wrinkles in the framework, very difficult to open and close. In addition, the wire hasps that hitch the gate crowns to the gate posts were too high and tightly bound for their hands to loosen.

In response, Los Padres Forest Supervisor Arthur Carroll reported that the locked gates on his forest roads "are being properly balanced and maintained in order to enable smaller employees to gain access" to the forest behind. Considering the fearsome beating these gates receive at the hands of pot growers, Carroll was filling a tall order. In an attached letter, he also digressed on the problem presented by combination locks, which had also been declared *gender hostile*. For reasons not understood, combination gate locks were presenting new employees with difficulties no pre-consent women ever encountered. He ended his letter by stating that on all five of his ranger districts, the combination gate and shop locks would be replaced by key locks.

Finally, Carroll informed region that a buddy system was being implemented for women in the field. In fact, this program was being implemented everywhere when it was discovered that a disproportionate number of women felt at risk when entering a forest alone. Conversely, in the past, the problem young men presented the agency was how to keep them out of the forests long enough to attend a meeting.

Through 1987, 1988 and 1989, as the sensing expert's reports poured into Meyer's office, she issued a torrent of directives to the forests—many acted upon, others not. Some were downright peculiar. On one occasion, she complained that the shoulder holsters worn by law enforcement officers were designed to favor right handed men and left handed women only. When she learned that almost every uniform issued a women had been of poor fit and that the shirt pockets were too small to slip a government issued calendar into, she ordered that all be replaced with proper fitting attire.

An impasse also occurred at the regional aviation center in Sacramento, where a tug used for shifting aircraft in and out of hangars was found too cumbersome for smaller persons to operate. Shortly thereafter, Jerry Sebastian, in charge of the facility, reported that he was purchasing a brand new, easy to operate tug (cost not stated). In addition, the Baron airplanes docked at the same facility and employed to fly firefighters to distant locales, were found to have seats that would not accommodate women. Here, the service simply decided to furnish each seat with extra cushions.

Regional Forester Paul Barker wrote several letters reminding foresters they must submit proof that they were purchasing *sex-neutral* tools. Copies of the purchase orders, photographs of the tools, as well as copies of newsletters from each forest highlighting *the neutralization of gender hostile equipment* were to be mailed to his office. Many forests obliged, while others offered the most disingenuous excuses, such as, "The staff misplaced my draft."

Still, Richard Henry of the Lassen Forest sent photos of his new Mark III pumps, "equipped with compression relief valves that released compression more quickly, thus allowing smaller persons to start them." From the Eldorado Forest, Jerald Hutchings reported "The snowmobiles have all been converted to key starters as opposed to pull starters, owing to the presence of new employees." "The District is purchasing more, and smaller pickup trucks on behalf of women." "Pallets are being piled in stacks of five only, while field tubs are being stacked four high only, in order to aid smaller persons." "An assortment of shorter and lighter wrenches and hammers are being purchased for the new and smaller employees."

From the distant Inyo, Forest Supervisor Dennis Martin wrote that "trucks and buses without power steering are being replaced." On a more worrisome note, he reported that women were not driving the heavy, flatbed trucks, or towing trailers in the numbers expected; nor were they taking sufficient All-Terrain-Vehicle (ATV) lessons.

His disappointment, common to every forest supervisor, was reported back to Meyer and Cables. With the aid of the *Sensor* the two sallied forth and attempted to persuade more women to drive more stake side trucks and ATVs. Quite often, while the monitors were present, the new employees obliged, but within a few days of their departure, operation of the stake sides and ATVs returned to previous levels.

The sensing expert also informed Meyer that the five-gallon containers, long employed by field personnel to transport gasoline and water, were oversized. In response, Dan Chisholm, supervisor of the Mendocino Forest, wrote that his three districts had replaced all five gallon containers with 2.5 gallon containers. Chisholm also reported that his firemen had been directed to encourage firewomen to only partially fill their portable back pumps when carrying water to the fire lines.

The forest service was relentlessly forced to deal with the conflicting demand to reach 43%, the innate reluctance of women to remain in physically demanding environments for any length of time and the high number of injuries they were suffering. The situation was judged so critical, that in 1988 Assistant Regional Forester Richard G. Deliessegues informed each forest supervisor that "all women have been advised to obtain assistance when undertaking a heavy job."

Meanwhile, under the direction of Forest Supervisor James Davis Jr., the Six Rivers Forest installed a shower at its plant nursery. The staff there had learned that their new employees possessed a much greater aversion to plant seed exposure and the chemicals used to treat the seeds than did their male counterparts. In addition the forest purchased seventy-five backpacks equipped with padded shoulder and padded waist straps. The padding was intended to prevent the straps from digging into the women's shoulders and to keep their hips from being buffeted by the packs—a major impediment while traversing rugged country.

In February 1989 Sierra Forest Supervisor James Boynton wrote that some of his fire engines "have been retro-fitted with steps, ladders, etc. to accommodate smaller people. One fire prevention vehicle has been refitted to accommodate a small person. (Documentation and pictures will be provided.)" Boynton also reported "...the Sierra has modified the chin up bars and dip bars on the physical fitness equipment. Trails are located at most fire stations. Also, some districts have purchased universal gym fitness machines which can accommodate any person regardless of statute [sic] or physical strength. (Documentation and pictures will be provided.)"

About this time John B. Hatch, Fire Management Officer of the San Bernardino Forest wrote that his forest had, "purchased a large stock of twenty pound backpacks for smaller persons working in the forest...the above referenced action plan addresses remedies for carrying packs that are very heavy for some people." Four months later, in July 1988, Richard Stauber of the same forest announced that because recruitment among women and minorities had failed to reach proper ration, he was now offering each potential female/minority recruit a $250 clothing allowance.

Living quarters at the various barracks around California did not come under the scrutiny of the tool sensory expert; rather it was the *housing sensor* who was apparently also appointed by the Equal Rights Advocates. Davis, Kurtz and company were sorely vexed when the sensor reported that the windows of many barracks in *South Zone OCC* could be opened by men only and issued a directive on the matter. Shortly afterward, the South Zone reported that all windows in all barracks on all forests could be opened by everyone.

Although the policy has since been reversed, in 1988 the advocates, Monitor Meyer and the regional committee decided that women should be housed in facilities separate from men. Within months, numerous single-wide mobile homes were being trundled into the forests. There, the windows were replaced by opaque glass panes in order to discourage the peeking proclivities of male employees. In addition, region reported that the approaches to various barracks were so poorly lit that many smaller persons were made to feel *vulnerable*. Additional lighting was installed at most facilities.

The housing sensor also informed Meyer that newer employees—many assigned to the most remote outposts in the state—were complaining about the lack of telephones. The forests responded by installing a great number of pay phones, a novelty many men to this day are still taking advantage of, and from which they would never have benefitted without the Bernardi Consent Decree.

From 1984 onward, with the great increase in numbers of women on the fire crews, it had become apparent that, with very few exceptions, they would never be capable of plunging through the underbrush with a hundred-foot hose pack in tow at the same velocity as a man. To compensate, in 1986 the forests began purchasing lightweight, single-ply fire hoses fifty-feet in length with plastic fittings attached.

By then every last forest supervisor understood the consent decree was here to stay. While most were now progressive, and eager to follow the directives as best they could, there were still a few conservatives of practical mind who simply rolled with the punches, hoping to gain a few more years before retirement. Unlike other forest employees, who could not be suddenly uprooted and transferred to any *god forsaken place* without good cause, a forest supervisor could be given two months to pack up and move to that god forsaken place.

Hence, by a wide margin cultural cringers ruled the forests. One of them even wrote a letter claiming the shortened length of his new fire hoses would "permit the new and smaller employees to make running attacks on the fires more effectively." He wrote this all the while knowing that the shortened hoses could not effectively reach the fire lines unless attached to a second, and often a third unit. He wrote it knowing that they severely impacted the effectiveness of his older, more powerful employees. He wrote it also knowing that his new, short, single-ply hoses had a propensity to kink, popped leaks by the score, and within what had once been a safe distance from flames, *melting*.

Also *melting* were his new, lightweight plastic fittings. Over a five year period the service squandered hundreds of thousands of dollars in material and man hours on some of the shoddiest equipment ever sold to a government entity. The precise amount of timber that went up in flames as a result will never be known, but one employee guessed that by 1991, the year the purchases were abandoned, California had lost one million acres of wild land to fire, owing to agency stupidity.

Chapter 8

THE EVENTFUL CAREER OF GARY

MCHARGUE

"*No education or training required...* " recreation technician position opened on Los Padres National Forest, September 1988.

"*Women only need apply,* " timber management position opened in regional office, San Francisco, September 1988

"*Unqualified applicants may apply,* " interdisciplinary analyst—Modoc National Forest, November, 1988

BETWEEN JULY 1986, when the Bernardi Decree was to have ended, and May 1988, it continued to bloom under the watchful eye of Magistrate Claudia Wilken. During that lengthy period, she began directly intervening into forest service hiring practices. That May Judge Conti himself decided to take another look at his legal entanglement. Prior to the hearing, he let it be known that Paul Barker had best carry an electric shaver and tooth brush to court, because if found in contempt he was headed for a correctional institution.

The forest service responded by flying out John R. Bolton, Edwin Meese's assistant attorney general and future U.S. Ambassador to the United Nations. Though long since recognized as a U.N. fire brand, Bolton would prove ineffective in Conti's courtroom, in large part because he was confronting a Judge who detested the client he was representing.

At the hearing the advocates informed the Judge that Region Five had failed to reduce its male representation within the all-important GS-11, GS-12 and GS-13 grades. It had also failed to come even close to filling its quotas in sixteen different professions and grades, which included electrical engineering, civil engineering, land surveying, aircraft piloting, automotive mechanic, construction specialist and cartographer. Also listed as failing to pass muster were personnel clerk, information receptionist and mail/file clerk, all which claimed over 70% female representation.

As noted earlier, in 1984 Zane Smith and his staff realized they would never place enough women to fill each of the targeted professions at 43%, and had opted for the *umbrella concept*. This meant staffing clerical positions with women in extraordinary percentages, as high as 95% in some categories. With adoption of the umbrella concept, they might reach 43% female employment overall, and praying for the court's blessing, demonstrate a good faith effort to abide by the decree.

But by allowing for percentages within numerous disciplines, in which women were well overrepresented, all region had done was create a second table of quotas to throw its money at. In essence, Smith and his staff had stumbled into yet another bear trap of their own making, a trap the advocates, and Monitor Meyer were no more inclined to release them from than the first. And so far as Judge Conti was concerned, all the agency had done was cut another deal behind his back.

Thus on May 28, 1988, he found the service again in contempt of court, and as such, would remain so until May, 9 1991. Barker was not carried off in a jumpsuit and chains, but he was ordered to fill a total of fifteen GS-11 through GS-13 positions with women only, and if necessary *create* all fifteen positions—whether they were needed or not.

In addition, Conti directed that 50% of all foresters hired be women. Further, the forests were to shift several clerical categories over to the higher-paying business management slots. Finally, the Judge ordered that any restructuring of forest operations that might have a negative impact on female employment, such as an increase in timber cutting, must be offset by a parallel project designed for their benefit. For example, development of a task force to study the "efficacy of multi-tasking within an office environment."

The Judge's most dramatic act of spite was to order region to appoint a second district ranger to each ranger district. The annual cost of this innovation was the near equivalent of 535 Congressional overseas junkets. Correspondence reveals that many forests, perhaps owing to fear of turf wars, evaded the order by creating an assistant district ranger position, a very pricey innovation nonetheless.

By now a fair number of forest supervisors and their staffs must have known that the 43% section of Article IV was not legally sound, and therefore a farce. Still, none had the stomach to bring the agency to accounts. To have done so would have been an admission of their own law breaking, opened the agency to a class action lawsuit and possibly draw thousands more individual suits.

Paralleling region's running assault on 43% were its sexual harassment problems. For reasons yet unknown, by the mid-1980s, the halcyon years of the Reagan Administration, sexual harassment had reached epidemic proportions throughout the federal government. As early as 1983, the advocates and its decree backers within the forest service announced that sexual harassment was having a devastating effect on workplace morale. Thus, beginning in 1984, scores of remedial classes were being held at ranger stations around the state. Within two years every national forest across the United States would be holding similar classes.

In fact, according to the employees interviewed, since 1972, when seasonal women were first employed, men occasionally used terms like *piece of ass* in their presence. But no one, including the woman, thought much about it. Physical contact, such as pinching a rear end did take place, but this was rare in large part because a self-governing mechanism was in place. The great majority of men on the crews viewed that kind of behavior with abhorrence; the harasser was ostracized, and within a few days ceased reporting for work.

Out-of-sight groping also occurred and if the woman reported the incident the offender was severely reprimanded, or if a seasonal employee, discharged. But among all employees interviewed, just five or six incidents of sexual harassment were recalled over their several hundred combined years of employment.

Jim Burton, the former engine captain recalled, "Sexual harassment was not an issue that the forestry employees, men or women, spent a lot of time thinking about. But after consent descended over the forests, it became an issue that everyone thought about. There wasn't any time frame that I can remember. They just kept tightening the screws, year by year."

Underscoring the dilemma Burton and others faced was a column Zane Smith placed in the *Southwest Pacific NewsLog*, in which he stated that America's societal norms no longer measured up to Region Five's standards. "The minority must be protected from the majority's mores." This in essence meant that he had rejected the ethics of the people who were underwriting his salary. Added Smith, "I would like to make clear to all employees that region does not recognize *minor* and *major* forms of sexual harassment. All forms are major and constitute a threat to the harmonious working environment we need, and our employees have a right to expect."

This was much like equating shoplifting with second degree murder, crimes not thought remotely comparable anywhere on earth. His announcement created so much antipathy and uncertainty, that it drove men and women even further apart. Indeed, the uncertainty as to how an employee, who was overheard to mutter the word *fuck* might be punished, undermined confidence everywhere. By 1986 many female hires, fresh out of college and who had taken numerous gender study courses, were pointing fingers at men for reasons no pre-consent woman would dreamed of.

This was one reason why the multiple lists of forty words, phrases, and subjects never to be spoken of in their presence was such a boon to the agency. A supervisor who repeatedly hoisted that list aloft while lecturing one of his men, understood that given a little more time and browbeating, that employees would resign and the agency be that much closer to reaching 43%.

By then, making life miserable for those passed-over for promotion had become an art form throughout the U.S. Forest Service. Those overheard criticizing the promotion of a woman over themselves, were often given an assignment without a job description, thus leaving them without a career path. By contrast, women who reported overhearing the criticisms of others were sometimes rewarded with a promotion.

Still, many men, determined to ride out the storm until retirement, adopted what the psychiatric profession calls the passive-aggressive approach. The employee would decline to speak—unless absolutely necessary—to a newly promoted woman. Or, upon seeing the newly promoted start down a corridor, dodge into an adjacent room. Many newly hired sensitized women found this distressing. Indeed, the ensuing arguments over who should have spoken to whom, or why someone vanished into a cubicle afforded a kindergarten-like aspect to the entire office workplace.

One individual who stated that sexual harassment was a problem was Eric Holst, a former employee union representative for the Eldorado National Forest. In addition to numerous other responsibilities, Holst's duty as a *union rep* was to resolve employee complaints at the forest level before they were passed to the regional office. Unlike the great majority of employees whose awareness of personnel problems was limited to those they worked with, he collided with all manner of conflicts.

He noted that during his years as a representative some incidents of sexual harassment were blatant, including guys asking women, "Hey, what cup size are you wearing?" He was particularly exercised over upper management's conduct, claiming some supervisors took certain liberties those in a lower position would never have dreamed of. Over his extended term as an employee representative (believed to be twelve years), he dealt with a dozen sexual harassment incidents—about one a year—in which the accused was found guilty.

In September 1985, Employee Relationship Specialist Chris Pyron placed a long article on sexual harassment in the *Pacific Southwest NewsLog*. She emphasized that aside from the physical groping of employees, other forms of sexual harassment included making lascivious remarks and lewd suggestions. These genuinely significant points however were undermined by the following. "Moreover, many types of routine interaction, such as harmless flirting is generally acceptable, but can be highly offensive to some [other] people. It is almost imperative that the harassed women make her dissatisfaction known. In no other way is employee conduct subject to this degree of subjective evaluation." Pyron here misjudged the general character of men and women alike. Even if a third party is witness to a flirtation and feels vulnerable for reasons of religion or jealousy, open interaction between the sexes has been on-going for many thousands of years. She concluded with the following:

> *I sympathize with the employee who has suffered harassment and am deeply offended by the harasser. I am also deeply frustrated that I realize now no matter what we do as an organization the situation for the victim will never be made completely right.*

This is untrue. Every day people are injured in automobile accidents, unfairly passed over for promotion, or swindled out of their homes by unscrupulous bankers. Yet friends and relatives alike, as well as society at large, expects the victims to place these misfortunes behind them.

The least credible portion of Pyron's presentation was her inclusion of a table created by Susan Webb, author of a piece that appeared in *Management Review* titled "Sexual Harassment, Court Costs Rise for Persistent Problem." Webb's table claimed that between May, 1978 and May, 1980, 294,000 out of the 694,000 women employed (42%) by the federal government had suffered sexual harassment. Presented as fact without credible origin, the numbers were placed in a large dark font much more likely to catch the eye than Pyron's text.

Yet strangely, in a paragraph just beneath the table, Pyron countered Webb's assertion, by stating that between 1983 and 1985, when she was Region Five's sexual harassment monitor, among roughly 13,400 permanent and seasonal employees, just 25 instances of sexual harassment occurred. Her revelation badly compromised the credibility of Webb's table and undermines her own judgment in placing it with her article. It also prompts the following question: why wasn't Region Five presented with an assortment of plaques for its superlative track record on managing sexual harassment?

Yet, by giving Webb and other like-minded sociologists credence, Pyron was performing as the forest service expected. Her article, like others, and the hundreds of sexual harassment seminars conducted by the agency, prompted many highly sensitized feminist employees to file frivolous suits, which in turn prompted many more men to depart.

Even employee representatives were not immune from sexual harassment charges. Lonnie Lewis, employee representative for the Modoc National Forest, had two sexual harassment suits filed against him. One was brought by a third party following a meeting, during which a woman he had not seen in several years, gave him a hug. The Modoc's consent decree monitor filed a sexual harassment complaint against Lewis. After an examination of the facts, the forest dismissed her complaint. But pointing to the entrenched hostility toward men among the forest staff, is the fact that no one considered filing a harassment complaint against the women who initiated the hug.

Confirmation of how institutionalized the hostility toward men, is the following—to this day, no woman has ever been discharged from employment for falsely accusing a man of sexual harassment. Nor are they compelled to offer an apology, which leaves the real victim in the incident unable to retrieve his reputation.

Lewis's second entanglement involved a joke that depicted Adam and Eve as foolish caricatures. The very same consent decree monitor filed a sexual harassment suit, charging that his joke depicted women as sex symbols. That too was dismissed.

The unspoken practice of inducing frivolous suits, such as the above, prompted many men to search for a thousand and one reasons not to go into the timber with a woman. Several interviewed stated they had no reservations about entering the forest with women on a work crew, but under no circumstances would they enter in the company of a single woman.

Meanwhile, as if the forests were not buried under enough paperwork, in August, 1988, each forest supervisor was ordered to file a quarterly, rather than a semi-annual progress report. At about the same time, an Employee of the Year Award was established. Each forest supervisor deemed to have done the best job of promoting the consent decree was awarded $1500; each first line supervisor who had done the best job of promoting the decree was to receive $350-$600; each non-supervisor was to receive $300 and a plaque. However, within the San Francisco office, the awards were dispersed somewhat differently. Each employee within each department—some with as few as five employees—who had demonstrated the greatest commitment to the consent decree was presented a $1,000 bonus.

Directly related to these awards were additional changes to an employee's annual evaluation. A dramatic example of the change in how they were arrived at was the case of Jim McGuirk, a fire control officer, who in 1989 was named region's supervisor of the year. A review of his evaluation reveals that resource management was just one of four criteria utilized to evaluate him. Other factors were work in *civil rights, safety,* and *concern for others.* A careful reading of his appraisal reveals that the number of words used to grade McGuirk for fire control officer came to just 17% of the total.

In yet another small event that speaks volumes for the times, an uproar erupted in the regional office in San Francisco when it was learned that its few remaining male staff members were putting in far fewer overtime hours on decree work than their female counterparts. Orders were issued, directing the men to buckle down and apply themselves.

As the above incident and McGuirk's evaluation demonstrates, throughout California achieving 43% was now deemed far more urgent than managing the forests. Among the reams of evidence in support of this charge, was a job posting issued by the Tahoe National Forest on August 5, 1988, stating that seven different positions were open. The forest collected eleven applications, eight from women—then proceeded to fill all positions with women. In yet another job announcement, the Tahoe placed three female on a listing for a single position, yet not a single male. A female was, of course, chosen, but per new agency rules, the selection panel was forced fill out a lengthy report as to why each of the other women were rejected.

By mid-1988 these announcements were commonplace on every forest in the region. The means by which they were concealed from the male employees varied considerably. In many instances, such as the following from the San Bernardino Forest, they were quite ham-fisted. After stating that the vacancy was being advertised for no more than a few days and targeted for women and minorities only, the applicants were told, "We would appreciate it if this information was not shared with others, as this would minimize your opportunity of becoming employed with our agency."

That September a position for a budget accounting analyst opened on the Grindstone District of the Mendocino Forest. The Selection Advisory Panel (SAP) consisting of three women interviewed eight applicants, all of whom were women. Just two were rated as strong, one of whom was hired. The advisory panel then sat down and wrote out in time-consuming detail why each of the remaining seven women were not chosen. But the agency's *sub rosa* system of listing jobs was yet to be perfected, and screw-ups continued to occur. In November, the Modoc Forest listed an opening and received a single application from a male candidate. The opening was immediately closed, rewritten, and posted under another discipline.

A truly curious incident occurred in the Lassen Forest when human resources hired a criminal investigator, drawing from a list of seven men and three women. A Sid Clark was chosen over a Cheryl Hall because he had much stronger firearm skills and better defensive tactics, which were considered *very critical to the position*. But the evaluator also concluded that Clark would be *useful* to the Lassen, because he was an Indian. By 1988, minority men were placing increasing pressure on the agency's female hiring programs.

In another incident that same autumn, a position was advertised within the electric shop, again in the Lassen Forest. Three women applied, one of whom was chosen. The very nature of this job suggests that region had become so adept at covertly listing its announcements, that possibly three-dozen eligible men were never made aware of its existence.

In November 1988, Jerold N. Hutchings of the Eldorado Forest reported that between August 9 and November 8 he had filled twenty-five positions with women, and just seven with men. He apologetically added that in all instances where the man had been chosen, it was because no women had applied, or if they had applied, declined his offer. Another example of this truly Orwellian approach to resource management occurred in July 1988, when an announcement was placed by the San Bernardino Forest. A single position was advertised in six separate professions, most of which were only remotely related to the job at hand. In effect, this presented the San Bernardino with a six fold increase in its ability to troll for female candidates.

The *Can Acquire the Ability to Perform* contrivance had been utilized in employee evaluations since 1984, but had yet to appear on any job announcement, no one seeming to possess the valor to take such a step. But beginning in September of 1988 every job announcement began with this statement: "Has, *or can acquire* the ability to perform."

More evidence of decay in the agency's workforce appeared a month later, when the Los Padres Forest placed ten job announcements with the statement "No Education or Training Required." The same forest also announced a position for a GS-05 archeologist trainee, who upon completing one year of work, would be vaulted to GS-07, and then GS-09, all without competition from other employees.

In September 1988 a timber management position was opened in no less a place than San Francisco. Within the *Knowledge, Skills, and Ability* section of the announcement lay this stark phrase: *Women only need apply*. This barefaced violation of multiple federal laws and court decisions as well as the Bernardi Decree itself, was followed by a generic footer at the bottom of the page that read, "The Forest Service does not discriminate in any way."

San Francisco also placed a request for a fisheries and wildlife biologist with the following stipulation, which henceforth would appear on all announcements: "Applicant must contribute to a federal work force reflective of the nation's diversity with respect to race color, religion, sex and national origin." This was correctly interpreted by almost everyone to mean that no white men need apply. Elsewhere, the Stanislaus Forest, in a posting for a district ranger, issued a notice that read "Applicant must contribute to a federal work force reflective of the nation's diversity with respect to race, color, religion, sex and national origin," and be "substantially qualified."

The last phrase was followed by: "Substantially qualified means an applicant requires not more than one year of specific job training...to be non-competitively promoted to the target position." In effect, the Stanislaus was trolling in the most profane manner for the second most important position in the entire U.S. Forest Service—that of district ranger.

Identically worded announcements were posted by the Sequoia Forest for the position of forest planning and budget, and by the Modoc for an interdisciplinary analyst. In November of 1988 the Modoc advertised a position with this statement: "Unqualified applicants may apply,"—another direct contravention of the Bernardi Decree.

The personal ordeals these job postings forced on thousands of employees was related in detail by Gary McHargue. Through his long career with the agency, he was at various times employed by the Lassen, Plumas, and Sequoia National Forests in fire, timber, and range management. He stands out among those interviewed because of his near photographic memory, and superb verbal skills.

Today he is hesitant to admit that he once worked for an agency that in his youth symbolized all that was important to him. His reticence is because the agency he once idealized had treated him so shabbily, and because of its notorious reputation among the agencies it now interfaces with. Despite occasionally raising his voice over a disappointment, he is remarkably cheerful. Even more surprising, he harbors no animosity toward the individual women who leap-frogged past him to occupy positions he had long been prepared to assume. This is why he asked that they be given fictitious names.

In 1987, hoping to leave firefighting because he was approaching forty years of age, he applied for the position of range conservationist on the Lassen Forest. Though he possessed a degree in range conservation, for an entire year the position sat vacant. Suddenly, in early 1988, the Lassen promoted an administrative assistant into the position. Forest Supervisor Richard Henry, who clearly hoped to jettison McHargue from the agency altogether, assigned him the task of training the woman for the position he had so long aspired to fill.

In the first of two taped interviews, McHargue continued, "Anyway, on Janet's first day on the job she comes over and says, 'Gary, I don't know anything about range management.'

"Well, I tried to give her some encouragement, but then she said, 'Gary I don't even know how to ride a horse. I was raised in the Bay Area.'"

He continued, "To be a range manager you must know how to ride a horse. In this instance there were seven allotments spread across possibly 300,000 acres of earth, grass and other growth. All must be analyzed to determine if the amount of livestock grazing should be reduced. Well, guess what they did? They sent her to a private horse riding school. For almost a month. At public tax payer expense."

After a pause, he continued: "In riding the range another important point needs to be taken into account—dealing with people—most specifically those who are leasing the allotments. And loggers who are likely to be encountered almost anywhere in the forest. One day Janet came over to the desk and said, 'Gary, I am terrified of those cowboys. They scare me to death.'

"So I explained to her that many were descendants from old pioneer families. They are rough, tough and rugged, but it's a hard life they lead. They may not be polite, but they are not going to beat you up, or shoot you…so then I explained that what we did in the forest was to take the initiative and learn *verbal judo* in order to gain their trust and reduce their hostility. But with Janet, verbal judo didn't count. She could not bring herself within shouting distance of a cattleman, let alone employ verbal judo. She was so intimidated, the district ranger provided her with a forest law enforcement officer when she went to formal meetings with them. After one or two meetings, both officers begged off, saying they had too many other things to do.

"By autumn the ground was pretty well pounded by the hooves of cattle, and no one had been out to check the allotments…with the first rainfall of the season, Janet, still unable to over-come her fear of horses, began using a four-wheel-drive truck. And in driving the truck over the muddy ground she ended up doing more damage to the range than any twenty head of cattle might have done."

"What happened?" I asked.

"The job never got done."

He paused, then made an observation that goes to the very center of the human soul, and the forest service's hostile work environment. "Some women did bust their butts. Even if they were not qualified, they did try. But others were in it for the free ride. They knew they didn't have to work, and flaunted it. We hated them."

McHargue turned to his second ordeal; that of being forced to train yet another woman for yet another position he had hoped to fill. "She was working for the forest as a clerk, then suddenly got promoted to a GS-09 trainee forester. I was furious when I learned that while I had been submitting my resume for forestry positions all over California, the service had been quietly paying the University of Nevada to give Andrea a forestry education." McHargue, who at the time was managing the Sequoia Forest's fall slash burning program, recalled his first meeting with the trainee.

"We had her coming on board. We needed to give her a tour of every discipline...well, I couldn't believe what I saw. She probably weighed one-hundred pounds and was extremely pale when I was introduced to her. In fact, Andrea did not even have a steady walk. And she had never been in the field. Well, I drove her all over the district, stopping to visit the different crews. Most of it was driving. Very little walking. But by mid-afternoon she was breathing heavily. On our way back to the station she sort of opened up about herself and said, 'I've always wanted to do something challenging, but I have a congenital heart problem.' A few minutes later she told me she had a pacemaker.

"Shortly after, she nodded off. Then she woke up. I actually thought that she might be having a heart attack. I picked up speed and drove back to the office as fast as I could go. On the way in she fell asleep and then woke up again for a few minutes and explained that the reason she kept falling asleep was because her pace maker could not keep pace with her heart."

"What happened?"

"We got back safely. Despite this she became the GS-09 forester. Even though she was never asked to leave her office. Her job, in other words fell on someone else's shoulders. Someone who probably was not making nearly as much money as she was."

"Did she ever tell you she felt guilty about this?"

"I do recall her explaining that things had always been handed to her on a silver platter. But that after a while she got use to things handed her on a silver platter. It can happen to anyone. No matter how well their intentions…anyway, I eventually took a liking to her and we are still good friends."

Shortly after, McHargue returned to the Lassen Forest. There, he learned that the forest had opted to send a seasonal clerk named Marsha to Humboldt State University— tuition, books, and transportation paid for—to become a forester. Though well qualified for that position, McHargue did not care as he was now marking time until retirement. In a development as darkly comic as Janet's fear of horses, it was only upon Marsha's return to the Lassen the following May that anyone learned she was afraid of insects. "She not only feared insects—worse, she was afraid of being alone in the forest."

"A forester afraid of the forest?"

"Her job was to be out there collecting data on fires, dispositions of the trees, the amount of slash on the ground and to locate groves of saplings that needed to be thinned. She had applied for and received a job that required her to be in the forest more than any other discipline in the entire service."

"What happened?"

"They tweaked her job. It was tweaked so that she had more work in the office. Then they told the fire captains to go into the field and do the job for her. There were four of us who had to assume her duties, even though they were not in our job descriptions. And we would never be promoted." Gary and the other captains easily dodged their assignments, and for the next two years the Almanor District of the Lassen Forest was without a forester. Yet the forest supervisor continued to furnish Marsha with books, board, tuition, transportation and a salary, knowing full well she would never become a forester.

These are not the last of McHargue's escapades with an outlaw agency he once idealized.

Chapter 9

THE MAUPIN WHITE PAPER

*ONLY APPLICANTS WHO DON'T MEET
STANDARDS WILL BE CONSIDERED*
—San Bernardino National Forest for GS-09
real estate specialist, November 28, 1991.

Only the Unqualified May Qualify.
—Announcement for a GS-05/06 dispatcher
by the Six Rivers National Forest, December
18, 1989.

THE CHRONICAL OF discrimination that brought Gary
McHargue's career to such a jarring finish was of course just
another tip of the iceberg. Each job notice that follows signi-
fies an instance where several professional careers were cut
off in similar fashion. To the lists of the professionally and
financially stricken men, must be added their wives and children, the many women placed in the most impossible positions, losses to the forests and losses to the American people.

In January of 1989, the Shasta-Trinity, Sequoia, and
Mendocino Forests all posted for an assistant district ranger.
Each announcement noted the "Applicant must be substan-
tially qualified." "Substantially qualified means an applicant

requires not more than one year of specific job training to be non-competitively promoted to the target position." In other words, no matter how poorly the candidate might perform, once over the selection hurdle, she was destined to become an assistant district ranger.

In February 1989, an opening for a forestry technician was listed by the Lassen Forest. Aside from the now ubiquitous diversity clause, the posting stated, "Applications will be accepted from both qualified and nonqualified employees." That same month, the Shasta-Trinity announced it too was looking for a forestry technician. In addition to the diversity clause were two more statements: "Unqualified Applicants Accepted," and, "An upward mobility position for employees who do not meet government qualifications." In September of 1988, the San Bernardino Forest announced it was looking for a supervisory district clerk. In addition to the diversity clause was this passage..."The unqualified may apply."

More job announcements follow. Again from the San Bernardino Forest under the supervision of George Irby, came a declaration in capital lettering for a realty specialist...

ONLY APPLICANTS WHO DON'T MEET GOVERNMENT STANDARDS WILL BE CONSIDERED.

In November 1989, the Sierra Forest placed an advertisement for a forestry technician, noting that "Unqualified Employees May Apply." "Unqualified will not be referred to the selecting committee if three qualifieds are found."

The following job announcement put out by the forest service circa 1920 offers a refreshing contrast to the criminally misleading euphemisms of postmodern forestry...

MEN WANTED!
A RANGER MUST BE ABLE TO TAKE CARE OF HIMSELF
AND HIS HORSES UNDER VERY TRYING CONDITIONS;
BUILD TRAILS AND CABINS; RIDE ALL DAY AND ALL
NIGHT. PACK, SHOOT, AND FIGHT FIRES WITHOUT
LOOSING HIS HEAD

ALL THIS REQUIRES A VERY VIGOROUS CONSTITUTION.
IT MEANS THE HARDEST KIND OF PHYSICAL WORK
FROM BEGINNING TO END. IT IS NOT A JOB FOR
THOSE SEEKING HEALTH OR LIGHT OUTDOOR WORK
INVALIDS NEED NOT APPLY

The Six Rivers Forest was the source of perhaps the most gracefully worded job announcement ever issued: "Only the Unqualified May Qualify." That forest, under the stewardship of James Davis Jr., went on to explain that this *unqualified* employee could schedule her work week as needed. Should a conflict arise between her personal needs and an obligation to serve the forest, personal needs would prevail.

The Six Rivers is located in the far northwest of California, between the state-owned redwood parks nearer the coast and the Klamath and Shasta-Trinity Forests inland. If it were placed in New Jersey it would have long ago been set aside in perpetuity and declared that state's greatest assemblage of natural marvels. But apart from the Siskiyou Wilderness, and the Smith River Recreation Area—both located in its far north—the Six Rivers is an ordinary piece of California real estate, a narrow, winding, string bean shaped forest noted for its huge black bears, stock-killing cougars, and mosquito-infested ravines ever lying in shadow.

Yet from the beginning it had been a consistent leader in the hiring and promoting of the unqualified. Its first quarterly report for 1989 informed region that the forest had declined to fill three positions for biologist because no women were on the list of candidates. Five other positions received applications from men and women both; women were chosen to fill all five. Further, the forest announced that it was applying the Peace Corps Appointing Authority in order to promote a woman to civil engineer, even though she had no background in civil engineering.

The Peace Corps Authority permitted forest supervisors to appoint anyone who had served in the corps to any position they felt suitable—a policy 180 degree at variance with the Bernardi Decree. The driving force behind this practice was the notion that anyone who had worked overseas in an undeveloped country would have little difficulty adjusting to a forest environment. I recall one employee shaking his head in mirth over the agency's Peace Corps fetish. "It was like watching a bear cub trying to open a jar of honey."

Another indicator of the corrosion enveloping the Six Rivers was a February 27, 1989 letter written by Mad River District Ranger Patricia Clark. After noting that recruiting employees for her remote district was extremely difficult, she proposed opening three GS-2/3/4/ rated firefighter positions for women and minorities only. In her words, "I feel it is essential we take the risk and fill all the positions if applicants are available. We have a tremendous opportunity to bring new people into the system which can only benefit the service."

The Six Rivers also reported that every week, each member of its management team was undergoing four hours of "discussions and activities that valued diversity and the acceptance of one another." Additionally, two female fire management officers were being sent to *The Woman's Diversity Mosaic for the Future,* a service-wide symposium being held in Denver, Colorado under direction of the Washington Office.

Perhaps the proximity of Humboldt State University was a factor in the Six Rivers' groveling approach toward Monitor Meyer and the advocates; or perhaps the engaging, bedside manner of its personnel department. On a number of occasions the Six Rivers posted such notices as: "It is always a good time to visit with a career adviser. They can assist you with any questions you may have regarding the professions. Career advisers can advise you on training, experience, and opportunities in their chosen field. They are all anxious to assist you."

One employee who never benefited from that forest's engaging bedside manner was John Fint, then an engineer on the Mad River District. He recalled how he had applied for an engineering position at the G-11 level. The forest never responded, and shortly after reposted the position at GS-09, the level he was working at. He again applied and again received no response. The forest then reposted at GS-07, below his level, and again after applying he received no response. Only after reposting at GS-05, far below Fint's rank, was the position filled. Upon being hired, the woman was informed that after a period of training, she would be promoted to his level. Three years of instruction followed and she was promoted, but her breadth of knowledge never approached that of John Fint.

He was able to escape the Six Rivers in exchange for a position at the same grade on the Sierra District of the Tahoe Forest. A year later, when a GS-11 position opened for an engineer writer coordinator, he applied. Despite twenty years of solid performance, he lost out to a woman with three years in the service—two working on a silviculture crew, a position not remotely related to the job at hand.

With his dashed hopes piling up, Fint filed a discrimination suit. In retaliation his district ranger reduced his yearly evaluation by one level in each category. According to Fint "The ranger then went to Forest Supervisor Geri Berg Larson and told her that [even though he had been on the district for just two years] I had been on the district too long."

"When I went in and appealed to Larson, she said she could not do anything about it, and that 'By far and away the one who knows your performance best is your district ranger.' I went back and asked him what he knew about my job. He didn't know anything about my job. Only my own supervisor knew. Yet the ranger had seen fit to downgrade me in every single category. It was retribution because I had filed a discrimination complaint."

By 1988, all across the United States forest service engineers had ceased applying for jobs anywhere, even though all avenues to advancement within their own forests had been closed off. Thus, like John Fint, most simply spent their days in the woods, glassing the ridges for deer, breathing in the scent of pine trees, escaping as many sensitivity round tables as possible, and waiting for retirement. Over the first twelve years of Fint's career, he had moved from a GS-05 to a GS-09 grade. Beginning in 1981 until his retirement in 2005, not once was he promoted.

Twenty-five job announcements similar to those that blocked the career paths of John Fint, Jim Burton, and thousands more lie in Box 23 at the Federal Records Storage Center in San Bruno. All were a breach of Section One of the Fourteenth Amendment, Title VII of the 1964 Civil Rights Act, and the Bernardi Decree itself. How many more were printed up and distributed between 1988 and 1994 no one can be sure, but the number is likely over a thousand. Nor were these postings restricted to Region Five.

In 1990, my wife, employed by the Bureau of Reclamation, learned that a torrent of *upward mobility* positions were being offered by the forest service. No one at the bureau knew what was taking place at the other agency, so she decided to apply and was soon carrying home dozens of job postings. For more than two months, I spent several hours, several days each week at the word processor painstakingly configuring her resume to fit the some forty jobs she applied for. Most were from California, but other equally deceptive announcements originated from Arizona, New Mexico, Montana and Wyoming.

Yet she never received a single telephone interview. It would be several years before we found out why. She had been working for the Department of Interior since 1972. Her resume reflected a wide breadth of experience, but the dating and wording also revealed that she did not share the agency's progressive sentiments. It is ironic, but simultaneous to its feminization, the forest service was also undergoing a coarsening of operations. A coarsening so profound that among the thirty or so human resource departments my wife contacted, not one had the courtesy to acknowledge receipt of her resume.

How many hundreds of thousands of hours were thrown away by other applicants across the country is another question that will never be answered. Days of toil wasted by job seekers never to be recovered, who never suspected that the jobs advertised were directed at so narrow a segment of the population as to make them fictitious. For the private citizen, time spent means money was spent. For the forest service, time spent doesn't necessarily mean anything was spent.

Shortly after the federal court's 1988 ruling, one of Paul Barker's aids, Ronald Crenshaw, employing state-of-the-art technology, launched yet another program, titled *Project*

Outreach for Women, an improvement over the renovated MARS program. The system enabled region to unveil the actual location of every woman residing in the United States who *might* possess an interest in working in the woods. One of the most exhaustive, expensive, intrusive programs ever launched by an agency—and among the most successful—it resulted in the hiring of 1,287 women and 118 minority men.

Never stated, but an ongoing dilemma that project outreach was never able to resolve, is how long the women and minority hires remained at their positions. All received paid transit, a salary, the pledge of a college education, and in the initial months, free housing. Yet very few remained at their stations remotely as long as the men they had replaced; in fact, many remained less than a year. The physical and psychological dichotomy between the sexes most definitely played a role in the lack of retention, but region's prevarication with regard to the actual duties performed played an equally important role.

Too many women lacked the credentials (no longer correctly stated on the job applications) to perform. This of course meant they had been lied to. Finally, there was the culture shock that resulted from the hiring of over 1,200 young women, mostly from suburban environments, flying them into a remote rural county, and then expecting them to embrace small town life.

A particularly excruciating example of these prevarications occurred on the Klamath Forest, which completely misrepresented a recreation position in order to coax a recent graduate from an Eastern college to fill it. On arrival the woman was shocked to learn, that as a recreation officer, she would be responsible for patrolling the campgrounds, and writing out citations to campers who broke regulations.

According to the employee interviewed (soon to retire), "Despite attending Forestry Protection Officer School, she never left her desk a single day. Everything in the building went *hush hush.* All this whispering going on; all this tiptoeing around. And no one had the nerve to tell her to go into the forest. But they couldn't fire her either. All that misery after dipping into the treasury to pay for her 3,000 mile journey. But in reality they had lied to her. They completely misled her. One day she just didn't show up for work and the ordeal ended." This is but one of many illustrations as to why Project Outreach for Women, despite being such a remarkable success, was such a remarkable failure.

By now the regional committee was placing large want ads in various newspapers. On October 3-4, 1988, *USA Today* ran what must have been a very costly three-by-seven inch advertisement, stating the forest service was in need of women employees only. Not one reporter among the hundreds working for this flagship publication of the Gannet news syndicate thought something hinky might turn up. The *San Jose Mercury News* also ran an ad, its header stating *Only Women Need Apply.* A column on the same page written by one of its more comatose staffers reported that Region Five solely desired women, but that not many were applying, because very few wished to relocate in the remote outposts most forests were located.

Forest Service Spokesman Matt Mathes countered by saying that agency offices ran the gamut, from the largest, most cosmopolitan cities in California to "the spot in the road." Whether intentional or not, Mathes revealed a little known fact—slowly and inexorably, region's workforce was being shifted out of the forests into the San Francisco Bay and other urban centers.

The regional consent committee was also drawing up 8½ by 11 inch posters and mailing them to any locale in the

United States, where it was thought women interested in forestry might reside. On April 14, 1988, Mike Causey, editor of the *Federal Diary*, ran a column on the subject, quite skeptical in tone. The *Federal Career Opportunities Report* ran reports in both its October 3, and October 15, 1988, editions. Yet none provoked any curiosity among reporters working for the nation's newspaper syndicates.

One stack of information that should have caught the eye of at least one reporter working for a major newspaper was the *Maupin White Paper* presented in June of 1989 by John Maupin, fire management officer for the Plumas National Forest. The Plumas is a remote forest, scenically less dramatic than the Sierra Nevada units to the south, and those of the Cascade and Klamath Mountains to the north and west. But covering 1.1 million acres, it has historically been a great producer of timber and among the top in livestock receipts. For these reasons, and because of its complex topography, it is one of the most difficult forests to manage. Maupin mailed a copy of his report to Plumas Forest Supervisor Mary Coloumbe, Regional Director Paul Barker, as well as the Washington Office. Many more copies were seized, copied and distributed by disgruntled forest employees.

He began by outlining the situation at the Frenchman Fire House, where the position of engine supervisor had been vacant for a year. A job notice had been placed, but no women had applied and none were expected. Applications were not being accepted from men living in the area. The position was being temporarily filled by a detailer, an undergrade, under-trained employee borrowed from another forest.

In addition, the position of engine assistant supervisor had been vacant for two years. It had been advertised twice without success, and was now being listed for a third time.

No female applicants were expected and no males were permitted to apply. Maupin noted that the position had been temporarily filled by three detailers and an inexperienced seasonal employee. Additionally, no engine driver was present at Frenchman's and no women had responded to that vacancy announcement either.

At the Laufman Fire Station, a crew assistant supervisor was badly needed. The report noted that *outreach* had begun the summer before and the position had been offered to an *unqualified female*, who declined to accept. At the Mohawk Ranger Station, two assistant fire captain positions and the position of engine driver were also vacant. There was no hope any women would fill those positions, and no detailers were expected anytime soon. Applications from men living in nearby Portola were not being accepted.

It is important to note that the pool of men who were willing to take on a detail was rapidly drying up. For them it meant the acceptance of a temporary position that was potentially dangerous, during which time they would find themselves on an atrociously steep learning curve. Even worse, a detailer understood that should he master that learning curve, at the first appearance of an interested woman, he would be removed.

Even more of a concern to Maupin was his inability to hire a fire prevention officer, a position that he had advertised twice since early 1988. One candidate certificate had been rejected because no female applicants were on it. A woman had been listed on the second certificate, but she had declined to accept after the Plumas refused to offer her husband a job. Wrote Maupin, "This is the most critical prevention position on the forest. We have suffered a serious setback in important prevention programs, such as local school fire programs, community involvement, residence inspections, and day to day prevention contacts."

At the Greenville Station the position of engine driver had been vacant since the prior summer. Attempts were being made to locate a detailer and to train a seasonal employee, who had shown promise at the wheel of one of the fire engines. Also at Greenville a fire prevention technician position had been vacant two years. It had been posted twice, but no women had applied. Applications from men were not being accepted.

At the Challenge Station there was no engine supervisor, and at the Strawberry Station no crew assistant foreman. There was no hope of filling either position with a woman. The equally hopeless task of advertising for detailers had been undertaken. Applications from men were not being accepted.

At the White Horse Fire Station the position of crew foreman had been vacant since 1988 and was being filled by a detailer. At the same location a search had been underway since December for an assistant forest dispatcher. That position was expected to be filled on July 15, but as Maupin noted, "By the time employee receives the necessary training, the fire season will be over."

In summary Maupin wrote: "Our ability to safely and effectively accomplish the fire protection mission on the Plumas National Forest is being compromised by our inability fill vacant fire POSITIONS in a timely manner. It takes an average of nine months to fill a position. Consequently we are using a large number of detailers, in key fire positions...our seasonal fire crews experienced an average of 48% in-season turnover last year. With such high turnover rates, it is not reasonable to expect short term detailers to deal effectively with major supervision challenges...our fire crews demand the highest level of supervision available. These crews are responsible for combating wildfires to protect lives, homes and natural resources on national forest and private lands. The work is hazardous, extremely arduous, and involves working with dangerous and sophisticated equipment such as chainsaws, helicopters, and complex fire engines. Our crew supervisors must be able to operate and manage their equipment effectively, and rapidly train a constantly changing crew in its safe and effective operation…

"We are competing with higher paying state and local fire agencies. The California Department of Forestry and fire crew supervisors are being paid the equivalent of our GS-11 wages. But forest service crew supervisors are grades GS-06 to GS-7. In spite of this higher pay and fewer remote stations the CDF is also having great difficulty attracting women…"

The locating and hiring of an experienced female fire captain or fire management officer is, in itself, fraught with hazards as Gary McHargue related in his second interview. When asked what his worst year of fighting fires was, he clapped his hands in the air and shouted, "*The siege of 1987* they called it! I got a couple of awards that year. Yes, there was the Turtle Fire, south of Susanville.

"A woman had been promoted to assistant fire management officer after just two years of experience fighting fires, and placed in charge of a division. Probably two hundred men. Normally it takes a man ten or twelve years to become a fire management officer. But they needed to have her [in that position] because they had plans to make her a district ranger. It was late in the fire season. And so they didn't want to send her to the Angeles, Los Padres, the Klamath, or some other dangerous forest. So they sent her here to the Lassen, where it is relatively flat, with a good road network.

"And we were not beating that fire [the Turtle]. The place was completely disorganized, a mess. There were some firefighters up slope from where the flames were moving and the vegetation was mainly sagebrush and bitter brush. Anyway, she directed the fire crews to use their dozers to cut two fire lines right in the face of that fire coming up the slope. Well, a center boss, a friend of mine, who was also under her, came over and said, 'Gary would you go over there and get those guys and their dozers off that slope?'"

Gary rushed down the hill and told the two drivers to "Get the hell up the hill!" They turned their dozers around and retreated with McHargue on foot beside them. "Suddenly the entire locale in which they were working blew up! Exploded into flames! That was closest I ever came to losing my life on account of the consent decree."

There was a pause as we stared at the still winding tape recorder. "Any other incidents?" I asked. He continued, reciting three more, one of which included this remarkable confrontation on the Klamath National Forest following a series of dry lightning strikes. The Klamath is yet another exceptional forest because of its huge size, over 1.6 million acres, extreme remoteness, extreme ruggedness, enormous trees, and what scientists term its remarkable biodiversity.

"We had five engines there, it was dusk, the men had settled down, and I was out on the road and a young woman pulled up in a forest service rig I had never seen before... well, she got out, came over, looked at me and said that I should order the men to construct some fire lines on the slopes below.

"'No, I am not going to do that,' I said.

"'What do you mean you're not going to do that?' she said irritably.

"I looked at her and said, 'I have my orders. You can see the fire down there. Do you realize how steep it is?' I threw a rock down the slope. You could hear it bounce, a second would go by and you could hear it bounce again, strike something, and then bounce again.

"She said nothing. Suddenly I asked if she was from the Klamath Forest. She said no. I then asked her position. 'I'm a trainer division supervisor' she said.

"Where is the person who is supposed to be training you?

"'They're back where the dinners are being served.'

"'Look, you go back and get that person who is training you. Then you come back with that person. Then we'll talk. And let me tell you something you need to know. You never send firefighters down a hill at night to do construction under these conditions. People are killed every year by stuff like that.'

"She started to cry, turned around and went back to her truck. I never saw her again. It was 1987. I had been fighting fires longer than she had been alive and she was going to be my division supervisor."

Despite these events, the Maupin White Paper and its out-of-this world revelations, neither the forests, the regional or Washington offices set out to correct conditions. Rather, each, with forethought and malice, set about further atomizing their workforce. Proof can be found in the documents...

The year after the White Paper was issued, Plumas Forest Supervisor Mary Coloumbe, who had been hired under the Peace Corps provision (she possessed a degree in horticulture), received yet another report, this one highlighting the dismaying effect the consent decree was having on the morale of her employees. A few weeks later the regional office reported that it was suspending seventeen different consent decree programs because its coffers were empty. Rather than attempting to reactivate her fire stations or raise the morale of her broken workforce, Coloumbe withdrew a substantial sum of cash from the Plumas operating budget, and applied it to the seventeen consent programs slated for suspension.

This ultimate cratering act by the U.S. Forest Service, aside from abandoning private in-holdings and adjacent ranches, effectively discarded the towns of Quincy, Greenville, Graeagle, Portola, Pulga and Forbestown, leaving them almost entirely in the hands of volunteer fire departments. Town structural fires may not be a forest's top priority, but fighting fires on service lands surrounding these communities are its major responsibility. If this operation cannot be performed, the agency's *raison d'etre* no longer exists.

Coloumbe was complicit in the destruction of her forest's reason for being. But a letter exists in San Bruno demonstrating that Regional Director Paul Barker was equally complicit. In 1990, a Klamath Forest District Ranger, Alice Forbes, a long-time employee, well grounded in resource management—who had somehow slipped beneath the decree's radar screen—received a startling memo. Of it she wrote:

"...Paul Barker put out a priority memo essentially stating that even though the Forest Service was facing a bad fire season the number one priority was the Consent Decree. As the District Ranger I was essentially told my number one priority was implementing the Decree." Forbes could not bring herself to believe that while a forest fire might be raging out of control six miles from her station, work on the decree within her complex was not to be disturbed. All other district rangers and forest supervisors received the same missive.

Through 1990 the decomposition continued unabated. Historically it had been a custom for a fire crew *strike team*, in its rush toward a fire on an adjacent forest, to pull the engine or buggy[5] over whenever a sufficient number aboard wished to relieve themselves. The strike team members then headed for the trees. This had never been a problem among women in the 1970s and early 80s, and for good reason. A strike team's route tends to pass through very few towns, and sometimes no towns at all. Most importantly, its mission is to arrive at the fire within the shortest time possible.

However, when the Equal Rights Advocates learned that female strike team members were being forced to relieve themselves in the trees, they sent a letter to region strenuously objecting. Region in turn mailed a memo to all forests, declaring that whenever a firewoman wished to relieve herself, the strike team was to detour to the nearest filling station or eating house. This would have effectively put an end to the strike teams. However, the directive was another one of those orders largely ignored by fire captains.

Despite the above memo, and scores of benefits the agency had conferred on women over the past six years, their numbers on the fire crews never reached 33% for any period of time. Thus, in order to hang on to the percentages they did attain, some units opted for extraordinary measures. In 1990, the Mendocino Forest promoted a woman to fire captain knowing that her legs were too short to operate the engine's brake, clutch and gas peddles. To remedy the problem the forest ordered custom finished wooden blocks, to be attached to each peddle. Unhappily the blocks became a source of ridicule among the captain's seasonal crew members, and she became discomforted. Shortly after, she was promoted out of her truck into an office.

By then all across the United States, every spring thousands of seasonal firemen, capable of carrying a full portable water pump (ten gallons) or sixty pounds of equipment to the fire lines were no longer being recalled for duty. Rather, they were being systematically replaced by firewomen capable of carrying three gallons of water and thirty pounds of equipment to the lines.

Yet no matter the year—1984, 1987, or 1990—agency progressives insisted on being caught off guard. In truth, the employees were being told by their superiors they *must* be caught off guard, even though their gut instincts—often referred to as *bullshit detectors*—warned them it was all wrong. Thus, the multitude of unyielding physiological mysteries that separate the sexes continued to present themselves each spring. The crumbling point for each ranger district varied across the land. Generally it was reached at that point in time where a majority of its permanent employees reconciled themselves to the fact that the ultimate reason they were drawing a paycheck, was for pretending these unyielding physiological mysteries did not exist.

Conversely, because they were being paid to ensure these mysteries did materialize each spring, the fire captains began delegating assignments by sex. On an average work day without a fire call, the men were sent into the woods to clear brush and thin timber, while the women remained behind to polish trucks, and sweep the shop floors. Needless to say, those performing the arduous duties of clearing brush and cutting slash received no pay differential. Hence, as spring advanced into summer, in forest after forest, the seasonals were clearing less and less brush and thinning very little timber.

In August 1990 Region Five's consent committee was confronted by yet another series of reports detailing additional biological mysteries regarding the sexes. The entire staff, now numbering 150 clerks, must have blanched at the details. But rather than attempting to resolve the many mysteries presented, turned its attention toward how to alleviate the distress of their new employees.

When it was learned that female hygiene products were not available at the fire camps, every effort was made to see there was a surplus. When it was learned that many firefighters were suffering from menstrual cramps, prescriptions were shipped off to the fire camps. In addition to experiencing a disproportionate number of sprains, muscle pulls and broken limbs, women were found to be far more susceptible to burns, gashes, poison oak and bee strings. This prompted Robert Tyrell, supervisor of the Shasta-Trinity Forest, to inquire if a special *female emergency kit* was available for his crew members.

By then it was known that most firewomen were not fond of camp food, which was too often restricted to hamburgers, hot dogs, and ham and cheese sandwiches. Thus, as early as the summer of 1988, cottage cheese, yogurt and fish were being trucked into the camps. By 1990, many cantonments were serving croissants, Jello and ambrosia salad. Piles of ice also began to appear in the forests—not in mid-winter, but in mid-summer. The ice was heaped onto mobile counter tops to form a bed for sliced tomatoes, iceberg lettuce, and carrot sticks.

Chapter 10

MAVENS AND CULLS HARD AT WORK

Smoke and mirrors is a metaphor for a magician's deceptive, fraudulent or insubstantial explanation. The source of the term is based on the magicians' illusions, where they use smoke and mirrors to accomplish illusions such as making objects disappear, when they really don't disappear at all. Smoke and mirrors is not recommended when displaying any program, as it can lead to expectations that turn out to be impossible or extremely difficult to implement.
—Unknown

One cannot expect to make an omelet without breaking eggs.
—Maximilian Robespierre, architect of the French Terror

IN 1989, UNDER pressure from the district court, the regional office began offering men occupying the high paying GS-11 through GS-13 grades *buyouts;* that is, they were offered the option of early retirement with benefits. Although the number of buyouts in many disciplines was high, for unknown reasons some of these highly ranked men, perhaps for reasons of family, or in some instances outright obstinacy, declined the offers. This was not the case among the younger, lower level workers whose on-the-ground presence was so important to forestry operations and where the mistrust lay everywhere. For four years they had been departing in droves without buyouts to work in state forestry, the private timber companies and city fire departments. The disappearance of these young- to middle-aged workers was a primary reason why Region Five would soon exceed its target of 57% men only in its workforce. The rate of departure was such that the remaining employees, many of them women with years of experience, realized there were no longer enough men on the ground for operations to carry on. This same realization belatedly dawned upon a sizable number of new female employees who had agreed (now regrettably) to replace the departed.

About this time California's black and Hispanic populations, at the express urging of Chief Forester Dale Robertson, began applying pressure for increased workplace representation. In 1988, a Hispanic core group collected enough signatures to file a class action suit. The numbers are not available, but it is known that its membership ran to several hundred. Yet the Hispanic Class was opposed by the Equal Rights Advocates, who regarded it as a distraction to the agency. Too much effort expended on hiring Hispanics would be injurious to reaching their target of 43% women.

Through 1989, a good deal of intrigue took place in San Francisco regarding the Hispanic lawsuit. In the end, at the insistence of Monitor Meyer and the advocates, the regional consent committee destroyed it by promoting its most powerful players into GS-11 and GS-12 positions. The remaining lower level members, now without leadership, abandoned the suit.

The advocates and the agency retained this same dog-in-the-manger sentiment toward African-Americans. Among several letters Region Five received from groups representing them, was one from Sam T. Cornelius of the *Advance and Enterprise Group*. In his letter Cornelius bitterly denounced Zane Smith for making every effort "to promote white women on the district [region] as opposed to black people. It is a violation of Title VII of the Civil Rights Act of 1964."

In 1986, the forest service entered into an agreement with the African American Class Complaint to increase the number of its black employees. Two years later the agency expressly agreed that black employment would come within 80% of that group's representation in California. However, by 1990, with its focus almost entirely on allotting jobs to women, it became clear that from the start the agency had not been earnest. In truth, it was not even necessary to railroad the African American Class Complaint. The suit was simply brushed aside because African American employees within the service were never as numerous as Hispanics.

This covert destruction of two class complaints places both the advocates and the forest service in the most damning light. In order to preserve the status quo, with a few strokes of a pen, they promoted a small number of Latinos into slots they were probably ill-suited to fill, while depriving the region of several hundred valuable firefighters.

In February 1990 the Washington Office notified all 175 forests and grasslands that a career counselor for women was to be placed in each unit. Within Region Five, Consent Decree Coordinator Marsha Glassner, despite numerous consent decree panelists already in the forests, dispatched the requisite number to fill those slots; she then backfilled their positions with freshly hired urbanites. Shortly afterward, as the counselors assumed their duties, they began issuing newly minted career guides to all recently hired women. They also implemented a mentoring program, in essence a sharing of wisdom and insight into life with the employees. Despite their self-confidence, much of it built up by a healthy string of promotions, many of the counselors were ill-suited for their new vocations.

A major distraction was the fact that they were not accustomed to working in small town settings in the proximity of men who talked about football, automobiles, fishing, hunting and dirt bikes—and whose very careers were at stake. Just as troubling, the counselors learned that many of their clients found the men training them difficult to work with. Here again arose the insoluble problem of a *hostile work environment*. Thus their own vocations in the forests were by-in-large reduced to providing their clients and themselves with work place solace, orientated toward victimhood.

At about this same time, the Washington Office also launched the nationwide *Job Fairs* program. Within Region Five, Assistant Regional Director Marsha Glassner hired a Floyd Thomas to direct the program. Thomas obliged by drawing up four purchase agreements and awarding $25,000 to each contractor who would provide recruitment services at entertainment functions, such as for example the *San Jose Fine Arts Festival.*

Between February and July 1990, over twenty of these events were held at various sites about the state, most notably in locales where it was felt the female talent pool was deepest. In the end they succeeded in hiring just thirty-nine women and one minority man. Worse, three of the contractors wound up recruiting employees for the wrong professions and wrong pay grades. The fourth did not even account for how he spent the money.

As a result, Paul Barker terminated Job Fairs, and as Zane Smith had done before him, turned his attention to education–specifically sending more women to more colleges. In a letter mailed to each employee of that sex, he wrote, "To all women... funding forms are attached to each letter and a list of colleges to attend. There are also practical training schools. It is a hiring opportunity for all women... this is a great opportunity that deserves your serious consideration. The funds must be spent by May 8 1991. Your long-term course of study can extend beyond that date as long as all fees, tuition, books, etc., can be paid by that date." The focus of the program was forestry, but numerous other curriculums of use to the agency, such as engineering, surveying, hydrology and range management, were also available. The difference between this very liberal undertaking and the prior education program, is that Barker was awarding students large chunks of cash long before they were to graduate.

A sampling of the record reveals that a total of fifty candidates signed a document stating they had no wish to undertake a four year forestry curriculum, even though it would be underwritten by the taxpayer. The same sample revealed that five candidates, or under 10% of the total, expressed a desire to be sponsored. As it is certain that this offer was made to every woman permanently employed in Region Five, which by 1990 totaled roughly 2,500, it is possible that 220 chose to attend college. The number who eventually earned a degree in these forestry related disciplines can only be guessed at.

After the official launching of Bernardi in 1981, no man was ever given that benediction. Rather, as an unnamed forester veteran told me, "I had to fight the forest service, tooth and nail for the right to attend a university...these women were being paid their tuition and housing, and [region wasn't] paying the tuition and housing of a decorated veteran who had fought for their country. They would not allow me to have an education!"

This employee, with the backing of a private fund, hired an attorney who clashed with Margaret Pasholk, the director of region's personnel department in a struggle that lasted three years. In the employee's words, "the director was as difficult, combative, and snotty as anyone I have ever known. But she was unused to such perseverance. One day she finally threw her hands into the air and caved." His court and college costs were paid for by the forest service, and upon finishing his courses, he was promoted. Yet because he raised such Holy thunder, fifteen years have passed and he has yet to receive another promotion.

It is worthy of notice that a very high percentage of privileged personnel within the agency disliked veterans, in part because they had been granted a ten-point application advantage by Congress after the Second World War. And, unlike the Peace Corps hires, who were regarded with a certain fondness, agency elites held a strong aversion to the military culture. This dislike was surpassed only by their hatred for Vietnam War Veterans. In 1990, Kermit Johansson of the Sierra National Forest, a member of the Male Class Complaint, reported that he did not know of a single Vietnam Vet who had been hired as a permanent employee in all the forests of California.

Underscoring the dilemma faced by the veterans, was a directive presented at a consent decree meeting held in Oroville, California that same year. There, Chairwoman Kathy Waller informed all present that every effort should be made to thwart veterans employed by the agency from learning of any new job announcements. Included in her notes was a reference to keeping *black males* out of the job loop as well. That same summer the Washington Office directed all nine forest regions to methodically single out veterans for discrimination. Dozens of *sub rosa* conferences were soon being held across the country where stratagems were developed to contravene the rights of the nation's veterans, mandated by act of Congress.

The largest confab in California convened in Yreka, one of the most remote towns in the state. There, on a July Monday morning, having registered for a full week at the Best Western Miner's Inn, forty members of the Regional Consent Decree Committee, led by its newly elected chairman, Richard Henry, gathered to *strategize* on how to best block the veterans in their career tracks.

By Tuesday, the committee had assembled a list of several hundred female candidates, and was matching them against a list of several hundred recently created job slots. Late that morning one of the women present, no longer able to stomach the proceedings, quietly left the room and phoned a member of the recently established Male Class Complaint. He in turn notified Jerry Levitoff, Gary McHargue, and several other veterans, who spent the next twenty-four hours phoning service vets up and down the state. Gathering in Fresno, Sacramento, Chico, and Redding, by the time they began the drive north, they outnumbered those gathered at the Yreka summit. McHargue described the drama that unfolded two mornings later as the veterans opened the door to their chamber, filed in and took positions against the wall. "They [the consent committee members] sat there absolutely stunned," he said in amusement. "Their faces turned ashen. It was as if they had been caught robbing a bank. But it was worse than robbing a bank. Add up the costs of housing and feeding all those people for weeks on end. And all to deprive the veterans of their rights!

"One of the guys then told them they were going to have to accept our applications, whether they liked it or not. Dick

Henry's face turned pink. Everyone was so blown out of the water they accepted them."

The informant later told McHargue and Levitoff that when the committee reconvened the following morning, everyone sat around wringing their hands, biting their fingernails and bitterly chastising the mole in their midst. But who was that mole? Finally it was decided to send an encoded message over the computer system to San Francisco, reporting that their cover had been blown.

The *Yreka Encirclement* threw Dick Henry and his mavens into a turmoil that lasted two weeks. Finally determining that too many well-qualified veterans were at the top of each newly created job slot, they decided to cancel them, a measure that suggests how unnecessary they were to forestry operations.

As McHargue put it, "We won the battle. The veterans stopped the evil developments from taking place. But it was a victory with no tangible reward." Indeed, within weeks the committee released another program that enabled each female employee to immediately update her skills and career interests via computer. Men, veterans and non-veterans alike, were completely left in the dark regarding the innovation. But within a short time, and in many instances with the aid of a female *sellout*, they too were accessing and updating their resumes. This so angered assistant regional director Marsha Glassner, she ordered her staffers to isolate the data base of each male employee and destroy it.

The number of new programs continued to mushroom. As far back as January 1990 the advocates had informed Paul Barker they believed a 43% quota could only be achieved by severing Region Five from the Washington Office of Personnel Management. This would in effect allow Barker to circumvent both the veteran's hiring preferences and the remnants of the U.S. Government's once vaunted *promotion by merit* system. He consented and asked U.S. Personnel Director Joseph Patti for what were termed *direct hire* rights.

As he explained, "Throughout the entire federal government and within the governments of all fifty states, there are not enough qualified women for the positions necessary to fill." In essence, Barker was simply stating that without direct hiring authority, he could not boost the number of ill-equipped, unqualified employees to a level that would enable him to manage his forests.

Patti denied the request, citing technical errors in the accompanying paperwork, and Barker gave up. This was largely because his staff was already both creating and canceling job announcements at will. He also knew the Washington Office was designing even more subtle programs to circumvent the rights of veterans. Finally, promotion by merit was now a concept of the past, not only within the U.S. Forest Service, but the entire federal government.

Rather, he turned back to the upward mobility program first conceived under the Smith regime, and now being improved by his aides. Hired at the GS-05 level, women were being trained for the position of management specialist at GS-07. Once promoted to that level they were to receive the undivided attention of an upgrade employee, enabling them to quickly pass on to GS-09 without merit consideration. This new upward mobility effort brought some spectacular *umbrella accord* results, and by 1991 the number of women occupying office positions below GS-11 had climbed to 75% of the total. But the new program had no appreciable effect on the number of female cartographers, hydrologists, silviculturists, surveyors and building inspectors.

In truth, although many *new women* favored *upward mobility*, they did so only within an office setting. Very few were eager to toil away the day in the environment of a cartographer, a silviculturist or a building inspector, which too often involved stumping through ankle deep mud, or swatting at insects under some very inclement weather conditions.

There was yet another problem unique to many new hires. As noted prior, women are known for their ability to communicate in a congenial manner both with individuals and at forums. Yet an extraordinary number of new hires, when placed into a high profile position were a disaster when it came to public relations. Their cold, brittle means of communicating with the local communities suggests they were not only emotionally ill-suited for their jobs, but products of an educational system that frowned on camaraderie with men. This was worsened by their lack of knowledge regarding the subject matter.

Particularly remarkable in this regard was a fire management officer named Jeannie Piccatori (three different spellings for the same surname), who in succession worked for the Mendocino, Plumas and Tahoe National Forests. Three different employees from each forest, none of whom knew the other, gave near identical assessments of her. No matter where employed, she was unable to confer in a friendly and informed manner with the personnel of the several counties, or the California Department of Forestry. The Mendocino employee, recalling her many messy misunderstandings, and the morning he learned she had departed for the Tahoe, shrugged, laughed and said "She became someone else's headache!"

He and other employees were prone to waxing nostalgic about the good old days when the forest service was a *forest service*. Whenever a question arose regarding forestry management or fire control, the Bureau of Land Management, the California Department of Forestry and personnel from the various counties would rush over in search of answers. By

1986, the employees of those organizations were scratching their heads, and asking themselves and each other, "What is the forest service doing to itself? No one over there is real anymore!"

1990 was also the year Paul Barker commenced the Joint Apprenticeship Committee, partially financed by consent decree funds and operated in conjunction with the California Department of Forestry. Known by the acronym of JAC, it was established to train badly needed firefighters. JAC was immediately attacked by the Equal Rights Advocates who, despite the recent heavy losses incurred by forest fires, would not permit any cash earmarked for the consent decree to be withdrawn for its training program. Only after the service pledged that women would represent 65% of all JAC candidates did they relent.

That June the first Joint Apprentice Committee class selected 75 women and 42 men, while the second class, which began in September, counted 31 women and 20 men. The curriculum placed great emphasis on reading books about fires, discussing those books, blackboard diagramming of fires, and writing summaries about the blackboard diagrams. By comparison, little time was spent in the field learning to suppress fires. This virulent form of instructional ineptitude would cost the service dearly in the years ahead—not only in regard to timber lost, but cash spent in defending itself against numerous discrimination suits.

Meanwhile, back at the office Barker took his swing at sexual harassment. After reiterating opposition to it, he ordered each quarterly forest publication to feature at least one article on either sexual harassment or the value of workplace diversity. He also urged that the hunt for gender hostile tools be resumed. Over the past three years, this pursuit, never successful in any forest, had prompted a good deal of ridicule among the men, and acute embarrassment among many women.

Testifying to the sentiments of the latter was Norman J. Walker, an engine captain on the Angeles Forest, who reported that the *sensoring survey* for tools was insulting to women. "The consensus among the women is that they preferred being given more physical training, and be allowed access to better workout equipment, as opposed to reinventing the various tools to address their weaknesses."

In early 1990, not long after taking over, Chief Forester Dale Roberson issued a memo to all regional foresters, stating that by 1995, he expected the work force of each forest to reflect the racial and sexual composition of all people residing in the United States. Perhaps in reaction to the Robertson order, Barker initiated a new quota system, the numbers of which follow: 15% of new hires would be minority men; 15% of new hires minority women; 45% of new hires white women; 25% of new hires white men. But within two weeks of the announcement, he rescinded it and implored Robertson to back off on his timetables. He simply did not have the staff to deal with any new gender/race rationing programs.

His rescission troubled several forest supervisors, who in studying Barker's numbers found them strangely comforting. One of the most troubled was Mike Rogers of the Angeles Forest who complained that "now there is too much uncertainty." After flatly acknowledging that white men were leaving the Angeles in unprecedented numbers, he followed with this odd suggestion. "Have region reestablish hiring targets for the forests so employees will know Consent Decree will not deprive them of opportunities for promotion. Employees will know the work force will continue to reflect the nation's diversity for all people and that each individual is important to the organization. The morale of the present work force would be enhanced and new applicants will not hesitate to work for the forest if they see a career ladder."

The gloom that had enveloped Region Five over the past seven years had by now seeped into every region in the country, all of which were in the midst of implementing programs that focused on minority, as well as female hiring. Yet as despondent as these forest employees may have been, California remained ground zero for morale. It had reached such a low point that women from other regions absolutely refused to transfer in. This so annoyed Chief Robertson, that he wrote a letter to Barker, insisting that he hold a meeting with the other regional foresters to emphasize the harmony among his job holders, and the welcoming environment his forests were certain to afford any new arrival.

At about the time Robertson dashed off his letter, Carol Hammer, the equal employment director for the Tahoe Forest, reported on a meeting she had chaired with consent decree staffers from all of California's national forests. An intense debate had taken place over whether men should be permitted to vote in the upcoming election to choose a new consent decree coordinator. In the end it was decided men *could not vote*, but they would be permitted to stand for the office (Indeed, Richard Henry of Yreka fame gleaned the most votes). Hammer claims the committee arrived at its decision only after a *careful review* of the Bernardi Decree.

At another meeting, this one in San Francisco, business management, heavily larded with consent decree advocates, complained that agency employees spent too much time in the woods, as opposed to inside their offices, where so much decree work awaited them. Further, the employees, through their many thoughtless remarks and irreverent manner, were implying that Bernardi was so much useless collateral. At yet another San Francisco gathering, decree committee members voiced their dismay regarding the number of poorly attended meetings.

Still, by massive scale of effort, feminization of the forests was proceeding. In February 1988 the *Pacific Southwest NEWSLOG* published a column by Roxane May Scales, presenting conclusive evidence to the fact:

> *Everything you need to know was there somewhere in kindergarten, The Golden Rule and love, and basic sanitation, ecology and politics and sane living. Think of what a better world it would be if we all—the whole world—had cookies and milk at 3 o'clock every afternoon and then lay down without blankets for a nap. Or if we had basic policy in our nation and other nations to always put things back where we found them and cleaned up our own messes. It is still true, no matter how old you are, when you go out into the world, it is best to hold hands and stick together.*

By now, the conservative Reagan Administration had been replaced by the moderate administration of G.H.W. Bush, whose two most important cabinet officials, so far as the forest service was concerned, were Secretary of Agriculture Clayton Yeutter, and Attorney General Richard Thornburgh. In the tradition of John Block and Richard Lyng, Yeutter had every intention of extending his department's long standing practice of "Let's keep Agriculture out of the Forest Service," and "Let's keep politics out of Agriculture."

It was under his watch that Region Five, under the umbrella concept, was closing in on 43%. On September 11, 1990 a hearing was held in the chambers of Magistrate

Wilken. Representing the service was Assistant Attorney General Stewart Gerson, who stated that among the remaining fifteen categories in which 43% had not been reached, four were *dead slots*, that is, the positions had been eliminated because they were no longer needed. In several other categories, there had been no opportunity to hire a woman, because no man had retired, transferred or quit. And, as he explained, region had also failed to maintain 43% parity in several categories because it had promoted *too many* women.

As Wilken listened, he explained how there was but a single GS-07 range conservationist in the state, a man with many years of service. There had also been a women range conservationist at that same grade until this past summer when she was promoted to GS-09. As combative as ever, Monitor Meyer rose and stated that without a GS-07 female range conservationist, region was out of compliance.

Gerson continued, pointing out that five women recreation employees, serving at the very low GS-02 level, were recently promoted to GS-03. This had the unintended effect of leaving the percentage of GS-02 female recreation employees below 43%. Meyer charged region with noncompliance.

Gerson then pointed out that for many years, just six landscape architects had been employed by region and all six were men at the GS-12 level who, despite repeated brow beatings, had refused to transfer, take early retirement or quit. Meyer charged region with noncompliance.

Similarly, for years, region counted on its payroll sixteen GS-11 and GS-12 geologists, all but one of whom were men. Though forced to repeatedly run the strong-armed gauntlet of their superiors, the geologists had also refused to transfer, take early retirement or quit. Meyer again charged region with non-compliance.

Gerson soldiered on, noting that at the position of public affairs, GS-09, there were three men and five women, which placed the number of women at 62.5%, or 19.5% above the quota. Meyer countered that under the *umbrella plan*, as devised and agreed upon by the forest service, female occupancy for that position had been placed at 87.5%, which was why region again was out of compliance.

Finally the court learned that none of the agency's GS-11 through GS-13 male administrative assistants, despite repeated brow beatings, had seen fit to transfer, take early retirement or quit. Region had created fifteen new positions for women at those levels per Judge Conti's order, but most of them had hurriedly departed in search of work elsewhere. This left their percentage well below 43%, thereby demonstrating the service had again failed to work within the spirit of Bernardi.

Gerson doubtless knew before his day of testimony that the court monitor was solidly in the box of the complainant, but he may still have imagined that he was dealing with a judicious magistrate, a class complaint, the members of which were of sound mind and body, and a client intent on making a heroic effort to save himself.

At day's conclusion, however, there can be little doubt that he knew that he was dealing with anything but a judicious magistrate, and a class complaint, the members of which were of sound mind and body. Moreover, his client, whatever his present positioning, had in fact masterminded his own debacle. Otherwise, why was he being forced to argue that limiting the number of male public affairs specialists to 37.5% was a good idea? And why had the promotion of one female range conservationist, and five female recreation employees left his client in non-compliance? It was all so Twilight Zone.

Indeed it was. Wilken thumped down her gavel and ordered the *contempt decree* continued until the following May. With Gerson's return to Washington, counsel was left in the hands of David Glass, Scott Barasch, Katheryn D. Ray, and Anne M. Gulyassy. During the autumn of 1990, on several occasions Monitor Meyer complained to Magistrate Wilken that these attorneys, as well as forest personnel had approached her on several occasions while she was conferring with a new employee. She considered these advances a form of harassment. Wilken agreed and ordered that no one was to approach Meyer while she was conversing with an employee of her own choosing.

In addition to Glass, whom Meyer found very annoying, she reported that the two women attorneys, Katheryn D. Ray and Anne M. Gulyassy had been hired for the sole purpose of harassing her. They did so by following her into private settings. On one occasion on after leaving a decree meeting, she became aware that one of the attorneys had entered the lavatory, and was in the stall adjacent hers. She claimed that attorney had entered the stall with the sole intent of making her feel vulnerable.

Wilken dashed off a notice, warning the forest service that the harassment of Meyer must stop.

In registering yet another complaint, Meyer stated that none of the forests ever seemed poised for her visits; that their staffs were often unfriendly and many newly hired employees were hesitant to speak with her. Wilken reacted by advising all forests that upon learning Meyer was to pay a visit, they were to see to her needs in full. She further warned that front line supervisors were not permitted to advise their employees on what to say, or not say to her.

With regard to Judge Conti, it doesn't take an astrologer to figure out why he detested the forest service. With

Wilken, the answer is more complex. Quite likely during her exchanges with Conti, she too developed a profound contempt for the agency. But there is more to it than that. At one of her more peculiar hearings, service attorney David Glass reported that the interim goals in several disciplines were at 6.6%, 5.8%, 10.2% and 18.9% respectively. Then, referring to an approaching court date, he said, "How are we to bring those [interim goals] up to 43%? There is no pool to draw from."

Ignoring all of what Glass said, Wilken retorted, "It's not interim goals, it's just final goals."

"What do we do when we meet 43% in all classes?" asked Glass, unsure of Wilken's, and perhaps his own frame of reference.

"Fire all the women?" she asked, mocking him.

By the time of this exchange the forest service had entered a realm of fatuity so immense it would have offered a nine-year-old child a cornucopia of targets for ridicule. Yet Wilken had chosen the same venue of derision that might have been employed by Davis, Kurtz or Meyer. It appears that she deeply sympathized with the advocate's objectives, which is why over a six-year period she never failed to rule in their favor. Further, over the same duration she never once turned down the Monitor's request for more money, routinely directing that she be compensated out of the forest service's budget.

Wilken's liberality is further evidenced in her decision regarding Mukhtau v California State University, Santa Barbara, when she ruled in favor of a Sudanese student who had filed a discrimination suit against the university, claiming he was denied tenure because he was black and a Muslim. Yet because Wilken had allowed blatantly improper testimony on the plaintiff's behalf, her ruling was overturned by the Ninth

Circuit Court of Appeals. Though overturned on a technicality, one cannot help but wonder if her political leanings were to the left of the most left wing court in America.

As 1990 evolved into 1991, in a rather strange evolution of events, the signatures of Davis, Kurtz and, occasionally Rose B. Fua, appeared with increasing frequency on correspondence with region and the court. This development and the events described above, lead one to suspect that Monitor Meyer was becoming unhinged. The possibility of her derangement is supported by the complaints of lawyers and individual foresters regarding her abusive behavior. But, though Meyer may have been losing her mind, she was destined to outlast Paul Barker.

Barker, who had initially thrown himself into the consent struggle with vigor, is claimed by some to have been suffering from mental exhaustion and declining physical health. Indeed, it was he who had sought to effectively deprive the veterans of their lawful rights, who informed all district rangers that the consent decree had priority over fighting forest fires and who had attempted to implement a new, and improved quota system. Between May 9, 1988 and May 8 1989, his forests had hired 386 professional women and just 235 professional men; between May 9 1989 and May 8, 1990, 414 professional women, and just 236 professional men were hired.

Several forest employees, one of whom knew Barker fairly well, claimed that by late 1990 he realized region had been so badly compromised, it was no longer a functioning entity. Possibly realizing the immense damage he had done, he may have peered into the mirror one morning and realized that he was gazing at a face he no longer recognized. This might be the reason for the events that followed:

During the past year various men's advocate groups had begun sprouting in the forests. After it was learned that one of them, the Male Class Complaint, had collected a total of $250,000 from its membership, Barker's regional counsel, Bob Simmons, urged that he impound the fund. When Barker declined, Simmons told him that since the forest service was tied to the consent decree, he was obliged to impound it. Barker told the Counsel that seizing the Male Class's bank account was tantamount to robbery. "It's none of the forest service's business!" he retorted. He then dashed off a letter to the organization—warning them of the Counsel's intention, which also had the support of the regional consent committee.

Then, beginning in the fall of 1990, upon learning of any new initiative about to be launched by the consent committee, Barker would pass the Male Class Complaint a *heads up.*

His record speaks for itself and he knows it. Yet because he took the above initiatives, members of the Male Class Complaint and other employees, speak of him with less hostility than any other regional director, or forest supervisor. On December 16, 1990 Barker retired. He was replaced by Ron Stewart, who for several years had been director of the Southwest Research Station where the Bernardi Decree had so long ago arisen.

Chapter 11

AN OUTLAW AGENCY

The government is the potent omnipresent teacher.
For good or ill it teaches the whole people by its ex-
ample. Crime is contagious. If the government be-
comes a lawbreaker, it breeds contempt for law; it
invites every man to become a law unto himself;
it invites anarchy. To declare that the end justi-
fies the means—to declare that the government may
commit crimes—would bring terrible retribution
—Justice Louis Brandeis

TALL AND ENERGETIC looking, if a bit overweight, Dr. Ronald Stewart, brought to his position a more sustained energy than either of his predecessors. He was not as creative as Smith, nor given to his expansive musings, but would prove a much more organized regional director. Whether this was because of, or despite his credentials is open to question. He was a fellow of the Society of American Foresters, the National Forestry Honor Society, a member of Xi Sigma Pi, the Phi Kappa Phi and National Scholastic Society. That he had also been overseeing the consent decree at the Southwest Pacific Experimental Station suggests he was not only aware of Region Five's two-tier quota system, but knew to a dead certainty that it was a legal farce.

Still, he was prepared to employ whatever means necessary to reduce the percentage of men in his forests to 57% within all grades and professions, and as quickly as possible. He was also prepared to reduce the number of men occupying clerical, personnel, budget, payroll and administrative positions to zero, if it would advance the feminist approach to forestry management. It was not simply the numbers Stewart and Chief Forester Robertson were seeking to transform. Lace curtain radicals almost without peer, they were determined to uproot by trencher, bulldozer and front end loader, every last vestige of the forest service culture advanced by Pinchot, Silcox and McArdle.

Betraying the brisk, commanding image projected in photos, Stewart composed an article in the Southwest Pacific *NewsLog* titled "Building a Healthy Work Environmen*t*." In it he revealed beyond any doubt that a culture with its focus on cherishment, nurturing and sensitivity had seized control of the agency:

> *In the past the Forest Service philosophy of dealing with new employees has been like throwing a baby into the swimming pool –if the baby swims, it's a good Forest person. If the baby drowns, then that Forest person just didn't cut it.*
>
> *We've lost a lot of good people that way. The philosophy of throwing them in and just letting them swim, just won' t work anymore. With the competitiveness of the job market we need to be able to recruit top quality people and hold onto those we get, especially women and minorities. We've got to get into the pool and swim around with them. I see the whole Forest Service philosophy changing in dealing with new people.*

We need to be more nurturing. We need to have more mentoring and more sponsorship. This is by no means a [negative] reflection on the talents and abilities of our new people. We've invested too much in recruitment and outreach and training to lose them. Retention is an absolutely key issue...in throwing the employee into the swimming pool it seems the girl babies were not receiving the help and never did receive the extra help boy babies were receiving... we have to in particular hold onto our women and minority babies. And we have to get into the pool and swim around with them, otherwise we'll all drown...

It is difficult to believe that Stewart could have penned such a kittenish feature as this, yet his name is appended to it. Other articles in the *NewsLog* similarly reflect the boutique nature of an outfit whose essential duties were once firefighting, managing timber, and keeping peace in the campgrounds. The following was composed by Phoebe Brown, employed by the Mendocino Forest.

People would take a break from their meetings and go play [ping pong]. They were [later] found in the break- room enjoying a brisk game. The visitor was encouraged to join and soon a doubles game was underway. After fifteen minutes they all went back to the meeting— refreshed, ready to cooperate and get on with business. It has become a stress relief tool for the district and everyone looks forward to participating in the activity together.

Another writer for the *NewsLog* reported that *The Salmon River Players* of the Klamath Forest had enacted several sexual harassment skits for the benefit of employees. According to the author, the skits covered "gender harassment, sexual harassment, personal space invasion, and crew hazing." No clarification as to the difference between sexual harassment and gender harassment was offered, but a large banner in the room carried the following message. "It's the effect, not the intent."

The same writer continued, ending her column with this contradictory weave of statements.

> *Employees saw themselves in the skits, and were confronted with some of their own actions in a new light. People realized for the first time that some of their actions were offensive to others. The result: positive changes in the work environment. Now people exhibit more concern and forethought during their daily interactions. Others are no longer inhibited or afraid to tell a co-worker when something offends them...a proactive attitude has replaced a reactive response.*

The entire Six Rivers Forest celebrated diversity day where another unnamed writer wrote the following:

> *The day opened with a speech on the common tie all Americans have to the U.S. Constitution. Later a speaker highlighted how many ethnic groups struggled to overcome prejudice in order to be accepted into American culture...the speaker pointed out the courage and conviction needed to make social changes. Another speaker highlighted the implications for diversity in California. All of this took place in a setting that encouraged pride in the*

diversity of heritage each person brings to the work-force. Employees created displays portraying their heritage and brought ethnic food to share at a luncheon potluck. There was a sense of shared unity when the day concluded.

While the *Newslog* ignored dozens of wild fires, resource management issues and accounts of search and rescue missions, it continued to burnish such columns as how Stanislaus Forest District Ranger Jan Ford directed a seminar on *clarifying values*. As she reported,

> *Values are those things which guide our lives and decisions such as Love, Money, Happiness, Religion, Family, Health etc. We constructed values charts and then auctioned off those values to the highest bidder who paid for them by using Monopoly money...participants also attended a one-day seminar on enhancing self-esteem among women. Future sessions are intended to build on this foundation and include topics such as assertiveness, self-imaging, and career planning...*

In August 1991 Region Five also began issuing a separate *Consent Decree Digest*, which, despite its clichéd material, all employees were expected to read. That December Stewart furnished his own article, a paragraph of which follows.

> *Knowing that the supervisor cares has a positive effect on the quantity and quality of work as well. When we are treated with respect and concern for our well-being, we feel part of a team, whether its [SIC] an office, district or forest. The supervisor*

may be the "team leader," but all members know
they play an invaluable role in accomplishing the
unit's goals. Employees are more willing to make the
extra effort to get a job done when they know that
their supervisor and co-workers have a real interest
in them as individuals...

Another article in the same issue, reported that a task force on the Six Rivers Forest, through applying cash from a consent decree grant, worked for three years to surmount a web of laws stipulating what was required to launch a day care center. The center was eventually opened and a handbook produced to assist other forests in establishing their own day cares. Over on the Stanislaus Forest, it was reported that a ten woman task force *worked diligently* for over a year to assemble *A Handbook for Managers,* to assist them in "making informed decisions on the use of job share/part-time jobs as an employment alternative."

In December 1991, Angeles Forest Supervisor Mike Rogers reported that he had bused all his seasonal employees to Pyramid Lake, Nevada for a consent decree meeting presided over by consultant Valerie Hunt. There, Hunt and Rogers urged the seasonals to speak out on such important issues as sexual and racial diversity. "Any questions can be asked at these meetings which are held quarterly," wrote Rogers—a real whopper on his part. Anyone questioning the value of diversity was told to shut up or leave the room. Consultant Hunt ended the three day confab with a question for each seasonal listener to ponder.

What is your boss losing sleep over tonight?

The same column revealed that the Angeles Forest held five two-day workshops for all its supervisors with the focus on "communications, listening, negotiations and conflict resolution." "We want to empower supervisors to be proactive in dealing with issues of the employees they supervise," said Rogers. The average cost of each workshop was $4,000. One seminar counted a single supervisor attended by seven consultants, each committed in her own bustling way to transforming that benighted forester into a *forest person*.

Despite the mentoring program already established by the Washington Office, Region Five determined that yet another program was needed for new employees settling into their jobs and communities. At its heart was the first line supervisor, a sponsor, and the new employee which constituted the *New Employee Sponsorship Team*, known by the acronym "NEST."

The above columns in concert reveal that extraordinary expenses were being vacuumed out of the operating budgets of each forest. They furnish further evidence that a feminized forest service was not proving to be the dynamic, high octane medium required to operate such a far flung agency.

It is of some irony that the agency's culture of cherishment and sensitivity presided over the severance of its *hotline* to Washington, DC. Prior to then it had been used by whistle blowers who observed their superiors violating forest service regulations. With the advance of the consent decree however, the hotline was increasingly used to blow the whistle on superiors who were violating Title VII of the 1964 Civil Rights Act. The Washington Office retaliated by reporting back to the forests the location and phone numbers used by the whistle blowers. Local management would then make a search of their units in hopes of locating the malefactor.

Still, as late as 1991, a few employees believed in the efficacy of the hotline. That year, a still current employee, then in the Mendocino Forest, phoned the capital, not to report an incident of discrimination, but to report that his district ranger had granted a rancher grazing rights to a section of forest without a permit. Washington responded by warning Mendocino management that a snitch was in their midst. A few days afterward the informer happened to be riding in the back seat of a vehicle driven by his district ranger and an assistant regional director. The ranger suddenly turned to the subject of the hotline and the caller—never suspecting that he was sitting in the back seat. The assistant director in turn cursed and wondered when someone would finger the snitch. .

Years have since passed and the caller has never again used the hotline; nor does he know anyone who has. Remarkably, the Washington Office never issued a memo, either assuring its employees that the hotline will never be abused or to announce that it was no longer operative. In the employee's words, "This is because the hotline still catches a few naive employees who think they are doing the government and the public a service. But in the end, they are brow beaten at the very least, or transferred out. To declaim anew that the hotline was now safe to use, would only discredit the service in the eyes of the public and their own employees even further."

The above incident may not have been related to the consent decree, but when employees are routinely forced to subscribe to deceit, lying, and breaking the law, the lack of a guiding principle inevitably spreads into other functions.

One of the quotas the advocates and regional consent committee were slow in coming to grips with was that of women in law enforcement. This was in large part because no law enforcement division existed until the early 1980s. Prior to the 1970s there had been little serious crime in the forests and the various violations, such as timber poaching, grazing stock without a permit, and campground violations had been dealt with by employees certified to write tickets for misdemeanors. Most ticket writers carried a natural gravitas and were adept at employing *verbal judo* in dealing with violators. However, when confronted with a felony, they withdrew and radioed the sheriff's office.

Still, as the old saying goes, "the public tends to carry its problems wherever it goes," and this came to pass with their discovery of the national forests. By 1980, timber thieves, poachers, arsonists, and others, who for one reason or another found it difficult to get along with others, had discovered this new playground. With each passing year more and more acreage was lost to marijuana growers, while simultaneously the number of human skeletons stumbled upon by visitors climbed.

Metal signs heavily ventilated by rifle fire, once a rare sight, are now a common sight, while wooden signs are simply cut down and, hauled away for firewood. An increasingly common sight are the battered, hulking trailers resting atop a knoll among some trees, often for a full season—the occupant not subject to taxes or user fees. Finally, there are the growing numbers of hillside dumps with their assortment of truck tires, stained toilet bowls, dented water heaters and half crushed washing machines.

What is so surprising is that the forest service waited so long to establish a law enforcement division. When the decision was finally made, it came at a most inopportune time—at that point it had decided to dispose of its more experienced, straight-talking employees. In addition, many job holders hired after 1984 were thunderstruck to learn that one or more armed employees, graduates of the Glencoe Georgia Academy, were working out of their buildings. These feelings were shared by many in the regional office, including Zane

Smith. All preferred to close their minds to the damning fact that well before Bernardi, many of those on the lam had abandoned the heavily patrolled state and national parks to take up residence in un-patrolled forest properties.

During the first years of the decree, while the agency was in the midst of clarifying values and drawing up phenotype charts, pot growers seized 200,000 acres of the Big Bar District of the Shasta-Trinity Forest, a part of the famous Emerald Triangle stretching from there into Mendocino County. The occupation took place not over a period of one year—but several years. The number of verbal threats, gun fire and booby trap incidents grew to such proportions that it became too dangerous for hikers, campers, fishermen and hunters to enter the district—property that had been granted them by an act of Congress.

Thus, the service was not caught by surprise. It simply had priorities and patrolling the vast reaches of its forests was not one of them. With but a handful of law enforcement officers on staff, the Shasta-Trinity was forced to call in a multi-agency task force to clear out the very rugged area. Because the operation was well publicized in advance, by the time the *feds* did arrive, all but a few of the planters had departed.

By the late 1980s the cultural shock regarding law enforcement officers, was abating and many were being accepted by members of the office staff as normal forest persons. It was about then that law enforcement requested separate funding from Congress, a move the service barons strenuously opposed. Their objection, though never publicly stated, was that the agency would no longer have access to the law enforcement budget. In the end, Congress decided to fund law enforcement separately, but the appropriation is so miserly that in California there are now approximately 160 officers, which breaks down to one lawman patrolling roughly

130,000 acres, eight hours a day, five days a week. The situation in the other eight forest regions is said to be worse.

With the establishment of a law enforcement division, everyone realized that tracking down an adequate number of women to reach 43% was an impossibility; about as challenging as altering our historical perspective as to who surrendered at Appomattox. This is why Smith and Barker placed law enforcement on the back burner. Not so Ron Stewart. In September 1991, he announced that a Joan Kushner was "rewriting the suitability standards for law enforcement personnel." Encoded in his words was the fact that Kushner was lowering the standards for women in law enforcement. The very challenging criteria for men would remain in place, while a second and much less challenging criterion for women was created.

Following their training at the Glencoe Law Academy, each of Kushner's recruits attended *a sensing meeting* where they were tutored on how to read the nuances of the men they would be working with. The sensing meeting was also intended to aid the women in interpreting the facial indicators and movements of the more adversarial pot growers, game poachers, arsonists and other felons they would be coming across in the field.

Stewart introduced the women of law enforcement in the following manner.

> *New employees are coming onto our Forests in large numbers and at all levels of the organization. Our new employees are bringing with them different perspectives and ideas developed not only through cultural and racial differences, but also from previous work experiences. This infusion is causing confusion within the workforce and must be managed*

*properly to prevent a hostile environment and to cre-
ate a positive change within the agency.*

As he implied, the agency was having retention problems with women and minorities in many disciplines, and he feared the same in law enforcement. Among the most important issues he digressed on was as follows: "Developing policies and procedures which will address such issues as child care at meetings and pregnancies of law enforcement personnel."

With each law enforcement officer in theory is now patrolling 130,000 acres, they are very thinly dispersed. Absenteeism, as well as retention, thus becomes an all-important concern. Hence, no matter how thoroughly Stewart chose to sugarcoat his words, he could not sugarcoat the fact that a pregnant law enforcement officer too often spells an a*bsent law enforcement officer.*

The absenteeism dilemma also compromised the safety of forestry protection officers. Following one week of special training, those employees deemed temperamentally suited, whether working in recreation, timber or fire are issued certificates granting them authority to write misdemeanor citations. FPOs, as they are known, often work in very remote areas, do not receive training in self-defense and do not carry handcuffs. Should personal risks arise, they are heavily dependent on a swift response by law enforcement. With the number of fulltime law enforcement officers already minuscule, their replacement by those subject to pregnancy tends to make FPO working conditions even more tenuous.

Rendering the dilemma yet more complicated, about the time the Bernardi Decree was entered into, the forest service began farming out its campgrounds to private concessionaires, who by-in-large do a fine job of maintaining and patrolling their assigned areas. This was one reason why, as the years advanced, and more and more campgrounds were leased out, the number of forest protection officers has declined.

Yet the criminal element has never left the forests. With immense acreage surrounding the campgrounds at their disposal, they have simply shifted their visitations to more remote locales where they continue to build the enormous fires they are fond of building, drink hooch and *cut and shoot* until their heart's content. Congress' failure to provide law enforcement with the funding it sorely needs and the reduction in the number of forest protection officers has impacted the forests to a tremendous extent. This is a big reason why the public, when it ventures out of the concession campgrounds, often undergoes a vexing forest experience.

As Stewart was in the midst of pondering his insoluble law enforcement problems, he created yet another issue of concern—the formation of a well-educated cadre of gays and lesbians who were to assist supervisors in educating their employees about the finer points of a homosexual lifestyle. All were directed to understand that their behavior was no longer *considered immoral conduct.*

His blueprint included a "networking program to break down that wall of isolation and loneliness gays so often encounter in a forest environment." Chief among Stewart's objectives was to compel local contractors, concessionaires and community leaders to understand that they must cooperate in achieving his sexual targets. After assuring several score of small towns that their input would be greatly appreciated, he gave his employees the following order. "If there are local and state laws that oppose the new forest policy then employees *are to ignore that law* [Italics added]." Finally, "Hiking or fishing or other licensed groups that do not permit homosexuals in their midst will be barred from using forest service facilities."

These measures brought a *revolt* within the ranks, as employees absolutely declined to discuss the gay/lesbian life style with local residents. When Stewart's gay/lesbian taskforces called at forest offices, they were often met with a vacant conference room and one or two employees in the front office attempting to explain the prevailing approach to life among locals. Thus, Stewart's dream of creating a truly diverse regional forest never came to fruition. It also resulted in a number of unseemly incidents, and some sharp exchanges with congressmen who charged that he was "out to cleanse the culture of small town America."

Still, he was moving toward triumph on another front. His predecessors and their subordinates had broken many laws and regulations on many thousands of occasions, but it was he who was now racking up the astonishing quotas they had worked so hard to attain. In March 1991, with Magistrate Wilken presiding, his attorneys presented the court with these figures:

Profession	10th Quarter Women hired/promoted %		11th Quarter Women hired/promoted %	
Professional	33	73	31	79
Administrative	22	90	38	90
Technical	88	65	81	72
Clerical	35	97	61	95
GS-111-13	29	68	49	82

In addition, agency attorneys offered the following figures. In 1981, when the decree commenced, the percentage of women in the regional workforce was 27.8%. By 1986 it was

31.9%. By January 1991, it had surpassed that mythical talis-
man—44% of California forest employees were female. The
court also learned that in 1990, the number of women hired
at the GS-05 level was 62.3% of those applying. In the same
year the percentage of female GS-08 technical employees
reached an astonishing 73.3% of those applying.

Not presented to the court, but readily deduced from
documents within the Federal Records Storage Center, is the
fact that men were now under represented in 83 different
positions and grade levels: 14 in the professional, 20 in the
technical, 20 in the clerical, and 29 in the administrative.

Also not presented to the court, but later posted in a letter to Congressman Wally Herger was this: during the year
1991, Region Five promoted within permanent positions 158
men and 527 women—for a staggering 77.2%. These figures,
breathtaking though they may be, do not in any way account
for the tremendous plunge in quality of work plaguing the
agency in so many professions—meaning, of course, that the
destruction of resource management was much greater than
the stark figures suggest.

But the tables and accompanying data did not seem
to make an impression on the advocates or the Monitor.
Rather, perhaps driven by a general sense of omnipo-
tence, they launched yet another courtroom assault on
the agency. Region had still not reached parity at nine
grade levels, in nine different professions. And under the
umbrella tier of tables, the percentage of female receptionists, admin assistants, and personnel workers (all ranging from 70% to 95% female) was still too low. Despite
a thoroughness of purpose that would have astonished a
Nazi Party spokesperson, Wilken once more found the forest service in contempt of court and ordered the decree
continued indefinitely.

On May 21, 1991, another hearing was held, this time with Judge Conti presiding. He listened as the service's prime witness, Ronald Crenshaw, reported that between 1981 and 1991 the percentage of women considered for employment overall, was 51% of the total, and that their selection rate was 73%. Over the same time frame they constituted 34% of the professional applicants interviewed and 70.4% of those hired. Among the technical positions, 41.8% of applicants interviewed were women, as were 62.8% of those hired. Among the various administrative appointments women made up 68.7% of the interviewed and not less than 87.4% of those hired.

Crenshaw also testified that Joyce Muroaka, who until recently was an assistant regional director, had informed him that between May 1988 and May 1991 Region Five had spent $22 million implementing the decree. This is not the real figure, as a large portion of the costs of relocating, training, retraining, counseling and re-counseling the new employees was vacuumed out of each forest's operating budget. For this reason, the full cost of the consent decree will never be known.

Conti sat and pondered the numbers before him. *62.8% of the technicals hired women? 70.4% of professionals hired women? 87.4% of administrators hired women?* He ordered the contempt decree extended, unaware that Wilken's earlier decision had set off a firestorm among the remaining long time agency employees, and that his would only add fuel to the flames.

All of the above events, as astonishing as they may be, should not leave the reader with the impression that the forest service was collapsing in a vacuum of its own. Its condition relative to other agencies was simply worse. *Multiculturalism* had by now infected every bureau within the federal government, including again most strangely, that other great landowning agency, the National Park Service.

As noted earlier, President Reagan was only vaguely aware of the affirmative action assault underway within his administration. Many of his cabinet members were aware of the revolt, but despite recognizing great voter antipathy for the rationing jobs by race and gender, they were reluctant to take on the Democrats and America's media moguls. For every Reagan cabinet member who opposed it, there was a combative supporter such as William Brock.

It may come as a surprise to many, but Brock not only had the support of the Labor Department, he had the backing of the National Association of Manufacturers and most Fortune 500 CEOs. The latter two groups, though non-governmental and *laissez faire* in economic outlook, supported *handicapping* by race and gender as a matter of *progressive principle*.

With the advent of the George H. W. Bush Administration, the situation only worsened. The new President was a strong advocate of racial/gender handicapping, a fact that few Republican or Democrat voters were ever made aware of. In an otherwise utterly barren news scape with regard to the subject, in 1992 Ruth Shalit of the *New Republic* wrote *The Unwhite White House*. In it she reported that the Bush Administration hoped to increase the number of women and minorities in government by a greater number than any previous administration. Katja Bullock, who was in charge of the White House computer system, was later quoted as saying, "Bush was just very concerned about it. We had statistics coming out of our ears. In the end we surpassed every other administration."

This is why Bush could not ride the coattails of hiring and promoting by merit, overwhelmingly favored by the American people. This was the real reason he lost the 1992 election to William Jefferson Clinton, an eager, but competently muffled supporter of diversity hiring.

C. Boyden Gray, special counsel to the president, and among the few *Reagan conservatives* in the Bush Administration, was caught entirely off-guard when he discovered that *norming*, or handicapping by race and gender, had become the primary means as to "who got the job and who didn't get the job." Other than the Shalit article and a few in such publications as the *National Review*, this *silent coup* was conducted entirely out of ear and eye shot of the American public. The news blackout by ABC, CBS, NBC and CNN, in conjunction with the Republican and Democratic Parties, and H. Ross Perot was so complete that Boyden Gray called it "the most significant silent policy revolution in American history."

Chapter 12

HOW TO LIE WITH WORDS

If thoughts corrupt language, language also corrupts thoughts. The great enemy of sincere language is insincerity.
—George Orwell

UNAWARE OF THE explosions set off by the district court's two recent decisions and the rapid growth of a group of employees known as the Male Class Complaint, Ron Stewart plunged ahead with his gender reapportioning. Between the date of his selection in December 1990 to May 1992, 52 out of 59 foresters hired were women, as were 24 out of 31 geologists, seven out of nine accountants and all four hydrologists. Other notations, referring to percentages only, state that 70.5% of the biologists hired were women, who now also comprised 54% of the archeologists on his staff.

A copy of the Maupin White Paper, revealing the dire status of the fire stations on the Plumas Forest was brought to his attention. He did not like its contents, and perhaps as a warning to other foresters about reports placing the achievements of the consent decree in a damning light, explicitly reminded all that any certificate of new hires that did not possess the names of three female candidates (qualified or unqualified) was to be canceled. Each forest was then to begin the search for new hires all over again.

At about this time, he also expanded the awards program by issuing $5,000 bonuses to each forest supervisor who had walked the extra mile to promote more women into higher places. The evidence is conflicting, but by 1993 it appears that 14 out of 18 forest supervisors received this windfall. Stewart and his predecessors had in fact turned the Civil Service System on its head. The discredited spoils system of the Nineteenth Century had been revived, but was now attired in an affirmative action toga. The key difference between the new system and that of the Nineteenth Century, was that the former was based on political affiliation, the latter on gender affiliation.

Stewart's liberality was such, that much as Barker had done he took time to remind employees that when a conflict arose between managing the forests, or managing consent decree, the latter prevailed. Proof lies in the Federal Records Storage Center, where a letter from a law enforcement officer on the Stanislaus Forest states, "If I had to make a decision between dealing with a Consent Decree administrative issue, or wrapping up a drug investigation, I was to put aside the drug investigation."

His energy and extravagance, as evidenced by his colossal hiring numbers, was remarkable. More was to come. In November 1991 he mailed a letter to each forester informing them that they were to attend a meeting at the Sierra Inn in Sacramento to review the joint apprentice cooperative fire program (JAC). At the inn, he presented a table cooked up by his task force maven, Barbara Holder. In an addendum to her table, Holder claims to have centered her picks on population projections and future school curriculum enrollments, meaning aside from physiological and psychological considerations, they were based on the most elliptical statistics imaginable.

Fully aware that the agency was targeting groups whose suitability for fighting fires was substandard, and subject to immense attrition, Stewart and Holder padded the JAC candidate list far out of proportion to population percentages. Thus the number of Hispanic women being considered for the academy was 290% above the percentage for white men, white women 363% above, Native American women 413% above, and African American women 430% above.

Within the same directive Stewart highlighted the fact that by 1995 he hoped to reduce the number of white firemen within region to 50.5% of the force. The above figures may not be a microcosm of forest service operations at large, but they are emblematic, and go a long way toward explaining the tremendous acreage lost to fire in the years that succeeded 1991.

The following portion of his directive (paraphrased for brevity) also offers testimony as to the unrelenting urbanization of the forest service workforce, yet another reason why so many millions of acres of wild land have gone up in smoke:

The JAC applicant list will first go to region which will then distribute them to the forests. The forests will review the applications, make interviews and then selections. They will then send their selections back to region where they will be reviewed by the Deputy Regional Forester, the staff directors for Fire and Aviation Management, the Consent Decree Panel, the Civil Rights Panel, Personnel Management, the Cooperative Education Coordinator, and the Apprenticeship Program Coordinator. In the end the Deputy Regional Forester will review the recommendations of all against regional criteria, negotiate changes as necessary, and then make the final selection.

In all, eight layers of bureaucracy were assigned the task of selecting students for an apprentice firefighting program, knowing full well that an over-whelming majority would be departing before the fire season was over. A master stroke in government criminality, Stewart's agenda took into its sights five targets: the soon to be disappointed candidates chosen, the disappointed better qualified candidates not chosen, the United States taxpayer, the sector of the public who has developed a passion for the forests, and the forests themselves, bereft of their "stewards of the land," pledged to them by the U.S. Congress and the President.

Despite Stewart's enormously swollen quotas, with one women listed to replace another, yet another, and yet another and so forth, less than half the 1991 graduates of the JAC academy were female. A deeply disappointed Stewart reacted by conducting a statewide dragnet to fill the 1992 spring roster, but found just twenty-five young women willing to sign on. In a nod to Chief Robertson, and to assuage his own frustration, he announced that he was dramatically increasing JAC positions for African, Hispanic, Asian and Native American men.

All of this took place at a time Congress decided to slash the forest service workforce from 34,000 to 27,000, with upwards of 1,500 in Region Five alone slated for suspension under what is known as "Reduction in Work Force." Commonly referred to as RIF, federal employees are laid off because of a lack of funding, but are eligible for reinstatement once the funds are restored.

Stewart reacted by suspending numerous men who had seniority over women in the same field. Here he specifically broke law addressed by the U.S. Supreme Court in Wygant v The Jackson Board of Education, 1986. The ruling expressly stated that the maintenance of a quota, or increasing a quota to the detriment of senior employees, was impermissible. He thus opened himself to numerous law suits filed by those he suspended.

As might be expected, his initiatives prompted many letters of complaint. Late in 1991 he received a long letter from a fire engine captain titled *A Consent Decree Opinion.* Though the Federal Records Center copy is unsigned, it is certain that the original letter was signed, because of the remarkable energy invested in writing it.

The Captain wrote after a Tahoe Deputy Forester pointed her finger at *fire* as having the most problems implementing the decree and creating a hostile work environment. The author freely admitted to a hostile work environment. But as one of his co-workers put it, "We didn't create the environment, we reacted to it." He added that fire itself was a very hostile environment and that within two hostile environments, fighting fires ensured that the blazes would never be extinguished within an acceptable time frame. He then went on to state, "The captains have discovered that almost no women want to be fire captains and they hope to rapidly pass through that post to a desk job that has much less pressure, but pays lots more money."

Referring to other positions in which women had leapfrogged over far more qualified men, the writer noted that in those professions, such as engineering, range management and recreation, a poorly designed road can lead to a wash out, a badly depleted range leads to erosion and a poorly designed campground leads to trash piles. "But in fire, decisions have to be made in an instant, without time to consult with more experienced personnel. The Fire Captains are talking about thousands of acres of timber, residential housing and lives lost."

Though the numbers cannot be precisely quantified owing to agency duplicity, as noted prior, it is a strange fact that more firefighters in other regions lost their lives owing to negligence than Region Five. This is because from 1984 onward, its fire teams understood that the women they were working under lacked the capability to organize, direct and lead a fire assault.

As a result, it became a routine function of everyday work in every California forest district for subordinates to coordinate their respective activities in working around the female captain. These *sub rosa* operations were expensive, time consuming, performed immense damage to the principle of equal pay for equal work and were profoundly destructive to morale. But it was the only possible means of fighting fires and saving lives.

In all other regions there was no *California Decree,* as the consent decree was everywhere else known. But beginning under J. Max Peterson, and later under tremendous pressure from Dale Robertson, all other regions began hiring many more women than was practical and promoting them into positions they were not qualified to fill. Still, because no other region engaged in Region Five's monumental law breaking, many of their employees reasoned, quite logically, that no district ranger would dream of placing their lives at risk with second-rate leadership. Laboring under this delusion, the awareness level of these firefighters was lower, and on numerous forests they failed to develop a contingency plan to work around their incompetent superiors.

Shortly after receiving the fire captain's letter, Stewart received yet another, possibly from the same individual. "Recently a new firefighter, an 18 year old male, was telling of his hopes and dreams for a career as a firefighter, what educational steps he intended to take, places where he'd applied and so forth. Then he said without any hostility or rancor, just matter of factly, 'I know since I'm a white male I'll just have to take anything I can get.'

"How can this be? This child never discriminated against anyone. What kind of country do we live in where we punish such an innocent person? Why must we tell him he'll have to put his dreams on hold while we virtually beg another person of less ability to steal his dreams?"

The writer continued with the following: "Many, who in the past, would have been considered excellent candidates for promotion today are not. Why? Because all they can offer is experience, knowledge and competence." Today the most vital component to the agency is "contributes to a federal workforce reflective of the nation's diversity with respect to race, color, religion, sex and national origin."

Another anonymous letter, also from the Tahoe, but of another style, read: "There is a waste of time, money and effort in repeatedly advertising the announcements, and interviewing the employees, a waste of time in assigning a teacher, and a waste of time while the employee learns. And then the countless consent decree meetings and counseling sessions that follow. If a private business was required to take the steps the Forest Service is taking, it would be run out of business in months. If an army was required to take the steps the forest service has taken it would be routed in four weeks. If the taxpayers turned into stockholders and decided to hold the board of directors responsible, the forest service directors would be replaced within a fortnight."

In early 1992 this anonymous employee submitted to Stewart *Two Short Essays on Statistics and Preferential Policies*, which applied the *Hypergeometric Distribution Method* in analyzing what are known as *rare events*. He assembled hiring data from 1991, focusing on fifteen different positions posted by

Region Five, which received applications from 105 men and 10 women.

Making the very unlikely assumption that physical and psychological abilities and experience are equally distributed among the sexes, region's ultimate hiring of six women and nine men was found to be an *extremely rare event*. This was because 60% of the women who had applied were chosen, while just 8.6% of the men were. In order for those results to reoccur, the job selection process would have to be randomly repeated 36,714 times, making region's hiring ratio *an extraordinarily rare and unusual event*.

In another study, after another hiring program was completed, the same author reported that nine vacancies had been posted. Sixty two men and twenty four women applied for those vacancies; all nine hired were women. The author states that according to the *Hypergeometric Distribution Method*, the event was so extraordinary the agency would have had to advertise the jobs on 352,113 random occasions to again arrive at the same result—the near equivalent of estimating the year and day a second meteorite will crash into Sunset Crater.

This unknown assembly of Tahoe Forest scribes mailed documents to such syndicated columnists as William F. Buckley, George Will and James J. Kilpatrick, the last of whom reported in a column that the managers in Region Five were "telling young men, off the record not even to apply. 'You are the wrong gender.'"

Kilpatrick's column caught the eye of consent committee director Richard Henry, who denied the assertion with the following statement.

> *Alert, alert…this program is an Equal Opportunity Program which is available to males and females alike—not one gender or another.*

Henry then went on to contradict what he had just written.

> *There is a consent decree requirement that we meet*
> *65% female if it's attainable given the applicant*
> *pool, but that still leaves 35% for other selectees.*

Another of the hundreds of prevarications that can be found at the Federal Records Storage Center is one by John Skinner, who had replaced Geri Larson as supervisor of the Tahoe Forest, and who in February 1991 issued a memo titled *Hostile Work Environment*. Skinner reported that a sarcastic male employee sent out the following message regarding a position posted on his district.

> *All females, please apply, no red card needed. White*
> *males, hit the five key [delete].*

Skinner apologized for the memo by saying:

> *I recognize a great deal of frustration on the part of*
> *the male author in this message, but it also inappro-*
> *priately transmits a message that women have been*
> *pre-selected without consideration of merit... it encour-*
> *ages a climate of hostility towards women that cannot*
> *and will not be tolerated on this Forest... although it is*
> *apparently hard for some employees to see women and*
> *minorities join the ranks of competition, it is unfair*
> *and unhealthy for the women or minorities in our*
> *workforce to constantly be subjected to the innuendo*
> *that because they are women or minorities they are*
> *less equal employees. It is unfair for them to hear that*
> *they, or others of their sex or ethnicity, could not have*
> *been selected based on their ability...*

Skinner then skewered himself by adding: "The selection rate for the Tahoe Forest from May 9 to November 8 1990 shows that even in the under- represented grades and series, six males were selected along with nine females."

A somewhat more skilled prevaricator was Mike Rogers of the Angeles Forest. When Fire Captain Norman J. Walker wrote that the women on his fire crew were embarrassed upon learning that tools were being specially designed for them, he convincingly misrepresented what Walker reported.

In fact, by 1991 many supervisors such as Dick Henry and John Skinner had become so accustomed to lying they made no attempt to polish their lies—affixing evidence of their prevarications on the same piece of paper in an adjoining paragraph. In short, from the GS-09 level to the regional director himself, mendacity was region's most important management tool.

Another letter, probably written by the same Tahoe employee who detailed the hypergeometric distribution method, reported that an East Coast think tank had recently produced a book titled *How to Lie with Statistics*, authored by Darrell Huff (1954). He noted the volume had become quite popular with pollsters and was stashed and dog-eared in numerous newspaper offices about the nation. He then went on to wonder why no one had yet written a book titled, "How to Lie with Words," observing that Region Five management had found lying with words about as natural as taking an afternoon nap. Should the day ever arrive when someone, somehow, surmounted his/her scandalous ignorance of the English language, that employee might one day write such a book.

The author was of course being facetious, knowing full well that should anyone in Region Five ever master the English language, he/she still could not pen a book about lying, because first-class liars were nonexistent. Unlike street criminals, who quite often must account for their crimes, no supervisor, personnel employee, SAP member or regional consent panelist was ever expected to account for their violations.

Still, in the face of the district court's two recent rulings and the presence of Davis, Kurtz and Meyer becoming ever more unbearable, by the summer of 1991 the consent committee was seriously looking for a way out of Bernardi. At a late May 1991 hearing Wilken formulated several directives for Meyer to use in micro-managing various grade promotions, and had gone so far as to insist that personal phone calls be placed to prospective female employees. If necessary, the agency was to pay a personal visit to their homes. The specter of Wilken and Meyer privately consulting one another over such matters was too insulting even for Ron Stewart, who wrote a letter of complaint to the court.

Perhaps annoyed by Stewart's letter, Meyer asked Wilken for the right to administer the hiring, firing and promoting of all personnel. She further argued that even though women now comprised 44% of the work force, many were leaving because of sexual harassment and a hostile work environment. There was merit to Meyer's hostile work environment charge. But in addition, as fast as women were hoodwinked into joining the agency, they were departing because the positions they had assumed had been so horrendously misrepresented. Only through the sheer monstrosity of scale was the Bernardi Decree ever able to reach 44% female representation.

On June 28, 1991, Conti held another hearing to again determine how long the decree should be extended. He made no mention of the court intervening in the hiring of forest personnel, but before adjourning, said in irritation, "Forty three percent. That was something everybody agreed to, not something I said. I approved it because you agreed to it." At long last the Judge had verbally approved of Article IV, but in doing so implied that he had not been in the loop when it was arrived at.

That August, at another hearing, he sat by as Nancy Davis presented the service with a $350,000 bill. The judge took note of the invoice then spoke on a wide range of topics, including the forest's hostile work environment. Then after complaining about the decree's great cost to American tax payers, he stated, "They are going to be paying $350,000 for the Region dragging its feet, to pay the complainant's attorney fees.

He could have ordered the advocates to cover their own expenses, rather than foist another encumbrance on the taxpayer, whose plight he so often expressed alarm for. Working himself into a rage, he shouted, "People are being hired now who were born when Consent Decree was born. I don't call this action a quota system. I don't call it an affirmative action system. I call it a contract action system. You people entered into this contract and you agreed to do one, two, three, whatever you agreed to do, and you are not living up to it…what you are doing is an affront to the Court, and I am not going to stand for it, and nor are the taxpayers of this country going to stand for it." In fact between March 1, 1988 and February 28, 1991, under his court's direction, the forest service had also been paying Monitor Meyer's wages, the sum total of which had come to $388,970.

Yet for a second time, using the words, "You people entered into this contract and you agreed to do one, two, three, whatever you agreed to do, and you are not living up to it….." the Judge had made reference to the elephant in the courtroom.

Despite all his bluster, by the fall of 1991 Conti was almost certainly losing sleep over the decree. The Male Class Complaint, a suit filed by the men of region, was now progressing through the Equal Employment Opportunity Office in Washington, DC. It had also gone before a three judge panel of the Ninth Circuit Court of Appeals–Robert Breezer, John T. Noonan, and Mary M. Shroeder presiding–and asked for an intervention into the consent decree. There, they were opposed by Judith Kurtz, who defended the decree with these words.

> *The Male Class lists seven complaints of discrimination claimed to be the basis for their complaint in intervention. All of these complaints involve practices which are in no way required by the consent decree. Even if they were proven to be true, they may indicate poor management policies or decisions [by the Forest Service], but they are not mandated by the Consent Decree. Thus, even if the Consent Decree was completely eliminated, the problems complained of could continue.*

Though she did not directly make note of 43%, Kurtz had referred to practices that directly arose from within Article IV, stated that they were in no way required, and were the result of mismanagement by the forest service alone. She may not have been under oath, but she did open herself up to disbarment from law practice. Fortunately for her, the ninth circuit decided that the Male Class suit was untimely. Still, the panel informed the plaintiffs that they had the option of challenging Bernardi under law provided by the U.S. Supreme Court's 1983 decision in Martin v Wilks.

On December 6, 1991, Conti held another hearing. Emblematic of these long running courtroom burlesques was forest service attorney Brook Hedges, who on one occasion complained that the directives the agency was working with were not a part of the original consent decree, but agreements arrived at to reach the overall umbrella figure of 43%. Conti dismissed her point and retorted that the agency had still failed to carry out its good faith pledge to see that women were represented in all professions in all grades at 43% and above. Hedges then turned to Monitor Meyer's monomania for detail, an obsession that had forced the agency to transfer 68 additional employees from as far away as Texas and Louisiana, to sustain its record keeping.

Conti ignored her, turned to Meyer and listened as she alleged that the agency had made unauthorized charges to the consent decree fund, and that it was now advertising jobs for sixty days, as opposed to the thirty days of recent years, thus permitting more men to apply for more jobs (forest service reaction to pressure from the Male Class Complaint). Meyer then pointed out that because of other challenges brought by the Male Class, the forests were now placing experienced men into positions that had been earmarked for women only.

Judith Kurtz then charged that the defendant had no mechanisms in place to ensure that consent would remain a fact of life after it ended. Those mechanisms must be emplaced and institutionalized. Conti in turn, assured Kurtz that should the decree end and the service renege on its pledge, she could always go back to court. He then turned to Hedges: "Well, I'll tell you this. My job here is to implement the decree and if the directives are...an integral part of the decree, I will order the directives to be implemented pursuant to the decree."

Note here the Judge was not directing the U.S. Forest Service, or the Equal Rights Advocates to implement any particular set of directives. He was simply stating that whatever directives they arrived at, he was going to see that they were enforced. Shortly after, he gave an interview to the *Recorder*, a small circulation Bay Area newspaper:

Judge Blasts Government Foot Dragging
Howard Mintz

Judge Samuel Conti blasted the Department of Agriculture for foot dragging and wasting tax payer's money. During his tirade Conti shouted "You people won't be hiring, firing and promoting. The Court will be hiring, firing and promoting." Described as an arch conservative appointed by Richard Nixon in the early 1970s, Conti has a reputation for an occasional tirade On this one he not only demanded the presence in court of people in authority, but took the unusual step of instructing his secretary to tip off reporters Wednesday of the possibility of fireworks. "I'm not mad, but I'm sure irritated. I'm getting sick and tired—sick and tired—of foot dragging by the forestry service."

The origins of his anger was a report filed by court monitor Jeannie Meyer who claimed that the Forest Service had passed over qualified women for positions such as forester. Meyer concluded that women were transferring out of the region because of harassment from male co-workers. In addition

> *Conti claimed Meyer charged the Forest Service had*
> *failed to account for half the 1.5 million dollars it*
> *had been assigned to implement the consent decree.*
>   *Conti did not give the Justice Department attor-*
> *ney a chance to respond before storming off the bench,*
> *threatening to seize all hiring and firing responsibil-*
> *ities. In 1988 his magistrate extended the Consent*
> *Decree herself for three years, because of Forest Service*
> *non-compliance, according to Meyer's reports.*
>   *The decree was to have expired in May, but*
> *ERA filed motions in June asking for another con-*
> *tempt finding. "My hit on what is happening here is*
> *that the judge is very irritated," said Nancy Davis,*
> *executive director of Equal Rights Advocates. "This*
> *is his way of saying to the Forest Service, You better*
> *take this seriously this seriously."*

Among events to follow that winter was another extraordinary statement, this one by Nancy Davis to the *Sacramento Bee*,
in which she also threw blame for the Bernardi quota system
on the forest service.

> *The courts have consistently upheld the consent*
> *decree which never intended or required a quota...*
> *and the consent decree did not require hiring or*
> *promoting anyone not qualified for a job...we*
> *had goals, something which we strived to progress*
> *toward. What went on in the actual day to day*
> *operations of the Forest Service I'm not privy to.*

Any investigation of the record will reveal that the advocates
had been privy to and were as culpable as the forest service
in building an illegal two-tier quota program so extensive

that it embraced every profession and grade within the organization.

Another statement Davis made also gives pause.

> *For any group which traditionally had the inside*
> *track on jobs, when its [SIC] no longer a foregone*
> *conclusion that you get the jobs or promotions, it*
> *is a bitter pill to swallow. Having to share is not*
> *always easy.*

This criticism of white men was made by an individual who had conspired with the forest service to obstruct California's underemployed blacks and Hispanics from gaining employment with the agency. The parties had colluded in order to preserve the advocate's inside track in the impoundment of government jobs, and the institutionalizing of a genderized spoils system. Davis, Kurtz, Meyer and their collaborators in the agency had never found it easy to share.

As noted earlier, the plutonium blast the U.S. Forest Service ignited in 1984 had not been detonated in a vacuum. It was simply among the first, and the most destructive bombs the federal government dropped. As late as 1970, there were still hundreds of gumshoe reporters with far more fiber than Howard Mintz who would have dug much deeper into so profound a scandal as the Bernardi Decree. Mintz's problem, like that of every other postmodern journalist, was that he was fearful of venturing into those realms of reporting that might not fit his progressive narrative. As has since been demonstrated over and over again, within every mainstream journalist in America, there exists a quiet dread that they will one day stumble upon yet another instance of malfeasance committed by a liberal interest group.

Indeed, by 1992, Washington DC high rollers and those in other major metropolitan areas were in the midst of shaping the greatest *silent coup* ever undertaken in a democratic society. Apart from the federal and state governments, among the worst offenders were such corporations as Digital Equipment, Hewlett Packard, IBM, Eastman Kodak, Motorola, AT&T, Kaiser Aluminum and Xerox. In fact, by 1990 Xerox had buried itself under affirmative action to such an extent that its bottom line was collapsing from low product quality. Owing to this, it was forced to reverse course.

Within the corporations, as in government, the guiding principle behind the rationing of jobs by gender and race was entirely driven from the top down. To justify each company's brand of affirmative action, these lace curtain radicals were fond of employing such phrases as follows.

> *I do it because it's the right thing to do.*
> *I believe in the free market, but I am also a social liberal.*
> *I graduated from a liberal arts college. I know what's right.*
> *I became a progressive when I was at MIT.*

The centuries-old narrative of greed-filled estate owners razing the homes of peasants tilling twenty acres of land has been succeeded by high-stepping bureaucrats, wealthy executives and well-to-do grievance mongers who go about brutally terminating the careers of hundreds of thousands of employees carrying mortgages on 1400 square foot homes. When white male employees protest discrimination, government and corporate activists retaliate with refutation and wrath. Because corporatists are not bound by any particular set of civil service rules, it is relatively easy for them to discharge a dissenting employee: "You've got till five o'clock to clear out your desk!"

In 1995 the *Wall Street Journal* estimated that one million white men in the prime of their lives disappeared from the public and private American workforce in that year alone. No one can determine the precise figure, but it is believed that between 1985 and the new millennium, over three million lost their jobs, owing to America's obsession with rationing occupation by race and gender.

However, unlike federal and state governments, the corporate world has a bottom line to ponder. When a lower profit margin and red ink begins to loom, much like Xerox, the balance of the corporate world tends to moderate course. Others, such as IBM have simply moved the bulk of their operations offshore to countries without a National Association for the Advancement of Women or an American Bar Association...where assessing people by phenotype is not the mad-cap fixation it has become in the United States.

Chapter 13

THE RISE OF THE MALE CLASS

COMPLAINT

Let the workers organize. Let the toilers assemble.
Let their crystallized voice proclaim their injustices
and demand their privileges. Let all thoughtful
citizens sustain them, for the future of Labor is the
future of America—John L. Lewis.

THE SCRIBES OF the Tahoe National Forest notwithstanding, the slowness by which the men of Region Five responded to the consent decree has often been remarked upon. Former Fire Management Officer Tom Locker states that one of the reasons employees were slow to respond was that the forest service paid so poorly compared to California agencies and the private sector, and that many were simply biding time. He was of course speaking of GS 07 rated employees and those below. Yet it is also a fact that beginning in 1986 the agency launched a buyout binge, directed at its higher rated members of staff.

Though no one can be certain, according to Bob Grate, between 1986 and 1994 the number of buyouts likely reached 1000 in Region Five alone. This of course means approaching a highly skilled employee and offering to pay that highly skilled employee a very sizeable sum of cash to leave. All of this was to enable the agency to hire an untrained employee whose suitability and willingness to remain on the job until retirement was doubtful, to say the least.

But back to the question of why it took the men of region so long to organize: The fact remains that when you've been run over by Judge Conti's fire truck, there are long-term consequences: particularly when it was your own regional director who shoved you in front of that truck.

In the beginning, many felt there was little to fear because the decree consisted largely of rumors. In May 1981, the decree was signed, but owing to dreadful planning, for another two years it remained little more than a bad cloud on the horizon. In 1983 it took hold in several forests and then in 1984 struck the balance of region with volcanic force.

Obliged to justify the humiliations heaped upon its employees and the enormous disruptions in work, the official line was that the consent decree was something Zane Smith and company had valiantly struggled against. Despite fighting the good fight, the fight had been lost and however unfair the decree was, it was now mandated by the Northern District Court and was the law of the land.

To this fable were added others: That the men of region had for too many years been inflicting anguish on their female co-workers. They had done so by sexually harassing them, providing them with an unfriendly work environment and denying them promotions they were entitled to. Men were to understand that they would no longer to be promoted in as great numbers, or as quickly as in the past. In the long term this lack of advancement would atone for past sins and permit them to feel better about themselves.

Omitted entirely was mention that in entering the decree, the Equal Rights Advocates had absolved the forest service of any wrong doing against women. The finding of innocence took place before Chief Forester J. Max Peterson signed the decree. Yet ever since the signing, the service had been inflicting these appalling falsehoods on its employees. They were nothing more than propaganda memes directed not from the bottom up by oppressed workers–but from the top down by highly paid social engineers.

Thus by 1985, increasing numbers of employees were departing while seasonal hires were no longer returning in the spring. Still, a majority of employees persevered because management insisted that so long as a good faith effort was made, the decree would be lifted in 1986. But in 1986, Judge Conti found the service in contempt and applied an indefinite extension. The attrition among veteran employees thereafter accelerated, and as anger mounted and work slowed those remaining gathered in the woods to discuss what was to be done.

Beginning in 1988, they organized in several forests, though without cooperating with their counterparts in other units. Then on November 10, 1988, what would become the most important group announced itself. Titled the *Male Class Complaint*, it was established by Robert Grate and Mark G. Levitoff, both of the Almanor District of the Lassen National Forest.

Jerry Levitoff, who would be the lead plaintiff in another suit that would one day reach the U.S. Supreme Court, was a native of the San Fernando Valley. After graduating from high school in 1965, he joined the U.S. Air Force and shipped out to Vietnam where he enlisted in a special forces unit and experienced combat. Upon returning home in 1969, he moved to Susanville, took several fire courses and became a hotshot in the Lassen Forest fire crew. He remained a hotshot for fifteen years before being promoted to assistant engine captain at a GS-07 rating.

In September 1988, Levitoff applied for promotion to engine captain at a GS-09 level, but one month later was told the job announcement had been canceled. Shortly after, he asked Lassen Forest Supervisor Richard Henry what had happened to the announcement. In reply Henry said, "If no females appear on the job roster for any position I will not fill it. The position will be filled with a female because the consent decree says it has to be."

Levitoff was a U.S. Army veteran, an eighteen year forest service employee and the North Zone backup air attack coordinator—skills the lives of many people depended upon. Yet, he was now being told that he would remain a lowly paid GS-07. He left the meeting in disbelief and in the days to follow met with Bob Grate. Both decided to contact employees in other forests; they quickly learned that events similar to Levitoff's were routine everywhere. A few weeks later male representatives from all forests gathered in Placerville and launched the Male Class Complaint. Though its membership initially consisted of fire-fighters, the class soon expanded to include employees in all disciplines.

As the Male Class lacked funding, in the beginning it simply acted as a clearing house, determining which individual plaintiffs had the strongest cases. The suits were then filed with the Department of Agriculture's Equal Employment Opportunity Commission. In the years prior to this event, employee union representatives such as Bill Shaw, Lonnie Lewis and Eric Holst were able to deal with employee complaints in a fair and just manner. But with the Bernardi Decree having assumed primacy, they were unable to cope with the tidal wave of discrimination suits that were now being *deep sixed* by the regional consent committee.

On January 13, 1989, with contributions pouring in the Male Class hired Louis Demas to represent them. A former government attorney who knew the workings of the U.S. Government inside and out, he prompted Levitoff to file his own civil suit. Word of the suit spread and within weeks Jerry found himself suffering retribution at the hands of Richard Henry, the Lassen personnel department and his district ranger. A few months later he learned that he had been *red flagged*—blacklisted, unable to transfer anywhere else in the United States as an employee of the forest service.

By then, some forty individual employees had launched civil complaints. Though the nature of their grievances varied, at the urging of Louis Demas it was decided to fold fifteen of them into the Levitoff suit, thus turning it into a second class complaint, distinct from the Male Class. Joining Levitoff were John Allendorf and Alex B. Cole, whose applications for promotion had been canceled because their forest supervisor felt too many men were employed in those positions.

Thomas B. Caves, learning that personnel, after failing to locate a female candidate, had scrapped a vacancy he hoped to fill, also joined. Stephen Matthews entered after learning that he had been rated the best qualified contender for an opening; yet it had been canceled after the woman interviewed turned down the offer. Baxter Virtue contacted the Male Class after learning the position he applied for had been left vacant for months, after two women declined the job offers.

Thomas Marks and Roger Evans complained of unqualified female co-workers being promoted, while they had been barred from gaining the same promotions. In addition, Wayne Bienowski and Thomas Caves filed complaints stating they had never been paid for work they had performed, even though the women in their unit had been paid.

Kermit Johansson, noted earlier, had compiled a detailed account of discrimination directed against himself and other veterans on the Sierra National Forest. Curiously enough, though its 1.3 million acres are located in the central Sierra Nevada and encircle much of Yosemite National Park, its headquarters then lay in Fresno—50 miles removed from the forest workplace.

While in Fresno, Johansson further learned that Consent Decree Coordinator Betty Smithers had recruited a substantial number of female candidates for several positions. Determined to purge all veteran applicants from the listings, she posted the announcements for three days only. Several vets, including Johansson, managed to rush their applications through, but all were tossed into what he termed a *black hole*. Thus he entered the class suit.

Almost as intolerable for him and the other veterans were the consent decree meetings they were compelled to attend. There, they were forced to sit and listen as the panelists, most of whom had spent their lives pottering about air conditioned offices, repeatedly denounced the character of armed service personnel, many of whom had spent two years fighting in a hell hole known as Vietnam.

The Male Class Complaint meanwhile began issuing *The Supporter*, a newsletter reporting on the various discrimination suits filed. In March 1989, the Department of Agriculture in Washington, DC, deluged by complaints, borrowed a phalanx of attorneys from the Department of Justice and packed them off to California. Paul Barker was so alarmed by events, he personally called Levitoff and Grate in for a meeting, and attempted to persuade them to abandon their class complaint.

Back in Washington Tom Beaumont, the director of the Equal Employment Opportunity Office for the Department of Agriculture, decided to fight the Levitoff suit. One of his objections was built around the argument that a class action suit called for a minimum of forty-five employees before it could be legally certified. Because each man's complaint was unique, the Levitoff Class could not be taken seriously. Beaumont's argument ought to be matched against the forest service's position in 1979, when it was agreed that *zero* employees were reason enough to launch a complaint.

In addition, knowing there was a ninety day time frame for processing the lawsuits, Beaumont sat on the Levitoff case well beyond that period, thus voiding it. His rationale, as he explained, was that he was not required to respond because no procedures for reaching a settlement had been set in place.

In August 1990, the U.S. Equal Employment Opportunity Commission overturned Beaumont's decision and reinstated the Levitoff Complaint. Louis Demas then sent the file to President Bush's Secretary of Agriculture, Clayton Yeutter. In his brief, Demas stated that Region Five was replete with positions *wired* for females only; that men were frequently detailed to vacant slots where they worked, but because no job description existed, no career paths were open to them. In addition, men were frequently being ordered to perform difficult tasks their highly paid and unqualified superiors were not able to perform.

Yeutter rejected Demas' argument, and sought the backing of Attorney General Richard Thornburgh, who filed a motion on behalf of the Equal Rights Advocates, thus denying Levitoff redress. He did so, even though in the recent case of Richmond v Croson, the U.S. Supreme Court had ruled that unless local and city governments (and by extension federal agencies) have been found guilty of *deliberate* discrimination, they cannot be forced to grant preferential treatment to certain groups. It was a sharp rebuke to government functionaries seeking to reconfigure their workforces, but a rebuke too often disregarded—Clayton Yeutter and Richard Thornburgh among them. This was not the last time the Bush Administration would sprint to the aid of a bureau that had erected a spoils system so extensive, it had brought its operations to a near standstill.

To underscore the forest service's pettiness toward the Male Class and Levitoff Complaints, on several occasions Ron Stewart invited Grate and Levitoff to meetings that included all other recognized forest employee groups. Though the pair were given seats at a very large and inclusive table, unlike every other employee association, they were forbidden to use any government time, equipment, or facilities to work their cases.

Nine months passed. Then in March 1991, Department of Justice Equal Employment Commissioner Jeffrey J. Goodfriend ordered Beaumont to process the Levitoff complaint. In turn, Secretary Yeutter, much against his will, was forced to write a letter to class members confirming their right of redress. Finally, in a separate motion, Goodfriend ruled that Levitoff and the Male Class must be accepted as class complaints in total, removing that most formidable of barriers—enlisting 45 aggrieved employees for each pattern of discrimination.

Yet another strange event occurred before 1991 passed into history. That October one of Chief Robertson's operatives called Richard Henry and offered to make a private settlement with Levitoff—that is, to buy him out. It was to be a replication of the year before, when Region Five pulled the plug on the Hispanic Class Complaint by buying out its lead members. Levitoff refused what he termed *this bribe*, and notified Louis Demas, who filed a complaint with the Washington Office.

Among forest supervisors, quite naturally it was Richard Henry, who had afforded Levitoff such barbarous treatment, who first felt the impact of the Male Class offensive. The previous fall he had added five women JAC graduates to his fire crews. All were hired at the GS-05 level after eighteen months of training at a time the Lassen already had on its crews five men at the GS-04 level, with three to five years of experience. Prompted by Grate and Levitoff, all five filed discrimination complaints; thus the Lassen dropped the JAC graduates and promoted the firemen.

Upon learning of the event, Monitor Meyer was furious and phoned Stewart. He in turn held a conference call with all eighteen forest supervisors, during which he instructed them not to settle any discrimination suits, but to send them to his office for review. In the end he proved unable to fend off the tide and was forced to send them on to Washington, where with a bit of luck, Tom Beaumont, beneath the Justice Department's EEOC radar screen, might pitch them into a shredder. Levitoff and the other plaintiffs would then become so dispirited they would quit the agency.

Among other Male Class members to file an individual suit was Thomas Locker of the Tahoe Forest, who from 1991 through 1993 applied for eighty different positions in forests all across the country. Unable to gain a single telephone interview, he began tacking pins onto a map of the United States, marking each forest where he had applied for work. He then placed phone calls to those forests. Locker stated that upon making each inquiry, "I always lost out to a woman, a minority, or a local white man. I never lost out to another white guy who wanted to transfer in...that was *my* big event in the forest service."

According to Locker, all nine regions of the agency had been practicing systematic discrimination for years. "They were definitely doing it everywhere. It wasn't as pervasive and horrible as it was here. But they were doing it everywhere." In one instance, he phoned the Cherokee National Forest in Tennessee to ask why his application had vanished into thin air. Fire Management Officer Don Corbin informed him that "[This] position is funded from out-of-region for us to hire a woman or minority. It's basically a way to gain a women or minority as a forest management officer. Just wanted to be up front with you." Corbin's unusually frank admission offered proof that a large share of the agency's discriminatory practices were being funded out of Chief Robertson's office. It also prompted Locker to file a discrimination suit.

Locker, who has a degree in journalism, then contacted the Sierra Forest to find out what had become of the resume he had submitted there. He recounts, "As everyone who has worked for the forest service knows, those submitting an application should place their yearly evaluations at the top of the resume. But I was told by the Sierra Forest that my resume did not contain any evaluations, which was why it was rejected. Further investigations of other forests showed that one, two and sometimes three of my evaluations were still present, but they had been placed at the bottom of the resume package."

Locker now knew that his *own* personnel department, in his *own* forest, was breaking down his resumes, casting out certain evaluations and sloppily reassembling the packages before mailing them off. He filed another discrimination suit. Most employees, confronted with sabotage of this magnitude, and without a degree in law or journalism, tended to throw their hands into the air and seek employment elsewhere. Not Tom Locker, who took pleasure in annoying those who annoyed him. Two years passed, during which time he routinely phoned or wrote each forest with regard to the fate of his missing resumes. By 1993 his roster of civil suits had grown to nine.

Finally that year, with the backing of Louis Demas, he ran the service into the ground. Region Five agreed to promote him to fire management officer GS-09, with all costs and back pay covered, provided he would drop his other eight suits. He accepted and shortly after transferred to the Inyo Forest on the east side of the Sierra Nevada. In a sidebar to this account, no action was ever taken against those who destroyed his resumes. If steps had been taken, as in the years prior to decimation of the Civil Service System, it is likely that members of the personnel department, as well as the supervisor's office, would have been discharged.

Back in Washington meanwhile, Secretary of Agriculture Clayton Yeutter had been replaced by Edward Madigan. A former member of the House of Representatives from Illinois, Madigan had served on both the agricultural committee and the committee responsible for marking up the budgets of America's public land agencies. In March 1991, when Wilken found the service again in contempt and ordered the decree extended, the new secretary of agriculture received an official summons. Madigan was so certain that his contempt citation would be followed by the appearance of several U.S. Marshals, he made a string of frantic phone calls in hopes of salvaging himself.

The Marshals never appeared, but the Secretary was so traumatized by the event that he became a consent decree truckler in the same tradition as Yeutter. Deciding to take a closer look at the Levitoff file, he determined that even though Levitoff had a case, none of the sub-plaintiffs did, and he disposed of them. Louis Demas was thus forced for a second time to seek redress before the U.S. Civil Rights Commission.

By now the advocates and the district court were being swamped with hostile mail. The deluge was in large part owing to Conti's and Wilken's rulings of March and May 1991, at which the service had demonstrated 44% of its employees were women. Shortly after the rulings, Conti received a letter signed by fifty women, informing him they were dropping out of the Bernardi Complaint. This letter, and others similar to it so infuriated the judge that at one hearing, he went so far as to wave his gavel at Bob Grate and warn him that his letter writing campaign was a failure.

"They don't even get read!" he shouted. In fact, Grate was unaware of the flood of mail the court was receiving. One of the more biting letters came from William Lewis of Yreka.

I understand that the Magistrate issued an indefinite extension of the decree. Judge Conti—ENOUGH IS ENOUGH and I urge you as presiding judge of this case to step in and look at the records.

To say that the Forest Service should be held in contempt of court is itself contemptible… The Forest Service has made every effort above and beyond the intent of the decree. As a matter of fact because of the efforts to comply with this decree the Forest Service has settled formal complaints filed by both Hispanic and Black special emphasis groups charging discrimination BECAUSE OF THE FAVORABLE TREATMENT OF FEMALES…

The amount of money being spent on this decision in the face of serious budget problems is

*horrendous. If you would like to check out just one
area of waste, look at the amount of money that was
spent to comply with the monitor's order to count
the number of toilets in the outlying areas in order
to provide satisfactory accommodations for women.
This one is politely referred to by our employees as
the 'Half Moon Task Force.'*

Conti also may have read a widely circulated article written
by Douglas Leisz, Zane Smith's predecessor in Region Five,
who stated that region had "compromised safe working conditions in emergency work and waivered qualifications and
experience in order to select and promote woman." Added
Leisz, "Morale for all employees is the worst I've seen for any
region of the Forest Service since my first employment with
the Agency [1948]."

The court was also receiving mail from a most unexpected
source: women. Women who had been forest employees for
many years, had slowly worked their way through the grades
and who intuitively understood the differences between men
and women. Many were appalled that the agency they had
once been proud to work for was breaking apart before their
very eyes.

One was from Alice Forbes of the Klamath Forest, who
had earlier expressed disbelief upon learning that consent
decree work had priority over fighting fires. Forbes reported
a discussion she had with Monitor Meyer over positions in
the fire organization.

*She stated that all positions could be structured
for trainees in cooperative education and upward
mobility. I tried to explain… my concern that certain
positions required experience to ensure safety for*

others during an emergency. Ms. Meyer accused...
me... of 'hiding behind the safety issue.'

Forbes then added, "Ms. Meyer stated that I was a 'good old boy in women's clothing.'"

She then turned to Judith Kurtz of the ERA, with whom she recently had an encounter. "When I told Kurtz about a decision made by the ERA that I and many others did not agree with, she said, 'The women in Region Five don't know what they want,' and that she could better see to our needs."

She also commented on the paranoia that had enveloped region. "Within six months of my promotion to district ranger... Ms. Meyer contacted my supervisors... and asked each of them whether I had been set up to fail and whether I was, in fact failing. On each occasion my supervisor contacted me, reported the substance of Ms. Meyer's call, and asked if I felt I was being set up to fail...I was and still am, disturbed that the Monitor contacted my supervisors and raised a problem I did not have, without ever contacting me...I have been told by other women that they had similar experiences."

A letter from Kathy Hammond of the Plumas Forest highlighted one of the consent decree's most disgraceful impacts.

> *In rural environments, the Forest Service may be the largest employer in the community. The Forest is thus a model and a leader in the community on many issues that have an impact on it. But communities no longer look to the Forest Service for opportunities and direction.*

To underscore her point, Hammond reported that one resource crew on the Plumas counted five women, two minority men and a single white youth.

In April 1991, Julie Vogan of the Lassen Forest warned Kurtz.

> *The Consent Decree has placed women in positions that are far too advanced for their careers. We are setting women up to fail, and I have seen it happen on many Forests since the Decree was implemented. The woman either quits the Forest Service or transfers to another job with a feeling of failure and disillusionment. Other employees view this situation with anger because the women had no qualifications to do the job in the first place...*
>
> *As a taxpayer I am very upset with the tactics. It has created many un-needed positions... I know a ranger district that has three wildlife biologist just because of C.D. Still, to hire anyone when we really need to fill a vacancy takes three to six months. But these key positions are not being filled, and the jobs are not being properly accomplished...*

As did Hammond, Vogan pointed to the extremely destructive effect the decree was having on the residents of towns adjacent the forests, leaving large numbers of them unemployed, and without fire protection. That same month Donna J. Bergstrom, writing from the Fremont National Forest in Oregon, told Conti...

> *I began my career with the Forest Service on the Klamath National Forest in Yreka in 1979...the morale when I started on the Klamath was very high. People were proud of their work, and the*

Forest Service. I was proud of my career and felt I could really make a difference...

I then followed my husband up to the Fremont National Forest, Oregon, two years ago. This was not something we had planned on doing, but due to the unnecessary stress and unhappiness that we felt was a direct result of the Consent Decree.... they started to hire UNQUALIFIED women to fill important positions. Work quantity and especially quality began to slide. The people underneath these unqualified women had to scramble to cover both theirs and their supervisor's work. Poor planning and decisions started forcing morale to an all-time low and it continues to decrease steadily...

One graphic example of the ludicrous interpretation being given to Consent Decree occurred shortly before we left the Region...if while working on a consent decree report with an upcoming deadline, and a wildfire broke out on our District, we would not be allowed to respond until the report was finished.

And again in April, Rhonda L. Barrett of the Lassen Forest wrote bitterly about the damage to...

...my agency, the U.S. Forest Service...it takes a special person to work for the Forest Service due to the nature of our jobs. The remote locations, the lack of child care, the public spotlight, the need to get "down and dirty" at a moment's notice, the continual crisis management, etc. I don't believe we could EVER reach parity with the normal civilian work force, no matter how many times you extend the Consent Decree...

Marcia Andre of the Olympic National Forest, Washington wrote begging the Judge to rescind the decree even though she had left California. Once a member of the Bernardi Class suit, she wrote, "No one outside the Forest Service can understand the toll it has taken on the work place, the atmosphere it has created and the hardships it has placed on individuals and their families. Not until the decree is terminated will the healing begin."

One woman was particularly furious over the day/night child care facilities established at fire camps. "This is the most ignorant idea I have ever heard of. Children have no place in fire areas. Besides the danger, the environment is so unhealthy for growing minds and bodies. How much parental attention could be derived after mom or dad works 12 to 16 hours per shift? It puts an added burden on the parent by making them become more exhausted and being unable to sleep while off shift. A very critical safety problem.... Exhausted people very often make bad decisions."

Another writer detailed why the decree was such a failure. "A woman fills a position in one quarter. The Forest Service has met compliance. But the very next quarter they are again out of compliance because the women has either quit or transferred."

Debora W. Fisher of the Plumas reported that the women of the Plumas, Klamath, Sequoia, and Sierra National Forest's had polled themselves and by overwhelming margins wanted the decree ended. The results varied from 86% on the Klamath to 95% on the Plumas. Yet when the results were transmitted to the advocates, the organization wrote back charging that they were *biased*, and refused to give them credence.

Among fifty-five other letters at the Federal Records Center is one from Terri Simon Jackson who informed the court that she and a group of other women had hired a law firm to represent them in the Bernardi case. Much as their Male Class counterparts had done, throughout California, working women were organizing to combat both the advocates and the regional office's entrenched functionaries.

Titled *Committee to End Court Oversight*, when CECO placed a phone call to the advocates to discuss an end to the decree, Jackson reported "We were informed that Ms. Kurtz declined to talk with us directly. They did tell me that Ms. Kurtz realized a majority of class members wanted the consent decree to end, but that Ms. Kurtz also said our questions were too general. CECO has twice written Mrs. Kurtz since, asking her to poll the class and tell us of her intentions in that matter. But she has not answered either letter. Over the last three years no member of the ERA has bothered to contact any class member as to how they feel about CD, whether the CD continues to benefit them, or what should be done in the future."

Of course this was what the misandrogonists at the advocates were all about. If an individual women happened to benefit from the consent decree that was okay, but secondary to the mission. Postmodern forestry's real mission was the tree by tree, acre by acre, employee by employee destruction of a male dominated institution that since its inception had performed with such striking success. If dismantling that male institution injured the interests of more women than it benefited, that was unfortunate, but incidental to the task.

The problem the Committee to End Court Oversight faced was truly daunting. Almost two decades had passed since the Equal Rights Advocates launched what was the most feeble class complaint in history. But no matter how unhappy CECO members were, the ERA was the only legal group Judge Conti would permit in his courtroom.

Chapter 14

CONSENT: A DEATHLESS DECREE

*Every revolution evaporates and leaves the slime of
a new bureaucracy*—Franz Kafka

*Every great cause becomes a business, and then a
racket.*
—Eric Hoffer

WITH LETTERS CASCADING into his study, and the formation of a woman's organization whose sole objective was to
end the decree, by the winter of 1992 Judge Conti had a lot
to think about. Over the years, watching Monitor Meyer and
the advocates shackle the forest service by its neckline and
jerk it around his courtroom had been a first-rate spectator
sport. But years pass, times change, and who can blame him
for reckoning that the consent decree had evolved into one
big headache. Two of the advocate's top attorneys had publicly admitted Bernardi was a *faux* decree. If an inquisitive
reporter was ever to stir himself, his legal legacy might be left
in tatters.

Another big headache was the Federal Equal Employment
Commission, which in 1991 still regarded the 1964 Civil
Rights Act with some regard and had twice overturned the

Department of Agriculture's decisions. Finally, in addition to the Levitoff and Male Class Complaints, hundreds of individuals had filed discrimination suits which were slowly winding their way through Madigan's house of agriculture and into the Department of Justice.

In mid-1991 Bob Grate's *Supporter* announced that an out of region male employee was offered a silviculturist job in California. When the regional consent committee found out, its staff informed the supervisor that he had hired a forester of the wrong sex, and that he was to be replaced. The supervisor did as told.

With the aid of the Male Class Complaint, the employee filed an informal discrimination complaint; the Department of Agriculture declined to respond. He then pushed the complaint to the formal stage (the Department of Justice's EEOC) and in March 1992 the service was ordered to reinstate him with all back-pay and costs accounted for. As was by then the rule, Grate declined to note the individual's name or the forest on which he worked. Once a plaintiff was identified, he quickly became a target of harassment by both the forest and regional consent committees.

Another suit was that of an employee who applied for a fuels management job and was turned down. When he learned that he had been rejected because of his sex, he contacted the Male Class, sued, and was awarded the position, including all back-pay and expenses incurred.

In yet another case, a fireman who for years was part of an initial attack team, was ordered by his doctor to transfer out of fire because of declining health. He requested a position in fire support, but was told that none was available. He was then dumped into an empty office where he remained for eighteen months, collecting a paycheck, but without an assignment. Payroll knew that he was among the living, but so far as the human resource department was concerned, he was dead. This enabled the department to cook its books, reporting that it had one less male employee than it really had.

It also left the employee's career in ruins. He sued, and represented by Louis Demas won a position in fire support with all back-pay and legal expenses paid for. This suit was not known to the Male Class Complaint until after events. The forest service was by now making a significant number of settlements, termed *non-disclosure cases*. This meant the agency offered a satisfactory settlement to a plaintiff provided he did not go public. Public disclosure too often prompted other aggrieved employees to file suits. Because the plaintiff, once his suit was made known, often suffered workplace harassment, he very often agreed to *non-disclosure*.

Yet other cases slipped quietly past Judge Conti's courtroom door toward the highest levels of the executive branch. One of the most egregious was that of William Putt, a GS-05 recreation technician who for six years was a seasonal employee in the Los Padres Forest. At the start of the 1991 season, he was sharing accommodations with a female co-worker when a second woman requested housing in the same quarters.

Despite seniority over both, he was forced to vacate his room and move into the Ojai District office complex at Temescal. He requested window coverings, a stove and table, but only the table was ever furnished. When Putt complained about the negligent manner in which he was being treated, the administrative officer told him he did not *give a damn* about his concerns.

During the summer Putt's major task was to patrol the adjacent Blue Point Campground, a heavily used off-highway vehicle area popular among binge drinkers. He frequently raised questions about the dangers he faced, his greatest concern being that he had not been afforded law enforcement (FPO) training—even though he was often the only employee on duty. When Labor Day rolled around, he and his immediate supervisor requested that the campground be closed for his own, and the public's safety. Forest Supervisor Arthur J. Carroll denied the request and that weekend Putt was injured when an intoxicated camper ran him over with his motorcycle.

Putt sued for injury owing to the forest's negligence, housing discrimination, and the fact that while residing in the office complex, he had never been reimbursed for answering the telephones or responding to the endless stream of visitors knocking on the front door. The regional office shelved his complaint. Putt's situation only worsened after he applied for participation in the JAC academy. Though judged fully qualified, he was rejected in part because he was not a woman and because he had made such a nuisance of himself by filing a discrimination suit.

One witness recalled that Forest Supervisor Carroll instructed the select advisory panel (SAP) not to consider Putt, because he had been employed on the district for over four years—a factor that should have improved his chances. A decision from Washington DC regarding the Putt claim was due anytime soon.

There was also the case of Michael C. Leveroos, a GS-06 forestry technician on the Sierra Forest who had applied for a GS-07 promotion, was evaluated by an advisory panel and the district ranger and found to be the best qualified among fifteen applicants, all but one of whom were men.

But the deputy forest supervisor determined that the panel and district ranger had not given the woman full consideration and judged her equal to Leveroos. He then pointed to the only provision of the Bernardi Decree that stated discrimination was permissible. If both candidates are found to be identically competent, the woman would be chosen. He selected the woman. Leveroos' attorney, Louis Demas, noted that the deputy forest supervisor's opinion was at great variance with the conclusions drawn by everyone else and took his case before the head of the Department of Agriculture where it was also awaiting adjudication.

In addition there was Barry Callenberger, a fire management officer in the Eldorado Forest, who in March 1991 submitted an application for district fire management officer. Thirty four candidates were interviewed, two of whom were women. While admitting that Callenberger was a close second, the acting district ranger selected one of the women. As the ranger explained, he chose the woman because she "could provide strong leadership...but Callenberger was clearly the most qualified in his range of skills and experience, and would have been chosen if the consent decree had not been in effect."

Callenberger's attorney, again Louis Demas, took note of the man-versus-woman being equal clause, saw that the district ranger had openly admitted his client's credentials were superior, and filed a discrimination complaint that had also wound its way to the Department of Agriculture.

It is very likely that the Male Class and Levitoff Complaints, cases such as the above noted, and scores of others known to be hidden in the legal woodpile, had much too often forced Kurtz, Meyer, Conti and Wilken to reach for their Rolaids. Thus, sometime in late 1991 (no document found), the court ordered the advocates to draw up a set of directives to be embedded in Region Five's personnel operations once the decree ended, which would not be long.

Indeed, on February 25, 1992, the advocates and forest service announced that they had reached a tentative agreement to end the decree, making note of some very general stipulations, such as the service would revise the directives as agreed upon, issue them ten days after the agreement and establish the position of *Special Assistant for Employment Progress.*

It appeared that a reasonable agreement had been reached; Grate and Levitoff were even invited to the directive meetings. There, however, Stewart and the regional committee announced they would embrace almost all the advocate's mandates without question. Grate wrote that "a large portion of the directives called for special treatment of certain classes of people, based on non-merit factors, such as race and gender." Some groups would continue to receive benefits that others were not entitled to.

Among the directives adopted and extended to May 18, 1994, was adherence to 43% female employment. This would be accomplished by continuing to send as many women as possible to universities, there to study forestry and forest related subjects–tuition, books and per diem paid for. In addition, the upward mobility, apprenticeship, and other training programs that men had long been denied, would be continued.

On learning of the agreement, Attorney General Thornburgh, who two years before had supported the advocates, announced his opposition to the directives and said that he planned to file suit with the Northern District Court. It appeared to him that 43% would become the forest service's recruiting mechanism for years to come. But something happened in Washington. According to columnist James J. Kilpatrick, President George Bush was so severely browbeaten by liberals on his staff that he directed Thornburgh to drop the suit.

Almost a century before the advent of G.H.W. Bush, Theodore Roosevelt warned the American people that

"Justice in the life and conduct of the state is possible only as first it resides in the hearts and souls of its bureaucrats." But Bush was no Theodore Roosevelt, and though Congress may not have realized—certainly their constituents did not— almost every interest group in the nation's capital understood that no matter who won the elections, or which party passed which bill, liberalism ruled Washington. No matter how finely Congress might word its legislation, there was very little its members could do to monitor some 280 agencies staffed by more than two million tenured employees. Employees whose workplace expectations were now so abysmal that ineptitude was the order of the day.

On March 27, 1992, Judge Conti agreed to the settlement. Though he had routinely used his courtroom as a forum to express alarm for the United States taxpayer, over the past three years alone, on his watch, the Bernardi Decree had officially cost those tax payers $21,245,418. This was of course far less than the real total, most of which was snatched from each forest's operating budget. The Judge's only stipulation was that the class members be polled with regard to the directives. A fairness hearing would then be held on May 18.

Yet, in a move breathtaking in its duplicity, on May 4, region quietly embedded the directives before the class members were given a chance to vote. Reflecting on the hostile mood among women, only a fraction of whom supported Stewart's directives, it is likely he realized that they would never pass muster. The ballots may have been mailed out, but there is no evidence a fair tally was ever made.

The forests were finally rid of their Mad Monitor, her voraciously time consuming reports and reams of monthly correspondence, but they would still be reporting to the *Assistant for Employment Progress.* The Regional Consent

Decree Committee was also disbanded, but an office berth for every last clerk was waiting. Already a shadow government was forming to ensure that whatever backstage stratagems were required, 43% would prevail into eternity. Free at last, Stewart and his staff could forge ahead with a patronage system uniquely their own, with all the postmodern, progressive baggage that accrued to it.

Yet the Male Class Complaint continued to forge ahead. Shortly after the decree ended, Grate and Levitoff reminded everyone who had filed a suit to pursue their cases to the formal stage within the Department of Justice. This invariably meant that a lawyer would be assigned the case. By one estimate, each suit reaching the formal stage carried a price tag of $20,000—not including the settlement outlays that almost invariably followed.

Both had also recently learned that a number of those who had filed suits were being smeared with *sexual harassment* and *creating a hostile work place* charges. These allegations were typically concocted by former consent committee members now assigned to the forests who sought to prod any new and unhappy employee into filing a grievance. Even though they almost invariably proved fallacious, the investigative process was made deliberately time consuming, leaving the accused employee under severe stress for months.

As a result, in the summer of 1992 the Male Class Complaint launched a support group whose mission it was to advise members on how to personally deal with bogus claims. Readers can imagine the waste of time, energy and money diverted into hatching these allegations, the waste of time, energy and money diverted into fighting them, and the tremendous animosities that developed.

In another fortuitous event for Grate and Levitoff, the very month the decree ended, the U.S. Civil Rights Commission ruled that Edward Madigan had wrongfully tossed out the fifteen plaintiffs attached to the Levitoff Class Complaint, in what it called "a violation of regulatory authority found to be flagrant and objectionable." The plaintiffs were reinstated and their attorney, Louis Demas, again began preparing for their day in court.

In the interim, *The Weekly Federal Employee News Digest* published two articles about the Male Class Complaint. Shortly after Grate reported that his website "is being flooded with inquiries concerning discrimination against white males from the U.S. Army, U.S. Navy, U.S. Park Service, U.S. Fish and Wildlife Service, the IRS, Postal Service, and F.A.A." The forest service remained ground zero for America's lace-curtain revolutionaries, but Grate's experience provided further evidence regarding the silent coup underway across America.

In October 1992, Louis Demas brought the Male Class Complaint before Judge Conti. The suit was filed on behalf of all men who had applied for promotions, employment, and training since 1981 and been denied. It also included those who would have applied for such promotions, but had not done so, knowing that their applications would have been dismissed out of hand. The suit also charged Region Five with taking punitive action against certain employees, after the decree was lifted the prior March. The sum total asked for was $36 million in restitution.

For understandable reasons, Conti decided to close the lid on his badly dented can of worms. He called the suit *untimely* and without explanation, dismissed it. But on that same day he admitted the Levitoff Class Action lawsuit with all its plaintiffs. Shortly after, the case was turned over to Judge Barbara Caulfield, within whose docket it would remain over the next fifteen months.

The past eleven years had brought Conti more indirect power over a greater expanse of acreage than perhaps any judge in American history. It had also brought him many puzzling, infuriating, and also amusing moments. But with hundreds of discrimination suits now being filed, each with the potential to defame his court, he was no doubt relieved to be rid of Bernardi.

Credit for his change of course goes to the Male Class Complaint, its founders Jerry Levitoff and Bob Grate and their attorney Louis Demas. Since its advent four years prior, by one count it had grown to 1500 members, many more than joined the Bernardi Complaint. The Male Class's aggressive defense of on-the-ground employees had in turn prompted many individuals to file their own suits. To this must be added *Committee to End Court Oversight*, the woman's legal organization founded by Linda Gross and Terri Simon Jackson.

Yet, as fast as Conti, Kurtz, Davis and Meyer may have been receding in Ron Stewart's rear view mirror, in mid-1993, in the face of newly mandated congressional budget cuts, he once again announced Region Five would eliminate all vestiges of discrimination against women. This would be accomplished by eradicating every tool known to be hostile to them, erecting more appealing housing facilities and updating the still existing thirty-odd women's development programs. In a closing statement to one letter, he added, "We must adhere to our new directives and special working group agreements." What is so remarkable here is that despite the already disastrous results *divide and rule* had wrought, he was prepared to reign over divide and rule with the same tenacity as during the consent decree era.

With the winter of 1993, there came a changing of the guard in Washington DC, as George H.W. Bush was replaced by

William Jefferson Clinton. While Bush tended to staff his administration with liberals, Clinton could be counted on to staff his with progressive liberals, almost as eager to test their social theories as Jeannie Meyer and Ron Stewart. Thus, the regional office likely welcomed the appointments of Janet Reno as attorney general and Mike Espy as secretary of agriculture.

Espy was an African American from Yazoo City, Mississippi, who earned his bachelor's degree at Howard University and his law degree at the Santa Clara Law School in California. In prior years he had served as Mississippi's assistant attorney general and was elected to Congress three times in succession. Following his appointment to agriculture, he chose Wardell Townsend, his former legislative director, as assistant secretary for the department. Another key member of his staff was Mike Alexander, a long-time friend and adviser, also African-American.

Five months would pass before Stewart and his associates learned just how mistaken they were in their assessment of Espy. While John Block and Richard Lying were little more than *time servers*, Clayton Yeutter and Edward Madigan had proven themselves downright hostile to forest service employees. Whatever motivated Espy, Townsend and Alexander to reverse the Yeutter/Madigan approach to social justice involves much conjecture. It may well have been that as young black men they had felt the genuine sting of prejudice; it is a certainty that their parents and grandparents did. Thus, it is possible that the three possessed a shared understanding of what *real* rejection was all about, a special torment that Nancy Davis, Judith Kurtz, Jeannie Meyer and the staffers at the regional office knew nothing about.

What is known is that Louis Demas learned of the unexpected change almost immediately. The first case to reach

Espy's office that he had prepared was that of Michael C. Leveroos, the forestry technician who had applied for a supervisory position and was judged the best candidate among sixteen applicants, even though he was not selected. In reviewing the case, Townsend and Alexander studied not less than twenty-six charts before arriving at a decision. The Article IV section of the Bernardi Decree, citing the percentage of 43, was not enclosed because it had never received a courtroom hearing, never received Conti's stamp of approval, and was not a part of the decree.

On August 6, 1993, they announced that the decree granted preference for female applicants only when their credentials were found equal to the male's. Three members of the selection advisory panel, after two days of reviewing the applications, had concluded that Leveroos was head and shoulders above everyone else. The district ranger reached the same conclusion after an eight-hour of study of the same documents. The deputy forest supervisor had reached his contrary assumption after just a half-hour study of the female selectee and Leveroos only. He had not bothered to review the other fourteen applications.

Wrote Townsend: "This is logically fallacious. If the Deputy Forest Supervisor had reviewed the other candidate's applications, he might have identified a superior candidate. It is obvious that the reason for his not reviewing the other applications was that they were not females. This interpretation was an abdication of his responsibility. It is not supported by the Consent Decree, merit promotion principles, or logic. The C.D. clearly states that the purpose of applying the evaluation criteria is to identify the best candidate."

Leveroos was awarded the promotion, with all back-pay and legal costs.

The second case presented was that of William Putt, who had been evicted from his quarters on the Los Padres Forest because he was not a woman, told to set up living arrangements inside a work center, been denied entrance to forestry protection school, had not been paid for months of overtime work, had been injured on the job owing to the negligence of his forest supervisor, and been denied entrance to the JAC academy because he had filed a discrimination suit. Even by its own standards, the forest service's treatment of Putt was barbarous in the extreme. Townsend, writing for Espy, noted that the consent decree required females to be treated with respect and dignity. But nowhere was a clause stating that male employees were *not* to be treated with respect and dignity. The forest supervisor had discriminated against Putt when it denied him forest protection training, failed to provide him with adequate quarters, denied him overtime pay, forced him to work under very hazardous conditions and then as a retaliatory measure denied him entry into the JAC academy.

Putt was awarded all back and overtime pay, sent to forest protection school, provided with proper living quarters and was selected for the JAC program.

There was also the case of Barry Callenberger, who in March 1991 applied for promotion to fire management officer (The same personnel case analyzed by the employee who had utilized the *Hypergeometric Distribution Method)*. Wrote Townsend, "For the 15 positions filed in this case, the ration of female selectees to female applicants was 60% (6 out of 10); the ration of male selectees to male applicants was 8.6% (9 out of 105). The difference is significant. We find discrimination based on sex was an impermissible factor in denying the complainant a promotion. The complainant will be promoted retroactively…all personnel documents will be revised, and the agency will calculate and pay the complainant's back-pay."

Townsend was so disturbed by the numbers that he recommended disciplinary action against the district ranger.

All three cases, though outside the Male Class's purview, presented clear evidence that the momentum was shifting in their direction. Shortly afterward, Grate and Levitoff reported that a handicapped man they represented, who had been terminated because of poor performance (very unusual), had been reinstated with all back-pay, and costs. Finally, the *Supporter* reported that twenty-one veteran firemen represented by the Male Class Complaint, who had been passed over by new JAC graduates, won their promotions, and with back-pay.

Another suit the forest service made hash out of was that of Greg A. Gregor. The case is pertinent because it underlines the primitive techniques employed by region before the rise of the Male Class Complaint. Greg Gregor was a forestry technician in the Plumas Forest who had applied for promotion and was rated the best qualified of twelve candidates, among whom were eight men and four women. After a select advisory panel recommended Gregor, the applications were passed to the district forester who also endorsed him while rating one of the women second. But the deputy forest supervisor reversed the order, and placed the woman first.

In reviewing perhaps the most complex case to reach their office, Townsend and Alexander resorted to the *Uniform Guidelines for Selection Procedures*, adopted by the federal government after passage of the 1964 Civil Rights Act. By this criteria, if it was found that members of a certain race or gender whose qualifications were roughly equal, but whose rate of promotion was not within 80% of the others, a case of *prima facie* discrimination was established.

With regard to Gregor, Townsend found that over a two-year span, of the 258 women who applied for promotion, the Plumas promoted 60, for a rate of 23.3%. Of the 368 male applicants who asked for promotion just 17 advanced, for a rate of 4.6%. The disparity came to a staggering 19.7%, a tiny fraction of the 80% required by the Uniform Guideline for Selection Procedure.

Townsend and Alexander then addressed the U.S. Forest Service's most important management tool: *prevarication.* The two noted that the woman promoted had been rated by the deputy forest supervisor as superior to Gregor in her ability to communicate orally and in writing; yet they found her application replete with misspelled words. Thus they decided to contact the silviculturist, who the deputy forest supervisor claimed to have spoken with in regard to the applicant's ability to communicate.

The silivculturist could not recall ever relaying that information on to his supervisor.

By contrast, Gregor's resume had no misspellings and for three years in succession he had been rated an outstanding employee. In his file was found a letter stating that he was "the most energetic and enthusiastic person I have ever worked with in the Forest Service."

Wrote Townsend: "In conclusion, the record reflects that the complainant was extremely well-qualified for the position. In fact, so well-qualified that it is difficult to imagine an equally qualified applicant..." On January 7, 1994, he ordered the Plumas to promote Gregor retroactively and to process all back-pay and benefits due. Disciplinary action was recommended against the deputy forest supervisor.

In mid-1993, Espy's office received another case, again filed against the Plumas Forest, this time by Kyle Felker. Among seventeen employees who asked to be promoted to timber sales specialist, the selection committee determined that Felker and one other male employee were much superior to all the others, among who were four women. All the resumes were then forwarded to the deputy regional forester in San Francisco, who selected one of the women. To quote him, "I did not concern myself with who was the superior candidate...[I] selected the selectee because she... helped to correct under representation of women as required by the Consent Decree."

Townsend and Alexander turned to the Bernardi Decree passage that stated promotion was by merit only, and that quotas were not permissible. Based upon the deputy regional forester's admission of discrimination, they ruled in Felker's favor. He was promoted with all back-pay, benefits and costs. These were not the last instances of discrimination overturned by Espy's Department, but the extreme nature of the cases was emblematic of forest service operations.

On the heels of the Gregor and Felker decisions, Espy learned that for two years running Stewart had been distributing bonuses to forest supervisors engaged in those very acts of discrimination that were costing his agency so much money. He ordered the director to cease awarding the bonuses, and reduce the performance ratings of those foresters he had favored. The Secretary then flatly warned that what he was doing was *illegal*.

Stewart chose to ignore Espy.

Chapter 15

TOWARD A KINDER AND GENTLER

FOREST

Creating a Positive Work Environment...we can often look right past negative messages in the work place when they are sent in an unconventional way. Such oversights give the distinct impression that we condone or tolerate negative messages that in many cases we haven't seen, but don't know how to handle.–composed by office cull, Samson Street, San Francisco

WHEN DALE ROBERTSON replaced A. Max Peterson as chief forester in 1987, he knew that Region Five had been in a state of decay for some years. He also knew the other forest regions had been following events there with great trepidation, as if analyzing some giant mushroom cloud on the horizon—a cloud that might one day sweep eastward and engulf them all.

The truth is, the radiation from the first bombs began sweeping into the other regions as early as 1985. That was the year Peterson suspended the seventeen-inch Harvard Box Step. Thus the regional foresters, in lifting their fingers to the winds and testing the cross currents, were able to determine that multiple explosions were being detonated in both San Francisco, and Washington. Ensconced at the nation's capital, Peterson and his staff were monitoring Zane Smith as he stumbled from one social minefield to the next. After assembling and analyzing the data, they did not trouble themselves to determine whether or not his experimentations resulted in improved forestry management. They simply determined which programs were encountering the most, and least resistance from the employees on the ground.

That same year, Washington ordered the forests of the other regions, its research stations and state and private forestry division–totaling roughly 25,000 permanent and 11,000 seasonal employees–to hire women and minorities in proportions far out of their representation in the country's professional and trade pipelines. The directive had a profoundly negative effect on several hundred towns and counties across the United States, for the most part located in remote areas where women tended to be conservative, and where minorities (other than Native American) were all but non-existent. Simultaneously, the forests were ordered to significantly slow, and in some instances abandon, the promotion of white men.

Leroy Johnson, then working in Minnesota, recalled having queried fourteen different forests across the country about submitting his resume for a promotional position. "The key phrase I received to all inquiries was the following: 'We already have a top quality candidate,' which was code word for 'don't bother to submit.'" Much like Tom Locker, Johnson is a meticulous individual who followed each rejection with an investigation as to the outcome of the appointment. In each instance, he found the position had been filled by a women or minority candidate.

According to him, as early as 1986 the hiring of unqualified personnel was apparent to everyone in every region and in all divisions of the agency. At one point, the branch he was then working for, the State and Private Forestry Division, appointed an employee with a degree in home economics as its North Central Deputy Area Director, encompassing those states ranging from Minnesota to South Carolina to Pennsylvania. "Because she could not answer any questions regarding forestry, I was assigned to go with her to all meetings," said Johnson. "They did finally get rid of her in the end."

On another occasion, the front office told him to fill a position that had been vacant four years, but with a woman only, even if she was not qualified. "Otherwise I would get no money for my project." Johnson obliged by bringing in a woman without any credentials. "She felt she deserved the promotion. Then she wrote a research paper, feeling that if she became published she would gain more visibility. I read the manuscript and was so appalled by the writing I decided not to edit the paper, but to hire an outsider...a university professor to do the review...two weeks later he called back and said he could not edit the paper. 'If a freshman from college had handed it in I would have to give her an F.'" The division later created a position for the employee that did not entail any written composition.

Being a geneticist, Leroy was often in the forest collecting tree samples. Coming upon a likely looking white pine, he would strap on his climbing belt, attach his cleats, and hitch his way into the upper branches where the best gene samples are found. The day arrived when he was forced to take a newly hired genetics graduate into the field to begin work. "It was simply part of the job I had been hired to perform, just as every other geneticist...Yet on the woman's first day in the field, after donning a strap and cleats, upon her very first attempt she balked. *She would not and could not climb trees.*"

Johnson was forced to hire a youth at a lower pay grade to accompany the new hire into the field, to perform this most critical aspect of a geneticist's work. Today, in order to maintain its requisite number of women, the agency farms much of its genetic work out to private firms.

In 1987, without formal announcement, the State Forestry Division blocked all promotions for male scientists within its St. Paul, Minnesota complex. The order had a devastating effect on the unit's research projects, the taxpayer and on the work habits of the scientists themselves. Until that time, despite the fact that the number of incompetent public servants was everywhere rising, all but a few scientists performed their research in the same diligent manner as in years past.

But that year, having determined their employer was no longer treating them in a professional manner, most of them ceased working in a professional manner. Few felt any remorse about spending their work week discussing last weekend's events, next weekend's events, fishing, football, vacations in Tuscany and anything else that did not pertain to the job. The amount of sick leave expended was phenomenal.

Thus the forest service, through all divisions throughout the nation, found itself hemorrhaging at both ends. A surplus of recently hired employees who could not perform the requisite tasks, and a surplus of veteran employees who refused to perform the requisite tasks. Leroy admitted that for a while he played the *quota game*, hoping it would gain him a promotion. It never did, and overtime his efforts to promote the unqualified over the qualified wore him out. No longer able to deal with the *stench*, as he put it, in 1993 he took early retirement. "When I walked out of that office in Minnesota and shut the door behind me, I never opened it again."

The year prior to Johnson's departure, Chief Robertson issued a blue covered booklet titled *Toward a Multi-cultural Organization.* The title is misleading in that it deals with the female perspective of culture only. While the tract does gives lip service to race, there is nothing in it directed toward any aspect of Asian, African or Latin American cultures. Indeed, upon reading it, one is left certain that if Robertson had learned that any of the social customs commonly practiced below the Mexican Border, were being practiced in his forests, he would have found some way to cashier every last forest supervisor.

The Blue Book's facing page carries the expression *The Vision,* and is followed by the following preamble.

> *The Forest Service is multicultural and diverse. Employees work in a caring and nurturing environment in which leadership, power and influence are shared. All employees are respected and accepted for their contributions and perspectives. As a result Forest Service efforts and services are highly innovative, effective and satisfying.*

The origins of the *Blue Book* do not hold the same great irony as the Bernardi Decree, but its genesis, and the reaction to it across the country, makes for fascinating reading. The source proved to be Robertson's own clique of clerks, all drawn from an urban/ suburban milieu. In truth the majority of his Washington, DC staff had never heard of a spotted owl, let alone a marbled murrelet, and were no more familiar with a grazing allotment or a clear cut, than the difference between a hardwood tree and a softwood.

What is known about the history of the *Blue Book* was furnished by Terry L. West, an archeologist who worked on several forests before transferring to Washington, DC. In response to the general outrage the book prompted, he reported by internet mail that "Only a few people had really read the report at the time it was written in March, 1991. It was a rush job and if I had written it, it would have included references, footnotes, etc."

The tract was pasted together by Mary Davis, whom West referred to as the forest service's *Shadow Deputy Chief.* Angered by its contents, West paid a visit to the chief of administration, Lamar Beasley. Failing to make any headway with Beasley, he sent a long letter to Christine Pytel, head of the Forest Service Task Force on Diversity, asking some pertinent questions, and making a number of caustic observations.

Among his observations, reported through computer services to forests across the country, was that before 1930, very few people had read *Mein Kampf,* but once Hitler seized power many wished they *had* read it. In his words, *The Blue Book* may seem funny, but the politically correct are already in power here, and their agenda is not at all funny...their only way to persuade is through power. One method is to 'ostracize.' The psycho fascism of the politically correct."

In making reference to page two, which states that cultural diversity is the law of the land and there is no room for discussing the matter, he wrote, "I was not aware that freedom to discuss the merits of law had been revoked in the United States. When did this happen? When does the preexistence of a law preclude debate over its merits?"

He turned to page thirty and the statement therein with regard to the classification of people by race. "How is the practice of typing people by appearance (phenotype) into groups...different from the apartheid of South Africa and

Nazi Germany? Will there be a race police to make sure everyone is placed in a slot?????"

Within two years West's hypothesis would become a reality. An enormous staff of phenotype racketeers whose specialty is the study of color in people's skins, and the nature of their gonads now operates both the Department of Justice Equal Employment Opportunity Commission and the Labor Department's Office of Federal Control Compliance. In addition, each cabinet within the federal government lays claim to its own staff of phenotype specialists.

He then turned to the central tenant of the *Blue Book*, the forest service's corrosive male culture. "Why should any of us labor hard for an outfit that denigrates the past contributions of white males and allows existing employees to disrespect us today?" For Pytel's benefit, he then identified that class of people being appointed to supplant the corrosive male culture. "Why does this class struggle leave out the working class? Because it is a system devised by wealthy, academic, upper class white females only."

Referring to the oppressive climate pervading the nation's Capitol, he wrote, "In Washington there is present at every staff meeting a diversity representative. Like a communist commissar. The commissar places loyalty to party line above job competence …a chilling parallel to the scenes drawn up in George Orwell's *1984*."

He then pointed to one of the *Blue Book's* most remarkable aspects, its cloying language—bizarre even by forest service standards. "There is no need for the obfuscating language of this report. If the Forest Service cannot think and express itself clearly on this topic, how can it do so on natural resource issues?"

Among other points Robertson, Davis and Pytel made, was that Americans were now rejecting the concept of a melting pot. Indeed, what if the trio happened to be right? What if Hispanics, African Americans, and Asians decided not to adopt American values in the same manner as European immigrants? Would separation of language and culture lead to, in Robertson's words, "a caring and nurturing environment in which leadership, power and influence are shared?" A place where "all employees are respected and accepted for their contributions and perspectives." An organization whose "efforts and services are highly innovative, effective and satisfying?"

As events have since proven, the answer is an emphatic no. Most East Asian employees are very circumspect in their approach to other people. Meaning that within the United States, a Caucasian forest supervisor might feel compelled to hold a second and third meeting with a new East Asian range manager, to learn what he *really* thought about tumble weed infestation on his forest.

It is also known that Latin Americans do not feel comfortable conferring in public with individuals they do not know personally. Meaning of course, the same supervisor might be forced to share several dinners with his newly hired Latin American hydrologist before a truly meaningful decision could be reached on a riprap project on his forest.

South Asians tend to be expressive and voluble, a situation that might compel the Caucasian forest supervisor, with the support of his Latin American and East Asian appointees to urge their Pakistani biologist to be more guarded in expressing his concerns about the forest's declining moose herd.

Regardless of culture, women are far more sensitive to criticism than men, a truth supported by study after study the world over. It is a factor that in turn might compel the Caucasian male forest supervisor, Pakistani male biologist,

East Asian male range manager, and Latin American male hydrologist to attend a series of seminars on how to better deal with their more vulnerable female employees.

Demonstrating that Robertson's *Blue Book* was so much rubbish was a study of 116,000 IBM employees in forty countries conducted by Geert Hoftadt. He learned that Latin American and Asian cultures were much more amenable to steep inequalities in power relationships. Throughout much of the world, the most important issues for workers were respect for the local language and culture, respect for more elderly employees, thrift, persistence and loyalty to the company. Female supervisors were not looked upon with favor. U.S. workers were as amenable as those of Great Britain and Scandinavia with regard to having a female supervisor, but most employees (men and women alike) from all three groupings preferred a male supervisor.

Finally, with regard to Robertson's, Davis's and Pytel's arguments in favor of multiculturalism, there is not a single country anyone can point to where the concept has created a "more caring and nurturing environment, where power and influence are equally shared, and where all citizens are equally respected and accepted for their innovative, and satisfying perspectives." Rather, those countries whose peoples most care for one another, and whose contributions and perspectives are most appreciated, are by-in-large mono-cultural. They include Japan, Korea, Finland, Denmark, Sweden and in former years Great Britain and the United States.

Conversely, today in multicultural countries such as India, Israel, Kenya, Lebanon, Malaysia, Nigeria, Sudan, Sri Lanka, South Africa and the United States, the tensions are everywhere roiling beneath the surface, often exploding into riots and civil war. In summary, the arguments cited in Robertson's book were intended to perpetrate upon forest service employees a form of social quackery not seen since the days Marxism was at high tide.

A few weeks after Terry West mailed his letter to Christine Pytel, he encountered her in a corridor. She stopped and said, "I have not forgotten your letter, and I will reply." She never did.

Lest the work crews on each national forest felt they were being singled out for abuse, West also reported that between January 1986 and 1989 62% of the employees hired by the Washington office were women, 22% were minorities of both genders (in a city where minorities made up 73% of the population) and just 16% white men. Two years later 62% of the Washington Office was in fact female. Though the minority population of Washington has since declined, the apportionment of jobs by race/gender has not improved. Despite all of Robertson's ballyhoo about a multi-cultural organization, the Washington Office remains a sorority of well-to-do, urban white woman.

That the *Blue Book* was not mailed out until May 1992 suggests the Chief had a full year to withdraw, reconfigure or at the very least, edit his tract. He did not bother to do so. Despite its shoddiness, the booklet was warmly received by Ron Stewart and his team, who for years had been accustomed to foisting similar quality material on their own job holders. By contrast, most forest employees, after scanning the book's first few pages, tossed it into a trash can. A small number however, recognizing its unique semantic maze, decided it might one day become a keepsake. They carried it home and stashed it in an unlikely corner of their closet, to be pulled out in the after years to entertain their grandchildren with passages about how people who once worked for the U.S. government, thought and wrote.

Peter Brost, a recreation officer for the Tahoe National Forest still has his copy. A native of the Midwest, he had formerly worked for the Siuslaw and Mount Hood National Forests in Oregon. It was a real pleasure to meet Brost, in part because he remains one of the few GS-13 white guys who has yet to quit or take early retirement. Nor was he afraid to go on record with his opinions. In an event as extraordinary as a solar eclipse, in 1986, at a time California was dumping its male employees overboard by the truckload, he was able to transfer into the state, and has been there ever since.

Shortly after Robertson's tract appeared, he responded with a detailed email to the Chief. He started off by stating that he was forced to read the booklet three times over before he could grasp its meaning. He then pointed to a sentence on page six, to wit: "Achieving consensus takes time and energy. In that respect an organization must 'go slowly to go fast.' Many white males claim to see little benefit in consensus and strongly resist initial efforts to seek it."

Brost called it "a weak effort at stereotyping white males that is insulting, offensive and sexist in content." From the same page he pulled the following quote. "Analyses of female culture draws attention to the use of 'power with,' in contrast to 'power over,' which characterizes white male culture." He noted the statement was not followed by any attempt to address the endless points of confusion that would arise from the "power with" concept.

He turned another quote on its head. "The Forest Service recruited young men with both the will and capacity to conform, so that they would do the job as the leaders of the agency wanted it done." He writes, "No great surprise. That is how every employer around the world recruits and deals with his employees. Otherwise the employer would face bankruptcy."

He cited another paragraph: "'Willingness to conform' was the initial criterion for employment. Once employed, men were indoctrinated and trained to have standardized discourse, attitudes, skills and interpretation. The result was an automatic conformity, not just because employees had to conform, but because they wanted to."

Brost noted the statement was "so extreme it begs confrontation."

In fact the paragraph inadvertently outlines how every last successful private and governmental institution has met with success. A *standard discourse* facilitates understanding; a *common attitude toward mission* enhances camaraderie; the desire to acquire the *skills* necessary to operate tools embodies the same values that made General Motors, the Space Program and the Los Alamos Project such successes in the past.

The Recreation Officer then presented a *Blue Book* platitude that a fourth grader would have recognized with very little reflection. "Increasingly organizations in America are recognizing that women, people in underrepresented groups, and people with disabilities have had different background experiences than able bodied white males."

"Of course they have," he retorted. "Everyone has a different background experience..."

He next addressed a sentence that underscored the sexism and racism intrinsic to the agency today. "Consider for example that we may be asking white, middle aged, Forest Service employees in positions of influence, to change their leadership style and their approaches to decision making."

Brost asked, "Why are we only asking white male employees to change their style and approaches? Why would we not ask everyone to change their style and approach to decision making?" As he and many others instinctively knew, white males were the repositories of almost all knowledge with regard to forestry management. To expect them to change their style and approach while teaching forestry to apprentices, would be an enormous affront not only to themselves, but to every similarly situated group across the globe.

Page ten carries the following: "Identify pools of diverse candidates as soon as possible for GS-13 and higher positions. Individuals who need additional training and development to qualify for target positions should be 'given' the needed 'qualifications' as quickly as possible."

Brost asked, "How do you 'give' someone qualifications as soon as possible? It is unfortunate that 'earn' has not been employed, or ever used anymore. The fact that Region Five has for the better part of a decade substituted the term "earn" with the term "give" has much to do with its decline."

Page fifteen offers more contradictory reflections. "All people who supervise must learn to empower, to loosen controls, to provide for the flexibility of a variety of styles, to promote self-responsibility and help discover individual potential."

Brost wrote, "And yet the entire booklet directs, demands, controls and sets quotas. How does this relate to sharing power and loosening controls? Throughout the booklet are such terms as 'require,' 'develop national policy,' 'set national standards,' 'define mandatory requirements' and 'establish uniform criteria.' 'Mandatory' is used everywhere. The underlying theme is control and conformity—not empowering, not flexibility, not promoting self-responsibility, but absolute conformity to predetermined values and norms. Indoctrination. Conformity. It is alive. It is well. It is here."

Brost's letter prompted scores of responses from across the country. One of the most notable was from Ralph Johnson, employed by the Lolo National Forest in Montana. Johnson wrote that he had contacted Kenneth M. Cohen, a general counsel to the Department of Agriculture, stating, "In order to achieve their 'quotas' it appears that the Forest Service will have to violate every piece of EEO/CR legislation on the books, and they are off to a high profile start with the publication of their 'blue book' policies." He then asked Cohen to mail him the document that had established the legal basis for the forest service's new policy of discrimination.

In his response to Johnson, Cohen might have drawn a passage out of *Darkness at Noon.* "It is the role of this office to provide legal support to the United States Department of Agriculture in the accomplishment of its mission as established by Congress, and not to provide legal services to employees of USDA in their private capacities. For this reason, this office is unable to provide to you the response that you have requested on this matter. Sincerely..."

Johnson then noted that the 1964 Civil Rights Act expressly required that no group be excluded from employment consideration and that quota systems were specifically prohibited. He took great umbrage to Robertson's claim that 'The Forest Service cannot effectively care for the land and serve the people without a workforce that mirrors American society," retorting, "In other words the present work force is not capable of effectively caring for the land and serving the people."

Despite the *Blue Book*'s eerie concepts and its fluffy assemblage of words, Robertson meant everything his staff wrote. All regional offices, forests, experimental stations and the state and private forest divisions were to dramatically scale back the hiring and promotion of white men. The reductions were to take place, even though the past nine years had demonstrated, again and again, that their removal was having a devastating effect on forest operations.

Additional proof that the purge taking place was nation-wide can be found in the *Southwest NewsLog* which in August 1989 compared Region Five and Six's hiring numbers. Six, which includes the states of Washington and Oregon and is the greatest timber producing region in the country, had a workforce 38% female, versus 36% in Region Five. Confronted with the very same pipeline problems that California was dealing with, 23.1% of its professionals, 34.6% of technicals, 54.7 of administrators, and 91.7% of its clerical employees were women. Simply put, Region Six and the nation's other seven regions were able to quietly proscribe the rights of men because their staffs were clever enough to avoid the embarrassing pratfalls Region Five was forever stumbling into.

To ram his objectives through, Robertson ordered each forest to assemble a staff of counselors, one of whose key objectives was to remind men of their shortcomings. Many of the counselors went so far as to declare that male chauvinism was a construct unique to the United States—all the while pretending it was unknown in Brazil, Japan, Kenya and just about every other place else on the planet: one more reason Brost received such a flood of mail to his response. Another email arrived from Richard Trochlil of the Eastern Forest Region who recounted his own encounters with the bureau's human resource department.

"When I first set foot in this outfit, the kiss of death in a performance appraisal was to say, 'Lacks Tact,' because there was no way one could prove that one did not 'lack tact.' It then changed to 'lacks sensitivity,' again there being no way one could prove one really was sensitive. In the last two years it has again changed to 'He, (they) doesn't get it.' (they always being a male). And of course there is no way to prove 'one gets it.' After reading your dissertation I can only say you 'lack tact,' 'lack sensitivity,' and finally you 'don't get it.' Three strikes, you're out! Good piece of work..."

Bob Peterson of Oregon's Mount Hood National Forest wrote, "During our recent downsizing and the possibility of a reduction in workforce there was a great effort to do everything possible to avoid a RIF because it would have an adverse affect on women and minorities. No mention of the effect on white males was ever made."

Jerry Wilkes of the Siuslaw National Forest, Oregon wrote, "More and more I'm beginning to feel like a "bootwipe" or worse. The ENEMY..." Michael Zan, also from Region Six wrote that "multiculturalism had been an everyday topic since I care to remember."

Commenting on the *Blue Book* and how little credibility management had left in the Northern Rocky Mountain Region, was Linda Buck. "We locally have learned to ignore management and its ever changing attitudes and do our own thing because management seems to take the tactic of divide and conquer. Open communications have kept the engineers together. Since management has lost credibility I would venture to guess that not even one-fourth of the work force here has read the book..."

Karl Brenneis of the Central Rocky Mountain Region wrote, "You have put into words what I feel has been "crushing down" on all of us in recent years." David O. Weber of the Eastern Region noted that most everyone on his forest, after reading one or two pages of the *Blue Book* had tossed it into the trash. He then summed up his thoughts.

> *Tis a shame as many of us after reaching this point in our careers had much to offer the organization in return for the training and experience given to us as we progressed. Now the store house of wisdom*

> *will be lost as most of us settle back, do only what is*
> *necessary to maintain our present status and mark*
> *the months, days and hours until we are outta here.*

This was already occurring on a scale that may have surprised Weber himself.

In contrast to the *Blue Book*'s almost total focus on a female culture, as noted prior, ever since the early 1970s the forest service at large had been attempting to employ increasing numbers of African Americans. It had met with little success, which was almost entirely related to that group's urban culture. An increase in hiring in the southern forests, where a large rural black population resided, did occur, but not in the numbers expected. Moreover, it was found that these employees invariably rejected transfer to such locales as the Cache Forest in Utah or the Gila Forest in New Mexico.

Just before the *Blue Book* appeared, Region Five, perhaps feeling remorse over its railroading of the Hispanic Class Complaint and demolition of the more modest suit filed by African Americans, set out to right its wrongs. Assigned to resuscitate its minority program was Equal Employment Coordinator Linda Nunez. At a meeting in San Francisco, she and her staff were reviewing a plan to transfer more black employees into California's rural counties. Suddenly the director of the Black Employees Association (name not cited) rose and announced that he would not allow his son to be *deported* to a small town in Northern California just so he could work for the M*odoc*. His station of employment was among his associates, those people he had something in common with. He then flatly stated, "His place is in San Francisco. And if you try to direct reassignment me, I'll quit."

Nunez is said to have blinked and murmured, "It was only a plan."

The above drama makes a powerful statement with regard to the forest service and its growing urbanization. It is likely that a few on Nunez's panel took note of the fact that very little timber was being cut in San Francisco. Conversely, many of the state's rural counties lay beneath some of the most extensive forests on earth.

But it is also safe to assume that her staff believed the service's primary mission was procuring enough cultural diversity to satisfy everyone. Marking trees, managing campgrounds, monitoring endangered species and fighting fires were components to forestry management, but incidental to the mission at large. Hadn't Paul Barker said so in his memo, directing every district ranger in his state to place a priority on hiring women over fighting fires? Logically, Robertson's booklet could only mean that hiring minorities also had priority over managing campgrounds, monitoring endangered species, and fighting fires.

Nationwide, one of the most egregious policies to arise from the Washington, DC Office, pertained to the hiring of temporary employees. As in California, many temporaries, most of them local, who proved their worth over four and five seasons, had been hired as permanent employees. But beginning in 1986, much as Region Five had done in 1984, the balance of the nation's forests began reaching out to metropolitan areas for temporaries. Not less than one hundred employees were assigned the task of designing a U.S. Forest Service workforce that would mirror the gender and skin pigmentation of the nation's largely urban/suburban populace. How many more on-the-ground forest employees were dragooned into assisting this task force is unknown, but the numbers severely crippled forest service operations everywhere.

Over the next several years, quite probably drawing upon Region Five's Project Outreach for Women, the Washington

Office developed a nationwide *temporary/promotional database* which Congress and the taxpayers were never made aware of. Despite this effort, the forests could not achieve their targets, partly because of a shortfall in applications from urban areas and because those applicants who did show up for work, just as hurriedly left.

Indeed, one would have thought that by 1992, with ten thousand and one blunders already folded beneath its belt, the agency might have learned a few lessons. Yet much as Region Five had done several years prior, the Chief and his directors remained adamant that no lessons were to be learned. Which was why, "Like the sorcerer's apprentice who could not stop bringing water to the flooded room," with every new year the forests were forced to backfill their initial roster of urban employees, with *undesirable* local youths.

The result was a sharp downturn in the effectiveness of recreation and resource crews. Within the fire crews, the problem reached crisis proportions. Very often it was not until September that the local replacements gained enough experience to fight fires. Worse, regardless of the youth's newly developed skills, as most subsequently learned, there was little likelihood that they would be called back in the spring.

In truth, the agency's single successful multicultural exploit continued to be white women.; as the agency's only *minority cluster*, their value was immense. Beginning in 1990 the paperwork necessary to fire a temporary female employee began to pile up—creating stacks vastly higher than the three thin sheets of paper required to fire a sea- sonal man. Leroy Johnson recalled the enormous store of documents he amassed in order to discharge one female *temp* who had stopped reporting for work. Washington direc- tives forced him to make numerous attempts to deliver the letter of severance in person. Six weeks later, after he finally located the woman, she refused to sign. Johnson estimates that the phone calls, interoffice memos, letter writing, conferences, and attempts to deliver the certified letter cost his office $10,000.

By now the agency was grappling with the gay/lesbian lifestyle. For years it had been a practice to make every effort to find a position for a man or woman whose spouse had been transferred. By 1991 gays and lesbians were also demanding, and very often receiving, the same benefit. The service even managed to ensnare itself in the transvestite controversy with no less than Jerry Levitoff coming face-to-face with the issue. Upon his first day of arrival at a fire camp, Levitoff, who had been appointed incident commander, was approached by an individual who said to him, "I'm half way through my change."

"Change??? What change are you talking about?"

"A sex change. I had another operation. Recently. And it seems that my breasts are growing again. But I'm not quite there yet."

Levitoff turned and walked away. No one had thought of sending him to a transvestite seminar. He had read about transvestites in newspapers, but regarded them as an unusual phenomenon, unlikely to be encountered in any forest.

He was not the only one confounded. That evening a furor erupted among the firewomen when it was learned that the transvestite was using their shower stall. This had a ricochet effect, as none of the firemen would now speak to the person. Finally someone drove back to forest headquarters, where a specialist decided that the women's shower would be closed for a short period each day for the transvestite's benefit. The following day, sensing rejection from all quarters the sex changer departed camp.

Chapter 16

THE EDUCATIONALLY DEPRIVED CHILD

What is genius?–It is the power to be a boy again,
at will.

—James Mather Barrie, creator of Peter Pan

UPON BEGINNING WORK for the Mendocino National Forest in 1999, within a few weeks I determined that the U.S. Forest Service's effort to reach gender parity in all professions and grade levels had been an unmitigated disaster. Fifteen years had passed since the agency had launched its grand social contrivance, an effort that had left it demoralized and utterly without a sense of mission.

Since its founding the service had established various barriers for employment to ensure that only the most capable applicants were hired and retained. Yet in 1983, the 18 national forests of California, directed by the Washington, DC Office, began eliminating as many barriers as possible in order to attain gender, and to a lesser degree, racial parity in its workforce.

As a result, over the past quarter century thousands of miles of recreational trails had reverted to brush, and those campgrounds not farmed out to private companies were in wretched shape. The law enforcement division was so badly depleted that large stretches of low elevation backcountry were by then occupied by cannabis growers, some operated by Mexican drug cartels. By the end of the first season, I was already wondering, who precisely were those forest supervisors who had quite literally set about destroying their agency from within.

What kind of educational background did they possess and what prompted them to so eagerly embrace Washington's fantasies? Zane Smith, who so long ago had launched the Bernardi Decree, received his bachelor's degree in forestry at the University of Montana and served as a fellow at the Institute of Public Affairs at Cornell University. His interests are so wide ranging, that after retirement he ventured into the wilderness of Northeast Asia in search of the Siberian Tiger. His successor, Paul Barker, former supervisor of the Los Padres Forest, also carried some impressive credentials and was once regarded by almost everyone as a man of honor. His replacement, Ron Stewart, possessed an educational and achievement background that is astonishing.

The employees who encountered all three regional directors describe them as personable. Photos reveal them to have been passable to impressive in appearance, and to some degree in possession of everyone's notion of what a forest ranger ought to look like. Tracing the myriad of forest supervisors who managed the forests under their direction is a bit like trying to trace pop-corn balls ricocheting around a hopper. Unlike their pre-consent counterparts, their terms were often quite short—the regional offices quickly disposing of those who were uncooperative.

Still, a goodly number of supervisors truly believed that a more feminized workplace was the answer to superior forest management. All of them must have eventually learned that the Bernardi Decree, as amended, did not have the district court's blessing and was therefore extralegal. I sometimes wondered aloud in the company of co-workers, what these supervisors actually learned as they passed through grade school, high school and onto college with regard to the physiological and psychological differences between men and women. This question is particularly apt, because it was these very differences that had plunged the agency into such chaos.

From the Chief Forester in Washington, right on down to the lowest consent decree clerk in the Inyo Forest, these individuals could look you straight in the eye and tell you that except for reproduction there were no physical and psychological differences between men and women—and if there were, they were marginal differences that could be tweaked. Most, if not all, could make this point in the face of the agency's extraordinary effort to track down every last tool, known to be hostile to women.

It is of course impossible to recount the education these supervisors received in human physiology and psychology, but I can relate my own education on the subjects which roughly parallels the years they also passed through school. Sometime in junior high school, my biology teacher provided our class with instruction on human procreation. He made no mention of the sex act itself, which of course everyone knew of; but he went over in some detail what took place within a woman's womb as well as her breast development. Later on he gave a short talk about vocal chords and how as boys matured their vocalizing underwent a change that resulted in their speaking with deeper voices Otherwise, he omitted any reference to differences between male and female.

In college I took general biology, and while somewhat more in depth than primary school, the professor took very little notice about the dichotomy between men and women. I took no courses in physiology, but did take two in psychology, during which I learned that men suffered more from various psychosis than did women, while women suffered more from neurosis/depression.

Otherwise there was nothing.

Yet in real life, from the third grade on, through personal observation I learned there were many differences between boys and girls. Boys tended to be much more physical and much more competitive. When the bell for recess rang, there was so much energy coursing through our systems, we were invariably the first out the door onto the playground. There, we organized ourselves into teams to play dodge ball, basketball or some sort of tag game. It was strenuous play, and other than an occasional scrap, good fun. On the other hand, if for one reason or another the physical education class, or morning recess, was cancelled, the afternoon brought on a great deal of pencil rapping, throwing of spit balls and other acts of rascality. All of this restlessness originated from the part of the room where most of the boys sat.

About this time I noted that overall girls received better grades than boys. Among ourselves we chalked these grades up to *goody*; that is, the girls always sat down when told, picked up their pencils when told and wrote down what they were told. By contrast, some boys made a point of talking back to the teacher or committing some other infraction, such as tossing a handful of peanut shells at another student. They were then sent to the office where the principal whacked them over the rear end with a ping pong paddle. But later that day came their reward, and from where it counted most—their peers. "Man, you showed a lot of nerve! What happened in the office? Got a lot of crap I bet. Did Alex[ander] beat you with his paddle?"

It was a real tightrope to walk, a fine line between being too obliging to the teacher and earning the good grades our parents expected us to—and punished us for if we didn't. Some boys were better at walking that tightrope than others and tended to become what are today termed *alphas*. By the time of college, it had become obvious through these observations, give and take among my peers, exchanges with girls, and informal talks with members of my own family and other adults, that the differences between male and female humans was far greater than any educator would allow.

Peterson, Smith, Stewart, Robertson and company probably underwent a similar trifling instruction on the same subject matter before moving on to forestry. For myself, however, I would sometimes lurch off on reading binges, into what is today known as *gender studies.*

The first of these projects grew out of a visit to my grandmother, who lived in a posh house in the middle of Pennsylvania owned by my Great Aunt Agnes. I was watching a boxing match with Agnes, who had made a lot of money in the stock market, swore like a sailor, and had never married. She hated men, as evidenced by her many acerbic remarks about them. Despite this, she was an avid sports fan and particularly fond of boxing. One evening following a match, annoyed by some comments she had earlier made, I rose from my chair and sarcastically said, "Notice there are no women in the ring? They can't cut it."

Agnes tossed her newspaper onto the floor, nearly leaped from her chair, called me "a god-damned puppy!" and shouted that the only reason there were no women in boxing was because they were not allowed to box and the day women were allowed to box, they would be winning more matches than the men. I was as jarred by her outburst as she was by my insolence, and since it was her house, and she was my elder, I was not about to argue.

On our return home I made a point of asking my father why no women were in professional sports. I further pressed the point that there were no female military heroes. In fact, there were no women *combat* soldiers anywhere in the world, and never had been.

My father was a chemist, with a doctorate in microbiology who spent his Saturdays and Sundays at his desk scratching out formulas on a yellow pad. I felt he should have been able to answer my questions, but all he could ever muster was something like: "Women are just not cut out for that sort of thing. Besides, we need them so they can get pregnant, and have—s*ay*, did you finish clipping the hedge? *You know,* you're supposed to work two hours around this place every Saturday! If that hedge isn't clipped I'll..." I would be off and Dad would return to his pad to connect one more element to his already trenchant looking molecule. It was about this time, I began visiting the pubic and school libraries to read what scant material was available about men and women.

It may have been that year-in and year-out, the forest service heads also suffered at the hands of a bombastic aunt, an evasive father and a childhood blotted by a multitude of teachers too *stricken* to examine, let alone explain, what I had come to feel was a series of truths.

A few years passed. The Vietnam War was underway and I made an attempt to enlist. I was rejected because of a skin infection no physician at Whitehall Street, New York City, could diagnose. I attended college and continued reading, my favorite subjects being history and natural history. I had no sympathy for the peace protestors of the time and tended to associate with the more sedate, pro-war students. During one of our coffee house sessions about *great wars,* in a tentative manner I asked, "How come no women have taken part in combat in those wars? Any wars? You guys ever wonder about that?"

Ronny, sitting across the table, set down his coffee cup, grinned, and said something to the effect, "What a dumb question! They can't fight! You know it!" His grin slowly turned to a grimace as he sought to cover his remarks with what he obviously thought was the better response. "It's the Christian way. It's chivalry. No civilized country would allow its women into combat."

Next to me Chester was laughing. I noted he had agreed with Ronny's initial remarks, as well as the obfuscation that followed. He then veered off-topic to focus on the concept of chivalry—when it developed and in which countries it became the norm. His spotlight was on Western Civilization and the role it had played in the development of chivalry. Great Britain, the United States, Australia, Canada, and France (the last reluctantly; he hated Charles de Gaul) were chivalrous countries. Everywhere else chivalry did not exist—which was proof of Western Civilization's superiority. Ronny and I, never having read about chivalry, simply deferred.

Chester then again veered off-topic, and jabbing me with an elbow motioned to Ronny and said, "I think Chris here is afraid of women. Otherwise, why would he ask such a stupid question?" He then nodded toward a tall, strapping waitress at a nearby table writing down an order, who also happened to be good looking. "Think you could handle her, Chris? I bet she could kick your ass. Wipe the floor with you." Ronny joined in the clucking, and after several vain attempts, I managed to change the subject. But the fact is, in their own uneven and demeaning way, Chester and Ronny offered me a superior assessment with regard to the differences between men and women than did my bombastic aunt, evasive father and stricken teachers.

Eventually I took a job with IBM, got married and fathered two children. During this time I noted that quite aside from procreation, my wife was very different from me. She was not as strong or mobile and her interests were not so focused. But her soft body with its well-rounded contours spoke of other assets I did not have. I noticed that she was more solicitous of our children, more meticulous about mailing Christmas cards and how the house should be kept. By then I had noticed that other women were better than most men in settling points of argument. At social events they were also successful at shifting conversations from one theme to the next. Some men were very good at this too, but on average more women were better.

We later moved to California, which was followed by our divorce. I got another job with another computer company, and remarried. Months before my second marriage, I could not help but notice that my future second wife was also smaller than I, less forward, less focused, more solicitous of others, more patient with children, and in possession of physical assets similar to, but unique from my first wife.

By the 1990s I was writing history articles for magazines and also venturing into California's backcountry. Finally I went to work for the U.S. Forest Service, where almost immediately I was confronted with the impasse that is the subject of this book. In truth, the gulf between making a living with a computer company and the forest service was jarring.

Not that my supervisors and co-workers were bad people. It was simply that the directives sent down from upper management forced them into on-the-job struggles that had little to do with forestry management and everything to do with regulations. Further, whether my supervisor's project was completed next week or next month never seemed to matter to the administrators. In fact, one second-level manager, tired of my supervisor's protestations against agency *rules*, intervened to make sure a project he attached great importance to never bore fruit. Of course, backbiting exists in private industry as well, but it was the service's ever lengthening lists of rules and the accompanying lack of urgency that was so striking when compared to IBM, where urgency was everything. If meeting a deadline meant breaking a few rules, so be it.

All of which prompted me, when the season ended, to resume the gender studies I had abandoned years before. As I quickly learned, today researchers are obliged to slide through an enormous quantity of feminist science before arriving at genuine science. This was because during the 1970s and 80s the vast majority of gender studies were undertaken by women seeking to demonstrate that gender parity existed in all aspects of human endeavor, and that the relationship between the sexes over the past several thousand years had been a theological misunderstanding.

Yet as the 1980s advanced into the 1990s, many feminist researchers became more and more convinced that the differences between men and women were genuine, and moreover biological. Most subsequently dropped their studies and spent the remainder of the decade seeking to obfuscate their own findings, with good success. Other more resilient women, formidable enough to deal with their discoveries, quietly continued work, and in addition were joined by an increasing number of men. This is a big reason why many libraries, as well as the Internet, can still be mined by anyone in search of the truth.

Inside the Chico State Library I found lying in print several revelations. For example, why so few women on the fire crews were, as they say, *living the dream.* For one, it had everything to do with body strength, a fact I had come across years ago, but over time had forgotten. An article in the *Journal of Applied Physiology* titled "Skeletal Muscle Mass and Distribution Among 468 Men and Women aged 18 to 88 Years," revealed that relative to body mass, the average amount of muscle in men was 38.4 kilograms, as opposed to 30.4 for women, meaning that a women of the same weight as a man would be 79% as strong, placing her at a very significant disadvantage.

But of course, we all know that the average woman does not reach the same weight and height as the average man. In fact, when the size differential is taken into account, she possesses just 61% of his body strength. David Put, professor of biological anthropology at Penn State and author of numerous articles on human evolution, states that the average upper body strength of a woman is just 52% that of a man. This is why a 130 pound firewoman, much as she might desire, is incapable of carrying away from a blaze an injured 180 pound fireman. According to Steven Rhoades in *Taking Sex Differences Seriously,* just 6% of women are as strong as the *average* man, meaning that if the strongest 20% of candidates applying at a fire academy are to be accepted, not a single woman will pass muster.

In another paragraph within Rhoades' book I learned that a woman's hands and wrists are capable of applying 57 increments of pressure for every 100 applied by a man, a major reason why so many women in the field, confronted by a flat tire, call the work stations for assistance. And why Gary McHargue, and so many others were forced to leave their projects to go in search of a stranded forester.

In truth, the physical dichotomy between the sexes with regards to strength is so great, it stands at 3.0 standard deviations, rated by researchers as enormous. Meaning, that no *sober-minded* employer would consider reviewing an application from a woman seeking to fight fires, fight crime in the streets, or fight the nation's wars. That these sorry developments have come to pass has led to some astonishing outlays and a precipitous drop in effectiveness. Over the past quarter century, the U.S. Forest Service has engaged in a frantic quest for that human anomaly: the extraordinarily rare woman equal in strength to the ordinary, run-of-the-mill man.

In hopes of creating that anomaly, the various forests began setting up elaborate exercise yards, complete with high tech nautical machines of up to six different settings. The average cost in 1990 dollars was $5,600 apiece. But the truth is, only if the physical disparities between the sexes stand at a 0.5 standard deviation or below can the exercise machines hope to level the playing field. As the author of *Co-Ed Combat*, Kingsley Browne, put it, "Why go through all the trouble of hiring women to give them extensive workouts when men can be hired off the street to perform immediately?"

With more pressing projects at hand, including forest service work, I placed the research aside. Five years later, suddenly with more time on my hands, I again commenced gender studies. Among the more startling discoveries was this...

Relative to height, men have significantly longer legs, allowing them to run faster, farther, and to jump much greater distances. Particularly startling was the discovery that the average male can leap 44% higher than his female counterpart. In addition, in proportion to their size, men possess larger hearts, larger lungs, higher systolic blood pressure and a lower resting heart beat rate.

These very pointed factors offer additional reasons why the agency was never able to sustain the proper ratio of women in any field that entailed strenuous work.

I also found that, on average, a man's endocrine system generates twenty-one times more testosterone than does a woman's: seven milligrams per day, as opposed to three tenths of a milligram in women. James Dabbs, in *Heroes, Rogues and Lovers; Testosterone and Behavior,* revealed that testosterone significantly elevates the production of hemoglobin, the oxygen-carrying protein found in red blood cells. As a result, each liter of male blood contains 150 to 160 grams of hemoglobin, compared to 130 to 140 grams for the female.

In addition, the blood of men contains higher amounts of clotting matter, such as vitamin K, prothrombin and blood platelets, assets that lead to a faster healing of wounds. These important differences are yet more factors that explain why the fire captains on many forests were ordered to permit their firewomen to carry half-filled portable water pumps to the fire lines. And why there was such an increase in the call for first aid kits.

Finally, testosterone carries agents that are able to neutralize the chemical byproducts that accrue during strenuous exercise—the byproducts that give rise to the aches, pains and stiffness that follow—an important reason why so many women employed in physically demanding positions, fail to appear after a strenuous day of work.

I also discovered that by age seventeen there is no overlap between the sexes when it comes to tossing a baseball, stick, wrench, or backpack. That is to say, that in offloading materials at a fire line, every single male firefighter will toss the necessary items to the right individual at the right moment, at a much greater distance with far greater accuracy and velocity than any female present. The standard deviation for throwing velocity and accuracy between the genders is 3.5—rated enormous. Yet another reason why women do not compete with men in professional sports, or the Olympics, and why they have never been *active* members of any armed services.

There was yet another study I discovered that goes a long way toward explaining why women working in fire and police departments, and any other physically demanding profession, go out on disability at a much higher rate than their male counterparts. A 2004 study reported that injuries to the anterior cruciate ligaments (ACL), was a common occurrence among athletes. Data from soccer, basketball and volleyball revealed the incidence of injuries among women was three to seven times greater than among men. This is because their ACL's are smaller and much less taut than those of men, which goes a long way toward explaining why so many firewomen were injured hauling fire hoses and other pieces of heavy equipment through thick underbrush to reach the fire lines. And why, when performing more routine tasks, such as post hole digging, many more are taken out of action.

The research continued, and by happenstance directed me to subject matter I never imagined existed. One magazine I came across contained an article about *mental rotation*. According to the author, equal numbers of each sex were subjected to a battery of tests to find out what a three dimensional image might look like if it were flipped over or rotated in one or more ways. It should be noted that mental rotation is strongly correlated with an assortment of capabilities such as mechanical aptitude, map reading, and finding one's way out of an unknown locale.

This study revealed that the discrepancy between adult men and women in mental rotation was 0.94; meaning the differences in their ability to use tools, read maps and to extricate themselves from unknown locales was large...which is one reason why so few women are found around repair shops and why a disproportionate number of people who become lost, whether in a city or a forest, are women.

I also came across the hitherto unknown subject of visual acuity. Men instinctively track and intercept—that is catch, block or dodge—objects thrown in their direction with much greater precision, which is why around any workshop, men toss tools to one another without a thought and why in the forests they are able to evade unforeseen dangers.

Visual acuity in turn is directly tied to what is known as *situational awareness*, the ability to focus the mind on immediate objects of concern; what might happen to those objects should there be a change in their direction or velocity, and what action should be taken if the object's direction and velocity does change. The greater one's situational awareness, the less exposure one has to irrelevant distractions. This factor has been cited in numerous studies regarding the competency of fighter pilots in the Navy and Air Force.

So far as the forest service is concerned, whether dodging the onrush of a 120 foot ponderosa pine that has unexpectedly lurched off its stump, or darting through a clump of chaparral that has suddenly burst into flames, men will move off the mark more quickly than women and much more often in the right direction. Yet one more expensive reason why long before retirement, so many women in timber management, resource management and firefighting apply for a desk job, depart the agency, or go out on disability.

Chapter 17

MANY SEASONS OF GENDER STUDIES

Courage is rightly esteemed the first of human qualities because it is the quality which guarantees all others. –Winston Churchill

VISITING LIBRARIES WITH gender research in mind can be as addictive as fishing, gold panning or visiting the Federal Records Storage Center in San Bruno. On yet another occasion, I came across an article that explained more about the puzzling mysteries that have over the past quarter century plagued the U.S. Forest Service and scores of other agencies, federal and state alike.

In a prior chapter I reported that firewomen suffered from gashes, burns, poison oak and insect bites in far greater numbers than firemen. The situation was so critical on the Shasta-Trinity Forest that Supervisor Robert Tyrell asked the regional office if a special women's first aid kit was available.

The following report on experiments conducted by the Department of Physiotherapy Studies at Keale University, Staffordshire, England, involved two pain tests—one between fifteen men and fifteen women, and another between fifty women and fifty men. Through applying increments of pressure the staff found that the pain threshold for women was 30.5, while that for men was 42.7. In the second test the scores were 29.5 and 42.3, establishing that men had a 28% higher pain threshold than do women. On the standard deviation scale, the gap stands at 2.3, which is very large. So large that by that criteria alone grave consideration should be given by any outdoor agency when considering a woman for firefighting, forestry, resources or recreation.

In support of the above examinations, I located another *pain test* under the title *Gender Competition: a Test Between the Sexes.* Carried out by Shannon R. Burnside of the University of Western Missouri, it involved two groups of subjects... twenty male and twenty female psychiatry students. All were to place their arms in stock pots filled with ice water and leave them submerged as long as possible before voluntarily removing them. Three different modules were created: Male versus male, female versus female and male versus female.

Burnside found that the men were able to immerse their arms in the ice water for much longer periods than the women, a result he and his researchers were not at all surprised at. What did surprise them was that the women, despite residing in a society that promotes the notion of sexual equality, withdrew their arms much more quickly when matched against men, as opposed to other women. Burnside was so puzzled by this phenomenon, he wondered if they were engaging in some sort of primal submissive behavior.

In addition, it has been found that men quite literally have thicker and more oily skin than women. These assets serve them well, whether scuffling with a criminal, deflecting tree branches while fighting fires, shielding their arms from work shop accidents, or scraping an elbow while conducting home repairs.

Also never reported upon by our newspaper chains and evening telecasts, is the fact that scientists have been conducting studies that quantify courage. In June, 2003 a *courage test* was conducted in Berkeley, California at the *Twentieth Annual International Conference of the Association for the Study of Dreams*, directed by Raymond Rainville. His psychologists selected a total of 1,500 men and women who were prompted, through stimulation, to undergo three different sets of *frightening* dreams.

There was some difference in the imagery used, women being presented with dreams in the following order...a one-armed male figure in pursuit, a one-armed male figure holding her prisoner, and a one-armed male figure confining and inflicting injury upon her. The dream characters presented the men were as follows: an armed male figure in pursuit, an armed male figure holding him prisoner and an armed male figure confining and inflicting injury upon him.

The overwhelming number of female responses to the three dream dramas were as follows, escape, placation, submission. The overwhelming number of male dream responses were as follows, attack, ambush, confront. The association concluded the reason for these vastly different responses was a much lower flight threshold among women; and that men, rather than fleeing their tormentors, were much more inclined to fight back. It should be noted that no attempt was made to present the men with one-armed female assailants.

A review of two other *courage studies* also revealed that men responded to threats much more aggressively than women. All three courage tests help to explain why in 1996, Ronald C. Johnson, in assembling his *Attributes of Carnegie Medalists Performing Acts of Heroism, and of the Recipients of the these Acts* found that over a seven year period, forty men had died attempting to rescue persons completely unknown to them, while only one woman gave her life in doing the same.

To this evidence must be added an annually compiled report titled the *Jobs Rated Almanac*. This review routinely notes that women almost uniformly refuse employment within the eight most stressful and dangerous occupations in the world—timber falling, deep sea fishing, piloting small aircraft, skyscraper construction, mining operations, roofing, building construction and truck driving. Men occupied from 96% to 98% of all positions and suffered even higher fatality rates, suggesting that even in those trades women tend to occupy positions of greater security.

Finally there is the matter of voice. Because of the hormone surge during their teens, men have much larger vocal cords than do women. Their voices tend to the range from 130 to 145 cycles per second, while those of women range from 230 and 255 per second. The difference is said to be as great as that between a violin and a cello. Many of us prefer listening to a romantic melody sung by a trained soprano, but a baritone resonates far more authority when issuing orders. This is a big reason why the voice of a male fire captain, police captain, or army captain will bring about and maintain a much higher level of attention and confidence than any female counterpart. Topics such as this and so many others here covered are never discussed by the Associated Press, the Gannet newspaper chain, television reporters, or the politically correct personnel now almost as thoroughly embedded in our armed forces as the U.S. Forest Service.

Which brings us back to a final look at the question: what sort of knowledge did most forest supervisors possess in regards to these subjects? During and after graduating from college there is little doubt that most engaged in the extra-curricular reading of natural history, history, psychology, current events, anthropology and perhaps the theory of evolution. But the hard fact is, by the early 1980s, whatever they had learned was no longer relevant since they had already rejected Darwinism and its derivations. Rather, they had bought into that highly commended meme of all post-moderns—Franz Boas' Frankfurt School approved theory of *evolutionary egalitarianism.* That is, over the millennia all races of humans and both genders have evolved equally. It is a presumption that carries as much scientific substance as witchcraft, and far fewer social and spiritual benefits than does the Bible.

Eight million years have passed since the proto-human separated from the ape that was also the proto-chimpanzee. Since that time, man and his closest relative, the chimpanzee, have either sustained or extended the sexual dimorphism of that common ancestor.

About 1.7 million years ago, man's early ancestor ventured out onto the savannah of Africa, and about a million years ago evolved into *homo erectus,* who developed a large cranium and began making use of fire. For hundreds of thousands of years afterward male *homo erectus'* traveled much farther from home than did females, left home more often and did so for many more reasons– to find mates, hunt, forge alliances with neighboring villages and take part in warfare. Thus, by the dawn of *homo sapiens,* more or less 250,000 years ago, male and female had already developed their respective and divergent aptitudes.

Hunting was often a dangerous endeavor. Conflicts between neighboring clans over preferred hunting lands and water sources were even more dangerous. Villagers often came under violent attack by hostile members of the same species intent on seizing their territory and killing as many clan members as possible. If the attack turned into a rout, most all the men were killed. Women of childbearing age and children were carried away and either consigned to slavery or assimilated into the triumphant clan. Often both.

On other occasions the villagers were able to beat off their assailants and months later, when the ideal moment arrived, set out to destroy them. Needless to say those villages that harbored the most physically capable, courageous and resourceful men tended to prevail, enabling them to pass their physical qualities and valor onto the next generation. Today our counterattacks and search and destroy missions are much more sophisticated, just as deadly, and as was the case 250,000 years ago, always carried out by men.

All of which might explain why a disproportionate number of women, as they decline to enter the Wildland Fire Academy, also decline to attend Forest Service Protection School. When they do attend FPO school and receive certificates, they are much less likely to write citations (a phenomenon noted among the nation's police forces). In a single season on a popular off highway vehicle area of the Mendocino Forest, one male forest protection officer wrote 112 tickets, while a second wrote 78. The sole woman on the staff wrote one ticket for the entire period. I listened one afternoon as her supervisor explained his dilemma. Two years prior he had reported that employee's lack of initiative to his district ranger, who then summoned her in for a meeting. There, she admitted that she did not feel comfortable approaching an assemblage of dirt bikers or a crowd of brightly tattooed itinerants. In fact, she did not even feel comfortable dealing with hunters.

He continued: "The ranger then took the step of sending her to forest protection school for a second time. It was unprecedented. They would never have done that for a man." He paused a moment, shook his head in disgust, but then breaking into an ironic grin said, "But good things happen. The next season she doubled her workload. She wrote two tickets."

"What happened then?"

"Well, one afternoon I drove into the SO [Supervisor's Office] and reported that I had a problem employee. And it was her. But [the district ranger] informed me that *I* was the problem employee. That there was only one female on the district with an FPO certificate. And she was going to stay, whether she wrote one ticket, two tickets, or no tickets!"

Evidence suggesting that the conflict between this supervisor and the timid employee is linked to yet another phenomenon, is supported by economist John R. Lott. Drawing upon U.S. Department of Justice statistics and his study of over 150 police departments across the United States, he discovered that a 1% increase in the number of female patrol officers on a police force increases the likelihood of assaults on all officers by 15% to 19%. Regarding women who patrol alone, he wrote, "Clearly if a physical attack takes place, it is much more likely to be directed at a female officer. Criminals are much more likely to attack if they believe the attack will successfully allow them to escape."

The significant sociological changes of the past fifty years (changes that have yet to reach much of the world) have not modified the basic nature of men and women in the least. Three decades of social tinkering has not unraveled what nature has bestowed upon us since the dawn of time. This is why in house-holds the world over, whether in Indonesia or the United States, when a mysterious noise is heard in the night, the man will investigate. When a street thug strong-arms an elderly citizen in Brazil or the United States, it is a man who will attempt to render aid. Similarly, when a phone call is received from a relative at an airport in the midst of a sleet storm, whether in Finland or the United States, it is the man who will drive to the terminal.

Finally, when the rain gutters fill with leaves, whether in Japan or America, it is almost always the man who ascends the ladder. A number of evolutionists, among them Steven Rhoades, Terry Burnham and Jay Phelan, the latter co-authors of *Mean Genes*, have concluded that the dichotomy between the human sexes is so great that when undertaking a study, they deal with men and women as if they were different subspecies.

There yet remains the critical point regarding the fact that so few men now work inside the forest service's regional, forest, and district offices. We know *why* it happened and *how* it happened, but beyond the wiping out of the forest militia, there are negative consequences to eradicating men from office workplaces.

One morning in Berkeley I came across *Male, Female, the Evolution of Human Sex Differences,* by American Psychological Association member David Geary. His conclusions confirmed the results of several other studies, but Geary was particularly deft at connecting the psychological dots that run from man to man, woman to woman, and man to woman, creating an image that was startling in its clarity. This was in sharp contrast to today's television newscasters and movie manufacturers, whose most important objective is to scramble all established, or newly revealed male/female character lines that might form a more comprehensive image of ourselves.

Geary undertook a study of several summer camps, studying how boys and girls in their early teens developed relationships with members of their own sex. At each camp, which included separate lodges with their own roster of youths, he repeatedly found that boys engaged in much more overt challenges to one another. The struggle for status within their hierarchy began immediately and involved name calling, shoving, fist fighting and the building of coalitions.

The *alpha boy* who eventually emerged was usually one of the strongest, brightest, most organized and good looking. Although shifts occasionally occurred within different lodges through the summer, the process of determining the alpha, the beta and the hierarchy below was generally concluded inside of two weeks.

Once the hierarchy was established and each youth understood his place, the alpha boy went about (within parameters set by adults) organizing the day's pursuits, which included a good deal of risk-taking activities and games involving competition between lodges—softball, badminton and volley ball. There were also task orientations, such as competing with another team to erect the best shelter in the shortest time possible to spend the night in. In describing their leader, the boys tended to use such terms as *organizes activities, knows what to do, makes the right decisions* and is *considerate at tolerating his underlings.*

Geary learned that girls at summer camps presented parallels, but with notable differences. Their moves toward dominance began more slowly, were much more subtle and seldom involved overt name-calling and shoving. Rather than directing a brusque remark across a lunch table such as: God, what a slob! as a boy might do, the soon-to-be alpha girl might turn to a friend and say, "Would you tell Cathy to take a napkin and wipe that jelly off her face."

The girl's dominance hierarchy, like the boy's, ultimately determined who was number one, two and so forth and again it was often through the use of coalitions. The hierarchy also settled such questions as who got the biggest portion for dessert, the most comfortable bunk, which TV programs to watch and who got to comb whose hair. Girls tended to describe their ideal leader in such terms as *she relates to my problems,* is *friendly, outgoing, patient,* and *considerate in respecting the needs and feelings of others.* The terms are in striking contrast to those the boys used, although there is some overlap such as in *is considerate at tolerating his underlings.*

Geary found two other important differences. When not watching TV or reading, the girls spent much of their free time walking and talking. They seldom engaged in any competition, even in such non-physical matches as chess, backgammon or card playing.

In their 2004 study, Joyce Benenson and Joy Schinazi found that girls tended to disapprove of those girls who outperformed them. In fact, many girls, correctly anticipating that their friends would react negatively toward them if they outperformed, very often *blew* the competition in order to keep their friends.

By contrast, the study found that boys actively sought out boys of higher status and took great pleasure in competing to see if they could outperform them in an assortment of tasks. Those who lost came back to try time and again, and despite the additional losses seemed to enjoy themselves. In another study, Sarah Hrd found that when a quarrel broke out among girls over the rules of a proposed game, the game was almost always terminated before it started. By contrast, the boys seemed to enjoy quarreling over the rules almost as much as the game itself.

Another important dynamic discovered by Geary was, however quickly and violently the boys began testing one another, once their hierarchy was established it was stable, lasting through the summer with each boy having more or less accepted his position. The changes that did occur almost always resulted from a coalition shift.

Strangely enough, he found that after the alpha girls had established themselves, they often disengaged from their group. Upon doing so they spent most of their time with one, two or three best friends, forming a select association that mingled with the others only on occasion and only at their own pleasure.

The dominant boys by contrast, never disengaged from their group, and spent most of their free time directing the *gang* in competitive activities against other gangs. In summary, the alpha boys were much more desirous and successful at controlling their groups than the alpha girls.

Within six weeks in the womb, boys and girls begin to behave differently owing a large surge of androgens into what will be a male fetus. With this in mind, our childhood experiences, as well as the above observations, there is every reason to believe that through high school and college, members of the two sexes will continue down parallel paths that ever diverge. It therefore follows that men will develop competencies that not only forge coalitions, but coalitions that are cohesive, and effective.

In its three decade quest to diminish men to just 57% of leadership positions, the forest service has demonstrated just how compelling Geary's findings are. Many of the agency's former alpha males tended to remain in their positions for years, often under the most trying circumstances. Today, the agency's alpha females become dismayed by unexpected events, take criticism much more personally, and transfer out at rates far higher than their predecessors. This is one more reason why so few forest supervisors, district rangers and administrative assistants know their forests—the terrain, vegetation, and climate like the *backs of their hands.*

Another important reason the service has deteriorated to such an extent, is that once a man has found his specialty, be it budget, hydrology, law enforcement, forestry, or mining, he will often work twelve hours a day, five days a week to achieve his objective. According to Warren Farrell in *Why*

Men Earn More, all across the spectrum, including office positions, men on average work three more hours a week than
women. More astonishing is the fact that men are four times
as likely to spend fifty hours a week at their desks, which of
course is why the vast majority of CEOs are men. They too
transfer from their positions, but tend to transfer only after
their projects have been completed or an opportunity for a
more lucrative position has presented itself.

Over the past six years numerous studies have been conducted about the human brain and the differences between
men and women. All emphasize the fact that women transmit information from the right side of the brain to the left
more frequently, which in turn means they are more cogni-
zant of subtle events taking place about them. And why they
are more responsive to the feelings of others. It is an asset
the forest service and every other government agency has
sought to take advantage of. Conversely, men do not transmit
information from the right to the left side of their brains as
frequently. This is why they are more focused, less likely to be
distracted by subtle events about them, and less considerate
of others. It is also why they are able to develop concepts and
then work out the steps necessary to apply those concepts.
It is a big reason why men receive well over 90% of the pat-
ents issued, And, as in centuries past, why they continue to
produce the overwhelming number of the world's technical,
philosophic, and artistic achievements. These are assets the
forest service and every other government agency, has absolutely refused to acknowledge, let alone take advantage of.

As Geary observed, once the alpha female succeeds in her
quest for dominance, her journey very often comes to an end.
Having become the most cherished person in her department,
she has achieved everything she has ever wished to achieve.
The next phase, striving to ensure the coalition she forged

meets the challenges of the office and its assigned mission, is often academic. Far fewer alpha women are willing to work fifty hours a week. Moreover, strong sensitivity to criticism, and conflicting emotional demands—both inside and outside the workplace—leave an inordinate number in depression.

Anthropologist Helen Fisher wrote that the norm for women was to seek consensus and harmony. If a women breaks from this mold she finds it very difficult to work with others, and is ostracized. Thus those immeasurable qualities of curiosity and office dissent, so often found in a man's workplace, are not present in a workplace dominated by women, simply because they are not welcome.

Men get upset too, erupting into terrific shouting matches, but the shouting and name-calling seldom severs the relationship. In the corridor the next day one man will make a comment about last night's football game, and the argument is all but over. Bitter as their disputes might be, there is very little ostracism among men; by contrast, ostracism is commonplace among women.

There is also a man's unique ability to remain *detached*. Interpersonal attraction does not necessarily translate into a group undertaking. Male supervisors often pick specific individuals as part of a team when assuming a task, yet when the day is over and it is time to exchange stories over a few beers, he often heads to the bar with someone entirely different.

Women do not possess the same detachment. When undertaking a project, they have a tendency to select friends who relate to their problems and are considerate in respecting their feelings. She cannot work with an employee she is not fond of or who raises uncomfortable questions, even if that employee is famously proficient at what she does. Thus, when selecting for a technological or commercial undertaking, they are less likely to choose a top-notch team.

This is not to claim that women should be systematically excluded from such teams. Should a choice arise between a man who is a learned civil engineer, but not adept at explaining himself or organizing presentations, and a woman with somewhat less technical expertise, but who is skillful at illuminating the task at hand, she should be chosen.

Finally, there are the absenteeism and retention factors. According to J.R. Meisenheimer—by no means an opponent of equal opportunity for females in the workplace—women have a 58% higher rate of absenteeism than men. No less a multiculturalist, than T.H. Cox reported that many companies had offered women flexible work schedules in order to attend to child rearing. Absenteeism fell, but within two years, it had returned to prior levels. Finally, women are 50% more likely than men to leave a management position.

Hence, among the biggest reasons the forest service has stripped both its forests and the taxpayers of the returns they are entitled to, is because of its methodical elimination of men from the office workplace. But the gender racketeers and sorcerers, entrenched as they are, continue to live out their lies—scandalous lies their far less educated, but far more intuitive grandparents knew to be such. They live out their canards with a great dread that any open discussion of the human sexual dichotomy, will reveal what their grandparents knew to be true. Thirty years of fabricating an egalitarian house of cards has produced a fright so extreme, a taboo on discussing the myth that rules, is a prerequisite for employment with the forest service, every other government bureau, and every last news agency.

Chapter 18

THE CAULFIELD DECISION

Our judges are as honest as other men and not more so. They have with others the same passions for party, for power, and the privilege of their corps. Their maxim is boni judicis est ampliare jurisdictionem [good justice is broad jurisdiction], and their power the more dangerous as they are in office for life and not responsible, as the other functionaries are, to the elective control... —Thomas Jefferson, 1820

BOTH JUDGE CONTI and the Ninth Circuit Court of Appeals had turned aside the Male Class Complaint. Still, it continued to play a powerful role as a clearing house for individual employee suits. Each plaintiff was advised as to what steps were necessary in presenting their cases before the Department of Agriculture, and failing there, the Justice Department's EEOO. It would also continue to play an important role in disseminating news to the membership as well as to Congressman Wally Herger, whose district covered more forest service land than any other House member in California.

Through the first half of 1993, the Male Class, applying what is known as the Freedom of Information Act (FOIA), pressed Region Five director Ron Stewart to pass on copies of all employee exit interviews; that is, those interviews of employees who had chosen to leave employment since Bernardi's beginning. Because a very high number cited discrimination and a hostile work environment, Stewart refused to issue them. Hence, the class was forced to appeal to the Washington Office, which under rules set by Congress, mailed not less than 2,000 pages of exit interviews.

Many of those affording the interviews were long-time employees who never received a forest service send-off and who attended an offsite party arranged by co-workers, sorry to see them go, but hoping to one day soon depart themselves. Frequently present at the offsite party were numbers of women who also hoped to soon depart. The exit interviews greatly aided Louis Demas in winning every case he filed against the forest service. They also aided hundreds of employees who filed individual grievances that reached the formal stage within the Department of Justice.

On October 28, 1993, Cathy Slobogin of ABC's *20/20* interviewed Bob Grate and Jerry Levitoff at Grate's home in Chester, California—a small town near Lake Almanor. Slobogin remained through the afternoon and well into evening, accepting an invitation to dinner. Grate described her as sympathetic to the Male Class. She confessed that her husband, employed by the FBI, had been greatly troubled over recently being *passed over* by a new female employee. Their six hours together was edited into a fifteen-minute segment of 20/20; nonetheless it was seen across the country and jarred many.

Again, most shaken were employees of other federal agencies. Although discrimination against men had been widespread since the early 1980s, nowhere had it yet reached the intensity of the forest service. Indeed, for reasons already

cited the agency had been able to detonate its own social
Chernobyl within a piece of political real estate that included
Berkeley, Hollywood, and Ghirardelli Square, all the while
managing to seal off knowledge of that blast from the outside
world.

When Congress passed the 1991 Civil Rights Act—in
some respects a badly flawed piece of legislation—it emphatically declared race or sex-norming to be unconstitutional.
Despite its illegality, handicapping by gender and race continued apace through almost all federal agencies. It was if
the U.S. Senate and House of Representatives did not exist.
The great enablers, of course, were the Bush and Clinton
Administrations, both caulked with social progressives, and
their fellow travelers within the news corporations.

Late that November, Catherine Crier of CNN's *Crier and
Company* also interviewed Grate and Levitoff. Crier, herself a
lawyer and former judge, assured the two they had an excellent case, but without the backing of the Clinton Justice
Department— then under the stewardship of Janet Reno—
they stood little chance of success. Crier's presentation created further turmoil among government employees at large.

The reaction was so strong that it prompted Phil Donahue
to design a program devoted to the merits of affirmative
action. Grate and Levitoff were invited to take part in the
broadcast, and both, naturally eager to bolster their momentum, accepted. Neither they, their wives or co-workers had
ever given the Donahue show more than a cursory glance.
They assumed they would be presenting their points of view
to a panel of affirmative action advocates of equal number,
and that the audience would encompass both supporters
and opponents. They had no idea that Phil Donahue was
not the fair and just master of ceremonies he pretended to
be. Indeed, the evidence is conclusive that it was he who lay

the groundwork for Oprah Winfrey and her most pernicious article of faith–*Every American a Victim.*

Fortunately, the day before the two were to depart for Los Angeles, they received a phone call from an unnamed member of the staff, warning them that they were being set up. Indeed, Donahue had already lined up a panel of seven rationing advocates to oppose them. In addition, he was packing his audience with affirmative action supporters, who were to interrupt Grate and Levitoff on cue. Following a hurried discussion, the two pulled out of the show and Donahue was left with a panel of seven quota advocates and a large crowd of their backers with no one to jeer at.

The *20/20* and *Crier and Company* segments did not take the press corps by storm. Once again, the news organizations either omitted the *California Decree* entirely, or did their best to impress upon the country that it was no more than a fight between two mice. When a reporter did ask Forest Service Spokesman Matt Mathes about the discrimination charges, he made two comments. "We're looking at it more as a matter of cultural change, rather than discrimination." And, "In the past, selection rates were totally out of balance. We, through the current consent decree, were trying to correct some past imbalances."

The first statement was in essence an admission that the forest service's objective was the elimination of its male culture. The second was intended to—and indeed was successful—in giving comfort to every major news outlet in the United States. Not one reporter was prompted to investigate the agency to determine what precisely was taking place. Within months of Mathes' statements, Richard Henry, supervisor of the Lassen Forest, having learned nothing from thirteen years of catastrophe, issued the following series of directives.

It was reported to us that the use of the Office of Personnel Management Register is being discouraged unless you have a minority veteran applicant that you would like to hire. Past experience with the Register is that it provides us with too many non-minority veterans.

An attempt was made to create full entry positions at GS-03 and GS-04 levels with women. We were not successful. There were too many males at the top of the registers....The registers were cancelled.

We are proposing GS-2/3/4 firefighter positions ... these positions will only be filled with women or minorities...we are also proposing a GS 3/4/5 in resources which we will only fill with a woman or a minority...the forest supervisor has committed to filling all new hire temporary positions with women... you must also keep in mind that regardless of whether or not an adverse impact occurs, selections of females must significantly exceed those of males...

...in a growing number of instances we are not filling positions when there are no women applicants. In the past three months we have either re-advertised, left vacant, or filled with unqualified temporaries eleven permanent fire positions because we could find no female applicants... I will not sign a 52 [a listing of applicants] without female candidates being identified who, if offered, will accept the position. If we can't find a female, then we may have to restructure who reports to who [demote], or drop a module [firefighting unit].—Dick Henry

Henry took these measures a full five years after the Maupin White Paper appeared and almost two years after Judge Conti, Monitor Meyer and Judith Kurtz had cleared out of his forest. In fact, all other units in California continued to operate in a similar manner, even though individual plaintiffs were winning case after case. Indeed, the litigation load was such that up to fifteen justice department attorneys continued to be rotated in and out of the state.

By now, from New Hampshire to Florida and Colorado to Washington State, each of the 155 forest supervisors in the other regions was conducting business in a manner similar to Henry, although generally with a good less zeal. None left behind a trail of paper quite so littered as his.

In another bit of arcane irony, as Mike Espy's office was in the midst of polishing its defense of Kyle Felker, it had flown an attorney to California with orders to defend the agency against the Levitoff Class Complaint. Nothing personal mind you...the Department of Agriculture stood to lose a fortune should Levitoff prevail. In addition to the class plaintiffs, thousands of aggrieved employees from across the country were likely to emerge from the woods and file their own suits. Hence, the schizophrenic position taken by his office—ruling in favor of individual plaintiffs, while simultaneously opposing the Levitoff Class.

That is how matters stood in December 1993 when the complaint was taken up by Northern District Judge Barbara Caulfield to whom the case had been turned over. Representing Levitoff was Louis Demas, who after outlining the means by which the class members had been denied constitutional protections, highlighted the reverse discrimination case known as Martin v Wilks, brought before the U.S. Supreme Court in 1983.

The suit had been filed by the firefighters of Birmingham, Alabama who had not been a part of an original consent decree that had ordered the city to hire additional black firefighters. Citing Martin v Wilks, Demas quoted the U.S. Supreme Court. "...a decree among parties to a law suit resolves issues among them, but does not deny relief to those employees who were not a part of the proceedings." He was of course stating that the Levitoff members had not been present in 1979, when the Bernardi Decree was arrived at. Martin v Wilks provided excellent legal authority, because in the years since, a number of federal courts had cited the same case in passing judgment.

He then turned to a Sixth Circuit Court of Appeals ruling in 1992, Vogel v the City of Cincinnati, wherein the city had successfully sued for relief from a consent decree because a lower court had reached far beyond the decree's original parameters. Here Demas argued that the forest service had ranged far beyond Bernardi by instituting quotas, when in fact the decree stated that only the best qualified candidates could be hired or promoted; and that the agency was continuing to employ quotas long after the decree had ended.

The opposing U.S. Attorney took his turn, arguing that when the Male Class Complaint's motion to lift Bernardi had been denied in 1990, it had left the forest service with no option but to continue the decree. Judge Conti may not have cited any aspect of law, but his ruling stood. Martin v Wilks and Vogel v Cincinnati therefore could not apply to the Levitoff Complaint.

He then cited GTE, Sylvania v Consumers Union, decided in 1975 by the Fourth U.S. Circuit Court. In its original form, GTE, Sylvania v Consumer's Union comprised a consent decree that put a stop to certain documents being released to the public. When a third party, GTE—not present when the decree was entered into—attempted to release the documents, it was barred from doing so until that decree was lifted. In effect, the attorney stated that third parties, even though not a part of an original decree, were bound by it.

The strength of Demas' case becomes apparent when one recognizes that GTE, Sylvania v Consumer's Union had nothing whatever to do with the denial of anyone's individual rights. And that Martin v Wilks, which succeeded GTE, Sylvania v Consumer's Union by eight years, identically paralleled the Levitoff Case.

Not yet out of ammunition, he turned to the Civil Rights Act of 1991, in which Congress had inserted the following provision: "Petitioners are entitled to prosecute complaints if they can establish that they did not receive notice of the consent decree; that they were not given reasonable opportunity to present objections to the decree, that they were not adequately represented by another party in the litigation when the consent decree is issued." 99.9% of the employees of the U.S. Forest Service had no one representing their interests when the decree was arrived at.

Finally there was the 1989 case of Richmond v Croson in which the swing justice, Sandra Day O'Connor, writing for the majority, made clear that local and city governments (and therefore by extension federal units) must be found guilty of deliberate discrimination, otherwise they could not be forced to grant preferential treatment in order to reach racial or gender parity. Demas was preparing to cite both the Callenberger and Leveroos cases, vindicated by Secretary of Agriculture Mike Espy, when Caulfield suddenly cut him short and adjourned court.

On December 14, 1993 she reconvened and ruled that since the Male Class Complaint's 1990 motion to intervene had been rejected, the forest service could not be expected to operate outside what its attorney had depicted as the rule of law. Which rule of law, Caulfield never cited, since the Ninth Circuit had not referenced any. It therefore followed that the Levitoff Class was barred from applying both Martin v Wilks, and Vogel v Cincinnati. She next stated, contradicting the text of the 1991 Civil Rights Act, "In any event as the district court recognized, it is well established (in this Court as elsewhere) that non-parties to the consent decree lack standing to interpret its terms or to challenge the parties interpretations of the obligation under it." Finally, ignoring the case of Richmond v Crosnon, she ordered the clerk to close the file.

Did Judge Caulfield enter the courtroom with justice in mind, or had ideological considerations prevailed? Was she running legal interference to sustain the reputation of a troubled fellow justice? The fact that she willfully misread the 1991 Civil Rights Act, the fact that Levitoff identically paralleled Martin v Wilks, and the fact that she would not permit Demas to cite Callenberger and Leveroos, suggests that either ideology, the salvation of Judge Conti's legal legacy or both were major factors in her decision.

On March 10, 1994, Demas petitioned the Ninth Circuit Court of Appeals regarding Caulfield's decision, a step fraught with hazards, as the Ninth Circuit was by far the most liberal appellate in the United States. Aware that his chances were less than sanguine, he also knew that each case was usually heard by a three-judge panel, as opposed to the entire twenty-eight member court (the number has since grown to 47). Hence, there was always a chance that one of the court's rare conservatives or a moderate might be chosen to hear the case.

The Caulfield decision prompted a stream of letters into Congressman Wally Herger's office. Startled by some of the material he received, in January 1994 he issued a press release in which he attacked the service's *Thought Control Program.* Citing four recent job announcements, he noted that two years had passed since the consent decree had ended, yet the agency was still posting notices that read, "Demonstrates a commitment to civil rights, or contributes to a diverse work force."

That year Demas mailed Herger the *Uniform Guidelines for Selection Procedures,* the post 1964 Civil Rights Act yardstick cited by Wardell Townsend in his decision regarding Greg Gregor. By that criteria, the hiring and promotion of racial groups and genders with comparable training backgrounds must be within 80% of all others. Yet, when the numbers for all nine forest regions were toted up, white male hiring stood at just 53% of female—far below what was legally permissible.

Grate and Levitoff also mailed Herger a letter documenting that over the past four years, some ranger districts had filled their fire trainee positions almost exclusively with female and minority candidates, a selection process prohibited by Public Law 102-166 of the Civil Rights Act of 1991. They also reported that management was now *strategizing* means by which positions irrelevant to forestry operations could be created for affirmative action purposes only.

These discussions on the best means by which employees could be awarded positions by phenotype were taking place in open forums, at a time everyone acknowledged that critical positions were being left vacant because no woman or minority could be found to fill them. They were also taking place in front of the same highly qualified individuals who had applied for those critical positions, and been rejected because they were of the wrong sex.

Upon reviewing the documents, Herger wrote a letter to Chief Forester Jack Ward Thomas accusing him of practicing discrimination. He noted that one of Thomas's own memos stated that "non-minority women, minority men and minority women have a higher rate of competitive promotions than their proportion in the applicant pool."

Thomas answered Herger in a letter filled with misconceptions, obfuscations and recitations not relative to the inquiry. By way of interest, he was the first chief forester not to have worked his way up through service ranks and in fact had been selected by President Clinton because of general unhappiness over Dale Robertson. Not that Robertson was forced out because of his lack of commitment to a more feminized forest environment. Rather, because he was held in disfavor by environmental groups, particularly those promoting the Northwest Forest Plan—the main object of which was protection of the Northern Spotted Owl. However stridently Robertson might hold forth on feminism, most environmentalists regarded him as little more than a logger attired in a skirt.

Shortly after Robertson's departure, Ron Stewart's sovereignty over Region Five came to an end. Early in 1994 Secretary Espy ordered him to cease awarding $5000 to those forest supervisors most committed to apportioning jobs by gender. When Bob Grate learned that, to the contrary, the director had actually expanded his gift giving, he informed Espy. He in turn phoned Stewart, told him to clean out his desk and report back to Washington. Grate claims Stewart flew into such a rage that he was heard shouting far down the corridor of his San Francisco headquarters, "I'm not going anywhere! I'm not going anywhere! You people can out and out kiss my ass!"

He was replaced by Lynn Sprague, a less combative director with an affinity for western wear, but whose liberality was known to everyone, and who was convinced that rationing careers by gender was the only means by which a forest could sustain its environment. In fact, the following year, two out of the four regional awards Sprague disbursed were owing to civil rights activities. He was as meticulous as Stewart in maintaining the blacklist against those employees who had filed discrimination cases. Under his regime, only through the sheer ineptitude of his staff was any man who filed a suit ever promoted.

One of those who won a suit and was never again promoted was Tom Locker, who has since left the service. His long struggle with the agency, resulting in his filing of nine individual suits, has already been told. Much like Leroy Johnson, he still holds a measure of guilt regarding his role with the agency before filing his first suit.

> *When I got ready to hire seasonals I was told to put men and women applications in separate stacks. I then interviewed or attempted to interview every women applicant before a single man was contacted.*

Locker reflected for a few seconds, then continued.

> *I should have fought it. It affected people's lives. But I didn't think about it very much.*

As a fire management officer in the Inyo Forest, he served on many fire teams throughout the Western United States. One of the most disturbing phenomena he came across was that not a single female fire management officer he worked with had any firsthand knowledge of fighting fires. Said Locker in a matter-of-fact fashion, "Not a single female I met had served in the all-important *initial attack module* positions. Yet they were all collecting the highest salaries possible among the forest service fire crews, without ever having taken part in fighting a fire."

This was one big reason why so few women—the Storm King Mountain and Thirtymile Fires not withstanding—lost their lives fighting fires and a big reason why so many millions of acres in timber went up in smoke.

Locker went on to make another point. By 1980 all forests in the United States realized they were entering a time of struggle so intense that it can best be likened to placing a human head on an anvil and pounding it with two hammers. Pounding the head with one hammer were the vested interests—timber, grazing and mining operators. Pounding the head with a second hammer were the environmental groups who filed numerous law suits challenging the agency's relationship with the traditional users.

The service should have been acting as a referee sorting out which environmental grievances were genuine and which were not, thereby averting many years of costly litigation. Unhappily, at this very juncture, the agency of its own volition passed out a third hammer, this one to the Equal Rights Advocates. According to Tom:

> *With promotions among managers based on their ability to carry out social programs, the service's most experienced employees departed. With their departure the ability to manage the forests plummeted in rough proportion to the number of lawsuits filed by the environmentalists.*

Present at the interview was Tom's wife, Nina, an Asian-American, formerly a landscape architect employed by the regional office, which has since been relocated to Vallejo. As she put it, "They wanted Asians badly, both men and women.

But the Asians did not want to work in remote sections of the state. This was because their parents lived in the Bay Area, and they did not want to leave their families..."

She continued, "For the forest supervisor it was 'Check off a box for the ethnic group.' That was even if the color of your face was white. That way they got credit for the racial preferences." She underscored the fact that the forest service's educational programs often duplicated those already in place by state and county agencies and ended the subject matter with the following quote.

> *But the forest service was glad to give those students an experience. Even if they did not come back.*

Chapter 19

THE STORY OF JACK WARD THOMAS

The fighting goes on and accelerates in frequency and intensity. The people, our sense of community and the Forests are bruised and battered in the process. The gladiators never tire of the fight—it is what they do. The fight itself provides their sustenance. I detect however that many concerned about Forests collectively have long since approached exhaustion—Jack Ward Thomas

A NUMBER OF significant points in this chapter are taken from a speech Jack Ward Thomas gave at the Horace Albright Conservation Lectureship in April 1992, the year before he became chief of the U.S. Forest Service. Others are drawn from his book, *Jack Ward Thomas, the Journal of a Forest Service Chief*, published after he left office. He was the first chief who did not rise through the ranks, and in fact was a political appointee. Possessed of ideals solidly founded within the environmental movement, it appears that he hoped to turn the agency into a bureau with objectives very similar to those of the U.S. Fish and Wildlife Service.

The many themes he made in his speech underscore the reasons why his impending tenure as chief would be less than successful. He began the talk by portraying the role scientists have played over the centuries in providing building blocks of knowledge, and then synthesizing that knowledge into applicable formulas. Until twenty years prior, this meant a scientist could depend on his technical expertise alone to win an argument in the realm of public debate. There were no worries about political ramifications, at least in the Western World.

But as he made clear, to be technically correct was no longer sufficient to remain a scientist in good standing. Scientists were now required to bring to the debate *an attitude*. In fact, as he explained, he and his associates were ill-prepared for the vicious name calling that arose in both the scientific and social arenas after the cultural upheaval of the 1960s. By the mid-1980s the reputations of many scientists, built up over decades of hard work and research, were being put to the stake by the gladiators of post-modern science, ever seeking an opening to attack their credibility, intelligence, and motivations.

It was not their powerful commitment to saving the red legged frog, the wolverine or the marbled murrelet that Thomas found so out of the ordinary. Indeed, in the past it was the vigorous commitment of individuals that had saved the bison, pronghorn and bighorn sheep from extinction. Rather, among postmodern scientists, all the glory lay in the struggle—their brawls and persecutions in many respects paralleling those of the Spanish Inquisition. The zeal of the post-moderns was such that they eagerly went about destroying the personal reputations of anyone who did not display a proper attitude.

At the time of his lecture, Thomas was unaware of the power the *social* scientists had assumed over the agency he was about to ostensibly lead. For Judith Kurtz, Jeannie Meyer,

Dale Robertson and Ron Stewart, all the glory had been in the struggle—a struggle in which they had emerged triumphant. That the forest service was now too crippled to manage its properties was not a concern of theirs.

Another point he made at the Albright Lectureship was the often unrecognized fact that when progressive environmentalists found themselves losing the battle of facts—which was more often the case than not—they invariably resorted to name calling. Even more effective than name calling was their talent for obfuscating the issues, as opposed to clarifying them. The master obfuscators were their attorneys hired to represent them in the courtrooms, and whose clamorous daubing of the facts quite often resulted in legal victories at a tremendous cost to taxpayers. It is easy to recognize the identical approaches used by the environmental extremists and the multicultural gladiators of the U.S. Forest Service, whose only talents lay in propaganda, obfuscation, and stratagems to ostracize the opposition.

Thomas then turned to the scientific method, noting that "when computers devour the data, perform the model's magic and then produce results that do not ring true in the light of theory, empirical data, experience, common sense and professional opinion, caution lights should be flashed on, and alarm bells rung." Yet throughout the service the functionaries had already switched off the flashers, and disconnected the alarm bells. They had long since ceased to study empirical data, engage in common sense thinking, or seek professional guidance.

At another juncture, he asked if scientists were still developing and testing protocols. Were customs and regulations dealing with formality, precedence, etiquette and ethics being adhered to? In the agency he was about to lead, multiculturalism had already brought about the extinction of ethics, etiquette, customs and protocols.

He also noted that "complexity seems to increase steadily with rapidly shifting public opinion, formulations of new laws, periodic court opinions and surges of gladiators into the arena." All true. The agency he would be leading possessed the most complex array of hiring formulas devised on the planet. As he would soon learn, because it operated in such secrecy, there was never a resultant shift of public opinion. Formulations of new laws such as the Civil Service Reform Act of 1978 and the Civil Rights Act of 1991 had been enacted, but the forest service had found it easy to circumvent them. Court opinions of a sort did exist, but because of collusion between the court and the agency, no *bona fide* legal opinions existed. And, other than the Male Class Complaint, all of the gladiator surges had originated within the ranks of feminists, both inside and outside the agency.

Thomas finally turned to the conflict between environmentalists and the needs of local communities, stating, "The welfare of these communities is a legitimate concern of elected officials—and all politics are indeed local. Furthermore the Forest Service has a policy of aiding in the creation and maintenance of community stability in such circumstances."

By 1986 the service had abandoned its decades-long principle of stabilizing the communities in its midst by hiring the locals. Strangely enough, this turn of events took place at a time the environmental movement on the African Continent had determined that setting aside large tracts of land for preservation and ignoring those who resided adjacent the tracts, was not working. Rather, it had led to bitterness among the villagers and relentless poaching and habitat destruction. By the late 1980's, environmentalists had concluded that the only means by which Africa's parks could be saved was by educating and hiring the locals to perform most of the work.

Over the past twenty years, this concept has been adopted by every African nation that retains a substantial wildlife population.

This revolution in resource management took place at a time the U.S. Forest Service was sacrificing local populations to the altar of metropolitan multiculturalism. By 1993, the residents of hundreds of communities across the United States could no longer identify with an agency that owned huge swathes of land in their midst, and which treated them as pariahs.

Even before Thomas assumed its helm, numerous outbreaks of vandalism had occurred to forest service structures across the country. As he later wrote, "A hostile local population, although small in number, becomes troubling with increasing violence directed at the agency and its employees." In 1998 alone, agency employees and the buildings out of where they worked were attacked or threatened nearly one hundred times.

In December 1993, upon becoming chief, Thomas knew the agency had its detractors, of which he had been one. Still, he appears to have believed that the general character of a forest employee—loyalty, trust, hard work, ambition— was still intact and with a bit of tinkering, his workforce would adopt a more preservationist outlook in managing its resources. This was probably why his first act as Chief was to issue a memo to all forest employees urging them to, "Tell the truth, obey the law, and practice ecosystem management."

He was not yet aware that for years *not* telling the truth had been the agency's primary management tool, that laws were being broken daily by the hundreds, and that even though many of his employees might wish to practice ecosystem management, few were left with the aptitude to do so. Across 175 forests and grasslands he found just 100 ecologists, which in large part was why, after numerous legal tangles with the environmental gladiators, he wrote, "The Forest Service lost much more frequently in court than it ever won."

In his book, *Jack Ward Thomas, the Journal of a Forest Service Chief,* he went on to explain his concept of personnel management, which in many respects paralleled that of Pinchot, Graves, and McArdle. Once his employees embraced ecosystem management, the forests would be managed from the bottom up, not the top down. Plans would be initiated in the forests, passed on to the regional offices, and then to Washington, where minor adjustments might be made. But he soon learned that his management model had long since been turned on its head and was a big reason why a good portion of his budget went to seed before it ever left Washington. Within months he learned the regional offices were also looting.

The forests aside, within weeks he found the entire Department of Agriculture was in turmoil. Mike Espy was in the midst of his departure and would soon be replaced by Dan Glickman. For the most part, he would find himself dealing not with Glickman, but his Assistant Secretary of Agriculture, James Lyons. Not only was Lyons a meddling micromanager, he was a cultural cringing multiculturalist, who almost immediately demanded to know what progress Thomas was making in his rationing of jobs.

The Chief reported back that nationwide, in 1993 white men represented 72.8% of the promotional pool, yet had received just 52% of the promotions. The following year white men comprised 71% of the promotion pool, but had received just 45.2% of the promotions. He also reported that in 1993 there were 261 retirement buyouts and that the great majority were among white males—thus enabling the service to recruit more women and minorities. The veteran employees who were bought out had of course taken with them the energy, the know-how and that immeasurable quality so important to forest management—curiosity.

1993 was also the year that Thomas and a group of environmental organizations put the finishing touches to the Northwest Forest Plan. In essence, it called for the preservation of all late succession and old growth forests, and that a 50 to 300 foot non-cutting zone would be established along each salmon and steelhead trout stream. These tracts of land covered large portions of seventeen national forests and seven Bureau of Land Management districts in Northern California, Oregon and Washington. Thomas thus had the seeming good fortune to be taking the helm of the forest service just in time to put what was essentially his own plan into effect.

Yet by mid-1994 he discovered that he could not implement it. The surveying and mapping had proved extraordinarily costly—running from $35 to $125 per acre, depending on the terrain. By the middle of his second year he was complaining about the incredible length of time required to conduct the surveys, in many instances projected to last three years. In truth, with so many cartographers, engineers, hydrologists and surveyors having left the service's employ, there were very few employees on the ground who could implement his plan. In addition, the massive cash allotments siphoned off by the regional and forest offices to sustain social programs all but ensured that the Northwest Forest Plan, as envisioned, would fail. Each unit was thus forced to curtail its surveys, and by-in-large vacate the forest. A less ambitious Northwest Forest Plan was developed then also shelved, to be followed by yet another, even less ambitious revision.

The Chief noted in his diary that his workforce was "badly demoralized and confused, filled with malaise and contention." But things were about to get worse. In 1995 the service, in the face of its fast-fading Northwest Forest Plan, unwilling to discharge any women or minorities, began offering additional buyouts of its remaining white males. In testimony before a U.S. Senate subcommittee, Thomas reported that 500 had been bought out in a single month. By the year 1999, 2,500 more were slated to be bought out.

Despite this mind-blowing disaster, the Chief was forced to watch from the sidelines as his more savvy functionaries went about decapitating his agency...the agency he had for so long aspired to lead into the realm of preservation. Rendered immobile by events about him, he could only register disgust in his diary. But the sorry fact is, even if he had managed to derail the buyouts, it would probably have made little difference. For years, these fellows had been subject to such rancorous dosages of *hate the white male* propaganda, on the mornings they did appear for work, they simply dodged out the back door into a green truck and disappeared for the day.

The Chief was frequently called upon to testify before the U.S. Senate Natural Resource sub-committee where he often clashed with its more conservative members. His accounts of those meetings also revealed the feeble state of his organization. When Washington Senator Patty Murray requested an increase in timber salvage operations in her state, he protested that he had too few skilled employees to do the assessments. "It takes time to hire and train the qualified people to do the work," he said, shortly after another buyout of those highly trained and qualified people.

At another committee meeting, South Dakota Senators Tom Daschle and Tim Johnson complained about the tremendous backlog of unprocessed national grassland grazing permits. Both suggested advancing the service additional funds to speed up the process. Thomas demurred, stating that money was not the problem. He simply did not have the soil managers, range managers and geologists to assess range conditions.

One of the most wrenching events to occur during his tenure was the 1994 Storm King Mountain Fire in Colorado, which cost the lives of sixteen firefighters—four of whom were women. He immediately flew to the site to console the survivors, after which the press peppered him with questions about who was responsible. The frenetic nature of the news conference irritated him, and he later observed, "We probably could start by appreciating firefighters a bit more than we have. It's pretty hard to build a career in the fire business. The grades are not high enough so you get diverted off into other things in order to make a decent living...you look at those heroes and everyone is applauding at the end of the fire season. And they go home and cough another three months. They've got no hospitalization, no retirement, we don't pay them enough..."

By then, Thomas was aware that the service had been criminally negligent in its rationing of fire positions by gender. But as the "new chief on the block," totally unfamiliar with agency operations, he had no control over the regional barons. It is curious that John N. Maclean, author of *Fire on the Mountain*, a detailed account of the Storm King Mountain Fire, noted that the service had debased its Harvard Step Test and that its firefighters were carrying 45 pound packs, as opposed to the 60 pound packs of former years. Yet nowhere in his book does he discuss the causes, merits or demerits of these changes.

An investigation later reported the agency was guilty of six acts of negligence that contributed to the deaths. No briefing had been given to the crews, there was much confusion in dispatching them, the escape routes were too lengthy and steep, the lookouts inadequate and there was an immense amount of flammable Gambel's Oak in the area. Further, even though the incident commanders knew that a wind front was sweeping in from the north, they failed to notify those soon to be caught in the flames. Never mentioned in the report is the fact that the firewomen on the crew were very likely to have possessed just 64% of the lower body strength of their male counterparts, an "effect rating" regarded by statisticians as enormous.

It is all but a certainty that a number of firemen on the crew returned to assist the firewomen and paid for their heroism with their lives. The families of the men who perished have likely never heard the term "effect rating." Nonetheless, they believe it was the presence of women on the crew that slowed their ascent out of the canyon, resulting in their deaths. The agency denies this, and when one reporter asked why a disproportionate number of women were on the crew, its spokesman very deftly evaded the question. Maclean himself wrote that the concerns expressed by the families of the lost sons produced no groundswell of curiosity within the forest service—the type of curiosity that might have led to an outside investigation. This cover up only served to confirm the misgivings of the families.

Shortly after this, and other fires that broke out around the West, Douglas Leisz, president of the National Association of Forest Retirees wrote a blistering letter, not to the forest service, or the Secretary of Agriculture, but to President Bill Clinton himself. For reasons of brevity, his letter is here paraphrased:

> Field organizations in the forest service have been decimated. Firefighting capabilities

have been reduced to dangerously low levels. Forces for protection of individual forests are only 50% of strength. Fire prevention personnel and initial attack forces of organized "hot shot" crews are at their lowest number I can recall. It has been impossible for the present fire organization to make prompt initial attacks when faced with multiple lightening fires. This insures that many fires will become large and destructive. Your administration's resource utilization policy has alienated or driven away most of the local folks (e.g. loggers, mill workers, ranch hands, construction workers) who in the past helped out in emergency situations.

The following passage by the same Doug Leisz is a direct quote: "Meanwhile the Washington Office of the Forest Service has been increased by 300 people who don't fight fires."

Sometime in 1996, Chief Thomas paid a visit to the Cleveland National Forest where he was confronted with the problem of illegal immigration. He found the forest's chaparral-covered slopes and woodlands, laced with trails cut by illegals who had left behind heaps of trash. Particularly disturbing were the large piles of human feces found along watercourses where many illegal families recreated. Wrote Thomas, "I am amazed the Environmental Protection Agency or state environmental agencies have not chastised the Forest Service for the conditions. I can't believe for example, that water samples would pass muster for fecal coliform and there are thousands of people (mostly children) playing in the water."

He went on to suggest that the Environmental Protection Agency had not taken action because "The pressure is so heavy in the city and the use so heavy, and the need so great that it is probably politically expedient to look the other way...as the city with all the problems moves into the woods these problems become Forest Service problems..."

Indeed. Had Rapid City, South Dakota, Bend, Oregon, or Branson, Missouri permitted their environs to disintegrate in a similar manner, the Environmental Protection Agency would have hauled those communities into court posthaste.

The Cleveland Forest Supervisor and his staff also warned him of increased anger toward forest service personnel among the illegal immigrants. Still, the same officials went on to say that forest personnel were very concerned about the well-being of the illegals. The two claims in adjoining paragraphs quite literally defy one another. In the face of increasing threats from illegal immigrants, it is inconceivable that forest employees had ratcheted up concern for their well-being. On the other hand, by 1996 the agency was heavily staffed by employees who relate to life in ways that run against the grain of both authenticity and survival itself.

The Chief further reported that three murders had been committed on the nearby Angeles Forest in the week prior. "The body count from all causes on the Forest is three to five per week...dealing with these fatalities plus the wounded is said to take a heavy toll on Forest Service people." He wrote that law enforcement officers were more numerous on the Angeles and Cleveland than any other forest, but that they were still woefully understaffed. He also reported that his own Washington Office was planning to phase out the forestry protection officer program—those employees trained to write tickets for misdemeanors, and who act as the eyes and ears of law enforcement.

As Thomas explained, "They [the law enforcement officers] are most concerned about the phase out of the [FPOs] over the next three years. The Washington brass have issued the edict in an attempt to reduce Forest Service liability that results from inappropriate action by inadequately trained FPOs. But LEOs feel that the [FPOs] do not cause legal problems, and that they should be given enhanced and increased training to deal with malefactors." It is possible that upon his return to Washington, Thomas himself put an end to the phase-out, as forestry protection officers are still present, although in greatly diminished numbers.

In addition to all the above, Thomas was in a constant battle with the timber interests and the legal challenges presented by environmentalists. Finally, there were his endless struggles with the Clinton Administration, the members of which he wrote, were more interested in preserving political power than in preserving the environment.

Indeed, he spent so much time in the field—as his immediate predecessors had failed to do—that he lost touch with the Clinton Administration, the core focus of which was task force meetings, personal power plays and the stroking of hundreds of egos. This may have been one reason he remained unaware that Secretary of Interior Bruce Babbitt was in the midst of selling off a large parcel of forest service land to an Indian Tribe—the rough equivalent of the forest service auctioning off a section of Sequoia National Park. Warned of Babbitt's tomfoolery, Thomas intervened.

In February, 1995, Congressman Herger sent him a job posting issued by the Cleveland Forest for a supervisory aviation and fire management officer. Among the announcement's prerequisites was the following, "Knowledge of civil rights program objectives, and has either demonstrated a commitment to the program or the contribution to a diverse work force." This was as good as admitting that in all likelihood this critical position would languish three years before being filled. By then, the service had the full backing of the Department of Agriculture under Lyons and Glickman, in sharp contrast to the opposition it had encountered from Espy and Townsend.

Thomas' thoughts on the announcement are unrecorded; it is only known that he passed it on to Assistant Chief Forester Lamar Beasley. Other, similar postings would be mailed him throughout his term, which he in turn handed over to Beasley. On several occasions he wrote about the "tiresome, politically correct mafia" that had seized control of the U.S. Government and his desire to move away from its very unpleasant proximity. At a ceremony in Portland, Oregon, a member of the National Forest Foundation, Sherry Sheng, gave a speech during which she made a point of ridiculing the capabilities of white men. Thomas was next to the podium, but before launching into his speech, he turned to Sheng and said, "By the way Sherry, that was a great speech for a girl." The crowd erupted into laughter. Thomas was later amused to learn that several women present murmured among themselves about his "insensitivity."

At another speech in Washington DC, he openly stated that he was tired of the anti-male observations made by so many in the forest service. Before a sizable assemblage, he announced to much applause, "I am white, a male and a southerner who grew up during the depression and World War II. As a white male, to surrender my personality is a price too high."

But the pressure was unremitting. Many on his Washington staff were enthused by a speech given by Commerce Secretary Ron Brown titled *New Models for White Male Leadership in a Culturally Diverse World* in which he asked, "Do you think of yourself as a white male when you look in the mirror?" Brown answered his own question with a "No. White male culture is very organized, rational, and mechanistic, designed to dominate and conquer nature, not live with it."

Given the thousands of white men who developed the National Park, the U.S. Fish and Wildlife Service, the U.S. Forest Service, the Bureau of Land Management, and the measures by which they were sustained and preserved, who was Brown kidding? Shortly after, in disgust Thomas stated that Gifford Pinchot and Theodore Roosevelt would have regarded the U.S. Forest Service of the 1990s with the utmost contempt.

In May 1996, he reported that a day-long Department of Agriculture civil rights forum was being transmitted to all national forests by satellite. The forum began with speeches by four new Clinton Administration appointees who piled scorn on the claim that the forest service was discriminating against white men. The feminists at the conference round-table were well prepared, having developed a series of pithy statements to rebut the complaints. Among them were "There's been an affirmative action program for white men for 200 years."

"The same old stuff," Thomas groused, specifically in reference to the subject of sexual harassment. "The problem is that those who make the harassment or discrimination charges can say whatever they wish and charge whomever they please. Those facing the charges must be cleared, as the mere accusation creates their presumption of guilt. And if there is no truth to the charges there are no consequences for the accusers."

By then, he had learned that personnel counselors were handing out grievance awards to *finger-pointers* in almost every sexual harassment and hostile work case filed—without an investigation into the facts. "This course of action leads to the belief on the part of some employees that any grievance will be settled in their favor. Such is both extremely inefficient and extremely costly in terms of troop morale...if we have a weak case we will settle with the complainant. If we have a strong case we will hang tough."

There is nothing to indicate that Thomas put his intentions to work, in part because by then he was planning to leave the agency. When he did resign in November of 1996, he listed nine very annoying problems he hoped never to encounter for the balance of his life. Among them were political correctness, civil rights, equal employee opportunities and sexual harassment, which collectively had destroyed his agency's ability to become the environmentally active organization he hoped it would.

Chapter 20

THE NINTH CURCUIT COURT OF APPEALS

So what is the job? Simply put, it is to change our work profile at every grade. At an accelerated pace to represent the demographic population found in the civilian labor force. If 43% of the civilian work force is women, then 43% of our forest supervisors should be women, This is what parity means. It's a requirement of law and therefore the policy of the U.S. Forest Service. –Arlen Roll, affirmative action director, Northern Rocky Mountain Region.

THROUGH THE MID to late 1990s, the forest service's all-consuming ambition to destroy its reason for being continued unabated, though sometimes by the most unusual means possible. Jim Burton, the former engine captain, spoke in amazement of how top management on the Lassen Forest assigned a man with an artificial leg to his crew. "The fellow loved reading literature about fires, and fire suppression, but he had only one leg. Management put him there knowing that a dangerous situation was waiting to happen. If a fire swung out of control he could have been killed, or worse; other crew members could be killed trying to rescue him. To

Burton's relief the disabled employee's season ended without incident. Yet the following year the same individual ended up on Bob Grate's fire crew. Grate recalls that on one four-mile run, his artificial limb became disengaged and clattered onto the rocks. Yet the mishap had no bearing in his standing with forest management, and he remained for the season.

In 1996, this same individual was placed in charge of a four member helitach crew. As the individual interviewed recounted, "I didn't like the whole business at all." But what was worse in this instance, is that he had learned a few days ago that his daughter had died. Somewhere near Los Angeles. He was depressed. And everyone could understand why he would be."

Because of financial reverses, the pilot was unable to attend his daughter's funeral. Despite unease over the disabled and now depressed pilot, management refused to relieve him of duty. When a series of dry lightning bolts ignited several fires, the helitach crew was ordered aloft and swept off in the direction of the strikes. As the pilot touched down the crew climbed out, and with tools in hand headed toward the fire, where they began cutting a line. As they hacked away the fire outflanked them, and began moving to their rear. A call was placed to the helicopter pilot who shortly after returned.

"We were calling for him [the crew leader]. But no one heard him. And no one saw him in the smoke Spontaneously, without signal, the four men retreated to the chopper, where they stood about yelling for their leader. With the smoke now a boiling mass of gray clouds, the crew clambered aboard. As the pilot prepared to launch, the crew member recalled, "Suddenly, there he was, about fifteen feet away. Coming toward us like a limping ghost." Never had the crew members been so relieved by the sight of what most would have perceived as a freak apparition. With their assistance, the disabled leader stumbled aboard, and the pilot lifted off, orange flames curling three to four feet into the air just beyond the helicopter tail.

Firefighters have always considered it their duty to rescue the disabled from a blaze, a tradition that began over two thousand years ago during the Roman Republic; and for perhaps two thousand good reasons. The U.S. Forest Service is thus the only outfit on earth known to have made a conscious decision to thrust a disabled person into the midst of a fire, with the lives of four others, including the pilot, dependent on him. In pursuing the genesis of this near tragedy, one need only turn to a sentence in Chief Robertson's *Blue Book*. "Increasingly organizations in America are recognizing that...people with disabilities have had different background experiences than have able bodied white males."

The agency's efforts to assemble a forest service representative of America's disabled population, has been less than successful, but not for a lack of trying. At the Lassen Forest's Butte Meadows Barracks, the forest supervisor ordered a wheelchair ramp and an accompanying deck added to the structure. When the fire captains protested that the building was intended to house the physically fit only, he insisted the additions be made regardless. "The total cost for the ramp and deck came to $30,000," said Bob Grate. "It's a work of art, a marvel to look at. But in all the years I spent at Butte Meadows, I never saw anyone in a wheelchair near that $30,000 deck."

By 1995 all nine forest regions had entered the seventh year of their frenetic search for employees of African lineage. Yet its repeated scouring of the campuses for black students majoring in forestry, hydrology, range management, and the various "ologies" had proved a hopeless undertaking; so too its quest for seasonal employees to work in fire, recreation, resources and surveying. Very few have been willing to move into a heavily timbered rural area, where white traditions prevail.

John Fint, engineer for the Six Rivers Forest, often began the season with one or more black youths on his surveying crew. But because his work projects were in such remote locales, he was never able to retain them a full season, most leaving within a few weeks, openly, freely and loudly proclaiming that the service could "take its forests and shove them...." Work on Fint's projects would often grind to a near halt as personnel rummaged through its listings in search of an employee with the right racial configuration. After which, the Engineer would once more begin the very time-consuming and expensive task of teaching him or her what a surveyor's job was all about.

In the Cleveland, Angeles, and San Bernardino Forests, which surround suburban Los Angeles and San Diego, African-Americans remained at work somewhat longer, but again, very seldom through the season. In fact, by 1993 the agency had begun hiring them without a background legal check. According to everyone interviewed, to hire an applicant without a background check was an invitation to trouble. One current employee recalled a fellow who reported every morning attired in a brightly colored toga, his finger nails painted bright red—much too long to perform any work around the fire house. "What was really unnerving about him was his lack of shame. He left after the first week without incident."

More often than not however, within days of hiring such an employee, the tools in the workshops began to disappear. Bob Grate related his amusement the day a deputy from a Bay Area county showed up at his work center with an arrest warrant for a recently hired felon. As the felon was driven off in handcuffs, the human resource department, frantically hoping to sustain its forest diversity, again began groping through the African-American files.

One of the most costly short-term projects ever undertaken by a U.S. agency was *Opportunity Los Angeles*, which arose out of the 1992 Rodney King riots. According to Bill Shaw, then employed by the Angeles Forest, forest service heads panicked during the course of the rioting. Determining that the Departments of Labor, Housing and Urban Development, and Health and Human Services had not done enough to alleviate poverty, they enrolled six-hundred African Americans in a special program to learn requisite firefighting skills. Fearing their objectives might not be reached, the supervisors of the Cleveland, Angeles, and San Bernardino Forests, with the backing of the Washington Office, suspended the agency's drug testing program. In fact, during the recruitment drive, interviewers were not even permitted to ask the applicants if they had any plans for the future.

Shaw, who knew those administrating the program and closely monitored events, recalled that not less than forty-two recruits quit in a single day. Two hundred left within six months, and by the end of the year two-hundred additional recruits had departed, leaving *Opportunity Los Angeles* with a 66% failure rate. About two-hundred hires did graduate from the academy, but the following year, almost every one refused agency job offers. Rather, they went to work for urban fire departments. One may well deliberate as to why at least a few black firemen did not remain, but one factor may have been the inordinate number of women occupying auxiliary and supervisory positions.

Prior to the 1980s Region Five had good success in hiring Hispanics who had a particular talent for working on fire crews. But with the enormous increase in women, the service found it increasingly difficult to hire them. Indeed, by 1986 it had evolved into an organization with such a shoddy reputation that few Latinos felt they could garner any satisfaction from a day's work. Worse was that ever-looming bogyman known as *sexual harassment?*

Thus, outreach to Hispanics, suddenly jumpstarted after demolition of the Hispanic Class Complaint, was not a success. Currently, California's northern forests are able to hire Hispanic Wild Land Fire graduates, but they routinely submit for transfer to the southern units before their first season ends. It is a phenomenon as predictable as it has been expensive, considering the telephone calls, paperwork and backfilling all drawn from each forest's operating budget.

Native Americans too were thought to be a part of the multicultural matrix. As late as 1993, the Northern Rocky Mountain Region was still having success in recruiting them. By contrast, in California the prospect of hiring Native Americans, whose *rancherias* quite often adjoined the forests was not good and with the influx of women, only worsened.

Attempting to explain this puzzle was Ken Gilbert, a Native-American, who rose through the service in the 1970s while working on the Mendocino, Shasta-Trinity and Lassen Forests, eventually becoming a fire management officer. In the early 1990s, he was designated Native American Manager for the Northern Zone. In his words, "I went to the reservations and made efforts to hire them. But it was difficult and I had very little success." When I asked why, he replied, "Well, a lot of it is they did not want to work for a structured government agency with all these rules to follow, and rules with how you were suppose to behave and look. I didn't meet with the success I wanted to." Ken, who retired in 1997, was asked what most Indians thought of the forest service. "It is not a popular agency. It is not trusted."

As a consequence, the agency's single remarkable success story remained white women, where diversity in its own curious way had moved into yet stranger realms. Among the employees I interviewed, the great majority still employed insisted on anonymity. Most are headed for retirement and simply hope to wrap up their last few years with as little disturbance as possible. One of the very few still employed, who stated "it wouldn't bother me in the least" if his name was placed in print, is Jeff Applegate, then employed by the Mendocino Forest.

Several of his worst experiences involved a single employee by the name of Mary Lepper. She was a highly paid GS-12 who possessed a Ph.D. in African Oryx studies. One of the big surprises the woman furnished him took place on their first drive up Trough Ridge on a narrow winding road noted for its precipitous drop offs, that in some instances reach 1000 feet. Still, it is a drive that since the years of the pioneers has been navigated daily by settlers, visitors and forest employees.

As they approached the summit Lepper became so traumatized she panicked. Jeff managed to turn the truck around to guide it back to the ranger station, when at an unguarded moment she explained that her unreasonable fear of heights began in college, following a number of experimentations with LSD. Some months passed before she consented to allow a chauffeur, assigned by the district ranger, to drive her over the ridge.

Part way through her first year Applegate noticed that Lepper was attaching the names of other employees to her purchase orders. He left the office to ponder what he had seen. Shortly after he returned, took a seat and questioned her about the propriety of forging the names of other employees. She took the criticism personally, and one unhappy word led to another, until she abruptly picked up a fistful of pencils and flung them at Jeff. Several ricocheted off his arm and face as he turned to avoid the volley. Seconds later she leaped from her chair, bolted from the room, out of the building and into the parking lot. Applegate also left the building for the parking lot, but upon approaching the oryx expert saw that she was sobbing. Although it was she who had hurled the pencils, because he feared sexual harassment charges, he turned and left.

Soon after, the Ph.D.'s practice of appending the names of others to all manner of purchase orders became common knowledge. The forest supervisor, fearful of discharging her, placed a series of phone calls and was able to foist her off on the Nantahala National Forest, claiming in Applegate's words, that "North Carolina owed him one," meaning Lepper would remain a big headache for the American taxpayer. Upon her arrival in the Nantahala, she received a government grant to conduct research on several Indian archeological sites. In the year that followed, she and certain members of the Cherokee Tribe purchased several power boats for recreational purposes, which resulted in their arrest and the termination of Lepper's career as a public servant.

At about the time of these epic events in Applegate's life, nine affirmative action committees representing all forest regions in the United States flew into Milwaukee, Wisconsin. There, they put up at the Marriott Brookfield Motel and spent the next four days discussing gender and racial norming in forests across the country. In a summary of the points made, it was determined "that the severity of the fire season was hampering the recruitment of women and minorities."

The following year, another committee of racketeers from all nine regions flew into Sacramento, rented the requisite number of SUVs and drove north to the Tahoe National Forest. There, they began *strategizing* on how to further advance their approach toward forest management.

On the morning of January 14, 1995, a discussion arose regarding the perception that the best qualified employees were no longer being hired or promoted. By mid-afternoon, the board resolved to make this perception "a fact of life." To quote Elana Brady, Art Umland and Joanne Roubique, among others:

> *A letter will be issued shortly explaining that there are many factors involved in the selection process and that the objective is to select a qualified person—not necessarily the most qualified.*

The next morning, a Sheri Elliott spoke about the advances the Washington Office was making toward crafting "a non-competitive eligibility policy." "Students with a grade point average of 2.0 can now be hired in place of someone with say, a 3.2 average." This Plutonium Rule of Law strategizing took place one year after Chief Thomas, in his first memo to employees, advised everyone to "tell the truth," and "obey the law."

Arlen Roll, affirmative action director for the Northern Rocky Mountain Region, then spoke. "The chief has therefore embraced these programs just as much as any other programs of the agency. As we all know…if we don't agree with them we have two choices: One, accommodate ourselves to the decisions; or two, find a new job. So it should be clear to all of us that affirmative action is here to stay and we need to get on with this job, the same as any other job of the organization."

Roll turned to the issue of promoting highly qualified candidates:

> *Greater tenure may produce candidates who are over qualified, but this is irrelevant to the issue at hand, which is getting on with the agency's affirmative action program, and filling positions with people who meet the position's legal qualification requirements.*

He then addressed the anxiety affirmative action had produced among employees across the nation:.

> *Reverse Discrimination. A buzz word that has come into being with the advent of affirmative action. It is typically used by Caucasian males to describe situations in which they believe they were victims of advantages given to women and minorities. In fact there is no such thing. Discrimination because of race, color, sex, national origin or religion... is against the law.*

He turned to another buzzword:

> *Backlash: It refers to the attitude/posture of those employees, usually Caucasian males who are opposed to the agency's affirmative action policies, and sometimes by mouth or deed actually sabotage these programs. Let us respond by first saying that as employees of this agency we are all expected to support the agency's policies. That's a condition of our employment.*

*We cannot tell employees how they should think.
We can, however, tell them what behavior is expected.
And, if they choose to pursue unacceptable behavior we
can deal with that through the agency's disciplinary
system. Put another way, we cannot legislate morality;
we can however legislate immorality, and we will.*

He then turned to the *Victim Game:*

*This is usually practiced by those who perceive
themselves as victims of reverse discrimination
and are, in fact, practicing backlash. It usually
translates into some kind of subtle or direct harassment against the affirmative action candidate...
the result is of course, that some innocent employee
becomes the victim of some other ignorant individual's actions...*

*Reverse discrimination is not occurring, and
we must not tolerate the existence of backlash and
more importantly the existence of the victim game.
Where we find these situations, and they are everywhere, they must be dealt with through the agency's
disciplinary system...*

Rolle then spoke rhetorically:

*So what is the job? Simply put, it is to change our
work force profile at every grade. At an accelerated
pace to be representative of the demographic population found in the civilian labor force. If 43% of
the civilian work force are women, then 43% of
our Forest employees at every grade level should be*

women, and 43% of our forest supervisors should be a women. This is what parity means. It's a requirement of law and therefore the policy of the U.S. Forest Service.

No lace curtain semantics or bureaucratic claptrap here. Arlen Roll was embracing the U.S. Government's greatest weapon of mass destruction, equality of outcome. What is so astonishing about him was his Hitlerian bluntness.

Meanwhile, discrimination complaints continued to flow into the offices of Congress. Finally, on May 25, 1995 Congressman Herger announced that he was introducing the *Forest Service Employment Act* to be referred to the House Committee on Agriculture of which he was a member. In addition to requiring the service to hire personnel without focus on race or gender, it demanded that political considerations be set aside and that the agency return to operating within the parameters of Title VII of the Civil Rights Act of 1964.

But by then, with Jim Lyons and Dan Glickman at the helm, the entire Department of Agriculture had slipped beneath the waves of a shadow regime ruled almost entirely by cultural cringing, *equality of outcome,* multiculturals. Indeed, by then the multicultural tide had swept into every other federal department. There, stealth governments quietly established themselves within each unit's equal employment opportunity commission. Among the most iniquitous were those who seized control of the over-arching Department of Justice EEOC, which until the advent of the Clinton Administration, had given the Male Class Complaint strong backing.

In fact, by the mid-1990s supervisors in all departments were being warned against discharging unsatisfactory employees if they happened to be of a certain race or gender.

Rules regarding worker integrity were also eased, and with promotion by merit—the concept that had built America into the great country it once was—now all but extinct, the politics of deconstruction would press forward. Still, the climate for Herger's Forest Service Employment Act appeared auspicious. The year before, the Republicans had taken control of the House of Representatives for the first time in four decades and again was in control of the U.S. Senate. A centerpiece of the party's 1994 campaign, in which it won 52 House seats, was *The Contract for America*, the thrust of which was to dismantle the regulations imposed on the country by the very functionaries over which Congress claimed to rule. Indeed, the House Committee on Agriculture began a six month investigation into forest service personnel practices.

At the time the Herger Bill was being considered, the Levitoff Complaint was undergoing review by a three-judge panel of the Ninth Circuit Court of Appeals. Attorney Louis Demas had again based his challenge on Martin v Wilks. Recall, this was the suit filed by the firefighters of Birmingham, Alabama who had not been a part of an original consent decree; in 1983 they had been vindicated by the U.S. Supreme Court. He again cited Vogel v Cincinnati (1992) wherein the Sixth Circuit Court ruled that a district court had roamed far beyond the original parameters of a consent decree. He also presented the cases of Barry Callenberger and Michael C. Leveroos, favorably adjudicated by Agricultural Secretary Mike Espy. Again he quoted Section 108 of the 1991 Civil Rights Act.

He then turned to Maitland v University of Minnesota, decided in 1989 by the Eighth Circuit Court of Appeals. In 1980 the university entered into a consent decree after it was confirmed that female teachers were receiving lower salaries than their male counterparts. In 1988 the university granted female teachers a salary raise, but denied an increase to male faculty members. A Mr. Maitland, not present when the original decree was arrived at, sued when the University refused to grant him one. The Eighth Circuit Court agreed with Maitland, ruling that his claim to a salary increase could not be obstructed by the consent decree.

On January 16, 1996 the Ninth Circuit Court issued its opinion. In their verdict Judges Goodwin and Poole wrote:

> *Appellants argument that they were not given a rea-*
> *sonable opportunity to object is absurd. Appellants*
> *not only missed two fairness hearings, but also*
> *failed to timely intervene in numerous proceedings*
> *in litigation that had been pending for 17 years*
> *before they chose to enter the fray. In summary, as*
> *discussed, we agree with the district court that none*
> *of the facts pled by the appellants indicate that the*
> *government did anything except follow the consent*
> *decree...*

It is of more than passing interest that both judges entirely ignored Martin v Wilks, the case which the Ninth Circuit Court recommended that Demas focus on during its September 1991 Male Class Complaint hearing.

In a powerful dissent, Judge Kleinfeld wrote that consent decrees by their very nature are collusive agreements. Yet no one had invited the employees targeted for discrimination to the initial negotiations that lasted from 1979 to 1981. "If the Levitoff Class Complaint had been presented in the sixth, eighth, or eleventh circuit courts they would have pursued their claims with success." Again referring to Goodwin and Poole, he wrote, "The majority said nothing brought forth by the appellant here indicates that the government did anything except follow the consent decree. There is great indication that in fact it did not follow the decree, as in Michael C. Leveroos v the Secretary of Agriculture, and Barry Callenbarger v Secretary of Agriculture."

He found it "distressing that the District Court and the Ninth Circuit Appeals Court had departed from the usual and accepted course of judicial procedure." While Judge Caulfield forbade Demas from presenting Leveroos and Callenbarger, Judges Goodwin and Poole pretended the cases did not exist. In conclusion, Kleinfeld quoted Section 108 of the 1991 Civil Rights Act, which under parameters set by that act alone, Levitoff should have prevailed.

Kleinfeld's opinion, of much greater length, and far more comprehensive than that of Goodwin and Poole, had no effect on the Ninth Circuit Court majority, which is why when Demas petitioned for a rehearing, he was denied. With no alternative, he decided to apply to the U.S. Supreme Court for a *writ of certiorari*. He would not be asking the high court to pass judgment on Levitoff. Rather, he trusted the high court would find the Northern District and Ninth Circuit Court of Appeals had so drastically departed from accepted norms of judicial procedure, it would order a jury trial.

Chapter 21

THE TURN OF CONGRESS

If you are out to describe the truth, leave elegance to the tailor.

Insanity is doing the same thing over and over again, and expecting different results
—Albert Einstein

THE YEAR AFTER the consent decree ended, 1993, was the high water mark for the Male Class Complaint, although many suits were won in the years to follow. Louis Demas, representing both members of the Male Class and Levitoff suits, won 45 cases in district court, not losing one. By then eight cases, also prepared by Demas, had reached the office of Mike Espy and were there adjudicated in favor of the plaintiffs.

In response to an inquiry from Congressman Herger, Regional Director Lynn Sprague sent him a table that noted from 1991 through 1994, Region Five was forced to settle 481discrimination suits for a total cost of $1,898,408. This does not include the extraordinary outlays in attorney fees which in 1993 alone ran to $10 million. Bob Grate states that the Male Class won about 100 cases that reached the formal appeals stage within the Department of Justice and that roughly 350 more were settled at the informal stage in the Department of Agriculture, bringing the total number of successes to over 500.

These figures do not include the unknown number of *quiet settlements* in which the forest service admitted to wrong doing and agreed to compensate the aggrieved on condition they not go public. No one has any solid numbers on these claims, but the gut feeling is that it was roughly equal to the number of informal settlements, possibly 500. This last process was how the other eight forest regions adjudicated most of the claims filed against them and why they lie beyond public purview.

This does not include the enormous number of buy-outs, the numbers of which are also beyond public purview. Thomas reports that in 1993, the agency bought out 261 employees, while in 1995, 500 buyouts took place in a single month. From then on through 1999, 2500 more men took early retirement, bringing the total to 3261, which does not include the years prior to 1993, the year of 1994 and balance of 1995. Within Region Five alone, the buyout number is thought to have been about 1000. It is anybody's guess, but nationwide the buyouts may well have reached 7000. The buyout process, though disastrous to the forests and tax payers, proved somewhat less costly to agency functionaries than going to court.

With but a handful of employees left who knew their districts like the backs of their hands, genuine forest management pretty much ceased to exist. Aside from a precipitous drop in the number of recreation projects, and environmental studies—the latter of which only added to the roster of suits in which the agency failed to even appear in court—tens of millions of acres went up in flames. Thus readers should not be surprised to learn that as the new millennium approached, the agency continued to stumble from one misadventure to the next. Misadventures that would never have been so graceless, if forestry could be practiced inside a building. The Social Security Administration for example, where the mission is carried out within compact and comfortable confines; where emergencies and unforeseen events are rare, relations with the public more remote and where built-in procedural safeguards are so far-reaching the daily routine is almost infallible.

Like all other forests, the Modoc is not housed within a compact and comfortable structure where procedural safeguards render the daily routine infallible. Rather, unforeseen events are the order of the day, and relations with the public all important. In the summer of 1995, as in every summer since 1941, a men's horseback riding club known as The Modoc Tribe Riders, submitted its application for a three-night stay at a group camp. The submission caught the eye of Modoc Forest Supervisor Diane Henderson who denied the permit, declaring the club was sexist because its members would not permit their wives to ride with them. In her words, "The men are discriminating against their wives. And discrimination has no place on the Modoc National Forest."

George Walker, a key member of the 100 member Modoc Tribe Riders, requested a FOIA on the matter, and opened legal proceedings. "It really blew up in her hands," he said. "The riders and their wives wrote dozens of letters to the congressman, the regional supervisor and to the local newspapers complaining about the forest service interjecting itself into their personal lives."

With its public image badly blistered, the Modoc was thrown into turmoil, unable to reconcile its progressivism with the conservative lifestyle of the people who camped, hiked and rode horses across its vast mountain and range country. Because of the ridicule Henderson had exposed the agency to, she received an order from Washington to "cease and desist." According to Walker she was shifted to another forest, and from there departed the agency altogether.

During my 2003 season on the Plumas, I was puzzled by the fact that the forest hired an overweight African American woman from Washington, DC, and an Indian from the Potawatomi Tribe of Kansas, who did not have a driver's license. Both were hired to work on one of its resource crews, and flown out to California, courtesy of the United States taxpayer. The woman was so obese she could not climb an embankment, let alone hike two miles into the forest to repair a washed out trail. Consequently, she spent most of her days sitting inside a forest service rig with the motor and air conditioner running.

The Potawatomi had a combination drinking and drug problem that was horrendous, and over a period of two weeks, so terrorized the two women in whose barracks he was housed, that a law enforcement officer was summoned. He was driven to Reno, Nevada and placed aboard an aircraft bound for Kansas. I was of course aware of the Bernardi Decree and the debilitating effects it was having on personnel, but so startled by the agency's hiring of two individuals— one downright dangerous, and the other so incredibly inept, that I questioned a staff employee about it.

She told me that it was the Plumas' goal was to reach out to minorities. Its passion for minorities was as all-consuming as it was far back in 1984. The prospective hires had been interviewed over the telephone, many, many states away. The interviewer had been directed not to ask any questions about the subject's physical condition, arrest record or plans for the future. The prospective employees were simply told the work would not be demanding. This was how the Plumas managed to hire an alcoholic drug abuser, who had long ago lost his driver's license, and another employee who was far too obese to enter a forest, let alone work in one.

To the south, on the Tahoe Forest, a woman with no background in engineering was promoted to engineer, where not surprisingly, she declined to accept most of her assignments; this of course meant they were foisted off onto her co-workers. In exasperation, the Tahoe's chief engineer went to the forest supervisor and informed him that he was "documenting her failures from here on out."

The forest supervisor retorted, "You will do whatever it takes to ensure that she succeeds!"

In the Sierraville District of the same forest, an interviewee recalled a crew composed of four women who were marking salvage timber. It may seem strange even at this point that a marking crew would not have included at least one man. But the rationale was, since all-male marking crews had been successful in the past, it was important to demonstrate that an all-female crew could perform as well. Unfortunately, while at work the crew came across a black bear with two cubs. They fled to their trucks and drove back to the ranger station, where despite management's pleas, none would return to work.

In desperation, management pulled a relatively highly paid man, a GS-07 surveyor, off his assignment and charged him with accompanying the women into the woods. He spent the next two weeks reading and otherwise passing the time, aware that only under the most extraordinary circumstances would a black bear, even with cubs, attack anyone. Said the employee relating the incident,, "They simply would not go back up there, because they were afraid of that bear. And he didn't even carry a gun…"

Again on the Tahoe, in 1995 the same employee recalled the hiring of an African American biologist. "They immediately found they could not send her into the woods alone because she always got lost. They had to keep dispatching search parties for her. At some point they determined someone had to accompany her at all times. A GS-05 was appointed to go out with her, even though he had other things to do. They were paying two people to perform one job."

And north to the Lassen, in response to a bid for sugar pine from Collins and Company, a crew was sent out to mark those trees for the sale. The crew, consisting of inexperienced seasonal employees, was led by a GS-07 woman who was unschooled at tree identification. When Collins and Company later examined the tract and found not a single sugar pine marked, forest management was forced to hire an outside firm to mark the trees. But by then its client had gone elsewhere for its sugar pine. As was underscored earlier, the agency's astonishing ignorance of its forests was in large part responsible for its endless string of legal defeats at the hands of environmental groups. In this instance however, as in many other occasions across the land, that very ignorance resulted in numerous small, unrecorded triumphs for wilderness advocates.

Mail meanwhile was still inundating the offices of those members of the House of Representatives who had large stretches of U.S. Forest Service land in their districts. In addition to hundreds of cases of discrimination, the letter writers complained of the relentless browbeating counselors were subjecting them to. Continually driven home was the point that while there was a female, Hispanic, African, Asian and Native American culture, there was no such thing as a white male culture. Or if there happened to be, it was an oppressive and illegitimate culture, not fit to make reference to. From time to time, when one of the men summoned the courage to point out the vast number of inventions devised by Caucasian men and the great pieces of art, literature and music they had produced, they were angrily told to shut up and sit down.

On January 17, 1997, five years after Bernardi ended, an exasperated Congressman Herger addressed a letter to Secretary Glickman, parts of which follow.

> *I have been deluged by hundreds of Forest Service employees with job announcements that contain bizarre preconditions which effectively preclude them from applying for an advertised position... by USDA definition non-minority males do not contribute to a diverse work force. This appears to require the passing of an ideological litmus test and has Orwellian overtones.*

He then presented portions of the Maupin White Paper and accused the agency of endangering the residents of communities adjacent the forests. Finally, he made reference to other letter writers who complained about the meticulously maintained blacklist against anyone who had filed a discrimination suit, as well as the destruction of the agency's hotline to Washington. Herger's letter was written at a time the forest service was reeling from the effects of several devastating forest fires that had ripped through the Western States. Decades of suppressing blazes that should have been left to burn naturally, and the vastly increased number of homes built on private property adjacent to forest lands (urban/wild land interface) are among the factors that caused the destruction. References to these last two causes can be found on several Internet websites. Yet there is no current website that dares make public the fact that for over thirty years the agency has been promoting the unqualified over the qualified into dozens of forestry related professions.

Herger concluded his letter to Glickman by stating that he was introducing *the Forest Service Employment Opportunity Act of 1997*. Yet much as the bill he had written in 1995 failed to make it out of the House Agricultural Committee, so did this one. This was in large part because the agency's proscriptive agenda had the full backing of the Clinton Justice Department, and was likely to arouse the wrath of the financially well-heeled National Organization of Women.

Weakening prospects further was the fact that Herger's bill represented the hopes and aspirations of people living in the most sparsely populated areas of the country. Which meant there was little to gain politically, and a good deal of risk in promoting such a bill. That the forest service was no longer managing its properties appears not to have resonated with any but a few dozen Western and Southern representatives.

I asked Dave Meurer, Herger's chief of staff, about the Forest Service Employment Act. Because so many years had passed, he could not remember its specifics. Nonetheless, he did recall the general disposition of the agricultural committee. While all Democrats, heavily dependent on the backing of the National Organization of Women, voted against the bill, a majority of Republicans voted for it. Unfortunately, several Northeastern Republicans, worried about losing the women's vote, joined the Democrats and blocked it from reaching the House floor. Simultaneously, Henry Hyde, Chairman of the House Judiciary Committee, had been following events within the forest service with great trepidation; but he too was stymied by an alliance of progressive Democrats and neo-conservative Republicans.

It may be difficult to conceive why women anywhere would have been offended by a bill intended to restore merit to forest service hiring practices and thereby reverse the destruction of its timberlands. But the fact is the National Organization of Women has the financial resources to subject women everywhere to a tidal wave of misinformation regarding any issue of importance to its membership. In truth, the Herger and Hyde bills were derailed without NOW ever having to kick off a high-profile campaign against them. Its very presence was enough to alarm a sufficient number of committee members. It is also ironic that most members of both parties who tabled the bills were environmentally friendly. Most were strong backers of the Environmental Protection Act and the Northwest Forest Plan.

Through 1997, Congressional discussion regarding the agency's shortcomings continued, finally reaching the House Committee on Government Reform and Oversight, chaired by Florida Congressman John Mica. After reviewing numerous letters from forest employees, on November 21, 1997 he wrote the agency a long missive. Actually more a questionnaire, it arrived in the office of none other than Ron Stewart. Since being relieved as director of Region Five, he had been kicked upstairs, and was then one of Chief Forester Mike Dombeck's deputy chiefs.

In his letter, Mica accused the service of discriminatory personnel practices under a program titled *Toward a Multicultural Organization*, shortened to TMO. He began by referring to a diversity task force statement that said, "Recognizes that everyone has valuable skills and perspectives and requires the organization to adjust some of its values and practices so that everyone will be fully recognized, accepted and utilized."

"What does this mean?" he asked.

He then followed with this, "In contrast to the Internal Revenue Service which appears to have curtailed portions of its affirmative action program after it was ruled unconstitutional by a federal district court, your testimony reaffirms your agency's policies will continue under the terms of the Department of Agriculture's Civil Rights Action Team. I find this troubling…"

On January 21 1998 Stewart responded to all of Mica's questions, prefacing his answers with the questions themselves.

"Does the Forest Service have a quota policy?"

"Other than Region Five in the 1980's and 1990's it does not." He then went on to say that its affirmative action plan was "…a legal requirement, [and] mandates that we make a good faith effort to recruit, employ, train, promote and *retain* [author's italics] members of under-represented groups."

What Stewart owned up to was that the service was going to ever greater lengths to retain its quota system even after the courts had turned aside similar programs undertaken by the Internal Revenue Service. "Retain" is the key word. To ensure women and minorities remained employed in numbers high enough to satisfy the Washington Office, a much greater effort was being made to oblige them. This meant that when dealing with fractious employees, management was pandering to so-called underrepresented groups.

"What guidance was given to selecting officials to manage a quota system?"

Replied Stewart:

> *No such guidance was provided. During California consent decree personnel managers and civil rights staff members presented managers with guidelines*

in California. This practice continues today and is
one of the procedures used in recruiting.

Stewart was admitting that the consent decree directives embedded by Region Five in 1992 were now being applied nationwide.

"What changes have been taken with regard to organization to implementing TMO?" asked Mica.

TMO coordinators were assigned to units to assist
with writing and developing a TMO strategy.
A recruitment board was instituted, a workplace
assessment was conducted, and a continuous
improvement plan survey training session for TMO
coordinators was developed and held.

Stewart breezed past the astonishing expenses incurred by these programs when carried out in every forest in the nation at a time when he and his associates no longer had the financial resources, or in-house talent to manage them.

Another Mica question follows:. "What steps has the FS taken to measure or monitor changes in the organizational culture?"

It is monitoring it through the Continuous
Improvement Project (CIP). All employees partici-
pate in a survey regarding workplace environment
factors. The results are analyzed, and problems
identified by work groups who then take aggressive
action to improve the work environment; an evalu-
ation is then made to the solutions being applied.
The CIP survey is expected to take three years.

Stewart had revealed yet one more program vacuuming great sums of currency out of sorely needed resource projects. Worse, he failed to admit that the "aggressive action to improve the workplace environment" was leaving his workplace environment in ever greater shambles.

"Has the FS done anything to modify the hostility toward white males that pervades the TMO?"

Stewart retorted, "We do not agree that the TMO report pervades with hostility toward white males." Aside from the mountain of documents at the Federal Records Center in San Bruno, readers can refer to the *Blue Book*, the analyses provided by Terry West, Peter Brost and Ralph Johnson, the multitude of affirmative action meetings, and the entire balance of this book.

When Mica asked where funding for Toward a Multicultural Organization originated, Stewart claimed the funds came from all over and that no special subsidy had been set aside. In fact the costs were being stripped from the operating budgets of each forest.

"What values and practices in the FS had to be changed in order to implement TMO?"

Replied Stewart:

> *Since 1990 the FS had learned a great deal about personal, individual, group and organizational values...people's believed practices in an organization is something that can be changed so that all may effectively contribute to achieving the agency mission and goals. The agency has made great efforts and spent significant resources in both preventative programs and EEO complaints before and after development of TMO to stop un-acceptable behavior and actions in the workplace.*

Stewart did not address what was specifically learned about "personal, individual, group and organizational values." Multiculturalism does not achieve the desired balance between timber falling, watershed management and endangered species protection. It does not provide the taxpayers with dividends in the way of recreation, safety and fire protection. It is downright hostile to local communities, and because of efforts to "stop unacceptable behavior and actions in the workplace," it has created the most rancorous workplace in the United States.

"What are the benefits of TMO?" Mica asked. Stewart answered with the following:

> *A workforce that is knowledgeable about leadership in a multicultural organization. A FS that is multicultural. An Agency that includes a diverse perspective in its decision making. Increased ability to guide and lead diverse teams. Mulitculturalism is a positive aspect in the leadership dynamics in the agency. An Agency that is a leader in adopting to change. Improving the work environment. FS employees that play a role in promoting social good and change.*

Among Stewart's multiple answers, not one addresses how multiculturalism translates into the superior management of natural resources and an agency's once renowned ability to "get down and dirty at a moment's notice." Nor does he make note of alterations to personnel policy so ruinous as to have destroyed employee trust, integrity, and morale. Nor does he address the broken relationships with hundreds of communities across the country.

Referring to the adverse mail he had received from those residing near the forests, Mica asked Stewart to "Provide examples where the FS identified or sought corrective action of inappropriate community behavior."
He responded:

> *The F.S. has limited influence over local communities. Employees mediate between various segments of communities to resolve conflicts resulting from miscommunications, a complaint appeals process [exists], building coalitions between parties. Town hall meetings have been held in order to keep residents aware of human resource issues.*

Tom Locker once said that the forest service "Was going to out and out culturally cleanse the small towns of America." As noted in a prior chapter, this endeavor never really got off the ground, but as a result of the agency's extremism, at town hall meetings across the country, its representatives were often placed on the *hot seat* and forced to explain why they were flying in so many outside seasonal workers. All the while local youths, whose transportation to the ranger stations did not require a two-way airline ticket, were being denied those very opportunities.

Mica then asked if managers were still being rated on their ability to recruit and retain women and minorities. Stewart was very blunt with his response, stating that the *headhunting practices* established in California were now being practiced everywhere.

The Chairman then asked about contracting goals with regard to women and minority businesses, another component of the agency's effort to reconfigure small town culture. Here Stewart assured him that every effort was being made. However, to this day the service has largely failed. Regarding this point, one supervisor interviewed said, "It became a matter of one more sheet to fill out. You just check off the right box. It makes them happy. They know there are no female contractors out here building restrooms, maintaining the roads, cutting salvage timber, or who are in the business of making signs."

For Mica's benefit, Stewart enclosed an agency racial/gender table for the years 1996 and 1997. Among those employed nationwide, women comprised 39.4% of the work force, of which 33.4% were white, 2% Hispanic, 2% Asian and 2% black. Men furnished 60.6% of the workforce of which 51.4% were white, 3.6% Hispanic, 2.9% Asian, and 2.0% black. No Indians were listed. Overall, Asians appear to be well represented, but it is safe to say that a great majority were working within urban confines; Hispanic and African-Americans are very poorly represented. In sum, despite all of Ron Stewart's claptrap about a multicultural workplace, he did not have one.

Chairman Mica had asked many pertinent questions. And the answers provided by Stewart were for the most part direct, if a bit misleading...a series of bare-faced admissions that his organization had erected a spoils system not imagined since the days of President Garfield. Still, Mica's Employee Relief Bill was sidetracked, the majority of his oversight committee evidently concluding that the forest service should continue building upon that spoils system.

A strong proponent of House Speaker Newt Gingrich's "Contract for America," and at heart a sincere man, Mica might well have realized that real power in government no longer resided in the hands of its elected representatives—such as himself. Two landmark civil rights bills (1964, 1991), and a Civil Service Reform Act had been passed by Congress to protect individual employee rights against the very abuses now being inflicted on them. Yet after all the legislative ballyhoo, the truth is real power in the United States rests in the hands of 2.25 million ideologically driven, tenured functionaries.

Truly dismaying was the behavior of Mica's own party leaders. Despite continued overwhelming opposition to affirmative action among the voters, they were utterly paralyzed by the issue. While supporters of the 1996 California Civil Rights Initiative saw their amendment pass easily, Newt Gingrich, Bob Dole and Jack Kemp could not race away from the initiative fast enough. The Republican leadership also failed to make a strong case for Adarand Construction in its successful suit against the state of Colorado, for choosing a minority contractor, despite Adarand's much lower bid. Gingrich and Kemp remained mute as well regarding the Hopwood v University of Texas decision, even after the Fifth Circuit Court of Appeals ruled that the Texas law school quota program was unconstitutional.

A number of political insiders, among them the well-known investigative reporter Robert Novak, were not surprised to learn that Newt Gingrich played a major role in turning back efforts to bring the Herger, Hyde, and Mica bills to the house floor. Despite overwhelming support for the bills among the American people, he simply did not have the stomach or backbone to lead the charge against America's lace curtain elites.

Most of the failures with regard to the fight against multiculturalism were centered in the House, but to that body's failure must be added the Senate. Not once during any of Jack Ward Thomas' appearances before its committees did any senator inquire into his agency's multitude of failures. In 1995 Thomas informed the U.S. Senate Agriculture Subcommittee that 500 seasoned forestry professionals had been bought out in a single month, and that by 1999, 2500 more would be prompted to take early retirement. The great fires that had swept through the West every two or three years, his reports on the lack of talent to manage salvage timber operations in Washington State, and explanations as to why South Dakota ranchers could not obtain grazing permits, should have told Patty Murray, Tom Daschle, Tim Johnson, and the balance of the committee something. Yet no senator had the good sense to question him about the devastating effects these buyouts might be having on the management of public lands.

Strange as it may seem, rather than turning the issue of hiring and promoting by merit into the great national issue of the 1990s, as it should have done during the 1980s, Gingrich, Kemp, Dole and other members of the "Republican Revolution" quietly established a détente with both the Democrats and big business. Most CEOs had come of age during the 1970s and while fiscally conservative, were also wealthy enough to align themselves with social progressives. Thus did the Republican Party leadership, heavily dependent on their contributions, roll over, forsaking the tens of millions of middle class citizens who had voted for them. Hence, the word—never heard on television, or seen in newspaper print by the people—went out. Government and corporate chieftains alike would continue to ignore employee antagonisms roiling everywhere beneath the surface, while engaging in "the mending, not ending" rhetoric assumed by Bill Clinton.

In October of 1996, the U.S. Supreme Court reviewed the Levitoff Class Complaint. Presented in detail were Martin v Wilks, Vogel v Cincinnati, Maitland v University of Minnesota, the Callenberger and Leveroos cases and a full narration of Section 108 of the 1991 Civil Rights Act.

Demas then-cited Foman v Davis settled by the Eleventh Circuit Court of Appeals. In Foman v Davis the court ruled that no court could dismiss a suit until the plaintiff had ample opportunity to present all the facts. The Northern District Court of California had done just that by refusing to admit Callenberger and Leveroos, which were central to the Levitoff Complaint. The Ninth Circuit majority, though pretending to be familiar with the complaints, having ample time to review Maitland and the 1991 Civil Rights Act, declined to make reference to any of them.

Demas then cited United States v Assay, decided by the Sixth Circuit Court of Appeals, to quote: "Courts do not permit parties to raise impossibility defenses when the inability to perform was intentionally caused by the party's own wrong doings." Here, the forest service was defending itself by claiming it was ordered by the Northern District Court of California to implement the Bernardi Decree. Yet the agency of its own volition, without Judge Conti's legal stamp of approval, had chosen to roam far beyond the decree when it reached for the all-embracing quota of 43%. Finally, Demas asked that the class be granted a trial by jury to make all members of the class whole.

The U.S. Supreme Court now had before it all the damning evidence and case law the two lower courts had chosen to ignore, as well as their unprecedented omissions of legal procedure. Yet on October 16, 1996, it declined to accept the Levitoff *writ of certiorari* without comment. The denial was also a denial of their request for a trial by jury. The decision not to review came as no surprise to Demas' clients, who had long since become habituated to losing. Most felt the writ was turned down because they were guys. And white guys at that. In view of fifteen years of relentless antagonism directed at them by their employer, and the hostility exhibited by the lower courts, who could blame them?

I spoke with Louis Demas eight years after the Levitoff Class was closed. He had decided to represent the Male Class Complaint and the Levitoff Class Action Suit because the injustices inflicted upon their members had been in the extreme. He suggested that Judge Conti had a tyrannical streak and at all times sought to ensure that whatever he ruled was enforced. He has no memory whatever of the court monitor or any members of the Equal Rights Advocates.

Every year the U.S. Supreme Court reviews several thousand appeals, yet accepts about 100 only, and for the most compelling reasons. Demas felt he had those compelling reasons after the Ninth Circuit had arrived at its decision—which ran counter to the decisions of four other appellate courts, and that both the Northern District and Ninth Circuit had so distanced themselves from the norms of judicial proceedings, his clients were entitled to a Supreme Court hearing.

Toward the end of the interview he pulled at his beard, and with a trace of sadness said, "You know some of those who became victims, who were punished by the consent decree, were three years old when Bernardi filed her suit. They had nothing to do with what went wrong back in 1972. And they were the ones who were punished. Never the higher-ups."

Chapter 22

THE DONNELLY SETTLEMENT AGREEMENT

The great masses of the people will more easily fall victims to a big lie than to a small one—Adolph Hitler

If the world will be gulled, let it be gulled
—Robert Burton

SHORTLY AFTER THE Bernardi Decree ended, the U.S. Forest Service found itself entangled in another civil suit. Strangely enough, the incident began at the Plumas Forest under the regime of Mary Coloumbe—the forest supervisor who for all practical purposes had shut down her unit's fire stations because not enough women could be found to operate them.

The suit was filed by Lesa Donnelly after Coloumbe turned down her request for a promotion. In retaliation, Donnelly wrote her a letter stating that if she was not advanced, she would file a civil suit. Coloumbe capitulated and promoted her, but with that promotion their relationship deteriorated to such an extent that Donnelly was transferred to the Tahoe Forest. Prior to the actual transfer, Donnelly contacted the Equal Rights Advocates, hoping that Davis, Kurtz and Company would represent her. They declined, claiming to be "sick to death of the forest service." She then telephoned

355

Gene Bernardi and was much disappointed to learn that she was not interested in discussing her civil suit of years past, let alone Donnelly's proposed suit.

As word of the pending claim spread across the Plumas, animosity toward her mounted; thus her eventual transfer to the Tahoe should have been a matter of relief. But no sooner did she report for work than she flew to Washington DC to protest her transfer. With the backing of the Equal Employment Opportunity Commission, she was able to retrieve her job on the Plumas—a pointless triumph to say the least. Still, despite the chaotic climate that prevailed there, she convinced a Ginelle O'Connor, to join her suit, thus making it a class action.

O'Connor started employment with the Plumas on its hotshot crew. Taking advantage of the agency's Woman's College Program, she began studying for a degree while continuing to work during the summer months. When the hotshots learned that she was receiving preferential treatment, they effectively froze her out of the unit. As a result a sexual harassment charge was added to the Donnelly claim.

On December 8, 1995, the Minami, Lew and Tamaki law firm formally cited Region Five for subjecting its female employees to a hostile work environment and for discriminating against them in promotions and training (Coloumbe had long since left the Plumas). The suit was certified by Eastern District Judge Lowell Jenson. Two years passed and the suit appeared to be going dormant. Then on February 24 1997, Jenson amended the complaint to include all past and current female employees who, since February 1, 1994, had been subject to a hostile work environment.

At this point, Regional Director Lynn Sprague agreed to sit down with Donnelly and negotiate a consent decree. However, since the term "consent decree" carried such odium, he insisted that it be called a "settlement agreement." Sprague expressed a willingness to intensify sexual harassment and work place hostility monitoring over a three year period. All employees would again be subjected to sexual harassment classes on a routine basis; and at each exit interview, women would be prompted to describe any harassment accounts that might carry credibility. During this negotiating phase, six more women joined the Donnelly Settlement, but almost as quickly dropped out.

Within a year of the agreement, the Plumas allotted Donnelly a desk in a corner of a room without an assignment. Between 1996 and 1999, she received three unsatisfactory performance ratings, and in 2000 ceased reporting for work, even though she remained on the government payroll. That year, in partnership with her brother, she founded the "Donnelly and Donnelly Employee Management Conflict Resolution Services." The title of the firm speaks to that field of expertise Lesa feels most comfortable working in.

After much prodding from their two clients, on January 8, 2002 Minami, Lew and Tamaki, asked Judge Jenson to find the agency in contempt of court. He declined to do so, but ruled on a continuance, choosing as a counsel (the term monitor being dropped) Judith A. Rosenberg. Cathleen Thompson was to represent the forest service, while Elaine Vercruysse would represent Donnelly and O'Connor.

By happenstance later that year, a strange and unusual event occurred in the Los Padres Forest. Through 2001 and 2002, Jennine McFarland, an archeologist, had been having difficulties with her supervisor, and, it appears, a number of employees at the fire house. The Los Padres is a rugged, scenic, and extremely flammable forest located in California's south coast ranges. Spread across five ranger districts totaling

1.75 million acres, it is more than twice the size of Yosemite National Park.

One day, a friend told McFarland that her boyfriend, a mechanic who worked in the garage at the Los Prietos Ranger Station, had noticed pictures of naked women pasted on the wall of a "hotshot buggy." Feeling that her presence in the garage would arouse suspicion, McFarland handed the friend a camera and suggested that while she and her boyfriend visited the garage, she take pictures of the nudes. The woman obliged and returned the next day with numerous photos of scantily clad women in suggestive poses, among them calendar girls and a clipping from *Maxim* magazine. All were affixed to the walls adjacent two buggy seats. In addition, the friend stopped by the hotshot barracks and snapped several photos of beer cans resting atop a table. Storing beer within hotshot quarters is against U.S. Forest Service regulations, though it is a measure seldom enforced.

The Archeologist gave the photos to fire management, the members of which decided that no corrective action was needed. Angry by their lack of reaction, on September 22, 2002, McFarland called Lesa Donnelly, whose own tumultuous career with the forest service had just ended, but who was still an official with the U.S. Coalition of Minority Employees. Donnelly immediately set out for the Los Padres where McFarland presented her the pictures, and gave her a rundown on her recent conflicts. She learned that the buggy's seven other hotshots (including one woman), and the two fire captains who drove the vehicle, were aware of the posted photos, but had not reported them. Worse, the Los Prietos District management appeared to be pleased with the performance of that year's hotshot crew.

The clips of the semi-nudes and beer cans convinced Donnelly that the Los Padres management team had completely lost sight of its priorities. She thus mailed the photos to the Washington Office, where they detonated an outrage that reverberated all the way back to Jack Blackwell, then regional director of California's forests. He in turn denounced the photos as insensitive and offensive, adding, "This behavior is intolerable." A few days later at a press conference, he told reporters from the *Los Angeles Times* and the *Santa Barbara News Press* that not less than twenty firefighters had known of the photos, had failed to report them to their superiors, and would be suspended for thirty days. In addition, ten fire captains and other supervisors, also caught in the photo dragnet, were being suspended for ten days. The forest supervisor herself was accused of fostering the conditions that permitted the events to occur, and was undergoing an investigation.

On being asked why the photos were such a concern to him when no one else, including the lone female hotshot, had been offended, Blackwell stated, "That is not the issue. The important point is that such photos are demeaning to women. They simply do not belong in government vehicles." In fact, the lone female hotshot had a photo of an underclad Sylvester Stallone-like hunk posted on the wall next to her seat.

Blackwell later held a conference call with all eighteen forest supervisors, ordering them to report back within one week to assure him that no pornographic material of any sort existed on forest property. He then ordered that all permanent and temporary workers attend "emergency" sexual harassment classes "to ensure that all employees understand our zero-tolerance policy." This was despite the fact that the forests had been conducting "sexual harassment awareness" seminars for almost twenty years. Still, in 2002 alone, within California, 58 civil suits had already been filed against the

agency. McFarland alone had filed fifteen, with charges ranging from sexual harassment to numerous hostile workplace
incidents.

Despite the steps Blackwell took, on perhaps the most
combustible forest in the nation, Donnelly called upon him
to discharge the entire Los Prietos hotshot crew and their
captains, and to remove from management all those who had
permitted such an environment to flourish. In her words:

> The pictures have given us tangible evidence of
> what we have been saying for years. The tone is set
> by management, and there are sexual harassment
> issues all over California. The hotshots are not pro-
> fessionals. They have brought shame on the entire
> Forest Service, They really think they are the hottest
> things around, and they act like they are a bunch
> of frat boys.

These were strong words from the director of an employee
conflict resolution service. Meanwhile McFarland, told a
reporter, "I am afraid somebody is going to get hurt, and it
could be me...I'm very concerned for my safety." Around the
ranger station, additional employees ceased communicating
with her, while within her living quarters she found several
"omens" left in the most unlikely places. Not long afterward
she was transferred to a forest in Region Six.

Though Blackwell had declared the sensitivity classes an
emergency measure, they in fact did not commence until
well into 2003. Still, for the forest service this was like turning on a dime. At the time I was working for the Grindstone
District of the Mendocino Forest. Because the district
ranger office was located in the town of Willows, forty miles
distant, it fell upon our immediate supervisor to present

the sensitivity class. It came in the form of a very long video cobbled together at the regional headquarters in Vallejo. The actors in the video portrayed various forms of sexual harassment in the workplace, in so officious a manner the level of mirth in the room quickly mounted. Adding to the mirth was the poor quality of the skits. That anyone would expend so much effort in assembling a series of performances as stilted as these, generated some amusing comments, and a few less than amusing thoughts–among them Victimhood.

Twenty First Century America loves a victim, and nowhere is this more manifest than in the U.S. Forest Service—an agency packed with sufferers. At the end of the production, the four of us left the office convinced that it was we who were the real victims, scapegoats for Region Five's sensitivity squadrons.

At the time of the incident, I had the good fortune to be working for the Mendocino Forest in its low-country off-highway vehicle area during the winter months and for the high country Plumas Forest during the summer months. For that reason I had the *misfortune* to attend not one, but two sexual sensitivity presentations. My immediate supervisor at the Plumas made a strong effort to remove me from the tutorial list, because I had already attended a session on the other forest, and because of a backcountry assignment we deemed important. She was turned down by upper management.

In June of that year, the entire district staff gathered in a private theater in downtown Graeagle to attend a performance by the "Mare Island Five." Whether they were an outsourced therapy firm or actual service employees, is incidental as the agency was footing the bill, including the cost of transporting, lodging and feeding the performers. Since the

presentation was live, the overall mood among the employees was subdued: mild curiosity mingled with annoyance.

The Mare Island Five tended to talk down to us, as
though we were scarcely aware there was a world outside
of Graeagle. A number of harassment skits were presented.
One featured an employee caught unnecessarily brushing up
against another; a second involved a man too persistent in his
efforts to obtain a date from an uninterested woman. A third
outlined the feeling of loneliness an employee might suffer
after witnessing a male and female staff member embrace
each other. Another presented the devastating affect an off-
color joke might have on the self-esteem of certain employees. Alone at the Grindstone District work station, we could
hoot to our heart's delight, but here on the Beckwourth
District, there was no scoffing because upper management
was present.

Still, two points sparked controversy. During what was perhaps the fifth presentation, a youth abruptly complained that
most of the skits showed men as the perpetrators and women
as victims. Amazingly, the troupe responded by pulling the
young man from his seat into the aisle. There, in impromptu
fashion, a matronly member of the cast tried to "put a hit" on
him. This produced a good deal of clucking in the theater.

Finally, toward the seminar's end, one of the lectors,
after sitting herself on a corner of a table, raised her forearm,
pointed a finger in the air and spoke:

> *Now, does anyone know when the issue of sexual
> harassment first entered the public discourse? When
> the country realized it had a deep seated problem.
> That had existed for generations.*

After a measured pause she continued.

*It was during the Clarence Thomas hearings. When
it was discovered that he had been sexually harassing Anita Hill.*

She had no more finished saying "Anita Hill" when a
middle aged employee almost shouted.

*I watched those hearings! That's not true! Hill
chased Thomas from one job to the next. Every time
he was appointed to another court, she up and
moved where he moved. Hill was the stalker! Not
Thomas!*

The lector, never expecting anyone present would recall
the details of the hearings, dropped her head, stretched her
legs outward and gazed at them, flummoxed. The silence was
broken a few moments later when another monitor noted
that the session had been very fruitful, and that it was time to
wrap things up.

A year later, I was conversing with Bob Grate about the
Los Padres hotshot incident, approaching it from every
angle imaginable, including Lesa Donnelly's insistence that
Blackwell had not sufficiently punished his employees. In the
midst of the exchange Grate shook his head.

*You know, firefighters are the real heroes in
America. They risk their lives in major catastro-
phes to save forests, lives and property. And then
the media knocks them to the ground for the most
trivial reasons. Posters of scantily clad women...a
few months back there was a picture of a marine in
Iraq on the cover of Time magazine with posters of
scantily clad women inside his tent.*

"I saw that," I said. "He had probably just returned from a search and kill mission. He was smoking a cigarette too, I think." Bob nodded then asked, "Why wasn't that marine, his captain and colonel removed from their posts? And the whole battalion sent to a sensitivity seminar?"

Sometime afterward I decided to give Lesa Donnelly a call to arrange an interview. My goal was to learn how her lawsuit against the service was progressing, discuss the Los Padres incident and obtain her analysis of the consent decree. In fumbling through the phone book, I found not less than four Lesa Donnelly numbers listed in the Chico-Redding area of Northern California, one of which read, "Donnelly and Donnelly Employee Management Conflict Resolution Services."

Almost certain my chances for an interview were zero I slowly pressed the phone buttons. When she picked up the receiver I introduced myself, told her I was researching a book about the Bernardi Decree, and that I would like to interview her. She cheerfully agreed.

I arrived at Donnelly's home south of Redding, not sure what to expect, but feeling that whatever passed, I would walk away knowing more than upon arriving. Of course, I wanted to know more about Donnelly herself. A number of agency employees had spoken of her civil case with great trepidation, as though another noose was about to be slung around their necks.

She proved to be a short, solidly built women in her late forties, who, after calling off her several dogs, led me inside. I took a seat on a stool in the kitchen as she brewed tea, switched on the tape recorder, and began what proved to be a friendly interview. She was born in San Francisco in 1957, raised in Visalia, had earned an associate degree in social science, and by 1986 was working on the Plumas Forest consent decree committee.

It was not long before the subject of Mary Coloumbe came to the fore. In going into detail about the forest supervisor's refusal to promote her and her own retaliatory step, she added that Coloumbe had "unleashed her hatchet men on me…they were very nasty and humiliating to me. There was more harassment of me too from a lot of other men on the forest. That is when I filed the suit." After providing thirty minutes of microscopic detail about her ordeal, she almost absent-mindedly, and without regret said, "Mary Coloumbe was very unhappy about being threatened with that suit."

With regard to the six women who had joined her suit and then dropped out, she reported, "Several had been called names by co-workers and been forced by their supervisors to sit at their desks with nothing to do. Others had dead animals put in their vehicles; one woman had her lunch box run over. In another incident, a guy pissed on a woman's apple, and then stuck the apple back in her lunch bag." On the several occasions when I asked Lesa why the six had dropped from the suit, she deftly changed the subject. My guess was that they either did not have a genuine grievance, or they found working with Lesa a very daunting a task. Perhaps both.

The single remaining plaintiff aside from herself, was Ginelle O'Connor, who had been working on the hotshot crew while attending a university. As Donnelly explained, "This resulted in the hotshots reacting on their resentments and freezing her out of their unit."

"She was not liked," I said.

"Yes, she got threats of rape and threats on her life." I turned to the consent decrees and asked if she felt it had been worth all the mayhem, to which she replied: "There was a lot of animosity toward women because of Bernardi. They were bringing women in off the street to work who could not do the job. They were not a majority, but management tried to make it seem as if they were a majority." After making that point, she veered off into the following incident: "One afternoon while driving out to mark timber with a male coworker, he pulled the truck over, parked, and said, 'Let's have sex.'"

"Just like that?"

"Yes, and I said 'No, that is not going to happen.' I was a staff officer. All my life in the forest service for the first fifteen years I had to put up with that kind of stuff."

"You mean being told to have sex in a presumptive way."

"Yes. It happened regularly."

She continued, reciting the harassment (not specifically sexual) of others, some rather jarring because they carried an echo of truth. One involved a woman airplane pilot in Sacramento, charged with training agency pilots. "The staff and her students went about destroying her reputation with such thoroughness she had a nervous breakdown. She didn't know she was being brought into a hostile work area."

She related the story of a female contract administrator who had earned a degree in forestry many years before, but had never utilized it. The service nonetheless hired her to manage several timber sales. "She could not drive a stick shift truck, had such difficulty dealing with the loggers, and dealing with her own crew, that she finally quit."

The stories continued, and again, unlike the telling of her own experiences, carried an echo of truth. In 2003, at the Lake Shore Work Station on the Shasta-Trinity Forest, a seasonal firewoman was upgraded to permanent status, while the men on her crew remained seasonal. The animosity grew so intense that one afternoon several crew members, from behind trees, repeatedly shot at her with air rifles. A few days later, members of the same crew seized her hat, painted "Lake Whore" across its crown, and left it in her truck. Management investigated the incident, but could not finger the culprits.

Donnelly then recalled that the year prior, in the Lassen Forest, a female seasonal employee was duct-taped to a chair and tossed into a dumpster partially filled with water. The forest investigated the incident, but could come to no conclusion regarding the malefactors. The following year the same woman was terminated for insubordination.

She continued, offering many startling insights into her personal views of forest management and people in general. Although she admitted that roughly 40% of the women appointed to various positions were unqualified and had replaced men far more qualified, the measures were justifiable because for so many years women had been circumvented. Speaking of the consent decree overall she said, "Management didn't have the right to make them [the men] that mad. They got screwed. But rightly so. They were not suppose to act on their resentments."

"Isn't that natural?"

"Acting on resentments?"

"Yes."

"No. You are supposed to overcome your resentments."

I shut off the tape recorder and asked for another cup of tea. Despite repeated questioning, Lesa had been ambiguous as to how her case against the agency was proceeding—other than to say that the forest service representative and her own law firm, Tamaki and Company, "are failing in their assignments."

She then revealed something startling. In June 2004, as vice president of the U.S. Department of Agriculture's Coalition of Minority Employees, she had joined nine female firefighters in Southern California who had filed another class action suit against the agency. The complaints ranged from sexual assault, to physical assault, to discrimination in hiring, training and promotion. "It all arose out of the forest service's failure to implement the Donnelly Settlement Agreement," she added.

Why didn't you speak with the monitor or your attorney Vercruysse, first?" I asked.

"When the female firefighters requested help from [them] a year ago, their request was ignored."

I stared out the window, perplexed. Sure enough, twenty minutes later, in response to yet another question, she reported that all but one of the plaintiffs had dropped out of the suit and that the remaining plaintiff had been arrested for destroying government documents. Here Lesa became a bit defensive, insisting that the prosecutor had a very weak case against the plaintiff charged with destroying documents.

Another point I brought up went to the very core of the forest service mindset: why over the past twenty years it was having such difficulty putting out fires, and why its cost of operations had reached such astronomical figures: "Why," I asked, "does the forest service, year after year, continue to seek out women—who are much smaller than men—in distant places, like cities, to fight its fires? Work in timber. Maintain campgrounds. When they could immediately hire half a dozen local yokels, who could begin work right away. Without all the expensive exercise yards, and airline tickets. Without all the courses in self imaging."

Said Lesa, defensively, "If a woman is not found to be sufficiently strong to fight fires or work in resources, she should be given the opportunity to be strong."

"What do you mean?"

She spread her arms vertically to amplify the considerable difference between ourselves in size, and said, "To get as strong as need be to fight fires."

"What if it took all season to get you that strong?"

"Then it should take all season. I should be given that chance."

I turned to the subject of Jack Blackwell, who had left Region Five after the Los Padres hotshot incident. Donnelly replied, "I've been accused of pushing regional foresters out, but I don't know. They wouldn't say it even though it's quite possible I had something to do with his leaving."

With regards to the other forest regions, Donnelly stated there is "an awful lot of sexism and racism in Arizona and New Mexico. There's lots of racism in the South, too. People have talked about finding nooses hung in their offices...the forest service is very fascist and very political."

Several years prior, as vice president of the U.S. Department of Agriculture's Coalition of Minority Employees, she toured the forests of the Great Basin, where she found the lack of women and minority employees "unacceptable." On one forest in Utah, she spoke with several trail crew members, most of whom were Mormon, who told her they did not feel comfortable working in the woods with women. Lesa took occasion to remind them that the forest service had "laws." Those laws were to be obeyed. And if the crew members didn't like those laws, they could find someplace else to work.

Another event Donnelly touched on was the dynamics of sadism, central to the nature of the Equal Rights Advocates, and Monitor Meyer. Recall back in 1991, long after the advocates had ceased to communicate with the women they were feigning to represent, those employees founded The Committee to End Court Oversight (CECO). Substantial sums were raised by its members, who then hired a legal team with the objective of ending the decree Quite naturally, they were opposed by the ERA and feminists within the forest service. According to Donnelly, at a hearing later that year, after listening to their arguments, Magistrate Wilken told CECO members, "I am not giving you the right to an attorney in this courtroom."

"You were at the hearing?" I asked.

"I was. And you know what?" she said, face beaming. "When they left the courtroom and went into the cafeteria they were in tears."

"They were?"

"Yes, I took pictures of them crying."

I had run out of tape, the first time that had ever happened in any interview. Late that afternoon, with dusk falling, we were heading toward my truck when Lesa made another remarkable comment relevant to the forest service, and its claim to be "the steward of the land." As we approached the vehicle, I motioned toward the mountains to the east and said, "There isn't much presence out there anymore."

Looking in the same direction, she said, "Oh, I wouldn't go up there alone. In the forest you're never sure what, or who you're going to run into. When I walk my dogs, I walk them down here. Where it's safe."

On January 8, 2006 Judge Jenson ended the settlement agreement.

Chapter 23

THE ROT STARTS AT THE TOP

Bureaucracy defends the status quo long past the time when quo has lost its status.
—Lawrence J. Peter

There is nothing so useless as doing efficiently that which should not be done at all—Peter Drucker

WITH WHAT SEEMS like a thousand years of blundering from one calamity to the next, any clear thinking individual might have thought that by the year 2000, the U.S. Forest Service would have been in the midst of clearing aside all vestiges of the social bombs it had detonated a quarter century earlier, and commenced with a new design to manage its lands.

This was all the more expected as a Republican President, who claimed to believe in initiative, hard work, promotion by merit and the Golden Rule, would soon become president. But the years 2000 and 2001 started off much the same as the years 1990 and 1991. Statements made by agency functionaries left little doubt that by 2015, whatever forest acreage not consumed by wildfire or seized by marijuana growers, would be flattened by nearly 20 million off highway vehicle drivers.

Standing in the distance in order not to be standing in their way, was George W. Bush, as committed to a culturally diverse U.S. Forest Service as was his father, and Newt Gingrich.

In the years prior to the second Bush Presidency, the agency managed to entangle itself in another dilemma arising from a book titled *Reinventing Government* by David Osborne and Ted Gaebler. The authors contended that institutions must be driven by mission rather than rules, that it is not the government's business to provide people with services, but to see that the private sector provided them, and that competition among businesses must be promoted, rather than to promote takeovers by other, larger businesses.

The service reacted by farming out its campsites, and hiring contractors to assemble its signs and erect public restrooms. Today, the agency also relies on private companies to mark timber, thin timber, conduct controlled burns, and repair roads. In fact, the fire division in California contracts out all its helicopter and airplane pilots, simply because those employees who were able to fly aircraft are now gone. Yet, even though the agency has essentially cleared out of its forests the costs of managing them continue to grow.

In part this is because agency experts determined that what *Reinventing Government* really meant was more rules and more monopolization. Proof lies in the fact that in the years following that volume's appearance, it transferred most of its human resource (personnel) departments to Albuquerque, New Mexico. According to employee union representative Lonnie Lewis...

> *It all started with the Gore plan to reinvent America. Bush picked up on it. Before, we could hire our personnel here [Modoc National Forest]. Now we have to go to Albuquerque to get good, sound advice. Lots of people retired after that, not wanting to move there.*

Now most human resource people come in from the Department of Justice, the Post Office, and pretty much from all over. They don't know the forest service at all, and thus we get terrible advice out of them.

Another employee representative, Eric Holst, was even more scathing in his assessment.

Albuquerque is divorced from the people on the ground and does not know what they do any more than in Washington. Many Albuquerque employees came from DOD (Department of Defense]. Unlike a forklift operator in another government bureau, or a social security worker who may handle one or two functions, each forest employee may be involved in twenty different functions. No one in Albuquerque understands this.

One of the severest critics of this consolidation and other aspects of forest service management is Randal O'Toole, a Cato Institute Senior Fellow and author of *Reforming the Forest Service,* published in 1988. Inspired by the writings of Henry David Thoreau and his dislike of big government, through 1999 and 2000, O'Toole wrote a number of columns explaining how agency functionaries might better grasp the means of managing the forests.

In *The Rot Starts at the Top* he declared that America's state owned forests, many managed by trusts, are much more effectively operated. To quote:

As it now stands, it takes approximately five forest service employees to perform the work of one state trust employee.

This means that the average service employee is idling along at 20% capacity, or putting in just eight hours of productive work a week. O'Toole further asserted that those states that manage their forests without trusts showed a return of 70% on investment, which *may* suggest their staffs are working at 70% capacity. In turn this *infers* that state forest employees, shielded from discharge by their own web of civil service regulations, are three and a half times more effective than their federal counterparts.

In O'Toole's opinion, the agency's worst unit is the State and Private Forestry Division.

> ...*a horrible role model for private land owners. Its personnel gives lip service to forestry management, and provides examples of how the forest service manages its resources.*

What he finds so offensive is that the division has access to the public treasury and when dispensing advice to private timber growers, does so under the premise that they too can garner the same assets.

In yet another article titled *The Financial Psychosis of Federal and State Forest Agencies*, he noted that in shocking contrast to the forest service's ability to earn a net profit in 1965, as of 1999 the costs of managing its properties outpaced income by an astonishing 4300%. If it were not for the generosity of a multitude of donors, the impact resulting from this nightmare figure would be many times more damaging.

As of 2010, the forest service budget stood at roughly $5.23 billion, of which 30% was officially spent on administration. In addition to the $1.57 billion officially consumed by the administrators, are heaps of additional costs levied against each of the 175 forests and grasslands in order to administer social programs. These figures do not include the costs of defending itself against environmental court challenges and the expense of fighting fires, which over the last four years have gone through the roof, forcing Congress to hand the agency a blank check. O'Toole proposed that "layers of bureaucracy be eliminated and replaced with decentralized new management teams," which in effect would close down every urban forest center in the United States.

It is unfortunate that few in the Congress have ever come across O'Toole's website or read his book (not that it would make any difference). Underscoring the chasm that separates hope from reality was the experience of J.W. Thomas's successor, Mike Dombeck. In the 1999 fall issue of *Wilderness* magazine, H. Michael Anderson reported that Chief Dombeck's principal objective was the restoration of forest watersheds. Over the years logging, road building, over grazing, and the debris left behind by mining operators has depreciated many streams.

Much as Thomas before him, Dombeck did not rise through the ranks, but transferred over from the Bureau of Land Management. Hence he may not have been aware of the mortal injuries the agency had inflicted on itself. Still, he headed a large public land agency that often interfaced with the forest service, and among the several extremists retained on his Washington staff, was Ron Stewart. Thus Dombeck's stated aspirations may have been little more than public window dressing.

His mission required a good deal more than a series of computer models sitting in the corner of a regional office. Rather, it called for crews of enthusiastic, sinewy employees toiling over the ground eight hours a day for five days a week on projects that ranged from riparian restoration and landslide stabilization, to the modification of dams, ladders, and fish weirs. Unhappily, as his predecessor discovered when he attempted to implement the Northwest Forest Plan, Dombeck found the agency had no aptitude to carry out his proposals—all of which called for a great number of hands on soil scientists, foresters, hydrologists, and surveyors, most of whom had long since departed.

As I personally discovered in 2002, even the biologists have cleared out, or at least the sort of biologists who find working in the woods a pleasure. That year, in the Mendocino Forest, I came across two individuals employed by a private research firm. Through the use of plaster casts and infrared cameras, they were taking inventory of marten and fisher, two rare fur-bearing mammals. In point of fact, the forests, having rid themselves of employees who took pleasure working in the woods, have resorted to contracting out their biological research to private firms. Unhappily, even contracting out biological research has its shortcomings. Much as those contractors who sign up to build restrooms, mark timber, thin timber and conduct controlled burns private researchers tend to visit the forests only when the occasion calls. They never learn the character of the districts they work in. And without that "sense of place," never develop the biological "breadth of knowledge" essential to managing the wildlife and the environments they inhabit.

The biologists doubtless reported their findings on marten and fisher to a provisional assistant forest supervisor sitting at a desk in Willows, and to the State Department of Fish and Game. But it is certain their findings were not shared with any interested forest employees, because those employees have long since departed.

In the same article regarding Dombeck's hopes for the watersheds, Anderson went on to state that even though timber production on the federal forests had fallen by 657%

during the 1990s, many of the agency's employees still viewed the forests as warehouses for timber and other commodities. In fact, by 1999 very few of the old-line foresters (timber beasts in the parlance of the Sierra Club) were left. The foresters may not have spoken resource management with the same accent as Wilderness Society members, but at least they understood the concept, unlike their metropolitan replacements.

The following report, issued by the National Association of Forest Service Retirees in April 2005, should provide the Wilderness Society, and any other organization hoping the agency will improve management of its lands, with a warning. The association reported that in 2002, the state of California alone lost 117,000 acres of timber to fire and that 30,372 had suffered from "high severity fire"—meaning those acres burned could not naturally regenerate themselves.

Yet three years after the Storrie Fire severely burned 10,647 acres of the Plumas Forest, just 3011 had been replanted. The Lassen Forest, which lost 17,000 acres in the same blaze, had replanted 1377 acres. In 2002, the McNally Fire severely burned 8400 acres in the Sequoia and Inyo National Forests. Three years later, just 4000-5000 acres had been *scheduled* for replanting. Another agency failure followed the 1999 Megram Fire on the Six Rivers Forest. Three thousand acres were severely burned, yet six years later just 1508 acres had been *scheduled* for replanting. The Association of Forest Retirees cited a lack of funding for controlled burns and reforestation, as well as "burdensome regulations." While 30% of the U.S. Forest Service is spent on administration, *just one percent is spent on reforestation.* As of 2009, nationwide, 900,000 acres of terrain slated for reforestation has gone unplanted.

By contrast, many private timber companies that suffered from severe burns quickly reforested. In 2004 W.M. Beaty and Associates, which lost 3200 acres to severe burn in the Storrie Fire two years before, announced it had completed its restoration project, its employees having planted nearly one million trees of mixed conifer species.

The agency is failing in other respects as well. In 1990, its forests produced 11 billion board feet of lumber at a time its budget for road building stood at $640 million. By 1994 the amount of board feet produced had plummeted to 3.4 billion; yet the cost of road maintenance remained at $435 million at a time the projected cost should have dropped to $198 million. Payments to contractors to close off roads that are no longer required may be part of the answer here. But, rest assured, the agency was padding its road building outlays in order to defray the costs of its social agendas.

The agency plays shell games with the taxpayers in other respects as well. Despite the fact that Congress annually increases funding for fighting fires, management pinches from those funds in order to maintain campgrounds, fence in grazing allotments, and repair signs, little of which would otherwise be accomplished.

Just prior to our second interview, Jeff Applegate had returned from a four-month stint at Region Five's urban office (Mare Island, San Francisco Bay), where he learned more about postmodern forestry than he ever wished to know. After stating that the forests were incapable of performing reforestation of any consequence, he turned to the Mendocino Forest's most recent ten year plan. Like all other forests, every ten years the Mendocino is obliged to compile a management plan.

In Applegate's words:

Much of the planning is done in the regional office,
where officials pour over maps, many of them years
old, each detailing the topography and describing
the vegetative types. They then compile the data,
and without anyone stepping into the forest, they
go forth with that plan, which of course is flawed.

In fairness to the regional office, not all planning occurs
there, as phone calls are sometimes placed to the forests
themselves in hopes of gathering information on timber
blow downs, insect infestations and fire losses. In addition,
on some forests a skeleton crew aids in developing the plan.
But as Jeff put it, "The last thing they desire, is to get into the
forest."

From a financial standpoint, the situation is a good deal
worse. From 1982 through 1992, as the urbanization of the
agency's workforce grew apace, its 175 units spent a combined
total of $1 billion dollars on their forest plans complete with
environmental impact statements. But their endeavors ran
well beyond the target date and by the time of completion,
were judged obsolete. They were thus shipped off to storage.

Unhappily, copies of an assortment of forest plans made
their way to several environmental organizations and resulted
in their filing a lawsuit that eventually made its way to the U.S.
Supreme Court. There, the service made the curious argument that since its forest plans never resulted in any decisions
being made, there was nothing for the environmentalists to
fear. The court saw merit in the argument and dismissed the
suit, one of the agency's very few legal triumphs. Still, it was
yet another policy failure—over a ten year period the agency
had spent one billion dollars accomplishing nothing under
the sun. As was customary the staff never informed Congress
of its triumph/failure, and the law mandating that each

forest develop a management plan every ten years, remains on the books.

Applegate went on to underscore a typical forest service employee's indifference to the agency's celebrated "Caring for the Land" slogan. He recalled how at a recent forum, an equal employment counselor boasted about her lack of interest in the forest. "She bragged that she was proud of the fact that she had gone into the forest just once, and only after donning some heavy boots, a helmet and gloves..."

Peter Brost of "Blue Book" fame spoke of the problems he has on the Tahoe Forest, in large part exacerbated by a staff that is similarly indifferent. By 2006 there were 82 squatters residing in trailers and cabins in various locales. His situation is not unique, as it is similarly affecting the Eldorado, Stanislaus and Sierra Forests, all located along the western front of the Sierra Nevada Range. Many squatters pretend they are operating gold mining claims. Owing to antiquated mining laws, the forests are thus forced to pursue them into civil court, where a lack of financial resources ensures that just a handful will be evicted in any given year.

"A lot of them have meth labs," Brost continued. "And they grow pot. We don't even go out there now, because we do not have the staff." Then employing words that ought to alarm every forest visitor in America, he added, "*We don't want to find out if it is really worse than it appears to be.*" Thus, with every passing year the squatters become bolder and each spring the woods fill with scores of their cronies buying, selling or trading in pharmaceuticals. This forces the forest visitor center to warn campers and hikers about which drainages to stay out of, and which ridges to stay off.

He recalled that when he arrived on the Tahoe in 1986, there were two law enforcement officers on each of its four districts. "Now we are down to less than one per district. All the while, crimes are rising in the field significantly." To effectually deal with the problems presented by squatters, itinerants building fires in the back country, myriads of roving dirt bikers and a multitude of timber thieves, he reckons that a half dozen law enforcement officers are required for each district.

Eric Holst of the Eldorado Forest also contends that trespassing is a big problem and that the forest is too shorthanded to deal with it. With four districts covering 668,947 acres, the Eldorado has just one law enforcement officer and two forest protection officers per unit. Unfortunately, feuding between the recreation employees over who will have Saturday and Sunday off, ensures that just one will be working weekends.

Elsewhere, the situation is worse. As early as 1995, the squatters and meth cooks found themselves struggling to retain their share of the public turf against the Mexican Mafia, several cartels of which had seized thousands of acres of land where they have established a booming pot industry. By 2005, the total number of plants razed in California had risen to 1,100,000, with 214,000 cut down in Shasta County alone. By then, the national forests of Oregon, Washington, Idaho, Utah and Arizona had also lost considerable acreage to the cartels. The environmental impact of this industrial-style farming has risen dramatically as every year the growers denude more hillsides, dam additional creeks, spread pesticides and add to the tons of garbage left behind from prior years. The number of human skeletons found in the forests rises annually.

Despite all of this, the service's law enforcement division—financially severed from the general agency—has never been able to convince Congress of its worth. It has thus had to rely on the assistance of agents from the Bureau of Land Management, the National Park Service, the Bureau of Alcohol, Tobacco and Firearms and various state narcotic agencies for backup. Even though the gardens are in low-lying country, it is also heavily timbered and rugged country, most easily accessed by helicopter. Adam Burke of the *High Country News,* in his column *Public Lands; Big Cash Crop,* reported on his eye-opening sortie with Dave Burns of the Bureau of Land Management and Ed Plantaric of the California Bureau of Narcotics.

Far back among the ridges and canyons of Shasta County, the agents spotted something below, banked the helicopter, hovered and slowly settled into an opening, as tree branches thrashed about from the ship's rotors. All about them, what seemed to have been a dense forest, was suddenly found to be full of fissures under which bright green cannabis plants grew.

Growers had cut off the lower branches of the trees with handsaws, and cleared the snarl of underbrush to the very edge of the garden to create an open air "room"—a red earth floor below, a lacy canopy above. On inspection, he and the officers found the slopes crisscrossed with irregular terraces that wound among boulders and tree trunks—each slung with a line of irrigation hose. At the far end of the plot, a narrow trail tunneled back into an enormous chaparral thicket leading to five more gardens very much like the first.

Burke related that just the week before, Burns and Plantaric came upon "a site where the growers had poached a bunch of animals. Deer meat was hanging in the trees. They'd killed a bear and kept its claws. And there were two owls impaled upon posts with their wings spread out."

Shortly afterward, members of the Campaign Against Marijuana Planting (CAMP) arrived at the site and within an hour cut down several thousand plants and stacked them into nets. The helicopter then hoisted the nets out over the forest and carried them several miles off where waiting sheriff deputies tallied and bound the evidence.

"These guys are like rabbits," Burke reported one deputy as saying. "They know every nook and cranny. We've never been out here before. And most of them are armed..."

Morning, afternoon, and evening, the illegals work the plots, leaving only to collect supplies dropped in burlap sacks at pre-appointed times and places, hoping to survive undetected until harvest time when, if they are not murdered, they'll receive their cash awards. Most are brought across the border by "coyotes", and until recently worked for the powerful Maganas family, members of which have since been captured and indicted. But so far as the forests are concerned, the arrests have not really mattered as the Maganas' have been replaced by other Mexican families.

Forest Service law enforcement agents, and those of other federal land-owning agencies charged with keeping the peace across millions of acres, have in fact become professional dope cutters. According to a patrol captain for the Sequoia National Park, "During the summer months, if we get a call about [another law-enforcement matter], we often can't deal with it because we're out cutting dope." Echoing Peter Brost's foreboding statement about not wishing to know how bad conditions really are, was Federal Narcotics Agent Tommy LaNier who said:

"Wherever I go flying, I find it. Sometimes, you don't even want to look down." No one knows the amount of land seized by the Mexican families in the six states named, but it is likely that several hundred thousand acres are now off-limits to the American people.

Chapter 24

THE DEMISE OF RECREATION

Everything secret degenerates, even the administration of justice; nothing is safe that does not show how it can bear discussion and publicity—Lord Acton

People occasionally stumble over the truth, but most of them pick themselves up and hurry off as if nothing ever happened—Winston Churchill

WITH THE DRAMATIC decline in timber cutting across the United States during the 1990s, the U.S. Forest Service's most important mission is now public recreation in all its forms: camping, hiking, hunting, fishing, botanizing, birding, gold panning, dirt biking, rock climbing and rock hounding. Year by year, the number of visitors grows.

Thus, ideally, with the departure of every employee working in timber, a replacement would have been found for recreation. With the same number of boots on the ground, there would have remained that all important factor known as "presence." But as readers now know, this didn't happen. What could have been the agency's definitive source of wonder has turned into its definitive disgrace: over the past quarter century, it has been busy cutting the heart out of its recreation programs.

One mitigating factor to this ongoing debacle is the utilization of private campground concessionaires to manage
its larger campgrounds. The quality of the concessionaires
varies considerably, but many do a fine job of keeping the
facilities clean. They are also able to explain and enforce
campground regulations, and their presence is felt and
appreciated by most campers. Still, many campground hosts
do not remain on a given district for any length of time
and thus are not familiar with its attractions. Outside of the
immediate campground itself, which is seldom more than
ten acres, they have no responsibilities other than to inform
forest law officers, or the county sheriff when a suspicious
character is seen lurking about.

This brings to the fore those campgrounds still under
forest management, as well as the balance of the forests
themselves. Peter Brost cited the insurmountable problems
he faces on the Tahoe Forest, much of it rooted in the cal-
lous disregard our "stewards of the land" have for the land
they are charged to steward. Said Brost, "Campgrounds are
not maintained. Restrooms are not maintained. The facilities
are in many cases decaying. The public is not being served.
Whether it is issuing maps, picking up trash, or repairing
signage. No one is replacing anything. The emphasis to get
out on the ground into the field does not exist anymore...
we don't have road maintenance, timber personnel, or recreation in the forest anymore. Thus thieves steal from wood
piles, and smash gates."

A second seemingly positive, but also illusory aspect to the
decline in the quality of recreation is that 41 million acres,
or about 23% of agency lands, have been designated wilderness areas, where firefighting becomes (or should become)
an incidental matter. Thus, it would appear there is no longer any logical reason for a service employee to tread across

those many acres. Yet as the wilderness system expanded during the 1960's and 70's, the agency pledged it would furnish the public with a network of trails through its wildernesses. In practical terms, this meant that local search and rescue teams would be searching for far fewer missing persons, and a corresponding reduction in the number of fatalities would be the outcome.

As a result, during those decades, most forests created trail crews composed of youths, many local, but also suburban dwellers majoring in outdoor disciplines who were eager to test themselves against the mountains. After packing their gear and grub atop pack horses, the crews would disappear into the wilderness for up to a month blazing trails along designated routes and erecting signs at trail forks. Once established, needless to say, these trails and signs required yearly maintenance.

For many, this was *the* ideal vocation, getting about as close to Jim Bridger, Kit Carson and Joseph Walker as anyone could imagine. The challenges were considerable. Crew members were forced to ford rushing streams, monitor themselves for dehydration and to locate a shelter on the approach of a thunderstorm. The rewards were inspirational as well: waterfalls, serrated snowy ridges, verdant mountain meadows, dramatic wildlife in the form of cougar, bear, elk and bighorn sheep, and strangely shaped trees such as the bristlecone pine and weeping spruce.

With the commencement of the Bernardi Decree trail crews were exempt from the arrangement. But with the passage of time and the rise of agency fringe groups, this exemption was weakened from one forest to the next. Much to the distress of agency culls, very few women and minorities were fond of trail maintenance. Other than among resource crews—which in those forests without extensive wildernesses tend to replace trail crews—the proper rationing of genders was never achieved. Thus trail work, having lost its allure to the urban planners, went into steep decline—a great loss to the American people.

Yet another setback to forest visitors occurred in the early 1990's when the agency all but ceased to issue updated forest maps. Today, visitors to public lands are continually confounded by the presence of roads that had never before existed, the disappearance of trails that were once of recreational significance and greatly annoyed to find private inholdings dotted with houses. In addition, there are a significant number of dirt bikers who have learned that the lack of an updated map is a perfect invitation to steer their vehicles into any corner of the forest they please.

Thus "misunderstandings" are the order of the day. Between 1972 and 2005 the number of off-highway vehicle owners rose from 5 million to 51 million. While a great majority of users are respectful of forest regulations, a fair percentage of those in their early twenties are not. As a result, the erosion of roadside banks, damage to locales of natural significance and trespass into wilderness areas is on an ever-spiraling increase.

In a December 26, 2005 internet article titled *Where have all the Rangers Gone?* Michelle Burkhart wrote that she and several other hikers arrived on the Eldorado Forest hoping to enjoy a few days of hiking over the ridges. Instead, they found 700 miles of forest trails, many of them illegally created by off-highway vehicles, closed to public access. They had been closed because environmental groups had threatened to take the Eldorado to court unless an environmental impact statement was made. Like most law-abiding people, Burkhart and her group decided to hike elsewhere.

She then went on to report that forests nationwide had similarly begun to restrict off-highway vehicles—except for snowmobiles—to designated routes. In her words:

> *However, the new rule allows individual districts to incorporate illegally-created routes—estimated to number in the tens of thousands of miles—into their permanent travel plans. And even if a district shuts down all such routes, enforcing the closures will prove difficult. Budget crunches have thinned agency presence in the field, even as the number of off-roaders skyrockets.*

Burkhardt has a good idea of how bad the situation is. In truth, the agency can enact six hundred regulations for the public's well-being, but if it does not have the manpower on the ground, it cannot enforce a single one of them. What is astonishing about the Sierra Club and other environmental groups is they know there is no longer any presence in the forests, and that in filing their suits, they are essentially hauling into court little more than a public illusion.

It is an illusion that brings to mind Mike Dombeck and his successor, Dale Bosworth. Both repeatedly declared that forest abuse by Off-Highway Vehicle (OHV) users must stop; and to stop it they were willing to print up maps and issue them in bulk. But creating an updated forest map requires the presence of on-the- ground cartographers and surveyors, both of which have been in short supply for many years. Thus, despite their declared intentions, neither chief (nor their successors) has ever come across the in-house aptitude, or funding to pay for the printing of current maps.

One of the most important components to recreation are recreation specialists (the FPOs commonly referred to as rangers by the public) who are able to explain what recreation opportunities their districts offer, what the rules are and write misdemeanor citations when occasion calls. Because so much of each forest budget is now siphoned into social programs, many now depend on donor trust funds to pay their dwindling number of recreation specialists. In fact, almost half the service's recreation budget is now derived from private funding.

These organizations run the gamut from the Blue Ribbon Coalition, a strong advocate of off-highway vehicle use, to the Wilderness Society whose objectives are 180 degrees at variance with the Coalition. The chairman of the Blue Ribbon Coalition insists that his organization is entitled to utilize a fair portion of the public land. The Wilderness Society concedes this, but claims that too many OHV users leave their designated routes and perpetrate damage in the forests elsewhere.

Yet, no matter how much time and cash is spent by either foundation, both are dealing with an agency whose only institutionalized feature is its ossification. This in turn leads to the question of how the service spends the donor funds it appropriates. The Blue Ribbon Coalition and several other private donors are the only reason the Mendocino Forest's Fouts Springs Off-Highway Vehicle Area remains open. But well before its recent reduction in staff, the district ranger had ceased providing his seasonal recreation specialists with uniforms, forestry protection school and training with regards to the area's extensive trail network.

A poorly paid seasonal employee out of uniform is thus forced to deal with a public that is often disrespectful of an employee out of uniform, who is not familiar with his district, is not forceful in explaining the regulations and who cannot write citations.

These are among the reasons why seasonal "recs" seldom return for a second year of work. This astonishing short-sightedness forces recreation supervisors to spend any number of days grubbing through their phone books in search of yet another green employee—leaving the Blue Ribbon Coalition and Wilderness Society without the services they have paid for.

This again brings us back to affirmative action and the agency's ongoing victimization phenomenon—and the immense damage both have inflicted on recreation. A current, long-time recreation employee for the Sierra Forest— one of the most scenic in the nation—was bleak in his assessment:

> *We have chosen to use our budget to make a higher priority out of piling up papers, and putting an awful lot of money into preferential treatment... the organization has developed and nurtured a victimization ideology, and it started with women. After they became victims, others joined in and they became victims too. We have a victim culture here instead of a "can-do" culture. We have no business settling the [sexual harassment] complaints we are settling. We are being blackmailed. People absolutely know that if they go [to management] with a complaint, they will get something out of it. Future preferential treatment, a promotion, a cash settlement, or maybe an early retirement.*

When asked how he would equate service effectiveness as an organization in 2005 compared to 1980, he replied, "In recreation the scale is 3 out of 10." With regard to recreation personnel, he guessed the Sierra Forest had five employees with forestry protection officer status, but few were willing to work weekends. "A line officer can try to change their work week. But they don't want to because of the fuss it will create and that a grievance might be filed."

Hence, on average, each of the Sierra's four districts has two recreation employees working weekends. The result is a pair of employees, often out of uniform, with perhaps one season of experience, who leave the public with a terrible impression of the agency. A far cry from the 1970's when the Sierra National Forest was the pride of the Sierras.

The same employee complained bitterly about, "The enormous waste of time the Clinton Administration spent on sensitivity training programs. When Bush won the election in 2000 I was almost certain a positive adjustment would be made. He has been a real disappointment." He then recalled a memo Ann Veneman, Bush's first secretary of agriculture, mailed to each forest employee, almost defiantly reminding them that certain groups of people would continue to receive favors others were not entitled to.

In 2004, a third of a century after Gene Bernardi filed her suit, Veneman granted Region Five permission to create twenty-two additional paper work positions for the sole purpose of tracking down more women and Hispanic hires. Again, the funds were drawn from the cash-starved forest budgets—cash that should have been earmarked for campground and trail maintenance. Jeff Applegate has his own insights as to how the forest service went about consigning recreation to oblivion. Like the Sierra recreation specialist and Peter Brost, he made his observations not in 1985, or even 1995, but in *2005*. He recalled how in the days before the decree, many forests presented each seasonal recreation employee with a two-week introductory course.

The curriculum was split into three portions, part of which was the host concept which was in order to make campers feel comfortable for the duration of their stay, and to familiarize them with the do's and don'ts of camping. In addition, the seasonal tech was tutored on what the district and forest had to offer the public with regards to hiking, swimming, fishing and hunting. Finally, they were given uniforms. The purpose for all of this had to do with the fact that the forest service did not want its employees to come across as ignoramuses to the public. They wanted professionals.

The recreation program varied from forest to forest with such scenery-spectacular units as the Inyo, Stanislaus, Sierra and Sequoia, placing the greatest emphasis on training its employees. With the advent of consent decree, and the ever-spiraling increase in social services and lawsuits, recreation died a slow death. According to Applegate, "Its death was not due to any decree issued by the regional office; the recreation program died at a pace unique to each forest."

Emblematic of its decline was a huge amphitheater near a camp in the Lassen Forest where school teachers from as far away as Chico (60 miles) were brought their classes to learn the area's natural history. Employees gave students talks about forestry management, firefighting and the plants and animals. One long-time employee who had just returned from the Olympic National Forest in Washington, where he had been working the past six years, stopped by and was shocked to find the amphitheater in an advanced state of decay.

"I asked the host at the nearby campground what had happened. He said, 'Oh, it collapsed two years ago. It doesn't really matter. No one from the forest service ever comes around here anymore, anyway.'"

The same employee digressed on the subject of search and rescue and how markedly it had changed over the years. The rescue operations, which more often than not take place on service lands, are described to one degree or another in local newspapers that often carry the names of the rescuers. But, said this employee with a shrug, "Anymore very often not a single forest employee is named, a circumstance that would have been way out of the ordinary in 1980. Even in 1990…

"The sheriff's department knows it. Search and Rescue knows it. Everyone knows it. Even though we own the land, rescuing the public when the public needs rescuing, is not our job. Its someone else's" He kicked at the turf and after reflecting a moment added, "You'd think the SO [supervisor's office] would want to do a little more than hand Search and Rescue a map."

Curiously enough, some old time employees spoke of their low opinion of the men hired over the past ten years. In part this is because the last employee a human resource clerk desires to work with is an eager overachiever with a robust personality, anxious to move ahead. Precisely the sort of employee, who upon finding himself illegally passed over for promotion, would raise Holy thunder and file a suit.

Indeed, today when a forest decides it is time for a Caucasian man to pass through its employee turnstile, personnel glances at the resumes, checks the racial/gender boxes, places the perfunctory telephone interviews, runs the rap sheet checks and then passes the resumes onto the select advisory panel (SAP). The panel, usually comprised of women, examines the resumes, then determines what sort of man they would like working in their forest. More often than not, they choose the wrong man, and for all the right reasons.

Referring to the low quality of employees, women and men alike, Eric Holst, who worked for the Eldorado Forest in several disciplines before taking early retirement, said...

> *I knew when it was time for me to retire. I was too frustrated at my inability to get the type of people in here to do the job. They lacked the concept of work ethic and lacked breadth and depth of experience to do the job. To hit the ground running. To see fire captains with less than six years of experience, to see supervisors not hold down a line job before becoming a district ranger or forest supervisor was too exasperating. For me, it was time to go.*

According to Holst, the average forest supervisor and district ranger remains at the job just five years. For most, sorely crippled by their lack of credentials in forestry, it is not remotely enough time to master their positions.

As he noted earlier, some forest supervisors and district rangers are simply transferred in from the departments of defense, energy, education and transportation. They don't know the difference between a white pine and a white fir, buck brush from buckwheat, a creeping fire from a crown fire or a marmot from a muskrat. Without the requisite educational background, without the forest work ethic, and without that "profound sense of place," it is impossible for them to prioritize.

A more benign result of transferring a supervisor onto a forest, where institutionalized memory has long since disappeared, occurred on the Lassen in July 2005, when a memorial was held for three firefighters who were killed when their fire engine plunged over a cliff three years before.

About seventy people, many of them relatives of the deceased, arrived at what proved to be an impromptu ceremony, rendered as such by Laura Tippen, the new forest supervisor. Until a few hours before she was not aware the tragedy had occurred. At the lectern, unable to correctly pronounce the names of the deceased, she gave a halting and rambling eulogy so offensive, that the relatives and friends of the deceased angrily turned on her before departing. But to paraphrase Tippen...

I didn't know.
And I was strapped for time

Chapter 25

THE TWILIGHT OF FIRE

Let no man's ghost ever come back and say his training failed him–firefighter quote from the National Fire Academy

Prudence which degenerates into timidity is very seldom the path to safety—Viscount Cecil

TWO PEAK FIRE years occurred in the 1980s, six in the 1990s and seven since 2000. Not less than 8.4 million acres of wildlands burned up in 2000, 6.9 million in 2002, 8.6 million in 2005, 9.8 million in 2006, 9.6 million in 2007, 8.7 million in 2011 and 9.3 million in 2012. From 1993 to 2013 fires have burned up 113 million acres, although not all losses were on forest service land. Ten of the thirteen worst fire seasons since the 1950's have occurred over the past twelve years.

Nothing like this has happened since the great Peshtigo and other fires of the 1870s, which prompted formation of the forest service. The agency tabulates the number of acres lost and the cost of putting out the fires, but never tabulates the losses of trees, wildlife and livestock, charred homes and ranches, and watershed damage in which entire creeks are boiled out.

True enough, urban interfacing, changing climate patterns, and the ever-rising numbers of youths brought up without supervision (today's arsonists, meth dealers, etc.) are contributors to these disasters. But the primary cause of these losses is the agency's madcap obsession with gender equity, which by 1987 had resulted in a tremendous drop in prescribed burns, clearing of fire lines and slash cutting. In many instances, the forests are so badly over-grown, they possess 10 to 100 times as many saplings per acre as those managed by the Indians of 180 years ago.

In the face of these setbacks, agency functionaries decided to enter the inter-agency wild land fire academy, an organization with much higher physical standards than, for example, the old JAC Academy. Despite a continuing hostile work environment, more young men who have graduated from the wild land academy are remaining with the service, for a few years at least. They are better paid than before and many remain long enough to be promoted to fire captain. But they quickly learn that the high-paying, prestige positions, such as district ranger, forest recreation supervisor, fire management officer, and forest management officer are too often closed off to them. Underscoring the problem is a report by the National Association of Forest Service Retirees which published the following:

> *Significant fire policy changes are appropriate only when fully supported by research and field experience. In NAFSR's opinion the Forest Service has failed to provide the required work to substantiate needs or likely results of recent policy changes. The current Forest Service leaders in Washington, DC, and a significant number of line officers in the field have minimal wild land fire knowledge*

or experience. Wild land fire is the most powerful and unforgiving change-agent that can impact the land. At its worst it is a killer of people. NAFSR members believe it is unacceptable to permit people to occupy line officer or leadership positions if they lack the will or the qualifications to redeem their responsibilities for fire management...

The scope of the needed fuels management program in the United States is massive and will require years to accomplish. Literally millions of acres are in dire need of treatment. Forest managers must be able to use all available treatment options and have adequate funding that is dependable over time. The Forest Service has an increasing shortage of people with the necessary wisdom, training and experience to carry out its fire mission.

Fire management has lost approximately 60% of its senior fire mangers and fire overhead during the last five years. Many senior fire suppression managers were from the militia (people working in other disciplines, but also qualified as firefighters). Unit consolidations have made it impossible for line officers and their staffs to know their areas "like the back of their hand." Emphasis has been on building teams to handle large fires rather than organizing staffing and training local people. (Forest Service and residents) to attack and control fires while they are small. Replacing and training senior fire mangers and militia is a slow and expensive process.

The fact is, that beginning in the mid-1980s, far fewer men were taking degrees in professions pertaining to forestry. This was because so many had correctly learned by word-of-mouth that there was no future for them in those fields. Though the percentage of forest supervisors who are women has never reached 43% (the actual figure is 34%), efforts to recruit them are so intense that often four and five men with superior educational background, and far more field experience are passed over every year.

At the same time, the fire captain, who has worked his way up from the hotshot crew, knows that with the passage of twenty years, he will be 47 years of age, and feeling that age. At that point, he knows he will find the great majority of staff positions occupied by individuals who have never earned their rite of passage. Thus, he departs early, taking with him all the expertise that has accrued during his nine years of fighting fires, leaving behind no institutionalized knowledge of the district. Regrettably, the dream of resurrecting the savvy fire crews of the pre-Bernardi years, and restoring the forest militia of old, will never become a reality.

In addition, even though the number of women serving on the fire crews has diminished, the agency's fixation with rationing by gender is so extreme that it cheats. It does so by hiring female non-wildland graduates and passing them through the most rudimentary training in order that they simply be listed as firefighters.

The prevalence of physically challenged firefighters varies from forest to forest, but in most, particularly in California, it remains much too high. The polite and genteel terms used to describe the attractive body types of women are "graceful," "slender," "willowy" and "elegant." Yet upon suddenly recalling the physical prerequisites essential for fighting fires the words "big," "powerful," "sinewy" and "dynamic" are what come to mind. These expressions do not include additional phrases that originate from the very significant hormonal disparities created by estrogen and testosterone.

Testifying to the services' continuing fixation with fire-women was a fire management officer near retirement, who lost a close friend of twenty years in a calamity, and whose unfortunate memorial was described in the prior chapter.

He was in the back of a fire truck, returning from fighting a fire in the Klamath Forest when night fell. The crew captain, thinking that it would be a good occasion to allow the woman in his truck to gain some driving experience, turned the wheel over to her. There was a Forest Service water tender ahead of them, and the driver, in making it around a sharp bend in the road, encountered two fellows standing on a log by the right of the road. On the other side was a drop off of several hundred feet.

The tender driver, with just six inches of clearance between his vehicle and the pair, shouted at them, "Get off the log!" and passed on. The woman behind, driving the fire truck, upon seeing the log and the two characters perched thereon, overreacted and swung too far left. The rear of the truck slid off the road, pitching the entire vehicle into the canyon below, killing all aboard. The fire officer paused, shook his head sadly and said, "The driver was inexperienced, and in that kind of country, at that time of night, should not have been at the wheel."

In February 2008, an article by Barb Stanton appeared on her website suggesting that, in California at least, even the Wildland Fire Academy had not been able to salvage the agency's fire division. In October 2007 fires in Southern California destroyed more than 2,000 homes and blackened more than 800 square miles from Los Angeles County to the Mexican border. In response, President Bush and Congress directed the forest service to examine its pay and personnel policies and present them with a plan to vastly increase retention for Southern California forests by February 1, 2008.

Stanton reported that the date had come and gone with no word from the agency, even though Bush and the Congress had asked for a rapid response. She noted the phenomenal lack of retention among firefighters and cited the usual culprit, the California Department of Forestry, which the forest service feels pays its firefighters too much money and offers them retirement packages they are not entitled to.

In fact, by 2008, forest service firefighters at the seasonal entry-level were earning $2,166 a month with no benefits. A CDF firefighter at the same seasonal entry-level was earning a minimum of $2,338 a month with overtime pay and a benefits package. The column went on to say that "CalFire" issued promotions on a regular basis for outstanding work that dealt with advancing the department's fire mission, as well as cost savings. In a sidebar to the above, in 2008 fifty forest service fire captains walked off their jobs and took positions with the California Department of Forestry and local fire departments.

These resignations added to region's already existing 470 full-time fire vacancies; in some areas of the state, the crews were said to be at half strength. This mass exodus has forced the agency to rely on firefighters working for private contractors and even prison inmates. In Southern California during the year 2007, more than one third of its frontline firefighters were employed by private companies, many of whom—as well as the prisoners—lacked the proper training.

The lack of expertise and initiative within the district ranger stations was so extensive that an audit revealed the agency in many instances had failed to make background checks into the training and know-how of its contract crews.

Their English language proficiency was too often found inadequate and numerous illegal immigrants were stumbled upon. In some instances, agency officials permitted contractors to both train their crews, then certify them as prepared to fight fires. Finally, the district rangers and fire management officers failed to monitor the contract fire captains themselves for proficiency. Readers should know that the vast majority of Southern California residents were so desperate, they preferred the presence of under trained private firefighters and convicts to the skeleton crews the agency was providing.

Concluded Stanton, "Whether it's due to a shortage of [US Forest Service] firefighters, or motivation, thank goodness that these inmates give of themselves and there seems to be some rehabilitative qualities to this also. Some released inmates do make the transition to full-time firefighters, according to the California Department of Forestry...' (since renamed CalFire).

The living hell that an unmanaged forest can unleash upon humanity is of course widespread throughout the United States. U.S. Senator Jeff Bingaman of New Mexico expressed alarm over the number of occasions the forest service failed to come to the aid of state and local firefighter units. "At times last year more than a third of the requests from fire lines for federal resources went unfilled during significant fires."

That same year, a congressional committee reported it was aware "that the Forest Service is facing challenges to recruit and retain wildland firefighters in Region 5 (California), particularly on Southern California Forests, due to the agency's vastly different pay scales and *personnel policies* [italics added], and the high cost of living in the region." U.S. Senator Dianne Feinstein stated, "The U.S. Forest Service is losing firefighters to other agencies in California. This is a serious problem that must be addressed, and we are working closely with the Forest Service on a long-term solution."

Feinstein, Bush and the House Appropriation Committee members may never have come across that "eerie" moment Tom Locker experienced—when he realized that none of the highly paid female fire management officers he was working with had any firsthand knowledge of firefighting. But Feinstein, Bush, and members of the House have long known that 43% female employment has been the forest service's overarching mission. They will not admit it, but all are well aware of those desk bound functionaries, whose cosmic insolence has guided the agency for more than thirty years now. That they appear to have come to terms with this appalling fact is all the more disturbing.

Another egregious instance of their coming to terms with some appalling facts took place in 2001, when a fire broke out on the Okanagan National Forest in Washington State. The incident commander sent four firefighters down a dirt road to the far end of a box canyon, there to await orders. Two of the firefighters were teenage girls, Karen Fitzpatrick, and Jessica Johnson, each with several weeks experience under their belts. A third, Devon Weaver, twenty years of age, had one week of fire experience, while the fourth, Tom Craven, described as "a grizzled thirty year old veteran," was the genuine article. All were part of a twenty-one member fire crew that counted eight rookies—twice the number considered prudent.

The Thirtymile Fire, as it became known, had been raging over the immediate ridge a full day, and in retrospect the plan for suppression stood little chance of success. As the four firefighters waited in vain for orders, the wind changed direction and the fire suddenly swept over the ridge and roared into the canyon. The unit fled to a comparatively open talus slope and attempted to erect their aluminum pup tents (shake and bakes) to take refuge in. Before they could do so, they were overwhelmed and killed. There is yet more to the story.

Tom Craven was not the grizzled old codger as sarcastically (the sarcasm was directed at the forest service) described, but a man in the prime of his life. He was an athlete of great ability, and according to his father could "run like the wind." The fact is another employee, a much greater distance from the inferno,, made his escape. Craven very likely could have run for his life too. Still, despite the gifts nature had presented him, he could not bring himself to leave the two teenage girls, and the untrained youth struggling with their pup tents. Thus he died with them.

Later that year, a U.S. Senate subcommittee held hearings on the fire, during which Senators Maria Cantwell of Washington and Ron Wyden of Oregon expressed surprise at the redactions (the inking out) of the names of those responsible for the catastrophe. The report was so chocked full of black outs "that it looked like the authors had used the pages to clean off a charcoal grill." Eleven managers and commanders were known to have been guilty of willfully disregarding ten out of eighteen fundamental firefighting warning signs. Yet the Senate subcommittee was unable to force the agency to name one of the eleven implicated.

Ken Weaver (Devon Weaver's father) wrote in *Forest Magazine*, "and so it is that an incident commander can abandon his responsibility to his crew, break every rule, ignore every watch-out point, suspend common sense, exercise no leadership, cause the death of his crew members, and simply be reassigned. No fines, no loss of wages or rank, just reassignment." Weaver then recalled he was recently issued a $10 parking ticket.

> *It occurred to me that parking thirty minutes over-*
> *time was a more heinous crime with a larger penalty*
> *than what happened at Thirtymile. How is this pos-*
> *sible? How can a department in government oper-*
> *ate by a different set of rules than the rest of the*
> *population? Aside from the legal questions, how is*
> *this morally possible?*

Having erected a firewall of secrecy around the tragedy, the following year the service raised a $32,000 memorial where the four firefighters were killed. The etching reads, "On July 10, 2001, high temperatures, low humidity and severe drought conditions caused an abandoned cooking fire to ultimately erupt into a devastating firestorm that swept up the Chewush River Valley, trapping 14 firefighters and 2 campers. Four dedicated firefighters perished in a valiant effort to battle the Thirtymile Fire."

The truth is, the service never gave them an opportunity to fight the fire. Worse, by failing to take weather readings, provide escape routes and having committed eight additional violations, it played a direct role in the deaths of Craven, Fitzpatrick, Johnson, and Weaver.

In January 2007, owing to pressure from relatives of the deceased, the U.S. Justice Department indicted the incident commander on charges of manslaughter. He was an African-American, Elreese Daniels, whose firefighting experience had been limited to urban structural fires in the Seattle area. Daniels was named incident commander because he had been placed on the Okanogan's "fast track for promotion." Sadly, no arrests were ever made of the race-fixated bureaucrats who placed him on that fast track.

Postmodern fire management has led to other deaths. In July, 2003, what became known as the Cramer Fire erupted when lightning struck a mountain in the Salmon-Challis National Forest in Idaho. Although the service has never released the names of anyone responsible for the deaths of firefighters Shane Heath and Jeff Allen, OSHA did release the names in a report, picked up by Alex Markels in the *U.S. News and World Report.*

Upon learning of the fire, Incident Commander Alan Hackett decided to clear a helicopter landing on the mountain slope. Yet, when Heath and Allen were dropped off with their chainsaws, no lookout system was established and although the commander identified four safety routes where they could flee in case of a firestorm, three were later found too hazardous.

Worried that Hackett, who was pulling double duty as a fire safety manager, was over-burdened, aviation officer Randy Lambeth recommended that he be relieved of duty. But District Ranger Patty Bates could not decide whether to relieve him or not. When later questioned, she denied that Lambeth had warned her of Hackett's burdens. Thus, did GS-13 District Ranger Patty Bates consign herself to dispatch duty (GS-07 level), and turn responsibility for fighting the fire over to five subordinates, all of whom were drawing *significantly lower wages than she.*

Shortly afterward, aviation officers spotted a flare-up downhill from Heath and Allen, but failed to alert them. Officials then decided to retrieve the two, but because of the dense smoke the helicopter pilot assigned to pick them up could not locate them and returned to base. When Allen called the base asking to be picked up, the dispatcher told him that another helicopter was on its way. Eight minutes later Allen radioed again: "Oh God! We've just got fire down below us. Just make them hurry up."

Unable to reach safety, the two were overtaken by flames so intense that the brass screws attached to the soles of their boots were the only remnants of body and clothing found.

In January 2004, Regional Director Jack Troyer showed the incident report to Shane Heath's mother, Jodi, who couldn't believe what she was seeing. "Everything was whited out about who said what to whom. So I asked him, 'Why aren't the names in here?'"

Citing privacy concerns, Troyer advised her that government attorneys had decided to conceal the identities of those who had failed to follow procedures which left Shane and Allen trapped in the path of a 2000 degree inferno. Then, revealing a gallant side to his nature, he assured Mrs. Heath: "I want you to know that the boys had no fault in this."

"Well, if the boys had no fault in it, then who did? The families and the public deserve to know that people are being held accountable…"

Shortly after the interview the service proposed disciplinary action against six employees. But, said Bill Allen, Jeff Allen's father, "We still don't know today if anyone has actually been punished. Meanwhile, the Forest Service is saying they're doing more training and safety. You can teach safety, safety, safety until you're blue in the face. But until you hold someone responsible, nothing's going to change."

A more recent, but much less tragic example of the agency's decline was the Davis Fire in Montana's Helena National Forest, which erupted in August 2010. Weather reports indicated that wind would be blowing at thirty miles per hour, that most of Montana was red flagged, and that open burning by county residents was banned. But the forest service decided to go ahead with a prescribed burn of 100 acres, an operation that in Montana is usually performed in September and October.

The following day, owing to the above conditions, the fire suddenly raced out of control, resulting in a 2,800-acre blaze that forced the evacuation of several families and cost the U.S. treasury $2.5 million. Later, after the fire was suppressed, Lincoln District Ranger Amber Kamps explained to fifty residents at a local school house, that the burn was intended to preserve the white bark pine, and the meadows that were being encroached upon by Douglas Fir. One of the women in attendance tearfully noted how her two children were at home alone when the fire burst forth. Had she known the agency was going to ignite a prescribed burn, she would have taken them with her.

Another resident asked Lewis and Clark County Commissioner Mike Murray, why the service was permitted to light forest fires when burning had been prohibited by the county. Replied Murray, "The federal government doesn't abide by county rules. "We don't like it. We work together, but they don't abide by our rules. They don't need a burn permit."

In truth, to bring the fire under control, the service appointed—not one of their own—but Greg Archie, employed by the Montana Department of Natural Resources, as incident commander. Archie brought with him sixty-five firefighters, nine engines, three water tenders and a helicopter to perform the tasks the Helena National Forest was expected, but could not perform.

District Ranger Kamps apologized to those gathered: "I cannot tell you how sorry I am that we have to meet under these conditions and that you are having to go through this...I can't make it up to you; I can just tell you I'm sorry and we will do the best we can from this point forward as we have been doing all day, to reduce the impacts on your lives and to get those of you evacuated back.

Still, the fact remains that five months later an investigation by the forest service assigned *no blame* for the fire. So far as known, Kamps is still drawing a paycheck from the United States taxpayer

Chapter 26

SOMEWHERE OVER THE RAINBOW

*Labor disgraces no man; unfortunately, you occasionally find men who disgrace labor–*Ulysses S. Grant

*The most barefaced lies die hard when influence and prejudice have a vested interest—*William Manchester

ON SEPTEMBER 6, 2007 an article by Dan Berman appeared on the *Red Lodge Clearing House* website titled, *Employees Say Their Agency is Adrift.* Twenty-six years after Smith and Peterson detonated the Bernardi Decree, Berman reported that forest service employees were confounded about the direction their agency was taking. Shortly after, a Massachusetts-based consulting firm, Dialogos, having interviewed 400 agency employees, reported, "The agency is experiencing confusion and drift in its central identity and direction and ambiguity in the way it allocates power and responsibility."

Even if they know their mission, employees said the agency's culture is not welcoming, as they fear ridicule or punishment for raising unpopular topics or questioning superiors. Individuals that raise

difficult issues can be accused of being negative and subsequently feel their input is not welcome. They may even be ejected from the system. Employees do not feel safe to speak up with such a climate, adding to the perception of suppression.

Dialogos stated that fire-related costs now account for nearly half the service's annual budget. Agency workers also "described firefighting as a burden and said it is unfair the forest service has to fight fires for other federal and state agencies

The guiding principle of promoting large numbers of unqualified personnel into positions such as district ranger or supervisor of personnel will invariably result in unhappy employees asking unhappy questions. Challenging the agency's creation of artificial office functions rather than filling on-the-ground positions essential to forest management, is certain to bring about suppression and reprisal.

In a March 2009 report, Mark Davis, the federal employee union chairman, blamed the low morale on "the general erosion of the ability of the employees to do the work they were hired to do, citing a particular loss of faith in the leadership of the agency'." His assertion, and that of Dialogos, was borne out by a "Best Places to Work" report published by the Partnership for Public Service and American University's Institute for the Study of Public Policy Implementation. Conducted through 2008, it ranked the forest service 206th in morale out of the 216 federal agencies surveyed. To quote:

Though the service can't get much worse than that, it managed to rank a pitiful 209 in the category that measures the level of respect employees have for senior leaders, and staff perceptions about senior

*leaders' honesty, integrity and ability to motivate
employees. In truth, it was found that prison guards
had a far more favorable opinion of their organizations, and supervisors than did service employees.*

It is of more than passing interest to note that prior to
Bernardi, the chief forester tended to remain at his position
for an average of 7.9 years. Since advent of the decree, the
average term has been reduced to 5.2 years. Within Region
Five the average length of a regional supervisor's term has
dropped from 7.7 years pre-Bernardi, to 4.3 years post. These
numbers suggest that even liberal progressives realize that
the manipulation of a hiring system, in which a candidate's
capabilities are placed far below that of gender and race,
brings with it great costs. The bickering, backstabbing, lying
and subterfuge that is the inevitable result of such management practices saps the will of all employees. Subliminally
progressives know the shabby treatment of those around
them, neglect of the forests they are charged to manage, and
the bilking of the public treasury is as heinous as it is contrary
to all the laws of nature.

Providing evidence for all the above is no less than the
agency's first female chief forester, Abigail Kimball, who—
herself sounding much like a victim from hell—called into
question the forest service's once celebrated "mindset of
can-do," that quality that so naturally fell into place under
the stewardship of Pinchot, Graves, Silcox and McArdle.
Said Kimball, "It is diluting our effectiveness, overtaxing our
workforce, and contributing directly to casualties."

The "can do" mindset she was referring to once led to
the thinning of slash, controlled burns, reforestation projects, and the maintenance of campgrounds and backcountry trails. Aside from the victimhood game, what was most

revealing about Kimball was her use of Einstein's famous quote, "Insanity is doing the same thing over again and expecting different results." She in fact was working for the agency over the past three decades, during which time the great purges unfolded; hence, she cannot plead ignorance to what took place. Further, she knows that thirty years of applied evolutionary egalitarianism has been a calamity. All the above are likely among the reasons she resigned in mid-2009, after little more than two years as chief forester.

Kimball's remarks bring to the fore the issue brought up by Peter Brost, the recreation supervisor on the Tahoe Forest—victimhood. An organization staffed by sufferers in continual need of emotional support, is no more likely to carry out its mission than an army of sufferers storming the beaches of Iwo Jima. Strange as it may seem, even though 26,000 casualties were taken in that 26 day battle, there were no victims.

Directly tied into victimhood is another curse foisted on the forest service—absenteeism. The number of employees who now chart ahead the Mondays and Fridays they intend not reporting for work is astonishing. Prior to the mid-1980's it was very common for a supervisor to remind his employees they had too many unused vacation days built up. "Use 'em or lose 'em!" was the phrase. Even as late as 2000, a few employees were still retiring with several thousand hours of accumulated sick leave. Among the post-moderns, this very seldom happens. Regardless of sex, sick leave is exhausted almost as fast as vacation time.

The lack of mission, lack of urgency, the profound sense of victimhood and accompanying absenteeism are why the average employee puts in eight hours of *productive* work a week. As a result, there exists within office buildings a profound listlessness. Within the regional and forest supervisor offices, parties are often held, but never in honor of some achievement that might have taken place. Rather, they are held ostensibly to honor some ethnic group, a member of which has been recently incorporated into the staff; or as the case may be, someone's birthday. Whether an ethnic celebration or a birthday party, for a few hours at least the lethargy and depression are kept at bay.

One long-time employee, soon to retire, related how in the pre-consent years, during the winter layoff months, he and several other employees would call the district office and set about organizing a day of work. They reported early as agreed—attired in winter clothing. Inside the office, while tossing down a couple cups of coffee, they reviewed the day's plan. The group then grabbed their lunch boxes, headed out to the workshop, loaded the chainsaws, Pulaskis, oil and gasoline into the rear of the pickup trucks, and headed into the forest.

Cutting brush in the brisk winter air is a challenging and invigorating experience, a time for rekindling whatever self-esteem may have slipped away over the recent weeks at home. At the end of the work day, with dusk rapidly falling, the men would return to the ranger station. Even if one had been nicked by a chainsaw, there was never a victim.

Today, these winter slash cutting excursions are unheard of. As the "graybeard" recalled, "It all stopped when the office butterflies took over." Currently, within each of the 175 forests and grasslands, just a score employees have any under- standing of what the forest service was about before consent arrived, much less an agency without its flotilla of victims.

This is in sharp contrast to the years former fire management officer Les Bagby was employed when spirits were high and parties were not only frequent, but held for good reason.

"There always use to be parties for something that had been done on the district. By the end of the 1980s, it was all gone. Since 1991 I have been to just three retirement parties, but years ago there was always a party, an end of fire season party, potlucks...now it is so impersonal."

His sentiments were echoed by Gary McHargue, who recalled with nostalgia the conviviality of the years gone by, alive with jest, jokes and laughter. "Now every retirement function I go to, and also at funerals, when we are socializing we walk over and say, 'How are you doing? Haven't seen you in three years.' After that, almost everyone you talk to, in any discipline, the next subject of conversation to come up is, 'When are you going to retire?' 'I've got five years left.' 'I got one year left.' 'Got four months to go. Think I can make it.'"

Hastening the desire to leave the agency, rampant among all groups, is the vandalism against property and physical attacks on forest service personnel, not only by pot growers and itinerants on the lam, but by the residents of the small towns scattered through the forests. Karen Mockler, a writer for *Bulletin Board*, reported that beatings, bombings, death threats and other acts of violence against the agency were commonplace.

One employee recently found a dead cat with a hangman's knot around its neck lying on his porch after a rock was hurled through his front window. In Idaho, a man phoned-in the following: "I used to poach moose; now I am going after rangers." In Oregon a female employee was abducted and held hostage for four days, a crime commonly known as kidnapping.

In November 1999, after little more than a year at the helm Gloria Flora, supervisor of the Humboldt-Toiyabe National Forest resigned, citing intimidation by rural Nevadans. Northern Nevada has long possessed a hostility toward the forest service as well as the Bureau of Land Management. At the same time Flora's personality was a poor fit for the area. Regardless, during the year 1999 seventy-three incidents of violence or intimidation against agency employees and structures occurred, largely in the area of Elko. The immediate factor was a dispute between the agency and locals over the rebuilding of a washed out road. But the underlying factor remains: when year in and year out, locals see an inordinate number of jobs awarded to people flown in from thousands of miles away, a tinderbox builds, waiting only for one match to ignite it.

During the pogroms of the 1980's and 90's, many employees driven from their positions were forced into psychological counseling. For a majority, it was a first time experience. Today, many employees seek psychological treatment, but for much different reasons: stress over the lack of urgency, failure to understand their mission, and knowing that whether they report to work or not will have no bearing on operations. There also remain too many subtle reminders of the agency's luminous past, as opposed to the living death of its present.

Yet, each employee, in conversing with a psychologist about their depression, will be solemnly assured they are suffering from "workplace burnout." In truth, there are very few psychologists alive who, confronted by such an employee, have the intestinal fortitude to tell them to find a "real job."

Meanwhile, volunteer organizations struggle to assume management of the public lands. Richard Knight writing for *High Country News* presented some genuine evidence regarding this trend. Like many recreationists, he could not recall the last time he saw a forest employee on a trail, remarking that he was far more accustomed to seeing them park their trucks in front of an office. He then recounted how he and a friend, horse-mounted and riding through an overgrown trail, chain sawed their way through eighteen downed trees on the Roosevelt National Forest in Colorado. He and his sidekick concluded that the forest was going "feral" because of neglect.

He then wrote:

> *The good news is that this forest won't continue to be a victim of neglect. Thanks to a group calling itself the Poudre Wilderness Volunteers, 180 Colorado residents have taken up the cause of their national forest. By foot, horse, or mountain bike, volunteers patrol forty-three trails on the Roosevelt National Forest, with about three- quarters of the routes through designated wilderness. They carry maps, answer questions asked by trail hikers, take notes on trail damage and have trained a crew to reopen trails that have been closed because of agency neglect. Members even do the dirty work of picking up trash.*
>
> *The idea was the brainchild of Chuck Bell, a retired diplomat, who recently worked as a seasonal ranger for the Roosevelt National Forest. In his three years with the agency, Bell says he saw the wilderness and recreation staff drop from three full-time rangers and 33 seasonals, to one full- time ranger and two seasonals. He also saw wilderness areas overused and abused, which led him to join with friends in organizing the Poudre Wilderness Volunteers.*

Perhaps it is a flight of the imagination to expect the success of the Poudre Wilderness Volunteers to be replicated across every forest in the United States. Yet, other organizations have sprouted on other forests. With more than 205 million visitors annually, and perhaps twenty million who visit them regularly, it is an under-taking worthy of consideration by anyone residing near a forest. Knight, in fact, refers to it as "almost a new form of outdoor recreation—people volunteering to work on the public lands, ensuring that their forests don't go feral. We can be grateful that these people are more worried about the health of our publicly owned lands than about what's in it for them."

In addition to volunteer groups, there are the trusts, which Americans have more confidence in than their government. Trusts not only run private schools, hospitals and museums, they successfully manage large tracts of timber land, including the state owned forests.

One of the most successful of them has been the Uncompahgre Plateau Project, also in Colorado, which performed a series of scientific studies the forest service was unable to accomplish. This included GIS mapping of the plateau, a landscape assessment, a fire history analysis, and a study forecasting vegetative succession over time. Since 1998, over eighty restoration projects covering 31,000 acres on the Uncompahgre have been completed, including controlled burns, thinning, seeding and road decommissioning. The number of mule deer, once in serious decline, has increased.

Elsewhere in the West, following the wildfires of 2002, a number of conservation groups, realizing the forest service was incapable of long-term scientific research, created the Red House Coalition and agreed to develop a community-based monitoring program that included timber salvage. The Wilderness Society, which had considered filing a legal suit against the salvage sales, changed its mind when they saw the group's overall effectiveness. With ten organizations now under its umbrella, the project membership counts hundreds of local citizens, including high school teachers and students.

Another positive project is the Lakeview Stewardship, formed owing to the failure of the Fremont National Forest to restore 400,000 acres of cutover timberlands in Oregon. Local contractors employing resident high school and college students, commenced work. In turn, scientists were brought in to follow their progress. In 2001 alone, more than 120 miles of roads were closed, 13,000 acres of brush and slash thinned and burned, and $1.3 million spent on forest restoration.

Environmentalists initially looked upon the Lakeview Stewardship Group with skepticism. But Mike Anderson, resource analyst for The Wilderness Society, soon became a participant. Many, but not all of members of the Wilderness Society now realize that without the backing of local communities, the task of managing the forests is hopeless. In 2004, after several visits to Washington, DC, the Lakeview Group and Wilderness Society together convinced Congress to assist in funding the program for ten years. Admittedly the trust draws from the federal treasury, but its employees put in a full day's work.

Another organization—one that has not fared so well—is the Quincy Library Group comprised of local citizens who were hoping to manage 2.4 million acres in the Lassen, Plumas and Tahoe National Forests. Authorized in 2004 by Congressman Wally Herger and Senator Diane Feinstein, the bill directed the three forests to employ local residents in creating fuel breaks, selective tree cutting and riparian restoration. But the Quincy Library Group's work was blocked by suits filed by the Sierra Club, and the U.S. Forest Service itself.

For all practical purposes, the forest service is flat on its back dead, its death brought about by a hundred thousand self-inflicted wounds. The world's largest coffin, its 193 million acres are almost as large as the states of Texas and Oklahoma combined. Yet it is a coffin that continues to drain the U.S. Treasury of more than $5 billion every year

Many of the units it has abandoned produced very little timber. They comprise the sort of acreage likely to attract such organizations as the Nature Conservancy and Conservation Fund, which time and again have proved capable of managing non-forested habitats. Furthermore, every state sustains several, and in many instances dozens, of non-profit conservation trusts, committed to managing public and private lands of all types. They tend to be *inclusive* in that they often heed the advice of local citizens, and in fact hire them to work for their organizations.

Those trusts that have demonstrated a capacity to effectively manage wild lands on a sustained multiple use basis should be given an opportunity to administer national forest *districts*, The emphasis should no longer be on the forests; rather, they should be on the districts, which themselves encompass anywhere from 12,000 to 800,000 acres. The public would retain legal title to the district wild lands, with overall management transferred to trusts, such as the Red House Coalition, the Lakeview Trust, and Nature Conservancy. They in turn would be entitled to apply user fees to manage the campgrounds and whatever timber or grazing projects are agreed upon. The result will be public lands managed by those living close by, not many hundreds of miles away. The public could be assured that employees working on one of the Mark Twain National Forest's (Missouri) nine blocks of land, will not be "clocking time," but working out of a personal commitment to managing that unit's resources.

Trust employees would perform a much better job of educating forest visitors with regards to rules and regulations, and the natural features of each ranger district than the tattered remnants of U.S. Forest recreation crews. These very qualities could be applied to managing a high country district in Wyoming, a bottomland district in Alabama or a desert and range district in New Mexico. Americans should no longer be forced to accept the bleak options of watching their public lands ravaged by neglect, or auctioned off to private timber firms and corporate ranches.

One exception to the trust management concept lies in the realms of fire suppression. Because of the catastrophic fires of recent years, the Wildland Fire Academy has cut into the U.S. Forest Service's obsession with race and gender. On this foundation, a new agency could be established and exempted from the oversight of extremists inside the Department of Justice's EEOC.

The other exception is law enforcement. Because of the rise of objectionable behavior within a vastly increased population, there are now great numbers of youths with little regard for regulations and laws: thus, the inevitable *misunderstandings*. Added to this dilemma is the tyranny of distance posed by the great size of most forest districts. This does not include the thousands of 640 acre parcels known as checkerboard lands, separated from the major forest blocks, and which most people do not even know exist. As matters now stand, these parcels receive a visit from a forest service employee every ten or twelve years, and have therefore become the perfect no-man's land—a haven for pot growers and methamphetamine manufacturers.

It is essential that Congress understand that to manage 193 million acres and to cope with the enormous number of Americans who have discovered them, requires presence.

That is, many more law enforcement officers with the probability of being on the scene.

Currently, even within major blocks of forest, once a law enforcement officer is contacted, it may be two hours before he arrives at the site of the reported incident. This impasse can only be surmounted by an increase in their numbers. In recent years there has been an increase, but still there are by no means a sufficient number on patrol. In turn, the addition of more law enforcement officers means the purchase of more four-wheel drive vehicles and dirt bikes, the drivers of which in their circuits might cover eighty miles in a single day, while consuming many gallons of gasoline.

The cost of these operations could not likely be sustained by a private trust. Much like the Wild land Fire unit, they would have to be drawn from funds that formerly disappeared into the black holes of Washington DC, Albuquerque, and the regional offices. Sometime, somewhere, over the rainbow, every American who has the least interest in their country's natural resources, might apply enough pressure to force the Congress and President to place our forests back into the supervision of genuine "stewards the lands"–beyond the grasp of the affirmative action racketeers, who thirty years ago seized, isolated, and then abandoned those lands

Chapter 27

A DEATH IN THE FOREST

Show me a hero and I will write you a tragedy
—Francis Scott Key

UPON LEARNING THAT the U.S. Supreme Court had declined to review his suit against the U.S. Forest Service, Mark G. (Jerry) Levitoff returned to work on the Lassen Forest. According to employees interviewed, like the other plaintiffs, he was pretty much philosophical about the loss. After all he was just a guy. Because he was such a skilled pilot, he was placed in charge of the fire air attack base near Chester. In the off-season he served as an instructor at the Wild Land Fire Engine Academy. Yet he found it impossible to be promoted out of his lowly GS-07 position. Like almost every other man who filed a discrimination suit, the agency had placed him on the blacklist.

Still, in certain respects, he was more fortunate than others. The consent decree and multicultural purges had driven thousands of forest employees into alcoholism, the chronic use of prescription drugs, in some instances hard drugs and the inevitable shortening of life that haunts those addictions. Levitoff never quite slid into the shadows that bedeviled so many of his fellow workers, their wives and children.

Surprisingly, after the decision he decided not depart for the California Department of Forestry, where his skills would have allowed him to earn twice as much money. There he could have placed to rest, once and for all, the painful remembrances that seemed to forever linger about the ranger stations. Rather, he chose to remain because, like so many before him, he was mystically drawn to the forests he worked in. Between firefighting, flying, conducting controlled burns and teaching at the Wild Land Academy, he found very little time to spend around the office.

In addition, well into the 1990s the price of housing in Northern California was still affordable. Some forest employees, including Levitoff, were able to purchase modest sized houses. As he approached retirement, he also began planning to marry. In fact, he and his fiancée Melany Lynn Johnson spent much of their time camping in and hiking across the meadows and ridges of the very country he had for so long worked in. As the Twentieth Century drew to its close, ospreys, bald eagles, cougars, black bears, and beaver lodges remained their preferred sights.

On the blustery day of January 21, 2000, he was fishing alone on the west side of Lake Almanor. Toward afternoon's end, with twilight closing in, he packed his gear and started across the snow toward his truck. In the distance, he noticed a well-worn pickup truck parked near his and next to it a figure awaiting his approach. When Levitoff reached the vehicles, the stranger told him that his truck would not start.

Levitoff said he would see if he could help and started toward his own vehicle. As he reached for the door, he turned and looked back. In the gloom stood the stranger with a shotgun raised and pointed. The weapon roared and its blast struck Jerry in the shoulder, knocking him onto blood spattered snow. The stranger stepped forward, stood over him and unloaded the second barrel into his head. He then rummaged through Jerry's pockets, removed his wallet, returned to his own truck, started it, and drove out onto Route 89.

Jerry's body was found the next day. A sketchy all-points bulletin was issued by Plumas County authorities. Eleven days later, some 600 miles to the east, at Flaming Gorge Reservoir, Utah State Conservation Officer Wade Hovinga, suspecting a lone camper of fishing violations, approached and asked the fisherman for identification. Noting that the camper, "Raindancer" Dickey O'Brien, was in possession of a credit card that did not belong to him, Hovinga called for backup.

Shortly afterward, O'Brien was driven to the county jail where, in addition to local charges, it was confirmed that he was a suspect in the shooting of Jerry Levitoff. He was extradited to California where a judge found him mentally incompetent, and ordered him sent to the Atascadero State Hospital for treatment. He remained there until November 2000, when ordered to stand trial. Plumas County District Attorney James Reichle placed a witness on the stand who implicated "Raindancer" in the slaying. The trial ended shortly afterward, when O'Brien admitted that he had murdered Levitoff for his money. He was sentenced to life in prison without possibility of parole.

Jerry's fiancée, friends, and relatives could not come to terms with his tragic death. Still relatively young and in good health, at the point of retiring, his most rewarding years lay ahead of him. His death was even more shocking than the multiple ordeals visited upon him by the agency he worked for, as his suit slowly wound its way through the United States court system

NOTES

Preface: Many Letters of Condolence

The interview with Ken Wolstenhom took place on August 5, 2004 at his house in Wildwood, California.

1 In 1973 Gene C. Bernardi, a female U.S. Forest Service research sociologist, filed a class action lawsuit charging the agency with sex discrimination. In 1979 the forest service entered into a consent decree with the plaintiff.

2 A helicopter and its crew, primarily used in initial assaults on wild fires.

Introduction: Significant Events in America

There are hundreds of books, magazines, newspapers and website articles that deal with the postmodern ideology, from its beginning in the 1920s to the present.

Chapter 1: Of Forests, Fires and Chiefs

For details of the Peshtigo Fire see website, "The Great Peshtigo Fire of 1871," Deanna C. Hipke.

An excellent account of the rise of the U.S. Forest Service is *The U.S. Forest Service*, Michael Frome, Praeger Publishing, 1971.

See also *The Forest Service: A Study in Public Land Management*, Glen O. Robinson, John Hopkins University Press, 1975.

Also read *Gifford Pinchot and the Making of Modern Environmentalism*, Char Miller, Island Press, 2001.

Pinchot's quote, discouraging any man from becoming a forester: Miller, 328.

Stewart Udall's reference to the "magnificent bureaucrat": Miller, 158.

President Eisenhower's quote: Frome, 27.

The close kinship among forest service employees: Robinson, 36.

Forest Service employee satisfaction was very high: Robinson, 37.

The Monongahela National Forest clear cut: Bob Cermak interview, January 6, 2006.

.

Six stacks of applications found at a Forest headquarters in New Mexico: Bill Dameron interview, April 9, 2005.

Chapter 2: The Strange Origins of the Bernardi Consent Decree

Much information, including all court records regarding the Bernardi Consent Decree, are stored at the Federal Records

Storage Center in San Bruno, California. The 37 boxes of material are stowed in no particular fashion, with many files unlabeled.

Some boxes contain quarterly reports from the agency's research station, and are not relevant to the book. Material can be found in boxes one through ten, and 29 through 33, but they essentially replicate information elsewhere. The most important sources are the following boxes: 11, 12, 15, 16, 17, 18, 19, 20, 21 and 23.

Bernardi never attended any Equal Employment Opportunity Advisory Panel meetings: Leroy Johnson interview, November 6, 2005.

Folkman's quote about Bernardi: Box 11, 01G Report.

The Washington Investigation finds no civil rights violations among the fourteen charges lodged by Gene Bernardi: Ibid.

Details of the Equal Rights Advocates are at website *www. charitynavigator.org*. In addition see Box 23, Docket 505 at the Federal Records Storage Center.

District Judge Samuel Conti ruled against both Bernardi's case and the class complaint she had filed: Box 11, 01G Report.

In October 1977 the Ninth District Court overturned Conti's ruling: Ibid.

In November 1979 Northern District Court Judge Samuel Conti acquiesced to the Ninth Circuit Court, approving the

Bernardi Decree as a class action suit on behalf of all women in Region Five. Ibid.

All aspects of the 1964 Civil Rights Act, the Civil Rights Act of 1972, and court decisions related to these acts can be found in Paul Craig Roberts and Lawrence Stratton's, *The New Color Line How Privileges and Quotas Destroy Democracy,* Regnery Press, 1995. The volume describes the efforts and statements made by Senators Hubert H. Humphrey, Clifford Case, Joseph Clark, Everett Dirkson, John Tower, and Congressman Emanuel Celler, to ensure that quotas of any type would never be considered by any agency of the federal government, the state governments, or within the private sector.

Lyndon B. Johnson and Richard M. Nixon's executive orders are accessible on the internet through *Wikipedia.*

The Civil Service Reform Act of 1978 is available in its entirety on the internet website of the same name.

Cermack's quote regarding the downfall of the U.S. Forest Service: Bob Cermack interview, January 6, 2006.

The Equal Rights Advocates were invited to the U.S. Forest Service's Washington Office: Box 18, folder not labeled.

The Department of Justice warned the forest service not to enter into the Bernardi Consent Decree: Box 18, folder not labeled.

The comments made about the small number of women who had joined the class action suit: Box 18, folder not labeled.

Before entering the consent decree, the Equal Rights Advocates agreed that the U.S. Forest Service had not been guilty of any illegal activity against women. The agreement is within Chief Forester Max Peterson's report compiled on October 7, 1980, and delivered to incoming Secretary of Agriculture John Block the following February. Box 18, file not labeled.

The consent decree was extended from the experimental stations to the entire Region Five: Ibid.

Affirmative action was to be employed by the U.S. Forest Service: Ibid.

The original decree stated women in forest service would roughly reflect U.S. work force at large. Still, there were no quotas, and only the best qualified candidates would be hired and promoted. Ibid.

Two thousand letters were mailed to all women who had been permanently employed by Region Five since 1972. Just 31 responded. Ibid.

Chapter 3: The Great Betrayal

Zane Smith was described as an easily distracted man, out of his element: Bob Grate interview of June 11, 2004.

The select advisory panels would always have one woman evaluator: Chief Forester Max Peterson's report compiled on October 7, 1980, Box 18.

The so called "contrived" qualifications for each position would be eliminated: Ibid.

The hiring of unqualified employees would not be permitted. Ibid.

Corky Lazzarno' quotation about forest service being over monitored: December 19, 1979, file unlabeled, box 12.

Anne Dow Hansen's letter: Box 18, file unlabeled.

Susan Wickham's letter: Ibid.

On January 18 just three plaintiffs were in Judge Conti's courtroom: Ibid.

Cermak's quote, when he was acting Region Five Forester: Bob Cermak interview, January 6, 2006.

At Judge Conti's February 2, 1981 hearing, Zane Smith pledged to have the needs assessment and long term goals finalized in early 1982. The proposed goals program however was not completed until August 6, 1982: box 11, file not labeled.

The Equal Rights Advocates second round of mailings soliciting plaintiffs for the Bernardi Decree: letter is dated April 28, 1981 and in Box 12.

Judge Conti's May 1, 1981 hearing and the consent decree's parameters are agreed to: Box 11, 01G Report. Letter is also in Semi Annual Report of July 1984.

Conti's quote to Smith, "I will hold you to this": Bob Grate interview, July 7, 2004.

Revolt of the Elites, Christopher Lasch. The book encapsulates how the hopes and aspirations of American and world workers were seized by educated elites, who then set about marginalizing the working class.

Diane Winokur's character and description: "Southwest Pacific NewsLog," 1985, Semi Annual Reports issued in July 1984, Box 11.

Smith's quote about correcting attitudes: letter in "Semi-annual Report" of July 1984, Box 11.

The death of Gilbert Lopez: interview with Bob Grate on March 28, 2005.

The section of Article IV dealing with 43% female employment was signed at a semi-annual compliance meeting in July 1982 by Zane Smith, without Judge Conti being made aware. Smith also pledged to have 77% of GS-09 administrative positions filled by women: page 5 of the Semi-annual Report of January 1983, Box 11.

Chief Forester Max Peterson signed off on the additions to Article IV. Semi-annual Report, January 1983, p. 10, Box 11.

Chapter 4: The Avalanche

Women were to be fully backed by management in any dispute they might have with men. Interviews with Ken Wolstenhom on August 5, 2004, and Bill Shaw on May 18, 2005. Many more employees stated the same when asked the question.

All events regarding Bill Shaw were related during the interviews of May 18, and October 27, 2008.

The Wes Bagby interview took place on September 22, 2004.

All events related by Britt Smith took place on the interview of March 26, 2006.

The Jim Burton interview took place on September 11, 2004.

The first of three interviews with Bob Grate took place on June 11, 2004.

The Pete Barker interview took place on May 23, 2008.

Other state and federal agencies were losing trust in the U.S. Forest Service: This was a common thread of opinion among all interviewed, when the subject was brought up.

Chapter 5: A Breadth of Knowledge

The Focused Placement Program: Consent Decree Report, p. 23, box 11.

The Accelerated Development Program: Consent Decree Report, p. 41, box 11.

The Potential to Perform Program: Consent Decree Report, p. 23, box 11.

The Human Resource Skills Program: Consent Decree Report, p. 30, box 11.

Credit for feminist studies is now given to employees: Consent Decree Report p. 30, box 11.

The Outside Skills Bank: Consent Decree Report p. 30, box 11.

The Shared Jobs Concept: Semi Annual Report, July 1984, docket 236, p. 21, box 11.

The Part time Employment Program: Ibid.

Weekend Worker Concept: Ibid.

Priority Placement Program: Semi Annual Report, July 1984, docket 236, p. 22, box 11.

Direct Assignment: Ibid.

Lateral Placement Program: Ibid.

Winokur states that 43% is achievable because Forest Service is a dynamic organization: January 1985 Report for Compliance, p. 5, Box 11.

Winokur recognizes there is no pipeline for women: Semi-annual Report, July 1984, docket p. 236, box 11.

The most cooperative forests: Semi -annual Report, July 1984, docket 236, p. 29, box 11.

The least cooperative forests: Ibid.

Women with two years of experience were being promoted to fire captain: This was stated in numerous interviews.

Winokur asks forests to provide "gender relief": Semi-annual Report, July 1984, docket 236, p. 23, box 11.

Winokur discovers that women are physically challenged: Ibid.

Quote from the Stanislaus National Forest Supervisor: within Third Quarter Compliance Report, 1985, Volume 3, box 11.

Front line managers are not absorbing material taught them during classes: Semi-annual Report, July 1984, p. 3, box 11.

"Qualified" is now an albatross around every woman's neck: Ibid.

The 43% quota was reached in 26 out of 60 disciplines: Semi -annual Report, July 1985, p. 44, box 16.

Awareness of the value of clerical work must be enhanced: Semi -annual Report, July 1984, p. 10, box 16.

Source for the very high percentage of women in office positions: Semi Annual Report, July 1985, p. 44, box 16.

Quote from the Sequoia National Forest forester: *Pacific Southwest NewsLog*, September 1985, box 16.

Shaw's observations on the sharing of news and information among the various disciplines: Bill Shaw interview of May 18, 2008.

Smith realizes 43% will never be attained in every discipline and level within discipline: letter within Semi Annual Report, July 1984, docket 236, box 11.

Region Five runs out of consent decree funds: letter of response from Diane Winokur, Semi -annual Report, July 1984, docket 236, box 11.

Judge Conti berates Smith for his failure to reach 43%: Northern District of California of California, court records, June 30, 1985.

Judge Conti extends the consent decree: Ibid.

Conti refers to the consent decree "as amended," Bernardi v Yeutter hearing at Northern District Court of California, May 23,1989.

Chapter 6: A New Forest Service Manual

Peggy McIntosh is referred to as the Pol Pot of the American education system: *The Diversity Machine*, Lynch, p. 11.

Symposium at the Hyatt Hotel in Berkeley: docket 596, document 292, box 21.

Dale Robertson gave talk on "Tradition and Values in our Present and Future World": docket 596, document 293, box 21.

Paul Guilkey: A female counselor must be present whenever a discussion is undertaken regarding a female employee's career path: Ibid.

Margaret Briscoe-Blake decides it is the district rangers who should do the hiring: Ibid.

A full time 122 member Regional Consent Decree Committee was established. At one meeting just eight were men were present: Figures were provided at the May 13 1991 District Court hearing called by the agency in hopes of ending the decree.

The consent decree meetings were poorly attended: Third Quarter Report 1989, Volume V, Forest Exhibit RAID report, p. 4, box 16.

Meyer targets 90 grades and profession for gender rationing: docket 596, Consent Decree Handbook. 10.1, box 21.

Number of positions targeted for rationing is continually expanded, eventually reaching 152: *The San Bernardino Bear Facts,* August 1988.

Meyer's quote about strategizing with engineering to hire more women: docket 596, Consent Decree Handbook. 10.1, box 21.

The Meyer MARS plan replaces the Outside Skills Bank: docket 596, Consent Decree Handbook, 30.1, box 21.

The Feeders Program was also developed: docket 596, Consent Decree Handbook, 314., box 21.

The Charged as Worked Program: docket 596, Consent Decree Handbook, 31.4, box 21.

The Red Card potential to perform controversy: docket 596, Consent Decree Handbook, 46.4, Box 21.

The elimination of "heism" is most critical." docket 596, Consent Decree Handbook, 43.7, Box 21.

The saga of the Feather River District of the Plumas National Forest, and the Grindstone District of the Mendocino National Forest was learned through exchanges with several employees, only one of whom would self-identify: Jeff Applegate interview of January 10, 2006.

"Exceeds Acceptable Standards" was thought to intimidate women employees: docket 596, Consent Decree Handbook, 43.1, box 21.

First line managers report that the consent decree was severely hampering operations on their Forests: docket 596, 41.5, box 21.

Letter from forest supervisors informing region that new employees must begin learning about forestry operations: docket 596, 41.7, box 21.

Wayne Strom's damaging four point presentation: docket, 596, 41.6, box 21.

Meyer refers to long serving women as "a good old boys in women's clothing." Alice Forbes' letter to the district court: June 14, 1991, box 15.

Forest Service was ordered by Magistrate Wilkin to compensate Nancy Davis: docket 596, box 21.

Attorney General Meese tries and fails to rescind Nixon's executive order: Lynch, pp. 30-32.

The prevailing attitudes toward affirmative action within the Reagan Administration: Lynch pp. 31-34.

Chapter 7: The Hunt for Gender Hostile Tools

The opening of a gender library at each forest supervisor's office begins: docket 711, box 21.

Quote of Daisy Chin-Lor, the director of Avon Products multicultural division: *The Diversity Machine*, Lynch p. 52.

Records for the gender hostile tool hunt are in Box 18, file 13.7, and file 13.7.2. The sub files are not numbered, and in no particular order. Additional documents are within docket 505, box 19, which also holds the Quarterly Consent Decree Reports for 1989. Boxes 18 and 19 hold dozens of letters attesting to the hunt for gender hostile tools, composed by forest supervisors, and their assistants. Reports and directives from Regional Forester Paul Barker, and Assistant Regional Foresters Michael Duffy, Richard Deliessegues, Joyce Muroaka, Margaret Nicholson and Consent Decree Coordinator Melba Leal are in those boxes as well.

3 McCloud's and Pulaski's are specialized tools developed by the forest service to maintain roads and trails.

The letters, reports and photos from the forest supervisors, such as Mendocino Forest Supervisor Dan Chisolm of October 5, 1988, Los Padres Forest Supervisor Arthur Caroll of November 1, 1988, Eldorado Forest Supervisor Jerold Hutchings of October 17, 1988, and Angeles Forest Supervisor George Roby, October 28, 1988, are all in boxes 18 and 19.

The letters and reports address all issues: "fixed nature furniture," the necessity to escort smaller employees off the premises, tools that allow for digging trenches without having to bend over, light chainsaws, smaller hand tools and mops, retrofitted fire engines to accommodate small fire captains, shoulder holsters that favor right handed men, and left handed women, problems with combination locks, opening road gates, driving all-terrain vehicles, and entering the forests alone. Present also, are documents relating to the $250 clothing allowances for women and minorities only, twenty pound back packs for smaller employees, and the installation of opaque windows. All are in boxes 18 and 19, files unlabeled.

The purchase of light weight, single ply fire hoses 50 feet in length, equipped with plastic fittings: Many Forests reported their success in locating these pieces of equipment. Typical was the Sierra National Forest's report in docket 505, Quarterly Report dated February 8, 1989, box 19, file unlabeled.

Consent coordinator of the Lassen National Forest, Deena Bible attempted to forbid fire crews from applying the term "lady's shovel": Gary McHargue interview of July 29, 2004.

Gary McHargue's estimate of the number of women who became stranded and who he went to aid: Ibid.

Chapter 8: The Eventful Career of Gary McHargue

Judge Conti's May 9, 1988 decision to extend the decree for three years, and his directives on how the forest service was to go about achieving 43% across the board, are detailed in the Northern District Court of California Decision, Volume Five of Third Quarter Report, box 23.

Jim Burton's quote about sexual harassment: interview of September 11, 2004.

4. The sexual harassment estimates exclude three employee representatives who ere interviewed and whose duty it was to deal with those suits.

Zane Smith's column, in which he stated that American societal norms no longer measured up to Region Five's expectations appeared in the "Southwest Pacific NewsLog," September 1985.

Employee Union Representative Eric Holst's experience with sexual harassment: interview of February 13, 2009.

Employee Union Representative Lonnie Lewis's sexual harassment suits: interview of February 22, 2009.

Various monetary awards given for consent decree work: First Quarter Report of 1989, box 11.

The evaluation of Jim McGuirk: Volume 5, Third Quarter Report, 1988, box 16.

Men at the regional office were found not to be working overtime on Consent Decree: memo of November 6, 1988, unlabeled file, box 18.

The Tahoe Forest's August 5, 1988 job announcement for a surveyor in which applicants do not have to meet X-118 requirements: Volume 3 of Third Quarter Report, 1988, box 23.

The Mendocino Forest September 27, 1988 job announcement: First Quarter Report, 1989, box 11.

Modoc Forest received a single application from a male candidate. The position was cancelled, rewritten, and posted under another discipline: First Quarter Report, 1989, November 8, 1988, box 11.

The Sid Hall and Cheryl Hill decision on the Lassen Forest: letter of October 14, 1988, First Quarter Report, 1989, box 11.

The job announcement for an electronics shop on Lassen Forest: Ibid.

A letter from Eldorado Forest announcing it had promoted 25 women and 7 men: November 12, 1988, file unlabeled, box 18.

Los Padres Forest places ten announcements that say, No education or training required: October 10, 1988, First Quarter Report, 1989, box 11.

San Francisco Regional Office places an announcement that says, "Women Only Need Apply": January 26, 1989, Second Quarter Report, 1989, box 19.

Stanislaus Forest advertises for a district ranger: "Substantially Qualified Means Not More Than One Year of Job Training": Volume 3, Third Quarter Report, 1988, box 23.

Modoc Forest places an announcement that reads, "Unqualified Applicants May Apply:" notice of October 15, 1989, box 18.

Modoc Forest places announcement, but withdraws it and places it under another description after one man applies: November 8, 1988, First Quarter Report, 1989, Box 11.

Gary McHargue's career events were detailed in the first of two interviews with him: July 29, 2004.

Chapter 9: The Maupin White Paper

In January of 1989 the Shasta-Trinity, Sequoia, and Mendocino Forests all posted the following: A substantially qualified assistant district ranger means one year of experience in the position: Volume 3, Third Quarter Report, 1988, box 23.

The San Bernardino Forest announces in capital letters: ONLY APPLICANTS WHO DON'T MEET GOVERNMENT STANDARDS WILL BE CONSIDERED: U.S. District Court of Northern California Transcript of December 6, 1991, hearing before Judge Conti, box 17.

The Shasta-Trinity Forest placed job announcement that says "Unqualified applicants are accepted." announcement of February 6, 1989, box 17.

Six Rivers Forest posts a job opening stating that "Only the Unqualified May Qualify": November 20, 1989; also, December 18, 1989, box 17.

Mad River District Ranger Patricia Clark desires women and minority firefighters only: Letter in box 18, no label to file. The reasons Peace Corp Provision was used to hire women: Volume 5, Third Quarter Report, box 23.

"The Woman's Diversity Mosaic for the Future" is being held in Denver Colorado: "The Six Rivers Quarterly," February 8, 1989, box 18.

The John Fint interview was held on March 9, 2006.

Project Outreach for Women," directed by Ron Crenshaw, was expanded to cover all of the United States, and to include blacks, and other minorities, resulting in the appointments of 1,287 women and 118 male minorities: docket 471, Volume 10, August 23, 1988, box 20.

Bridge Positions are set up. A woman will receive extensive on the job training to develop qualifications. After conversion to personnel management specialist, GS-07, the employee will then be promoted to a GS-09 level without competition: docket 471, Volume 10, August 23, 1988, box 20.

8 ½ by 11 posters are sent out to all locales where it was thought women were present in high numbers. *USA Today* ran a three column 7 inch high advertisement on October 3-4, 1988, as did *San Jose Mercury News* on September 16, 1988, docket 471 Volume 10, August 23, 1988, box 20.

The Maupin White Paper: June 1989, Box 15. Copy also in Dave Meurer's papers.

Gary McHargue's second interview regarding his consent decree firefighting experiences: August 22, 2004.

Plumas Forest Supervisor Mary Coloumbe diverts funds from forest operating budget to sustain the consent decree programs: letter of February 8, 1989, folder untitled, box 23.

5 A hotshot buggy is a bus used to transport firefighters.

Mendocino Forest has custom made fire truck pedals created for a woman fire captain with short legs: Jeff Applegate interview of January 10, 2006.

Physiological factors force the forests to assign women to lighter duty: Bob Grate Interview of November 8, 1994, and Gary McHargue interview of August 22, 1994.

Robert Tyrell, supervisor of the Shasta-Trinity Forest, inquires if a special "female emergency kit" is available, letter of November 1, 1988, box 18.

Cottage cheese, yogurt, fish, carrot slices and ice are trucked into forest service fire camps: Ibid. Also Bob Grate interview of November 8, 2004.

Chapter 10: Mavens and Culls Hard at Work

The Washington Office notified all 175 Forests and grasslands that a career counselor for women was to be placed on each unit: docket 596, box 23.

A letter dated February 16, 1990 from Scott Barisch of the Federal Civil Division informed Kurtz and Meyer that a career counselor would be available on every Forest by March 1, 1990. Ibid.

All career counselors will be women: Mentoring is quite an issue. Ibid.

On March 2, 1990, Region Five began holding Job Fairs to provide the service with an opportunity to expand its female talent pool.

Floyd Thomas placed in charge Job Fairs Program drew up four blanket purchase agreements of $25,000, with each contractor to provide recruitment services: docket 615, box 19.

On January 6, 1990 the ERA informed forest service that Job Fairs should be dropped and direct hire authority obtained from OPM: docket 615, box 19.

Fifteen additional job announcements discriminating against men; and 15 contracts signed in order to send women to college, with tuition and living costs paid for: Volume 4, Third Quarter Report, 1988, box 23.

Paul Barker's letter to the women of Region Five regarding the great opportunities in education is dated September 30, 1988: unlabeled file, box 23.

In a sampling, a total of 50 women signed a written statement stating they did not wish to attend colleges paid for by the U.S. Forest Service. Five accepted. Volume 3, Third Quarter, 1988 reports, box 23.

Veterans are singled out for discrimination in Region Five: "Report of Prohibited Personnel Practices or other Prohibited Activity," mailed to the U.S. Merit Systems Protection Board by Kermit Johansson, February 8, 1990. A letter by Jerry Bertagna, dated October 13, 1988, quoting Kathy Waller on the efficacy of purging vets from the rosters: Both in unlabeled file, box 11.

The Great Yreka Encirclement: interview with Gary Mc Hargue of August 22, 1994.

Paul Barker's letter of January 16, 1990 to U.S. Personnel Director Joseph Patti, Office of Personnel Management: Barker told Patti that throughout the entire U.S. government and state governments, there were not enough qualified women to fill many positions: docket 615, box 19.

Details of Paul Barker's new upward mobility program: Letter and tables in Fourth Quarter Report, December 26, 1989, Box 16.

Women must comprise 65% if the JAC fire program and Engine Captain Norman J. Walker's letter about women being embarrassed because special tools were being designed for their use. Letter is in Volume 5, Third Quarter Report, 1988, box 23.

Chief Forester Dale Roberson's directive expects each forest in the United States to represent the racial and gender composition of the United States at large: Third Quarter Report, Volume 3, exhibit RAID, box 16.

Region Five's new quota program: 15% of hires minority men, 15% minority females, 45% white females, 25% white males: Volume 5, Third Quarter Report, 1988, box 23.

After Barker rescinds the quota system, Mike Roger's complains about the uncertainty caused by not allotting jobs by gender and race: Volume 5, Third Quarter Report, 1988, box 23.

Chief Robertson writes Paul Barker, urging that he hold a meeting with other regional foresters, emphasizing the harmony among his employees: Volume 5, Third Quarter Report, 1988, letter dated December 12, 1989, box 23.

The consent decree committee, chaired by Tahoe Forest assistant forester Carol Hammer decides the Bernardi Decree prohibits men from exercising their right to vote: Tahoe National Forest Fourth Quarter Report, box 16.

The *Pacific Southwest NewsLog* of February 1988 presents a column by Roxane May Scales, indicating that the female culture drive was in the midst of a very successful launch.

Jeannie Meyer complains to Magistrate Wilken she is being harassed by forest employees when conversing with them; and that Department of Justice's female attorneys are following her into the restroom to make her feel vulnerable: letter of October 18, 1991, file unlabeled, box 21.

Conti announces he is not interested in 43.5% overall; only interested in that all the grades are at 43.5% and above—despite the fact region hired at an overall 71.4% rate female since 1986, and up to 96% in some categories: U.S. District Court of Northern California Transcript of December 6, 1991, box 17.

Forest Service's extraordinary percentages in the hiring of women: U.S. District Court of Northern California Transcript of December 6, 1991, presented to Judge Conti, box 17.

Paul Barker begins passing "heads up" to the Male Class Complaint: Bob Grate interview of July 28, 2004.

Chapter 11: An Outlaw Agency

Ron Stewart begins using "Reduction in Work Force" to reduce the number of men in Region Five: *The Supporter,* December 12, 1992.

Ron Stewart's kittenish feature about swimming in the pool with girl employees: *Southwest Pacific NewsLog*, September 23, 1991, box 21.

Ping Pong acts as a stress reliever on the Mendocino Forest: Ibid.

Sexual harassment skits were enacted on the Klamath Forest: Ibid.

The Six Rivers Forest celebrated diversity day: Ibid.

The Orleans District of the Six Rivers Forest reported on the three years it spent developing a Day Care Center. A handbook to assist other forests was produced and distributed: *Southwest Pacific NewsLog*, September, 23, 1991, box 21.

On the Stanislaus National Forest, a task force was assembled to compile information on potential job/share/ part time positions on the Forest. The ten women "worked diligently' for over a year in assembling "A Handbook for Managers." Ibid.

Stanislaus Forest District Ranger Jan Ford directs a seminar on clarifying values: Ibid

In August 1991 Region Five began issuing a separate *Consent Decree Digest*. Ron Stewart composed a column emphasizing how important all employees are to the supervisor, and when that importance is lost, the agency is also lost: *Consent Decree Digest*, December 2, 1991, box 21.

Angeles Forest Supervisor Mike Rogers reports on his employee diversity meeting at Pyramid Lake: *Southwest Pacific NewsLog*, September 23, 1991, box 21.

Joan Kushner is "rewriting the suitability standards for female law enforcement personnel": *Consent Decree Digest*, September 5, 1991, box 21.

Regional Director Ron Stewart launches gay/lesbian taskforce: directive of February 24, 1992, file unlabeled, box 21.

Stewart desires to contact local community leaders, and businesses regarding the efficacy of gay/lesbian lifestyle: March 3, 1992, file unlabeled, box 21.

The forest service's hiring/promotion tables within the Semi-annual Report from Monitor Meyer to the Northern District Court was presented on March 8, 1991: box 15.

Men were underrepresented in 83 different professions/job levels. They made up less than 25% of employees in 14 professional, 29 administration, 13 technical and 20 clerical positions. Figures were deducted by author from the tables on female hiring presented to the court: box 15.

Percentage of receptionists, administrative assistants, and personnelists ranged from 70% to 95% female: Report of June 21, 1991 to Northern District Court of California, box 15.

Ronald Crenshaw's presentation of hiring percentages to the court: Ibid.

National Association of Manufacturers, and most Fortune 500 CEOs decidedly approved of job rationing by race/gender: Lynch, p. 34.

Katja Bullock's quote on George H.W. Bush: Lynch, p. 31.

C. Boyden Gray's quote: Ibid.

Chapter 12: How to Lie with Words

Region Five figures report that 52 out of 59 foresters hired were women, etc. The forest Service's hiring/promotion tables are within the Semi-annual Report compiled by Monitor Meyer, and presented to the Northern District Court on March 8, 1991. Box 23.

A Stanislaus Forest law enforcement officer reports that consent decree work had priority over drug investigations: Letter was undated, but within the Tom Locker files, furnished May 4, 2005.

Stewart's extraordinary numbers for the JAC firefighter apprentice program: directive of November 13, 1991, docket 596, Box 23.

The Tahoe Forest Fire Captain's "Two Short Essays on Statistics and Preferential Policies," using the *Hypergeometric Distribution Method*. The essays, written in early 1992, are unsigned copies of the original: Tom Locker files.

Under qualified women were very defensive, and tended to file sexual harassment grievances far out of proportion to their numbers: The observation was made within the text of "Two Short Essays on Statistics and Preferential Policies," using the *Hypergeometric Distribution Method*. The unsigned essays are in the Tom Locker files furnished May 4, 2005.

The letter about the young male firefighter having to place his dreams on hold: Ibid.

The use of the *Hypergeometric Distribution Method* in analyzing what are known as "rare events:" Ibid.

James J. Kilpatrick, syndicated columnist, reported that fire management officers were telling young men, off the record not even to apply. 'You are the wrong gender.' *Union Vision*, National Federation of Federal Employees, Summer 1992.

Consent Decree Coordinator Richard Henry contradicts his own argument within same letter one paragraph below: June 25, 1992. Tom Locker files, furnished on May 4, 2005.

Tahoe National Forest Supervisor John Skinner's memo about a hostile work environment: February 28, 1991. Ibid.

Magistrate Wilken directly meddles in U.S. Forest Service hiring policies: letter of May 21, 1991, by attorneys Brook Hedges, and Scott Barisch, regarding that day's hearing: box 15.

"Forty three percent. That was something everybody agreed to, not something I said. I approved it because you agreed to it." District Judge Samuel Conti at August 1, 1991 court hearing, box 15.

Conti's quote during the August 1991 hearing about not being interested in 43.5% overall, but in 43.5% for each grade within position: December 6, 1991, court hearing, box 17.

Between March 1, 1988 and February 28, 1991 the forest service paid Jeannie Meyer's salary, a sum total of $388,970: May 13 1991.

District Court hearing, box 18, U.S. District Court for the Northern District of California.

Equal Rights Advocate Judith Kurtz' testimony before the Ninth Circuit Court of Appeals: September 26, 1991, box 17; also see *Union Vision*, National Federation of Federal Employees, Summer 1992.

Brook Hedges says the directives, later arrived at for women in many office positions are not a part of Article IV, and Judge Conti's retort: court hearing of August 2, 1991, box 17.

"Judge Blasts Government Foot Dragging": Mintz, Howard, *The Recorder*, August 2, 1991.

Equal Rights Advocate Nancy Davis' quote to Jane Braxton Little, *Sacramento Bee*, November 8, 1992.

The corporations employing large scale affirmative action: Lynch, p. 34.

The 1995 *Wall Street Journal* estimates the number of jobs lost by white males: Lynch, p. 338.

Chapter 13: The Rise of The Male Class Complaint

Estimates as to the number of buyouts in Region Five from 1986 to 1994 *may* have reached 1000: interview with Bob Grate, November 8, 2004.

Levitoff is told by Richard Henry a woman must be promoted to GS-09 fire captain; he will not be considered: Interview with Bob Grate, June 11, 2004.

Document listing those joining the Levitoff Class Complaint: Within the binder presented to the United States Supreme Court for its October 1996 term.

Kermit Johansson's "Report of Prohibited Personnel Practices or other Prohibited Activity," presented 18 exhibits of the Sierra Forest depriving its veterans and men in general of their civil rights is in report of February 8, 1990: Dave Meurer files.

Sierra Forest consent decree panel members denounce the character of U.S. military veterans: page 3 of item 6, Report to the District Court of February 8, 1990: Dave Meurer files.

Tom Beaumont, director of Equal Employment Opportunity Office for the Department of Agriculture, decides to fight the Male Class and Levitoff Class Complaints: *The Supporter*, March 28, 1990.

On March 23, 1991 Bob Grate received from the Department of Agriculture EEOC a denial of their right to establish a Class Complaint: Ibid.

Bob Grate and Jerry Levitoff are granted seats at very large inclusive table, but are denied the right to use government computers, stationery, etc to pursue their case. *The Supporter*, September 28, 1991.

U.S. Supreme Court decision, Richmond v Croson, is disregarded by Secretary of Agriculture Clayton Yeutter and Attorney General Richard Thornburgh: *The Supporter* November 19, 1990.

Levitoff refused the Washington Office's "bribe," and class attorney Louis Demas files a complaint: *The Supporter,* December 15, 1991.

Tom Locker traces the rejection of his applications to forests across the nation by placing a pin on a map of the U.S for each unit.

Investigates each rejection, and finds out he lost to a woman every time. Tom Locker interview of April 27, 2005.

The Cherokee National Forest's Don Corbin's, quote: Tom Locker interview of April 27, 2005.

Locker concludes that his own personnel department was improperly rearranging his resumes for jobs elsewhere: Locker interview of April 27, 2005. Also his letter of October 28, 1991 to Martha Twarkins, EEO Counselor of Tahoe Forest: Tom Locker files.

Locker was offered a promotion, costs and back pay if he would drop his nine other suits: He accepted: Ibid

Secretary of Agriculture Edward Madigan was traumatized by contempt of court citation: Tom Locker interview of April 27, 2005.

On June 28, 1991, Judge Conti receives a letter from fifty women, informing them they are dropping out of the Bernardi Complaint: Tom Locker files.

Klamath Forest employee William Lewis sends letter to Judge Conti, making note of the "Half Moon Task Force, "dated May 4, 1991: unlabeled file, box 15.

Alice Forbes' letter to the district court, regarding the fact that consent decree had priority over fighting fires, dated June 14, 1991: unlabeled file, box 15.

Letter of Public Relations Officer Kathy Hammond of Quincy to Magistrate Wilkin informing her that a group challenging Bernardi, titled CECO, is being formed: dated June 6, 1991, box 15.

Julie Vogan, dispatcher at an interagency fire center, wrote a letter to Equal Rights Advocate Judith Kurtz, dated April 19, 1991, four pages in length. unlabeled file, box 21.

Donna J. Bergstrom's letter to Judge Conti stated that working on consent decree had priority over fighting fires, April 26, 1991: Ibid.

Rhonda L. Barrett's letter to Judge Conti stating that it takes a special kind of employee to work in a forest: April 30, 1991: Ibid.

Marcia Andre of the Olympic National Forest, Washington, wrote a letter (undated) to Judge Conti, stating that conditions are so horrible in California, that no woman working in Oregon and Washington will consider transferring there: Ibid

Debora W. Fisher reports to the ERA, that a poll of women on the Plumas, Klamath, Sequoia, and Sierra Forests indicated that 86% to 95% wish the consent decree to end, April 9, 1991: Ibid.

Terri Simon Jackson informs the ERA that they are forming a class complaint titled, "Committee to End Court Oversight" to fight Bernardi Decree, May 6, 1991: Ibid.

Chapter 14: Consent, a Deathless Decree

In May 1991 U.S. Civil Rights Commissioner Jeffrey J. Goodfriend ruled that Secretary of Agriculture Edward Madigan, and Agricultural EEO counsel Tom Beaumont, were in flagrant violation of the law: *The Supporter,* June 7, 1991.

Region Five is ordered to reinstate a displaced silviculturist with back pay and costs: *The Supporter,* May 19, 1992.

Fireman asks for a desk position on doctors orders, but is told none exists: Ibid.

The consent decree ends with directives fully embedded. Joyce Muroaka states the cost of the decree from 1988 through 1991 were $21,245,418. Figures are from the May 13 1991 District Court hearing, box 18.

Bob Grate notes at the meeting that "a large portion of the directives called for special treatment of certain classes of people, based on non-merit factors: *The Supporter,* May 9, 1992.

The Department of Justice intends to intervene against the U..S. Forest Service because of its intention to follow the directives, but abruptly reversed course. James J. Kilpatrick's stated that President G. H. W. Bush then lost his nerve. Also *The Union Vision*, published by National Federation of Federal Employees, Summer 1992.

Levitoff and Grate learn that many who have filed discrimination suits are being targeted with sexual harassment smears. A support group is established for them: *The Supporter*, May 19, 1992.

Bob Grate reports that his website is being flooded with emails from men employed by the U.S. Army, U.S. Navy, U.S. Park Service.

Service, U.S. Fish and Wildlife Service, the IRS, Postal Service, and F.A.A. with accounts of discrimination: Grate interview of July 28, 2004.

Ron Stewart's statements about adhering to our new directives and special working group agreements after decree ends: *The Supporter*, March 28, 1992.

The forest service implements the directives before the class complaint members are given an opportunity to vote. *The Supporter*, May, 9, 1992.

Secretary Espy's office rules in favor of plaintiff Michael Leveroos: signed by Wardell C. Townsend Jr., August 3, 1993: Louis Demas files.

Espy's office rules in favor of plaintiff William Putt: signed by Wardell C. Townsend Jr., August 19, 1993: Louis Demas files.

Espy's office rules in favor of Barry Callenberger: signed by Wardell C. Townsend Jr., October 8, 1993: Louis Demas files.

Twenty one firemen who filed discrimination complaints against Region Five for promoting JAC graduates won their cases: *The Supporter,* December 12, 1992.

Espy's office rules in favor of Greg Gregor: signed by Wardell C. Townsend Jr., January 7, 1994: Louis Demas files.

Espy's office rules in favor of Kyle Felker: signed by Wardell C. Townsend Jr., May 20, 1994: Louis Demas files.

Espy is informed by the MCC that Stewart is awarding discrimination bonuses to his forest supervisors: Bob Grate interview July 28, 2004. The figures are in unlabeled file in box 21.

Chapter 15: Toward a Kinder and Gentler Forest

Leroy Johnson's account of his being forced to hire a female employee who was barely literate, a geneticist who could not climb trees, and the refusal among scientists to engage in any more work, after learning they stood no chance of promotion: Leroy Johnson interview of November 6, 2005.

The Blue Book was issued with Chief Robertson's memo of February 2, 1993: Peter Brost file.

Terry West's critique of Chief Robertson's "Blue Book," appeared on April 9, 1993, although he wrote the original essay shortly after the book was composed in March 1991: Peter Brost file.

The natural sensitivity of women to criticism and stress: Studies have focused on the stress hormone, corticotrophin releasing (CRF), which plays a role in human psychiatric conditions, and helps to explain why they are twice as vulnerable as men to stress-related disorders. It is a major reason why they are less able to contend with rejoinders, criticisms of plans, and divergent opinions. M. Valenzuela, D. Bartrés-Faz, F. Beg, A. Fornito, EMerlo-Pich, UMüller, D. Öngür, A W. Toga and M. Yücel *The Journal of Molecular Psychiatry*, Philadelphia, May 31, 2011.

See also ehast, Aaeron, "Women are more sensitive to stress than men," *Kinetic Movement and Stress Relief.*

The percentage of women employed by the Washington Office, 1990: figures were furnished by Terry West, and in the Peter Brost file.

The behavior of employees in various parts of the world is described in Geert Hoftadt's study of 116,000 IBM employees working in 40 countries: *Foundations of Management*, Robert Kreitner, Arizona State University, 2007.

Peter Brost critique of Chief Robertson's "Blue Book": March 9, 1993. In reaction to Brost and West's critiques, among the hundreds of emails was that from Ralph Johnson of Lolo, Montana; his letter to Kenneth M. Cohen was written May 16, 1993: Peter Brost files.

Richard Trochlil of the Eastern Forest Region, writes of his encounters with the bureau's more "vulnerable employees" in email of May 9, 1993: Ibid.

Bob Peterson's quote on RIF policies toward men in Region Six, Mount Hood National Forest, appeared on email system May 9, 1993: Ibid.

Northern Rocky Mountain Region Linda Buck's quote appeared on email system May 9, 1993; Ibid.

Karl Brenneis of Region Two wrote that "You have put into words what I feel has been "crushing down" on all of us in recent years is an email of April 16, 1993: Ibid.

Email of David O. Weber of the Eastern Forest Region, on the evaporating institutional knowledge of the forests appeared on May 9, 1993: Ibid.

A comparison of Region Five and Region Six's hiring numbers for women: *Southwest Pacific NewsLog*, August 10, 1989.

One hundred employees were assigned the task of designing a forest workforce mirroring the gender and skin pigmentation of the nation: Chief Robertson's letter to all forests, dated February 2, 1993: Peter Brost files.

The forest service at large now focuses on a "temporary/ promotional data base" in order to increase minority employment: The directive was referred to in The Forest Service Manual," Title 1700 Civil Rights: from Peter Brost files.

Jerry Levitoff's encounter with a transvestite: Interview with Bob Grate July 28, 2004.

Chapter 16: An Educationally Deprived Child

"Skeletal Muscle Mass and Distribution Among 468 Men and Women aged 18 to 88 Years": *The Journal of Applied Physiology*: February 23, 2000.

Just 6% of women are as strong as the *average* man: Steven Rhoades, *Taking Sex Differences Seriously*, p. 144.

A woman's hands and wrists are capable of applying 57 increments of pressure for every 100 applied by a man: Ibid.

The upper body strength of women is 52% of that of a man; the lower body strength is 61%: David Puts, and company, "Beauty and the Beast: Mechanisms of Sexual Selection in Humans," Penn State, Department of Anthropology, 2006, 31: 157-175.

One Standard Deviation: denoted as "g," or "effect size," is the number of deviations separating two means. By convention an effect size of 0.2 is regarded as small, and can be overlooked. An effect size of 0.5 is labeled as moderate, and can be overcome with aid. An effect size of 0.8 is labeled as large, and cannot be compensated for. Most physical differences between men and women range from *very large to enormous;* that is, from 1.5 to 4 effect sizes, or standard deviations: Rhoads, p. 20, 21.

Relative to height, men have significantly longer legs, allowing them to run faster, farther, and to jump much greater distances.

They possess larger hearts, larger lungs, higher systolic blood pressure, and a lower resting heart beat rate: Rhoads, p. 213.

Each liter of male blood contains 150 to 160 grams of hemoglobin, compared to 130 to 140 grams for females, James Dabbs, *Heroes, Rogues and Lovers; Testosterone and Behavior.*

By age seventeen there is no overlap between the sexes when it comes to tossing a baseball, stick, wrench, or backpack: Rhoades, pp 213, 214.

Anterior cruciate ligament injuries among women are three to seven times more frequent: R. Alexander Creighton, M.D, *ACC Sports Sciences Main Page*, Oct. 1, 2004 (internet). Other more recent studies have placed the number of injuries at the median of the above figures, that is five times as many injuries are likely to be sustained by women.

Mental rotation differences between men and women: "Sex Differences in Mental Rotation and Spatial Rotation in a Virtual Environment, Parsons, Larson, Kratz, Thiebaux, Bluestein, Buckwalter, and Rizzo, August 2003 (Internet).

Visual acuity differences between men and women: "Spatial ability and Throwing Accuracy," Behavior Genetics, Volume 13, February 28, 1983, Rosemary Jardine and N.D. Martin. See also *BRAIN SEX: The Real Difference Between Men and Women*, Anne Moir, Ph.D. and David Jessel (Internet).

Chapter 17: Many Seasons of Gender Studies

The two pain tests conducted by P. Chesteron, P. Barlas, N.E. Forest, G..D. Baxter and C.C Wright were titled "PAIN gender differences in pressure pain threshold in healthy humans" Department of Physiotherapy Studies, Keele University, Staffordshire, UK.

The pain test conducted by Shannon R. Burnside of the University of Western Missouri was titled, "Gender Competition: a Test Between the Sexes," 1999. Only the abstract is presented in the most confusing manner on the internet.

Men have thicker skins than women; their skins secrete more oil: A number of websites confirm these traits.

Raymond Rainville at the "Twentieth Annual International Conference of the Association for the Study of Dreams," Berkeley, California, June, 2003, reported on his "courage test."

Over a seven year period forty men died attempting to rescue persons completely unknown to them, while a single woman gave her life in doing the same: Ronald C. Johnson's "Attributes of Carnegie Medalists Performing Acts of Heroism, and of the Recipients of the these Acts, 1996. (abstract only online).

In men, because of the testosterone factor, the vocal cords are much larger and tend to the range from 130 to 145 hz, or cycles per second, while women's voices are from 230 and 255 cycles per second: A research article by Hodges, C. R., Cárdenas, R. A., and Gaulin, S. J. C. (2007) titled, "Men's voices as dominance signals: Vocal fundamental and formant frequencies influence dominance attributions among men," Penn State, Department of Anthropology (internet).

With the addition of female patrol officers there is a large increase in assaults on police officers, most particularly on women: "Does a Helping Hand Put Others At Risk? Affirmative Action": *Police Departments and Crime,*" 38 Econ. Inquiry, 2000, John R. Lott, pp. 35, 36, 37 (internet).

A detailed study on how boys and girls in their lower teens go about organizing their activities, as well as their status at summer camps: David Geary, Psychological Association member, *Male, Female, the Evolution of Human Sex Differences,* 1998, pp 262-268.

A 2004 study found girls disapproved of girls who outperformed other girls, while boys took pleasure in challenging those with superior capabilities: "Sex Differences in Reactions to Outperforming Same-sex Friends," Joyce Benenson and Joy Schinazi, *British Journal of Developmental Psychology* (internet).

Alpha boys are more successful at controlling their groups than the alpha girls: Geary, 269.

For 8-11 year olds it was found that boys in England had 50% to 200% greater play ranges than girls. Similar discoveries were made in studying children in Peru, Kenya and Guatemala. With the advance of age boys or groups of boys continue to explore ever further. Geary, pp. 232-236.

Women and Absenteeeism: "Cultural Diversity: Implications For Workplace Management," Donatus I Amaram, *Journal of Diversity Management,* Fourth Quarter 2007, Volume 2, Number 4.

Women are 50% more likely than men to leave a management position: "Gender Differences in Absenteeism," Scott, McClellan, *Public Personnel Management,* pp. 2, 19, 229-253.

Men on average are four times more likely to spend 50 hours a week at their desks: "Unequal Pay for Unequal Work," Carey Roberts, January 12, 2005 (internet).

There are many sources for this statement regarding male achievement. Read in particular Charles Murray, *Human Accomplishment: The Pursuit of Excellence in the Arts and Sciences, 800 BC to 1950,* Harper Collins, 2003.

Chapter 18: The Caulfield Decision

Louis Demas did not lose a single plaintiff's case: Interview with Louis Demas July 20, 2004; also Bob Grate interview of November 8, 2004.

Bob Grate and Jerry Levitoff 's interview with Cathy Slobogin on ABC's *"20/20,"* October 28, 1993: *The Supporter,* November 19, 1993, and Bob Grate interview of July 28, 2004.

Bob Grate and Jerry Levitoff 's interview with Catherine Crier of CNN's *Crier and Company,* November 28, 1993: Bob Grate interview of July 28, 2004.

Phil Donahue fails in his attempt to design a program devoted to the merits of affirmative action: Bob Grate interview of July 28, 2004.

Forest Service spokesman Matt Mathes statements to the press after the Slobogan interview: *The Supporter,* November 19, 1993.

Richard Henry, supervisor of the Lassen Forest, well over a year after the Bernardi Decree ended, issued a series of crippling directives: *The Supporter,* December 19, 1994.

The Northern California District Court decision by Judge Barbara Caulfield is in the Mark G. Levitoff v Dan Glickman file, December 14, 1993, Federal Records Storage Center, San Bruno, CA.

Congressman Wally Herger's office issues a press release on the forest service's "Thought Control Program," January 14, 1994: Dave Meurer file.

Herger writes letter to Chief Forester Jack Ward Thomas, accusing him of practicing discrimination: Letters of January 25, 1995, and March 7, 1995. Dave Meurer file.

Mike Espy relieves Ron Stewart as director of Region Five: Bob Grate interview of July 28, 2004.

In fighting fires throughout the Western states, Tom Locker was disturbed to find that he never come across a single female fire management officer with a firsthand knowledge of firefighting: Tom Locker interview of April 27, 2005.

Nina Locker's quotes regarding Asian Americans and the U.S. Forest Service: Ibid.

Chapter 19: The Story of Jack Ward Thomas

Scientists are now required to bring an attitude to the debate the speech by Jack Ward Thomas to the Horace Albright Conservation Lectureship, April 14, 1992 (internet website).

When deconstruction environmentalists find themselves losing the battle of facts, which is more often the case than not, they invariably resorted to name calling, and obfuscating the issues: Ibid.

Thomas' quote: "When computers devour the data, perform the model's magic and then produce results that do not ring true in the light of theory, empirical data, experience, common sense and professional opinion, caution lights should be flashed on and alarm bells rung": Ibid.

Thomas' quote: The welfare of these communities is a legitimate concern of elected officials—and all politics are indeed local. Furthermore the Forest Service has a policy of aiding in the creation and maintenance of community stability in such circumstances." Ibid.

Thomas informs James Lyons that in 1993 white males represented 72.8% of the promotional pool, received 52% of the promotions, and that in 1994 they comprised 71% of the promotion pool, but received 45.2% of promotions: Report of May 3, 1994, Thomas, Jack Ward, Dave Meurer files.

He also reported that in 1993 there were 261 retirement buyouts: Ibid.

The surveying and mapping for the Northwest Plan proved extraordinary costly, running from $35 to $125 per acre: *Triplicate Staff*, Jennifer Henison, August 11, 2003. Thomas, Jack Ward, *The Journal of a Forest Service Chief*.

A less ambitious Northwest Forest Plan was developed, then also shelved, to be followed by yet another, even less ambitious revision:" Ibid.

Thomas notes in diary that his employees "are badly demoralized and confused, filled with malaise and contention," p. 91.

He will not give up his white male culture: "For me to give up my personality is a price too high," pp. 92, 93.

According to Thomas, during 1995 500 white men were bought out in a single month; 2,500 more were to be bought out by 1999, p.170.

Thomas informs South Dakota Senators Daschle and Johnson that he did not have the soil managers, range managers, and geologists available to assess the cattle allotments, p. 170.

The causes of the Storm King Mountain Fire in Colorado: p. 116. Read John N. Maclean's, *Fire on the Mountain* in its entirety, Harper Collins Perennial, 2009.

Retired Region Five Forester Douglas Leisz's letter to President Clinton was written on August 29, 1995, and can be accessed on the internet by entering the website of the "National Association of Forest Service Retirees."

Thomas is astonished that the Environmental Protection Agency has not taken legal action against U.S. Forest Service because of poor quality water conditions in Cleveland Forest. "The pressure is so heavy in the city and the use so heavy, the need so great that it is probably politically expedient to look the other way," Thomas, p. 114.

Author states "The body count from all causes on the Forest is three to five per week.....Dealing with these fatalities plus the wounded is said to take a heavy toll on Forest Service people." Ibid.

Law enforcement officers on the Southern California Forests were concerned about the phase out of forestry protection officers by the Washington office, Thomas, p. 155.

An announcement for a supervisory aviation fire management officer on the Cleveland National Forest; only those who contribute to Forest Service diversity will be hired: Attached to Congressman Wally Herger's letter of January 30, 1995 to Jack Ward Thomas: Dave Meurer files.

A Civil Rights forum spent almost an entire day denouncing the protests of white men about discrimination, Thomas, p. 318.

The Chief's quote to Sherry Sheng, and the crowd erupting into laughter, Thomas, p. 92.

The Chief learns that personnel counselors are handing out grievance awards to "finger-pointers" in almost every personnel complaint filed, without an investigation into the facts: Thomas, pp. 93, 387, 388.

Thomas' list of very annoying problems he hopes to never come across in private life, Thomas, pp. 387, 388.

Chapter 20: The Ninth Circuit Court of Appeals

Jim Burton's account of the disabled fireman: Burton interview of September 11, 2004.

Bob Grate's account of the disabled fireman: July 28, 2004.

The Lassen Forest builds a $30,000 ramp and deck for the disabled: Ibid.

Black employees refuse to stay with the forest service any length of time, resulting in turnover, and training problems: John Fint interview of March 9, 2006.

The Lassen Forest hires an urban felon: Bob Grate interview of July 18, 2004.

"Opportunity Los Angeles," the Rodney King riots and the forest service's reaction: Bill Shaw interview of May 22, 2008.

Native Americans do not trust the U.S. Forest Service: Ken Gilbert interview of February 4, 2006.

Jeff Applegate's experience with the African Oryx specialist: Applegate interview of February 22, 2006.

Nine affirmative action committees from each forest region across the U.S meet to determine how to increase numbers of women and minorities. Answer: The devastating fire season was discouraging them from seeking work: Document is titled "Service Wide Civil Rights Commission Report," Marriott Brookfield Milwaukee Hotel, October16-20, 1996: Tom Locker files.

Nine affirmative action committees from each forest region across the U.S. met on the Tahoe National Forest. It was determined to make it officially known that the best qualified employees will not always be promoted: "Report on the Crag Meeting, Truckee Ranger District, Tahoe National Forest, January 11, 1995: Dave Meurer Files.

Sheri Elliott announces that "Students with a grade point average of 2.0 can now be hired in place of someone with, say, a 3.2 average": Ibid.

Arlen Roll's long address concerning opposition to affirmative action: Ibid.

The special efforts to accommodate "under represented" employees was posted on one of the U.S. Forest Service's website links as late as 2008. It remained on site for some months, but appears to have been withdrawn.

Congressman Herger announces that he is introducing the "Forest Service Employment Act": Letter of May 25, 1995, Dave Meurer files.

By the mid-1990s supervisors in all branches of government were being warned against discharging unsatisfactory employees of certain races and genders: commentary by former head of the office of Personnel Management, Donald Devine, *Washington Times*, October 14, 1997.

The Ninth Circuit Court of Appeals decision: Mark G. Levitoff v Dan Glickman folder, January 16, 1996: Federal Records Storage Center, San Bruno.

Judge Kleinfeld's powerful dissent citing case law, the Civil Rights Act of 1991, and the circuit court's departure from the usual and accepted course of judicial procedure: Ibid.

Chapter 21: The Turn of Congress

The number of legal victories by the Male Class Complaint were arrived by a table presented to Congressman Herger by Region Five Director Lynn Sprague, dated April 7, 1995: Dave Meurer files.

They did not include the attorney fees for the Department of Agriculture, which ran to $10 million in 1993 alone: *The Supporter*, June 8, 1994.

The notion that there was no such thing as a culture of white men was a common complaint, noted by many interviewed. One rhetorically asked, "Who in hell invented forestry?"

Florida Congressman John Mica, Chairman of the House Committee on Government Reform and Oversight, and his lengthy exchange with Assistant Chief Forester Ron Stewart, is within Mica's letter of November 21, 1997, and Stewart's reply of January 21, 1998: Dave Meurer files.

The California Civil Rights Initiative of 1996 to eliminate quotas was passed by the voters by a wide margin. Yet Newt Gingrich, Bob Dole and Jack Kemp could not sprint away from the initiative fast enough: Lynch, 170.

The Adarand Construction Company was successful in its suit against the state of Colorado for hiring a minority contractor, despite its much lower bid. Yet Gingrich and Kemp declined to support Adarand: Ibid.

Gingrich and Kemp remained mute also regarding the Hopwood v University of Texas decision, even after the Fifth Circuit Court of Appeals ruled that its law school quota admissions policy was unconstitutional: Lynch, p. 361.

The word went out to the government and corporate chieftains, that despite employee antagonisms roiling everywhere beneath the surface, they could engage in "the mending, not ending" rhetoric assumed by President Bill Clinton: Lynch, p. 367.

The U.S. Supreme Court decision not to review the Levitoff Class Complaint is within the Supreme Court of the United States, Mark G. Levitoff v Dan Glickman folder, October 16, 1996. Term Petition for Writ of Certiorari: Federal Records Storage Center, San Bruno, CA.

Louis Demas cites the dramatic departure of the Ninth Circuit Court from the usual and accepted course of judicial procedure, Louis Demas interview of July 20, 1994.

Louis Demas furnished numerous documents regarding the cases he had handled, as well as providing back ground on the case law that preceded Bernardi and Levitoff: Ibid.

Chapter 22: The Donnelly Settlement Agreement

Accounts of the events at the Los Prietos Ranger Station were related in *Wildlife News*, October 10, 2002.

A very inferior accounting of the nude photo incident was presented by CBS news, titled "Sex bias at the Forest Service," October 12, 2002.

6: Self-contained fire service vehicles (box or cargo trucks) that carry gear and tools.

Jack Blackwell's quotes: *Wildlife News*, October 10, 2002.

Lesa Donnelly's quotes about hotshots: Ibid.

McFarland expresses concern for her safety: interview with Lesa Donnelly, February 15, 2008.

All material regarding Lesa Donnelly and the Donnelly Settlement Agreement: Ibid.

Bob Grate wondered why the Marine in Iraq was not discharged from the Corps, because of the photos of scantily clad women in his tent: Interview with Bob Grate on July 28, 2004.

Chapter 23: The Rot Starts at the Top

Some contend that the Bush Administration thought it was outfoxing the U.S. Forest Service by directing the agency to contract out much of its work. In doing so it would circumvent the agency's all-consuming numbers game. It did not work out that way, as the costs of paying the majority of agency employees, now lodged in the regional and forest supervisor offices, continues to climb.

The negative effects of the Albuquerque, New Mexico personnel office move: interview with Lonnie Lewis on February 22, 2009.

Eric Holst points out that unlike other agencies, such as the post office, where employees are responsible for two or three tasks, forest service employees may be expected to perform twenty tasks: Interview with Eric Holst, February 13, 2009.

America's state owned forests, many managed by trusts, are much more effectively operated than those of the forest service. *Thoreau Institute*, "The Rot Starts at the Top," Randal O'Toole, February 8, 2000.

Randal O'Toole reports that the costs of operating the agency, outpaces the income from timber and recreation by 4300%: "The Financial Psychosis of Federal and State Forest Agencies," *Thoreau Institute,* December 30, 1999.

Chief Forester Dombeck's principal objective was the restoration of forest watersheds: H. Michael Anderson, 1999 fall issue of *Wilderness* magazine.

The failure of the forest service to restore its burned over timber lands: "National Association of Forest Service Retirees" report of April 2005.

In 2004 W.M. Beaty and Associates, which lost 3,200 acres to severe burn in the Storrie Fire two years prior, announced it had completed its restoration project: Ibid.

Much of the planning for each forest's ten year plan is done at the regional office without anyone entering the woods: interview with Jeff Applegate, March 16, 2006.

The forest service spent $1 billion dollars on their forest plans, complete with environmental impact statements. But their endeavors ran beyond the target date, were deemed obsolete, and shipped off to storage: O'Toole, Randal, "Forest Plans that do Nothing," *Seattle Times,* May 18, 2003.

A forest service human resource employee bragged at a public forum that she has entered the woods just once in all her years of employment: interview with Jeff Applegate, January 11, 2006.

By 2006 there were 82 squatters residing in trailers and cabins in various locales of the Tahoe Forest: Peter Brost interview of November 21, 2006.

"We don't want to find out if it is really worse than it appears to be." Ibid.

Estimate for the Tahoe National Forest is that a half dozen law enforcement officers are required for each of the four districts: Ibid.

The Eldorado Forest has just one law enforcement officer, and two forest protection officers for each of its four districts: Eric Holst interview of February 13, 2009.

The Mexican Mafia has seized many thousands of acres, where they have established a booming pot industry: Adam Burke, "Public Lands; Big Cash Crop," *High Country News.* Oct 2, 2006.

Even though the marijuana gardens are in low lying country, it is also heavily timbered and rugged, most easily accessed by helicopter: Ibid.

Forest Service, Park Service, and Bureau of Land Management law enforcement officers have become professional dope cutters: Ibid.

Chapter 24: The Demise of Recreation

Comments about the dramatic decline in the recreation department of the Tahoe National Forest: Peter Brost interview of November 21, 2006.

The lack of updated maps of the Forests: Jeff Applegate interview of November 21, 1995.

The countless trails cut by dirt bikers and lack of foresters on the ground: Burkhart, Michelle, "Where have all the Rangers Gone?" *High Country News*, December 26, 2005.

Secretary of Agriculture Ann Veneman's memo informing forest employees that certain groups would continue to receive favors that others were not entitled to: I saw the memo myself while working on the Plumas National Forest in 2003.

In 2004 Veneman granted Region Five permission to create 22 additional paper work positions for the sole purpose of tracking down more women and Hispanic hires: Peter Brost interview, November 21, 1995.

The demise of recreation programs was unique to each forest: Interview with Jeff Applegate, November 21, 2005.

The sharp decline in the work ethics among forest service personnel: Interview with Eric Holst, February 13, 2009.

The memorial ceremony on the Lassen Forest angered the relatives of the deceased: interview with Bob Grate, June 11, 2004.

Chapter 25: The Twilight of Fire

Figures for the timber losses to fire can be found on numerous internet websites.

The National Association of Forest Service Retirees' report on the lack of capability of the forest service fire crews is dated March 29, 2001.

Today young white men regard colleges and universities as hostile learning places. Seminars and student orientation meetings focus entirely on the needs and importance of women and minorities only. Focus on the interests and desires of white youths have been entirely dispensed with. This is one of three major factors in the dramatic decline of young men attending college.

The great difference in pay scales between the U.S. Forest Service and the California Department of Forestry: article by Barb Stanton on her website, February, 11, 2008.

The U.S. Forest Service is forced to rely on private firefighting firms, and prison inmates to fight its fires: Ibid.

Agency contractors made little effort to check the backgrounds of many companies assigned to fight the fires. Many employees were not proficient in English. Ibid.

U.S. Senator Jeff Bingaman expresses alarm over the Forest Service failure to aid New Mexico fire teams and local units: Ben Goad, *Inland News, Press Enterprise*, Riverside County California August 7, 2008.

U.S. Senator Diane Feinstein is working to bring to an end to the hemorrhaging of firefighters from the U.S. Forest Service: Ibid.

The U.S. Forest Service presented the Senate a report on the Thirtymile Fire so chocked full of black outs "that it looked like the authors had used the pages to clean off a charcoal grill": Michelle Malkin, "The Forest Service Smokescreen," *Jewish World Review,* June 21, 2002.

Other details on the Thirtymile Fire can be found at website firecrew77.com. It is a forty four slide presentation of the blaze, with commentary. Also see *Las Vegas Sun,* "Forest Service Blamed for Deaths," February 8, 2002. The last is available on website www.fseee.org/forestmag/0205.

OSHA did release the details of the Cramer Fire in the Salmon-Challis National Forest in Idaho on April 1, 2004; in turn it was reported by Alex Markels in the *U.S. News and World Report.*

The Davis Fire in Montana is at the website *Wildfire Today.* Background information about the Davis escaped burn was provided by Bill Gabbert, August 30, 2010.

Chapter 26: Somewhere Over the Rainbow

Low morale in forest service was caused by "the general erosion of the ability of the employees to do the work they were hired to do, citing 'a particular loss of faith in the leadership of the agency': Mark Davis, federal employee union chairman, March, 2009 report.

"Best Places to Work Report," published by the Partnership for Public Service and American University's Institute for the Study of Public Policy Implementation, 2008." It was found that prison guards had a far more favorable opinion of their organizations and supervisors than did forest service employees. Of the 216 federal agencies studied, the Forest Service ranked 206 in morale.

There always use to be parties for some achievement or event: Les Bagby interview, September 22, 2004.

After greetings each other at gatherings and funerals the talk always turns to "when are you retiring": Gary McHarge interview of August 12, 2004.

Beatings, bombings, death threats and other acts of violence against the forest service is on a steady rise. In 1998 alone, agency workers and the buildings out of which they worked were attacked nearly 100 times. Karen Mockler, *Bulletin Board*, November 22, 1999.

The 1999 resignation of Gloria Flora, supervisor of the Humboldt-Toiyabe National Forest, is discussed at length on several websites accessed by her name.

Richard Knight and his sidekick concluded that the forest was going "feral" because of agency neglect: "When a forest goes feral it's time for volunteers," *High Country News*, September 2004, Richard Knight.

The Poudre Wilderness Volunteers: 180 Colorado residents are taking on the responsibilities of Forest Service recreation technicians and trail workers: Ibid.

Chuck Bell, who recently worked for the Roosevelt National Forest within three years saw the recreation staff drop from three full-time rangers and 33 seasonals, to one full-time ranger and two seasonals: Ibid.

Uncompahgre Plateau Project, also in Colorado, completed a series of scientific studies the Forest Service was unable to undertake. Uncompahgre Plateau Project, Red Lodge Clearing House, Robyn Morrison, June 21, 2005.

In May 2005, the Red House Coalition held a conference on the Uncompahgre National Forest, attended by over 300 scientists, resource managers and local citizens. Object was a plan to managing the forest: Ibid.

The Lakeview Group and Wilderness Society are working to restore public lands on the Fremont National Forest, Oregon.

"Cultivating Common Ground," The Wilderness Society, Andrea Imler, November 7, 2008.

The Quincy Library Group's efforts to assume management of 2.1 million acres of timberland in the Lassen, Plumas and Tahoe National Forests have been stymied by both the Sierra Club and the U.S Forest Service: "Property and Environmental Research Center," C Report, Volume 23, No. 2, Summer 2005.

Chapter 27: A Death in the Forest

Details of the death of Jerry Levitoff were provided in a letter from by Bob Grate of February 27, 1995. His fiancé Melany Lynn Johnson wrote a column about Jerry that appeared in the *Chester Progressive* (date clipped from copy of paper).

BIBLIOGRAPHY

Books

Dabbs, James, *Heroes, Rogues and Lovers; Testosterone and Behavior*, McGraw-Hill, 2000.

Farrell, Warren, *Why Men Earn More: The Startling Truth Behind the Pay Gap*, Amacon, 2005.

Frome, Michael, *The U.S. Forest Service*, Praeger Publishing, 1971.

Geary, David, *Male, Female, the Evolution of Human Sex Differences*, 1998, American Psychological Association.

Kreitner, Robert, *Foundations of Management*, Arizona State University, 2006.

Lasch, Christopher, *Revolt of the Elites*, W.W. Norton Company, 1995.

Lynch, Fred, *The Diversity Machine*, Transaction Publishers, 2005.

Murray, Charles, *Human Accomplishment: The Pursuit of Excellence in the Arts and Sciences, 800 BC to 1950*, Harper Collins, 2003.

Robinson, Glen, O. *The Forest Service: A Study in Public Land Management,* John Hopkins University Press, 1975.

Miller, Char, *Gifford Pinchot and the Making of Modern Environmentalism,* Island Press, 2001.

Moir, Anne, Ph.D, David Jessel, *BRAIN SEX: The Real Difference Between Men and Women,* Dell Publishing, New York, 1992.

O'Toole, Randal, *Reforming the Forest Service,* Island Press, 1988.

Rhoades, Steven, *Taking Sex Differences Seriously,* University of Virginia, 2004.

Roberts, Paul Craig and Stratton, Lawrence, *The New Color Line How Privileges and Quotas Destroy Democracy,* Regnery Press, 1995.

Thomas, Jack Ward, *The Journal of a Forest Service Chief,* Society of American Foresters, 1999.

Articles

Amaram, Donatus I, *Women and Absenteeeism: Cultural Diversity: Implications For Workplace Management,* Journal of Diversity Management, Fourth Quarter 2007, Volume 2, Number 4.

Burnside, Shannon R, *Gender Competition: a Test Between the Sexes,* University of Western Missouri, 1999.

ehast, Aaeron, *Women are more sensitive to stress than men,* Kinetic Movement and Stress Relief.

Henison, Jennifer, *Tripilcate Staff*, August 11, 2003.

Johnson, Ronald C., *Attributes of Carnegie Medalists Performing Acts of Heroism, and of the Recipients of the these Acts*, 1996.

Partnership for Public Service and American University's Institute for the Study of Public Policy Implementation, *Best Places to Work Report*, 2008.

Raineville, Raymond, *Twentieth Annual International Conference of the Association for the Study of Dreams*, Berkeley, California, June, 2003.

Scott, K.D., McClellan, E. Schwartz, N., *Gender Differences in Absenteeism*, Public Personnel Management.

Internet Web and Article Sites

Anderson, H. Michael, "Reshaping National Forest Policy," *Wilderness magazine*, 1999 fall issue.

Benenson, Joyce, Schinazi, Joy: "Sex Differences in Reactions to Outperforming Same-sex Friends," *British Journal of Developmental Psychology*, 2004.

Burke, Adam, "Public Lands; Big Cash Crop," *High Country News*, October 2, 2006.

Burkhart, Michelle, "Where have all the Rangers Gone?," *High Country News*, December 26, 2005.

Cárdenas, R. A., and Gaulin, S. J. C., Hodges, C. R., *Men's voices as dominance signals: Vocal fundamental and formant frequencies influence dominance attributions among men,* Penn State, Department of Anthropology, July 13, 2011.

Chesterton, P., Barlas, P., Forest, N.E., Baxter, G.D., and Wright, C.C. "PAIN gender differences in pressure pain threshold in healthy humans," *Department of Physiotherapy Studies, Keele University,* Staffordshire, UK.

Creighton, R. Alexander, M.D: *ACC Sports Sciences Main Page,* October1, 2004.

Equal Rights Advocate Website: www.charitynavigator.org.

Fields, Suzanne, January 17, 2008 townhall.com

Forestmag Website, www.fseee.org/forestmag/0205

Gabbert, Bill, "Background information about the Davis escaped prescribed fire in Montana," *Wildfire Today,* August 30, 2010.

Hipke, Deanna C., *The Great Peshtigo Fire of 1871.*

Imler, Andrea, *"Cultivating Common Ground,"* *The Wilderness Society,* November 7, 2008.

Jardine, Rosemary, Martin, N.D.: "Spatial Ability and Throwing Accuracy, Visual Acuity Differences Between Men and Women," *Behavior Genetics,* Volume 13, February 28, 1983.

Lott Jr., John R, *Does a Helping Hand Put Others at Risk? Affirmative Action, Police Departments and Crime,"* 38 Econ. Inquiry, 2000, (internet).

Knight, Richard, "When a Forest goes Feral it's Time for Volunteers," *High Country News,* September 2004.

Malkin, Michelle, "*The Forest Service Smokescreen,*" *Jewish World Review,* June 21, 2002.

Markels, Alex, "OSHA Report, Cramer Fire ": *U.S. News and World Report.* April, 4, 2004.

Mockler, Karen, "Risks Multiply for Land Managers," *High Country News,* November 22, 1999.

Morrison, Robyn, "Uncompahgre Plateau Project," *Red Lodge Clearing House,* June 21, 2005.

National Association of Forest Service Retirees Report of March 29, 2001.

_____-Report of April, 2005.

—————Letter of Regional Forester Douglas Leisz to President Bill Clinton, August 29, 1995.

O'Toole, Randal, "The Financial Psychosis of Federal and State Forest Agencies," *Thoreau Institute,* December 30, 1999.

O'Toole, Randal, "The Rot Starts at the Top," *Thoreau Institute,* February 8, 2000.

O'Toole, Randal, "Forest Plans that do Nothing," *Seattle Times,* January 11, 2007.

Parsons, Larson, Kratz, Thiebaux, Bluestein, Buckwalter, and Rizzo, *Sex Differences in Mental Rotation and Spatial Rotation in a Virtual Environment*, August 2003.

Property and Environmental Research Center, C Report, Volume 23, No. 2, Summer 2005.

Putts, David, et al, "Beauty and the Beast: Mechanisms of Sexual Selection in Humans," Penn State University, Department of Anthropology, 2006, 31: 157-175 (Internet).

Roberts, Carey, "Unequal Pay for Unequal Work," January 12, 2005 (Internet).

Stanton, Barb, web article drawn from her radio show of February, 11, 2008.

Thomas, Jack Ward, Speech before Horace Albright Conservation Lectureship, April 14, 1992.

Valenzuela, M., Bartrés-Faz, D., Beg, E., Fornito, A., EMerlo-Pich, UMüller, Öngür, D., Toga, A. W., and Yücel., "Neuroimaging as endpoints in clinical trials: Are we there yet? Perspective from the fires Provence workshop," *The Journal Molecular Psychiatry*, Philadelphia, May 31, 2011.

Williams, Clarence A., "Sex Differences: Applying the Naturalist Paradigm," June 6, 2007, www.clarencewilliams.net.

Interviews

Applegate, Jeff, William, interview of January 10, 2006.
————February 22, 2006.

Bagby, Les, interview of September 22, 2004.

Barker, Pete, interview of May 23, 2008.

Burton, Jim, interview of September 11, 2004.

Cermak, Bob, interview of January 6, 2006.

Dameron, William, interview of April 9, 2005.

Demas, Louis, interview of July 20, 1994.

Donnelly, Lesa, interview of February 15, 2008.

Fint, John, interview of March 9, 2006.

Gilbert, Kenneth, interview of February 4, 2006.

Grate, Robert, interview of June 11, 2004.

————interview of July 7, 2004.

————telephone interview of November 8, 2004.

Holst, Eric, interview of February 13, 2009.

Johnson, Leroy, interview of November 6, 2005.

Lewis, Lonnie, interview of February 22, 2009.

McHargue, Gary, interview of July 29, 2004.

————interview, August 22, 2004.

Shaw, Bill, interview of May 18, 2008.

————interview of October 27, 2008.

Smith, Britt, interview of March 26, 2006.

Eighteen additional employees consented to interviews on condition they remained anonymous. A dozen more declined to interview because they had placed those years of their lives behind them. Others refused because they had too deeply compromised themselves during and after implementation of the Bernardi Decree.

Personal Files

Brost, Peter

Demas, Louis

Grate, Bob

Johnson, Leroy
Locker, Thomas
Meurer, Dave
Shaw, Bill

Newspapers and Journals

CBS News Report, *Sex Bias at the U.S. Forest Service*, October 12, 2002.
Consent Decree Digest, September 5, 1991.
————December 2, 1991.
Inland News, Press Enterprise, Riverside County, California, Ben Goad, August 7, 2008.
Las Vegas Sun, "Forest Service Blamed for Deaths," February 8, 2002.
Sacramento Bee, November 8, 1992.
San Bernardino Bear Facts, August 1988.
San Jose Mercury News, September 16, 1988.
Seattle Times, May 18, 2003.
Six Rivers Quarterly, February 8, 1989.
Pacific Southwest NewsLog, September 1985.
————————— February 1988.
————————— August 10, 1989.
————————— September 23, 1991.
The Recorder, August 2, 1991.
The Supporter, March 28, 1990.
————November 19, 1990.
————June 7, 1991.
————September 28, 1991.
————October 14, 1991.
————December 15, 1991.
————March 28, 1992.
————May 9, 1992.

————————December 12, 1992.

————————October 28, 1993.

————————November 19, 1993.

———————— June 8, 1994.

————————December 19, 1994.

Union Vision, National Federation of Federal Employees, Summer 1992.

USA Today, October 3-4, 1988.

Washington Post, June 10, 2009.

Washington Times, October 14, 1997.

Wildlife News, October 10, 2002.

The Federal Records Storage Center, San Bruno, California

Case # C73-1110-SC, Accession # 21-95-0050, Location #445697.

Material can be found in boxes one through ten, and 29 through 33, but they essentially replicate information elsewhere. The most important sources are those here numbered: Boxes 11, 12, 15, 16, 17, 18, 19, 20, 21 and 23.

INDEX

AUTHOR

ABOUT THE AUTHOR

Christopher Burchfield has worked for the U.S. Park Service, the U.S. Bureau of Reclamation and the U.S. Forest Service. In the more distant past he has worked for IBM, and prior to that operated a landscape businesses. During the last decade of the last millennium, while working for two of the federal agencies noted above, Burchfield became aware that personnel alterations were impacting the performance of individual employees in each unit. But it was only after his employment with the U.S. Forest Service that he became truly aware of the devastating affects political correctness was having on the performance and morale of federal employees.

During the course of his inquiries he came across a massive store of documents located at a federal record storage center. Following a lengthy study of the material he began a series of interviews with forest service employees in various disciplines. Finally in 2012 *The Tinder Box: How Politically Correct Ideology Destroyed the U.S. Forest Service* was published. Aside from history, the author has a passion for natural history, and is at his happiest exploring America's wild lands and the national parks and reserves of the African Continent. He is married, has a multitude of children and grandchildren and lives in a small town in Northern California.